REFLECTIONS AND OPINIONS

REFLECTIONS AND OPINIONS

Désirée Patricia Bernard, O.R., C.C.H.
Former Judge of the Caribbean Court of Justice

HANSIB

First published in Great Britain by Hansib Publications in 2018

Hansib Publications Limited
P.O. Box 226, Hertford
Hertfordshire SG14 3WY UK

info@hansibpublications.com
www.hansibpublications.com

ISBN 978-1-910553-93-0

A CIP catalogue record for this book
is available from the British Library

Production by Hansib Publications Limited

Printed in Great Britain

DEDICATION

To my dear daughter, Carol Ann Bernard, Attorney at Law, for her support and encouragement over the years.

Also, to my deceased parents, William and Maude Bernard for instilling in me the core values of honesty and integrity which I have endeavoured to uphold throughout my life.

CONTENTS

FOREWORD

I am extremely happy that Mme. Justice Désirée Bernard asked me to write the Foreword to this collection of her speeches. They provide an opportunity to benefit from the excellent intellect, research and reasoning, that make her one of the leading contemporary judicial and legal thinkers in the Caribbean.

Désirée Bernard went into practice in Guyana and soon held office in the Guyana Bar Association. I knew her when we both were young practitioners working in regional organizations. Even then, she showed her leadership and interest in the broader legal picture. Through the Organisation of Commonwealth Caribbean Bar Associations (OCCBA), she was engaged in the discussions on abolition of appeals to the Privy Council and the development of Caribbean jurisprudence, thinking which was the foundation of the Caribbean Court of Justice (CCJ).

In those days, while metropolitan countries like the United Kingdom and the United States of America were maintaining a male image of the Judiciary, Mme. Justice Bernard was elevated to the Bench in Guyana becoming the first woman to be so appointed. She rapidly rose to the post of Chief Justice, incidentally becoming the first woman in the British Commonwealth to hold that office. She later became Head of the Judiciary of Guyana when she was appointed to the post of Chancellor. Upon its inauguration, she was the first and only female judge to sit on the Caribbean Court of Justice (CCJ). It was her trailblazing that has led to women being judicial leaders in several jurisdictions at both high and appellate court level. No small credit is due to Mme. Justice Bernard for female judges to be now well received and respected by their male colleagues as a matter of course, as they contribute to building public confidence in the Judiciary.

Reading these essays has been an enthralling experience. They are replete with case law and legal reasoning, and address topics which could guide judicial and legal deliberations on many issues making them valuable as a research tool, but delightfully written, making reading pleasurable. Many of them I have read more than once. In writing this Foreword, I have been severely tempted to write a synopsis of the speeches, a temptation that I have not entirely resisted.

Mme. Justice Bernard's speeches show her to be a leader in pro-active judicial thinking. She examines the role of women, "the power behind the throne" in the home, the society and in the legal profession, with characteristic and incisive humour as well. She has portrayed the thinking that has become mainstream: that women's rights are in reality human rights. She powerfully confronts gender-based violence. Her essay on "Saving Caribbean Children" delivered at the launch of the Caribbean Women Judges' Association, traces regional initiatives and informs reforms still needed. Her discussion is grounded in the constitutions and international law. The adoption of the Convention on the Rights of the Child (CRC) by the General Assembly of the United Nations on 20 November 1989, first of two other U.N. instruments concerning the world's children – The Millennium Declaration adopted in September 2000, and A World Fit for Children adopted on 10 May 2002.

She discusses the work and steps relating to the prevention of AIDS, and describes the Caribbean responses with positive recommendations for improvements. In reference to the UN Convention on the Rights of the Child, she brings into focus the regional strategic framework, revealing alarming statistics in the Caribbean. Mme. Justice Bernard discusses the CCJ. Her speeches set out its origins, its relationship to economic development in the CSME, and even recalls its early jurisprudence.

Her essay on *The Impact of the Common Law on the Caribbean* is a tremendous piece of work. The content of this essay, both in terms of ideas and fullness of research, could be developed into a full text book. This essay truly qualifies as a must-read. It is replete with scholarship, wit and advocacy. It exposes how English Common Law, based on English customs, sometimes inapplicable in the Caribbean, perpetuated the stereotypical role of women, discouraged adaptation to accord with the peculiar customs and culture of a particular colony and sometimes produced ridiculous results. She showed the desirability of developing a jurisprudence peculiar to our needs, culture, traditions and regional objectives with the establishment of our own final court of appeal.

Mme. Justice Bernard dedicates several essays on judging and on being a judge in the modern world. Her address delivered at a lecture series by the Diversity & Development Team College of the Judiciary of England & Wales Royal Courts of Justice on 25 November 2013 is a classic. She defines the "modern world" and discusses new and emerging issues: computer crime; surrogacy, when a woman carries a baby for another who is unable to do so or to conceive. She tackles the issue of same-sex marriages and all of the legal problems which can arise from such unions, e.g. adoption and custody of children, maintenance and division of marital assets. She identifies the emerging issues, such as:

the worldwide increase in human trafficking
the use of modern technology in the judicial process
the impact on judiciaries of large numbers of women entering the legal profession
the world-wide concern over preservation and protection of the environment
the developing concept of cloning, fraught with legal and ethical ramifications.

She advocates the adoption of judicial codes of conduct based on Guidelines such as the *Bangalore Principles of Judicial Conduct* which have been accepted by judiciaries of the Commonwealth and elsewhere.

In her seminal essay on *The Independent Judicial Mind,* Mme. Justice Bernard discusses what informs the judicial mind in arriving at decisions, and in official and personal conduct on and off the Bench. In her discourse titled, "Securing and Enhancing Judicial Independence" delivered to Heads of Judiciary Conference in 2003, Mme. Justice Bernard discusses the fundamental importance of the independence of the Judiciary. One theme that appears in several of these essays is that of judicial activism. Mme. Justice Bernard refers to human rights and the proliferation of international instruments for their protection. Her essays are all full of insights on international law and its influence on domestic jurisprudence. Thus, a common theme in her essays is the impact of the UN Convention on the Elimination of Discrimination Against Women (CEDAW). Her examination of judicial activism traces its evolution from tentative beginnings to contemporary times when women enjoy greater rights.

In this context, she honours former Chief Justice P. N. Bhagwati of India, in her presentation on "Creating a Judicial Culture to Promote the Enforcement of Women's Human Rights" where she discussed the creative function of judges that is necessary to reconcile rules with the wider objectives of justice encapsulated in the international norms of women's human rights. So long as judges are sensitive to women's human rights and are prepared boldly to advance the law through a process of creative interpretation, women's human rights will be safe.

Mme. Justice Bernard's classic essay on the duties of the advocate is a work of scholarship, citing case law, statute law from England, Australia, Canada, the USA and the Caribbean, with cases from Guyana and Trinidad & Tobago. It sets out principles which should guide the practitioner today and should be read by all practitioners.

It is always fascinating to examine the voyages upon which life takes one. Some 40 years ago, like many other Caribbean nationalists, Désirée Bernard and I first became convinced of the inadequacy of the Judicial Committee of the Privy Council as a court of final resort for the Commonwealth Caribbean. In our discussions, though our faith in the eventual creation of a Caribbean Court of Appeal was strong, we were nonetheless aware of the then reality which was not overly sympathetic to the emergence of such a court. The retentionist lobby was strong, as it continues still to be in some quarters.

Both as jurists and as Caribbean nationalists, we found illogical that the court of final resort of the Commonwealth Caribbean should lie outside the Caribbean itself. It seemed to us that logically, Caribbean matters should be settled in the Caribbean in Caribbean institutions. It also seemed to us at least incongruous that the highest judicial authority for the Commonwealth Caribbean should be completely insulated against regional input, as the structure, staffing and organisation of the Judicial Committee of the Privy Council lie completely outside of regional purview.

We had no inkling, neither one of us at that time, that the day would dawn on which both Mme. Justice Bernard and I would be both sitting on the Bench of the Caribbean Court of Justice. The experience has for me been a dream come true indeed – not only to be sitting on an originally, genetically Caribbean court of final resort, but also to be doing so at the same time with Désirée Bernard, with whom I had for numerous years debated the need for exactly such an institution. With the passage of time from those early days to which I refer, our legal and professional paths diverged, hers through private practice, then the High Court and Court of Appeal in Guyana, and eventually the Chambers of the Chief Justice and of the Chancellor of the Judiciary.

My own career led me through various levels of adjudication in the Eastern Caribbean Supreme Court, prior to the United Nations International Criminal Tribunal for Rwanda before returning to the Caribbean and the CCJ. I have said elsewhere and I repeat here that having been appointed President of the CCJ was for me the summum of juridical accomplishment. What I must express further is the degree to which my sense of personal achievement was heightened and enhanced by being able to share accession to the Bench of the CCJ with Mme. Justice Bernard, my co-conspirator, as it were, from those early days when the Caribbean Court of Appeal, as it was then styled, was merely a gleam in the eyes of the CARICOM Secretariat.

I feel no small sense of pride to have adjudicated together with Mme. Justice Bernard as my sister Judge in a number of matters. The reader will understand the catharsis of seeing, feeling, hearing and *making* the reality of a Caribbean aspiration solidified into reality. That is not all, however. My deep sense of having been privileged to have shared experiences and a common judicial destiny (albeit under different jurisdictions) with Mme. Justice Bernard does not stop there. It is important to acknowledge that much of the international legislation to which many of the world's states are now signatories have benefitted from the sterling contributions of Désirée Bernard.

Legislation treating with the rights of women, the rights of the child, and human rights in general have all benefitted from the insights and perspicacity of Mme. Justice Bernard in all of these areas. Her ground-breaking research, analyses and recommendations have found their way into deliberations upon these matters in the highest echelons of international legal drafting.

It must of course be mentioned that Mme. Justice Bernard served as both rapporteur (1982-1984) and Chair (1985-1989) of the United

Nations Committee on the Elimination of Discrimination against Women. She was therefore admirably positioned to contribute significantly to legislation resultant from the work of said committee. It is no doubt in recognition of such an invaluable contribution to the architecture of the legal framework under which Caribbean women in particular live, that Mme. Justice Bernard was awarded in July 2005 the CARICOM Triennial Award for Women. Recognition of her legal acumen was further burnished by her appointment, in February 2011, as a Judge of the Inter-American Development Bank Administrative Tribunal, based in Washington DC, USA, once again positioning her to make valuable input into the administration of international law.

My objective in the preceding paragraphs is to highlight not the results of her work which are well known and speak for themselves. It is to allow the reader to grasp the behind-the-scenes history and activism which have combined to give to the Caribbean - and indeed, the wider polity – the legal brainchildren of a distinguished daughter of the soil.

We are often accused in the Caribbean – and admittedly, with some degree of justification, of a lack of rigour and follow-through in our undertakings. This has been dubbed a lack of "maintenance". My point in emphasising the quiet, understated personal labour which has characterised my dear colleague's work is to demonstrate indeed what our Caribbean can accomplish when the need for "rigour and follow-through" is respected, when "high maintenance" is the primary characteristic in an individual's efforts. Placed in a position to indicate what can be achieved through similar methodology, and able to grasp with both hands as it were what Désirée Bernard has wrought, I feel it is incumbent upon me to invite the Caribbean to consider what great heights can be scaled in the construction of a genuinely Caribbean jurisprudence by individuals such as Mme. Justice Bernard sitting on the Bench of the Caribbean Court of Justice.

My colleague has been among the trailblazers, since our early, fledgling discussions on the Caribbean Court of Appeal, all those decades ago, to have shaped and moulded the first notions of the Court. She has, and very creditably, also had the great good fortune to actually sit on the Court and see the seeds planted many years ago, bear fruit. Those jurists and parliamentarians coming later will have no need to do the ground-breaking work. The path will already have been cleared by such as Désirée Bernard, who has not only, through her writing as contained in this volume, cleared the way intellectually and psychologically. She has also, by dint of commitment to success, arduous toil and conscientious engagement, provided the nuts and bolts of the actual instruments and implements which the latter generations will need to continue and perfect the construction of the edifice whose foundation she has so adroitly and expertly laid.

Ultimately, and this must absolutely be said, my personal knowledge and experience of her as well as my dispassionate reading of her texts in this volume lead me to attest to her unequivocal, unqualified understanding of the need for and her indefatigable commitment to the social transformation of the Caribbean through the buttressing of that third pillar of national administration, the Judiciary, whose especial and tremendous charge is the administration of the rule of law. Mme. Justice Bernard demonstrates unfailingly through these essays, which transparently reveal the polished pearl of her accumulated years of experience, understanding and application of the law, the singular importance and terrible weight of that remit. It is not a charge from which she flinches. Her essays demonstrate to us that we cannot, *must* not do so, either.

I reiterate that it is for me both a privilege and a pleasure to have been invited to write this Foreword. Privilege, for obvious reasons. Multiple parties have long attested to the signal importance of Désirée Bernard's contribution to the rule of law and administration of justice in the Caribbean. To have been asked to usher in, as it were, this collection of her thoughts on a wide expanse of the law in the Caribbean into the collective public consciousness, I consider a rare privilege indeed. The task that I have been so graciously invited to perform has also been a source of great pleasure. It has required me to immerse myself into the enlightened thinking and crystal-clear analyses of the author. I confess to having frequently forgotten what my task was when I abandoned myself to the sheer pleasure of reading these highly instructive and finely-crafted documents.

Beyond the personal, as a jurist, I feel honour-bound to assume the role of advocate for this volume. Contained herein are the distilled thoughts and examinations of one of the contemporary Caribbean's finest legal minds. True, these writings are of historical significance in that many of them commemorate milestones in the evolution of Guyanese in particular and CARICOM law in general. In that sense, these essays are tools to be used as a magnifying glass through which to observe that which has already been accomplished. More significantly, to my mind, much of the content of these essays looks towards the future.

With characteristic foresight, Mme. Justice Bernard has tackled these questions analytically, thoroughly and with rigour, so as to provide for the reader, the scholar, the researcher, the activist the wherewithal upon which to construct a plan of action. One of the founding principles of the Caribbean Court of Justice was/is the creation of a genuine Caribbean jurisprudence. The content of Mme. Justice Bernard's collection provides not only examinable evidence of what has been already done and how it has been done. It also identifies the next challenges for Caribbean jurisprudence, proposes targets, suggests the way towards them and most pragmatically, the tools the Caribbean jurist may use to craft our response to said challenges. In a marvellously logical way, my friend and colleague Désirée Bernard illustrates where we must go and how to get there by exposing to us whence we have come and what has brought us from there to here.

My admiration for this material is unbounded. I can give no higher recommendation to the reader.

Dennis Byron
President
Caribbean Court of Justice

PREFACE

The book comprises a collection of speeches and addresses delivered at the invitation of organisations and groups on the celebration or observance of an event as well as discussion of a particular topic.

The collection is in four parts - the Judiciary, the Legal Profession, Issues Pertaining to Women and Children as well as commentaries on topical Social Issues of the day.

It is hoped that it will stimulate interest in the particular topic and encourage further expressions of opinion.

ACKNOWLEDGMENTS

I wish to acknowledge the invaluable assistance of my Secretary, Mrs. Chandra Jagnandan of Guyana and my Executive Assistant, Ms. Andréa-Rennétte Sohun of Trinidad and Tobago when over the years in Guyana and Trinidad and Tobago I delivered speeches and lectures to various groups and organisations. They assisted in no small measure in the written preparation of these speeches.

I must extend special gratitude to Andréa for her extensive assistance in the preparation of this book, her scoping expertise and her meticulous adherence to the specific instructions of the publishers.

PART I

JUDICIAL

CHAPTER 1

RESPONSE UPON FIRST SITTING AS A JUDGE OF THE HIGH COURT OF GUYANA

There are certain occasions in one's life when words are wholly inadequate and inappropriate as a medium of expression of one's feelings. This is one such occasion, and I therefore ask all those who have spoken here this morning and my many well-wishers to pardon me and understand if my remarks are few and words of gratitude seem inadequate. Be that as it may, I wish to thank all of you for everything you have said. As I sat and listened it seemed to me as if this event concerned someone else and not me.; it was as if I was a spectator and not the recipient of all of your good wishes and expressions of goodwill.

I wish especially to pay public tribute to Mr. Frederick Wills who is responsible in no small measure for my legal training, and to whom I was articled for five years. He has produced many eminent lawyers, among them three judges – my brothers Aubrey Bishop, Stanley Moore (who acted for three months) and me; also Natalie Stephenson, Norma Jackman, Elvy Edwards, Ayube McDoom, to name a few. He will always be remembered for his outstanding contribution to the jurisprudence of our country, and I wish him well wherever he is at present, and every success in whatever he undertakes.

I wish also to express heartfelt gratitude to my mother for all the help, guidance, prayers and encouragement given to me throughout my career. I am indeed grateful that her life has been spared to savour this moment with me. Special thanks also to my Aunt Monica and all other relatives and friends who assisted me in small and large ways throughout the years.

I cannot conclude my expressions of gratitude without paying tribute to my two faithful clerks – Hassan Khan and Frank Goppy – for their help and cooperation during my years of legal practice. Their loyalty will always be remembered.

There is a great disadvantage in being the first in any field of endeavour. There is no precedent, no rules or examples to guide and follow. One has to strike out on one's own and become a trail blazer thereby leaving a path for others to follow. It is my sincere hope that my appointment will be the forerunner of many more appointments for women not only in the legal field but in all top-level and managerial positions in our country. This is indeed a significant day for the women of Guyana, and one tinged with a touch of history. I feel deeply honoured and humbled to have been chosen as part of that history.

Thank you all again for your good wishes. I pledge publicly that I shall hold the scales of justice evenly, and be patient with the poor and unlearned who may appear before me. I know that I can count on the cooperation of all practitioners (male and female), and with God's help I shall succeed.

Guyana Law Courts
3rd October, 1980

Swearing in as Judge of the High Court of Guyana 1st October 1980

CHAPTER 2

THE JUDICIARY AND THE CITIZEN

The public generally has always regarded the Judiciary with a sense of awe and mystery, and considers the persons who hold the office of Judge as one occupying the rarified stratosphere in our society. This was certainly so in colonial times, and though in the immediate post-independent era some of the awe has diminished with the advent of local Judges known to the majority of the population, there is still a certain mystique attached to the office born of the fact that the average citizen has no idea of how the system of justice works. This has led to misconceptions and simplistic assumptions among them being that a judge (or a magistrate) has an unfettered discretion to decide on the guilt or innocence of a person appearing before him/her or to enter judgment or dismiss a case at will. There is absolutely no understanding of what is involved in dispensing justice. There is also the perplexity in trying to understand how one can be morally right but legally wrong or *vice versa.* Sad to say the law does not always follow morality. Before proceeding further, I shall discuss the structure of our court system.

The courts comprise Magistrate's courts, High Courts, and the Court of Appeal as well as the Full Court which is a division of the High Court, and the Land Court. Summary matters i.e. less serious criminal offences (including minor traffic offences) are heard in the Magistrate's courts as well as preliminary inquiries into serious or indictable offences. Civil matters involving claims under a certain statutory amount, for example $50,000, are also heard in the Magistrate's courts as well as claims for maintenance of spouses and children up to a certain statutory limit. Claims for possession of land and rents up to a statutory limit as well as inquests fall within the Magistrate's jurisdiction.

In the High courts, over which Judges preside indictable and serious offences are heard in the criminal jurisdiction as well as civil claims over a statutory limit, personal injury claims, divorces, custody and adoption of children, and other civil matters. The High Court jurisdiction is extensive, and I have mentioned just a few of the matters which are heard in these courts. There is a court held every Monday called the "Bail Court" (which has nothing to do with bail) where claims for specified amounts such as claims under promissory notes, mortgage foreclosures, sale of goods or other transactions are heard. It is intended for speedy resolution of summary matters, but this is sometimes defeated by an ever-increasing case load and fewer judges as well as an inordinate amount of postponements. The list of cases on any Monday can surpass 200.

On Tuesdays certain matters are heard in chambers, and include applications for custody and adoption of children, injunctions, division of matrimonial property, matters pertaining to the estates of deceased persons, and any other applications which statutorily can be dealt with in chambers. These too can reach 200 on any Tuesday.

Generally, appeals from the decisions of magistrates and rulings from a judge sitting in Chambers are heard in what is referred to as the Full Court of the High Court by the Chief Justice and one or two Judges.

Appeals from decisions of Judges of the High Court sitting in open court as opposed to chambers, decisions of the Commissioner of Title and some appeals from the decisions of a Magistrate as well as appeals from the Full Court are heard by the Court of Appeal. This so far is the final court in the court structure, and is presided over by the Chancellor sitting with two Justices of Appeal. If the Chancellor does not sit the most senior Justice may preside at a hearing. In matters of great importance jurisprudentially the Appellate Bench could comprise as many as five Justices.

The full complement of the Court of Appeal is the Chancellor and five Justices; the High Court's complement is the Chief Justice and eleven Judges, and the statutory number of Magistrates is twenty-two. The High Court and the Court of Appeal are referred to as the Supreme Court of Judicature.

Sad to say in all of the courts there is a shortage of personnel. There are at present sixteen Magistrates instead of twenty-two, eight Judges instead of eleven, and three Justices of Appeal instead of five excluding the Chief Justice who is ex-officio a member of the Court of Appeal.

In addition to the courts mentioned earlier there is a Land Court which is presided over by a Commissioner of Title often referred to as the Judge of the Land Court and who hears petitions for declaration of title to land and applications for land registration. There are two Commissioners of Title – one sits in Demerara and the other in Berbice.

The courts are serviced by a Registry headed by the Registrar of the Supreme Court and other members of staff such as clerks, marshals and an accounts section. There is also the Deeds Registry which deals with transports, titles to land, mortgages and other deeds.

I shall now explain what is involved in having a case heard in court. It is said that a lawyer is the only person who gets rich fighting other people's battles. I mention this to indicate that it is desirable although not obligatory to consult a lawyer if one intends to file a claim or defend an action in court. If the claim is a small one or is one of landlord and tenant, a document called a plaint is filed in the magistrate's court. A date is fixed for hearing and it is served on the other party who is being sued. This person, called the defendant, may be given time to file a defence. At the hearing the plaintiff, i.e. the party who has filed the plaint, is required to give sworn evidence and be cross-examined by the lawyer for the defendant or the defendant personally. Witnesses, if any, give their evidence and are also cross-examined; the same process applies to the defendant. After all of the evidence is led the magistrate then considers submissions made by both lawyers, if any, on the facts and the law applicable to the particular case before rendering a decision. A Magistrate is required to give reasons for arriving at a particular decision, and either party, if dissatisfied with the decision may file an appeal to the Full Court of the High Court within a specified time setting out the grounds on which the appeal is brought. The Magistrate is then required to submit written reasons for the decision, and a record of the proceedings including the evidence led is prepared. The Full Court at the hearing of the appeal considers whether there is merit in the appeal and may allow it or dismiss it if there is no merit. The procedure I have outlined also applies in large measure to actions filed in the High Court and appeals heard in the Court of Appeal from decisions of judges.

Criminal prosecutions are launched by the police in the Magistrate's Court and by the Director of Public Prosecutions in the High Court. Indictable or serious criminal offences are conducted in two stages – a preliminary inquiry in the Magistrate's Court where the Magistrate decides whether a sufficient or *prima facie* case is made out against the accused after hearing evidence and submissions by Counsel for the accused; if he/she so finds then the case is remitted to the High Court to be heard before a Judge and jury. There a jury of twelve persons is empanelled and evidence led by the prosecution. The accused is given three options - make an unsworn statement from the dock, give sworn testimony from the witness box, or remain silent.

The onus of proof in criminal matters rests at all times on the prosecution to prove the guilt of the accused beyond a reasonable doubt, and no burden rests on the accused to prove his innocence. After all of the evidence is led by both prosecution and accused and both Counsel (or the accused himself if not represented by Counsel) have addressed the jury the Judge sums up the evidence and advises the jury on the law before they are requested to consider their verdict. If that verdict is a finding of guilt, the Judge imposes a sentence. This is entirely within the discretion of the Judge in cases other than murder having regard to the nature of the offence and the statutory provisions as to penalty. If it is a case of murder the Judge has no discretion as there is only one sentence that can be imposed, and that is the penalty of death.

Much to the surprise of lay persons all evidence led in the courts is recorded by hand. It is a tedious, tiring and time-consuming exercise; in several instances the handwriting cannot be discerned sometimes even by the writer. In many countries of the Caribbean there is simultaneous recording of evidence, but we still cling to this archaic form of note-taking.

A Judge or Magistrate is also required to observe the demeanour of witnesses in order to ascertain whether they are truthful as well as rule on objections by Counsel, all of this while concentrating and recording the evidence. It requires one to be focussed and attentive, and not be distracted.

Sometimes a decision is reserved by a Judge or Magistrate after all of the evidence has been led. This requires analysing and researching all relevant case law before coming to a decision depending on the complexity of the matter. This ought to be done within a reasonable time, and not be delayed for an inordinate length of time which could give rise to justice being delayed and consequently denied.

The life of a Judge is very lonely. It requires a large degree of self-discipline, dedication and commitment. One has to make decisions based on the law and not on the identity of the litigant. Justice is blind, and a Judge ought to be concerned only with doing justice between litigant and litigant and litigant and the State. The independence of the Judiciary is sacrosanct, and must always be preserved.

I shall now discuss an aspect of the law with which all Judges, Magistrates and members of the public should be familiar – the law pertaining to contempt.

To a layman unskilled and untrained in the niceties and complex twists of any legal system displaying contempt for a court in its ordinary meaning means to show disdain and disrespect for that institution. The common law definition of contempt is any "act or omission calculated to interfere with the due administration of justice". Contempt of court may be manifested in a variety of ways for a variety of reasons. It may be either civil or criminal, and may occur in the face of the Court, e.g., by refusing to answer questions or disclose the source of information, disobedience of orders of the court or the commission of any act calculated to obstruct or interfere with the administration of justice or prejudicing a fair trial. In fact it is felt that there should be no distinction between civil or criminal contempt.

A criminal contempt is an act which threatens the administration of justice and which occurs in the face of the Court, scandalises the Court or prejudices the fair trial of a cause to such an extent that it requires some form of punishment, e.g., a fixed term of imprisonment.

Statutorily our law of contempt is governed by the Contempt of Court Act, Cap. 5:05 which was enacted in 1919 "to define and regulate the law with respect to Contempt of Court". Contempt can take place in the face of the Court, i.e., where some insult is offered to a Judge or Magistrate or by any interruption of the proceedings, or where, although not committed in the face of the Court, is calculated to obstruct, interfere with, or improperly prejudice the administration of justice in proceedings before the Court.

Very many, and I am sure little known acts of contempt, concern using or threatening violence or using abusive language to a juror in or near the precincts of the Court as well as where anyone intentionally personates any juror by answering to his name when called or where anyone liable to serve on a jury does not answer to his name when called.

Of even greater interest is that a majority of the Supreme Court of Canada in a case in 1971 regarded a barrister as having committed a contempt in the face of the Court by absenting himself from the Court and thus preventing a trial from continuing.

A striking feature of criminal contempt is that it is usually dealt with summarily and immediately if it is committed in the face of the Court. This is in keeping with the inherent jurisdiction of the Court to punish interference with the administration of justice in an effort to keep its streams pure. Although this power to deal condignly with contempt in the face of the Court may be criticised by liberals and human rights advocates it is absolutely essential in order to maintain respect for our courts and their functionaries who dispense justice. If this power were to be removed or eroded in any way the consequences would be too terrible to contemplate. Judges would be abused with impunity, and our judicial institutions would plunge headlong into abysmal disrepute. I adopt the statement made by Lord Denning in his book "The Due Process of Law", at page 8:

> The course of justice must not be deflected or interfered with. Those who strike at it strike at the very foundations of our society. To maintain law and order, the judges have, and must have, power at once to deal with those who offend against it. It is a great power – a power instantly to imprison a person without trial – but it is a necessary power. So necessary, indeed, that until recently the judges exercised it without appeal.

Since then in England, in fact in 1960, the right of appeal was granted to the Court of Appeal, and in a suitable case to the House of Lords.

The important feature of criminal contempt being that it should be dealt with summarily, the offender is usually asked to show cause why he/she should not be committed for contempt. If no or no sufficient cause is shown the Judge can immediately impose a penalty which could be either a term of imprisonment or a fine consistent with the seriousness of the contempt.

One of the most important functions of our judicial system is the Judge's capacity to issue orders. These orders are intended to be obeyed, and if not obeyed are regarded as a contempt incurring punitive sanctions. Section 3 of the Contempt of Court Act gives a right of appeal to the Full Court from an order for committal or the issue of a writ of attachment or other proceedings for contempt through disobedience of a Court's order. However, before a contemnor can be committed or a writ of attachment issued against him the procedural rules must be complied with, and he/she is entitled to take advantage of any irregularities.

The breach of an undertaking given to the Court is generally regarded as civil contempt and one which should be treated in the same way as contempt of an order of the Court. Breach of an undertaking given to the Court by or on behalf of a party to civil proceedings has been regarded as tantamount to a breach of an injunction with similar consequences.

Every day in our courts as Judges we encounter persons breaching orders for injunctions or undertakings given to the Court to desist from committing certain acts until the hearing and determination of an action. I do not think the solemnity of such undertakings or the implications of injunctions made are appreciated by litigants; this must be brought home forcefully to the minds of such persons by the imposition of harsh penalties after following the established procedures. Persons who volunteer undertakings should have explained to them the seriousness of the duty they have assumed, and that its breach may incur punishment for contempt. This should be stressed by the Judge before whom the party is appearing and before accepting the undertaking or ensure that Counsel representing the party has explained the implications to his/her client.

We have encountered situations where persons raise in defence when summoned for contempt that the order made was illegal or made without authority.

The popular misconception is that one is not bound to obey such an order. This is totally false; as long as an order remains in force whether properly or improperly made disobedience of it is a contempt; it remains in force until it is set aside. It will, however, be a defence to a charge of disobedience to an order that it was made without jurisdiction; also, the order must be capable of being obeyed and not be impossible to comply with. Nevertheless, the sanctity of orders made by courts must be preserved, and this underlines the need to obey orders whether properly or improperly made.

There is a never-ending backlog of cases due in no small measure to the fact that we are a litigious nation. Litigation has tripled over the last twenty years since people have become more aware of their legal rights. At the same time the number of Judges has been decreasing for a variety of reasons – retirement and in some cases resignations to take up more lucrative positions overseas. Hence, cases cannot be heard as speedily as they should.

There is also the litany of adjournments which continues to plague the system, and for which both Bench and Bar must bear responsibility. Adjournments are sought and granted too readily, sometimes for inconsequential reasons. This results in prolonging the hearing of an action for an inordinate length of time. We have to endeavour to reduce and eliminate as much as possible the number of adjournments which are granted if we are to reduce the large backlog of cases clogging up the system.

One aspect of the administration of justice that is misunderstood frequently by the public is the granting of bail. Most persons regard bail as a form of punishment and penalty for the commission of an offence, and feel that once a suspect is arrested he/she ought not to be granted bail, but should be kept in prison, and even if bail is granted the amount fixed must be very high to reflect the severity of the offence and the public's abhorrence.

Bail is a surety lodged to ensure the attendance of an accused person at his/her trial. The issuance of bail is provided for under the Criminal Law (Procedure) Act, Cap. 10:01, Section 81. In certain circumstances a person charged with an offence has a right to be admitted to bail, e.g. where the offence is a misdemeanour, i.e., a minor offence, punishable with a fine or with imprisonment for a term not exceeding two years. If the offence is a misdemeanour not punishable with a fine or imprisonment in excess of two years or is a felony, i.e., a serious offence, a magistrate has a discretion to admit an accused person to bail. The only offences which are not bailable, i.e., for which no bail will be granted, are treason, misprision of treason, treason felony and murder.

An accused person under Section 82 may be admitted to bail upon providing a surety or sureties sufficient, in the opinion of the magistrate, to secure his/her appearance at court. The fixing of the amount of bail is at all times in the discretion of the magistrate, the amount fixed being always to ensure that the accused attends court, and is not a fine or penalty.

One hears repeatedly opinions expressed that the bail fixed in relation to a person accused of a crime was too low, and satisfaction expressed when bail fixed is high. Of course, one has to consider that we live in times when it is possible to leave the country undetected or to induce someone in authority to look the other way. Persons on bail sometimes fail to attend court for hearings of cases involving offences for which they are charged. Without seeking to justify a magistrate's reason for fixing bail in enormous sums, may be to discourage such persons from fleeing the jurisdiction before the hearing is concluded. One of the conditions of the grant of bail is that the bailor, i.e., the person who lodges the surety must produce the person charged at the trial; if not the bail is escheated, i.e., forfeited. One is, therefore, less likely to flee and have thousands or millions of dollars forfeited than if it is a relatively small sum which a bailor can afford to lose.

Whatever the reason excessive bail which is beyond the reach of an accused person to lodge may be regarded as being tantamount to a refusal of bail. Of course, conditions can be attached to the grant of bail, e.g., surrendering of travel documents or causing the accused person to report to the nearest police station on specific days and at specific times.

I hope that I have been able to clarify certain misconceptions about the Judiciary due in no small measure to a lack of appreciation of how the court system works. I trust that you now have a better understanding of the Judiciary and some of the issues which our courts have to determine, and the difficulties which arise on a daily basis. For our courts to function satisfactorily there must be cooperation between Bench, Bar, the support staff, the police and the prison service. A chain is as strong as its weakest link, and deficiencies in one area invariably result in the entire system being clogged. All of us are involved, and it is only with cooperation from everyone that we can achieve the commendable goal of providing justice to the citizens of this fair land of ours.

Georgetown, Guyana
June 11, 2001

CHAPTER 3

SECURING AND ENHANCING JUDICIAL INDEPENDENCE

The independence of the Judiciary has been the watchword and mantra of all who administer justice in jurisdictions of western democracies. It is usually safeguarded in written constitutions, and preserved by years of tradition and conventions in the unwritten constitution of England. The Judiciary has been described as the third arm of the State (a term which I prefer instead of arm of Government), the other two being the Legislature and the Executive. Those who choose to regard the Judiciary as the third arm of government labour under the misapprehension that it is part of the elected government, and so subject to its dictates.

Unfortunately, much of this misapprehension can be found in some developing countries in the infancy of independence and governed by rulers enjoying the heady euphoria of power with its attendant consequences. They regard the Judiciary as a wild horse which needs to be tamed and controlled lest it gets out of hand. Even in developed countries with entrenched constitutional provisions which safeguard the independence of the Judiciary, judges though respected, are privately regarded as humbugs and hindrances standing in the way of advancement of political objectives. The courts are bulwarks against abuse and violations of the rights of citizens in disputes between citizen and citizen and citizen and the State. The courts through their judges have conferred on them the power to declare legislation enacted by the legislature to be unconstitutional, and it is very often in so doing that they incur the wrath of the Executive. In some jurisdictions, such declarations are usually followed by the passage of new legislation to counteract the effect of the courts' decisions.

Because of its unique status in the hierarchy of State institutions, the Judiciary must be protected from interference (whether covert or overt) from any quarter. Judges must be free from pressures either of a financial or psychological nature if they are to render justice according to law and established precedent. By their oath of office judges are enjoined to hold the scales evenly, and they know not the persons before them, only the cause itself. Integrity is the *sine qua non* of every judge, and an integral component of judicial independence. Consequently, nothing should be done to affect this integrity, and we should spare no effort in preserving it.

In this regard the ugly spectre of corruption in the Judiciary which is rearing its head in some jurisdictions must be snuffed out.

Accountability is an integral part of judicial independence, and we must accept that we have an obligation to the public whom we serve. Hence it has become increasingly necessary to formulate codes of conduct to guide both judges and magistrates in the performance of their duties and in their day-to-day relations with members of the legal profession and the public. It is a suggested list of "do's and don'ts" which draws attention to circumstances and situations which a judge may encounter and which he/she should be prepared to confront.

Codes of conduct may be useful guides for judicial conduct, but at the end of the day the judge's moral character and personal code by which he or she lives will always be the best criterion to be followed.

David Pannick in the introduction to his book "Judges" made this profound statement; "Judges do not have an easy job. They repeatedly do what the rest of us seek to avoid: make decisions". Everyone throws their problems at you, and expects you to find a solution sooner rather than later invariably complaining about your incompetence if the decision goes against what was expected. The successful litigant hails the trial judge as brilliant while the loser regards him/her as incompetent. Alas! These are occupational hazards which one learns to take in one's stride. The important consideration for a judge is acting fairly and doing justice according to law.

One important factor which will enhance judicial independence is its financial independence. A Judiciary which does not regulate its own finances or does not have a sufficiency of funds allocated to it cannot be said to be truly independent. One should not be obligated to the Executive for periodic expenditure or, for that matter, increased emoluments. In some jurisdictions, the Judiciary invariably has to take the initiative in requesting an increase in salaries, and adopt the role of bargaining agent in negotiations for better working conditions. This can be a most humiliating and embarrassing experience particularly if it takes place shortly after a court has struck down some bit of legislation or ruled against the government in a politically sensitive matter.

This unsatisfactory state of affairs should be avoided at all costs by establishing a non-partisan independent commission to regulate periodically the emoluments and conditions of service of judges. This was one of the recommendations included in the Limassol Conclusions coming out of the Commonwealth Secretariat's Colloquium on combating corruption in the Judiciary held in Limassol, Cyprus in June 2002. It was endorsed recently by nineteen (19) Chief Justices and Heads of Judiciary when they met at the Commonwealth Magistrates' & Judges' Association Conference in Malawi in August 2003. The text of the recommendation reads thus:

> In order to strengthen judicial independence and integrity the Colloquium requests the Commonwealth Secretariat to facilitate the carrying out of a comprehensive survey of the methods of determining conditions of service of judicial officers throughout the Commonwealth so as to provide guidelines on prevailing best practices. The Colloquium notes the practice adopted in some jurisdictions of determination of judicial salaries and terms and conditions by an independent commission.

In similar vein, another recommendation within the Limassol Conclusions urged Governments to ensure that the remuneration of judicial officers is fixed at a level that will ensure that they enjoy financial security during their tenure of office and that upon retirement they continue to enjoy such security. In this way recruitment and retention of persons of the requisite integrity and competence will be assured.

The Colloquium during its deliberations welcomed the 1999 commitment of the Commonwealth Heads of Government to the Framework for Commonwealth Principles on Promoting Good Governance and Combating Corruption in which this statement was made:

> An independent and competent Judiciary, which is impartial, efficient and reliable is of paramount importance. This requires

objective criteria for the selection and removal of judges, adequate remuneration, security of tenure and independence from the executive and legislative branches of government.

However, judicial independence does not imply a lack of accountability. Judges should act properly in accordance with their office and should be subject to the ordinary criminal laws of the land. There should be procedures to discipline or dismiss them if they act improperly or otherwise fail in the performance of their duties to society. These procedures should be transparent and administered by institutions which are themselves independent and impartial.

The independence of the Judiciary is a precious and fragile gem. It can be destroyed easily if not safeguarded and protected. We have a vested interest in its preservation, and we must do everything we can to ensure that it remains intact and inviolable. That eminent jurist, Lord Denning in his book "What Next in the Law" in the course of discussing abuse of power by governments stated that the only admissible remedy for any abuse of power in a civilised society is by recourse to law, and it follows as a necessary corollary that judges must be independent. They must be free from any influence by those who wield power; otherwise they cannot be trusted to decide whether or not the power is being abused or misused. They must not be diverted from their duty by any extraneous influences; not by hope of reward nor by the fear of penalties; not by flattering praise nor by indignant reproach. It is the sure knowledge of this that gives the people their confidence in the judges.

This summarises in full measure all that can be said and all that I have said about judicial independence; I can do no more than endorse the learned jurist's conclusions. I commend them to you as well.

Heads of Judiciary Conference
Belize
September, 2003

CHAPTER 4

THE IMPACT OF CORRUPTION WITHIN THE COURT SYSTEM ON ITS ABILITY TO ADMINISTER JUSTICE

I commend the organisers of this 14th Commonwealth Law Conference on the choice of the theme "Developing Law and Justice" and the various streams which include human rights and corruption within the Courts, issues which are inter-related and important in the administration of justice.

One of the fundamental rights of humankind is the expectation of reciprocity of treatment in the conduct of one's affairs. This translates into being just and fair, and expecting to be so treated in the courts which are charged with administering justice. In discharging this obligation, the streams of justice must be kept pure and unadulterated, not clogged or polluted.

The right to be treated fairly is recognised in international human rights treaties. The Universal Declaration of Human Rights[1] stipulates that every human being is entitled in full equality to a fair and public hearing by an independent and impartial tribunal in the determination of his rights and obligations of any criminal charge against him.

The 1966 International Covenant on Civil and Political Rights[2] similarly provides, and the Human Rights Committee has unambiguously held that "the right to be tried by an independent and impartial tribunal is an absolute right that may suffer no exception".[3] Other international treaties have similar provisions, e.g. the African Charter on Human and People's Rights, the American Convention on Human Rights and the European Convention on Human Rights.

The common thread woven into all of these treaties and which is relevant to the topic under discussion is the impartiality of the court or tribunal. The objective of every court in the judicial system of any nation is to administer justice by protecting the rights of citizens. Justice can only be achieved by holding the scales evenly which involves being impartial. No party should come to the court with an unfair advantage over the other.

Preservation of the integrity of the judicial system is a *sine qua non* of its effectiveness, and this can be tarnished by the corruption of its functionaries no matter how lowly. The whole structure becomes infected resulting in loss of confidence and trust in the persons responsible for safeguarding the rights of a state's citizens.

CORRUPTION

Corruption in its ordinary meaning connotes dishonest or fraudulent conduct, typically involving bribery, and in the context of this paper attributable to persons who are in positions of authority or in a position to influence those in authority. It has also been defined as the abuse of public office for private gain.[4] Members of any Judiciary by virtue of their eminence are expected to be pillars of rectitude in their communities, and above reproach. They are expected to provide solutions to problems and redress for violation of rights. They are expected to be objective in assessing evidence and determining guilt or innocence.

Oft times in some jurisdictions the failure of governments to ensure the independence of the Judiciary by according to it adequate and reasonable financial resources lead to corruption within the court system. If judges and support staff are inadequately paid or remunerated for their services, they will inevitably become vulnerable to external pressures and corruption.

In 1985 the Seventh United Nations Congress on the Prevention of Crime and the Treatment of Offenders adopted the Basic Principles on the Independence of the Judiciary which was later unanimously endorsed by the General Assembly of the United Nations.[5] One of the Principles is to this effect, "*It is the duty of each Member State to provide adequate resources to enable the judiciary to properly perform its functions.*"

The whole issue of the independence of the Judiciary has been debated and discussed repeatedly at different fora. One wonders whether any Judiciary can ever be totally independent having regard to the fact that its whole existence requires some dependence on the legislative and executive branches of government. The Judiciary cannot stand in isolation. It needs to be funded by the government, and some postulate that this compromises its independence and violates the doctrine of separation of powers. This is a notion to which I do not subscribe since of necessity every state must provide for the establishment of a court system which must be adequately staffed and funded. To request and expect adequate financing in no way compromises the independence or integrity of those who work within the judicial system. The compromise results when little or grossly inadequate financial resources are allocated to the administration of justice in a government's budget, and the Judiciary is relegated to the position of a mendicant in order to keep the court system on an even keel.

The symbiotic relationship between the Executive and the Judiciary was fully ventilated in the Report of the American Bar Association Commission on Separation of Powers and Judicial Independence[6] where it was stated that the success of any cooperative and constructive relationship ultimately depends upon meaningful communication. The Executive must appreciate that the Judiciary is usually in a better position to determine the most efficient and effective means of administering the courts, and must remain attentive to the Judiciary's needs and concerns. By that same token, the Executive is in a better position than the Judiciary to decide upon fiscal priorities, and it behoves the Judiciary to be sensitive to those priorities when communicating its own needs and concerns.

A balancing act of competing priorities for finance is always performed in developing countries with scarce financial resources. This results in the administration of justice being placed at the bottom of the scale when cash-strapped governments have to decide whether a school or hospital should be erected rather than a new court building or whether the emoluments of the Judiciary should be increased.

The inevitable result of persistent failure to address the needs of a state's Judiciary is that the scourge of corruption rears its ugly head. Judicial officers may be tempted to devise ways and means to augment their limited earnings. This also spreads to an underpaid and overworked support staff within the court system. These lowly persons are the main focus of my attention in that they can influence adversely the public's perception of a judicial administration which strives valiantly to uphold standards of fair play and principles of impartiality.

In the judicial systems of most developing countries the support staff which comprises clerks, typists, marshals and bailiffs is drawn from the traditional public service with fixed salary scales which are invariably low and hence attract persons with minimum qualifications. In most instances the wages earned can barely meet their living expenses. They are, however, expected to conform to high moral standards of behaviour befitting an institution charged with the responsibility of preserving the law and dispensing justice. They are expected to be scrupulously honest and fair in their interactions with the public, but are exposed on a daily basis to temptations and requests from parties to litigation in the courts to alter and remove files and documents or misrepresent facts or try to influence judges with whom they work.

The problem of corruption within the court system has gained momentum in proportion to the growth of the drug trafficking and narcotics trade. As law enforcement personnel seek new ways of prosecuting drug offenders these wily fiends devise methods to infiltrate the court system by targeting the persons who work within it, particularly those at the lower levels who are the most vulnerable and easy prey to temptation having regard to their fragile financial situations.

One may posit the view that all support staff in the court system should be adequately trained not only in the procedures to be followed in the performance of their duties, but also in the ethics and moral norms of behaviour which they are expected to uphold. This is a laudable and commendable objective, but is it easily achieved by personnel whose earnings are minimal? The temptation to transgress may be too great to resist.

The answer to this may not be easy for poor developing countries, but efforts must be made and methods devised to increase the emoluments of the support staff in the court system. Failure to do so and do so effectively will result in an infection of the system with a virus of no mean proportion with justice being sold to the highest bidder, not to mention loss of confidence by the public in the ability of judges to effect justice fairly and without favour.

Having identified the problem, one may ask quite naturally what can be done to eradicate corruption. For a judicial system to function effectively, justice must not only be done but be seen to be done. Public perception is very important, and those who administer the court system must be perceived to be acting firmly and resolutely in eradicating any form of corruption. Several initiatives can be taken to maintain public confidence and restore it if it is perceived to be lost.

One such initiative mentioned earlier was increasing the emoluments of the support staff, and I may also add the emoluments of judicial officers where necessary. Before proceeding to discuss other initiatives, I wish to make reference to the Limassol Conclusions.

LIMASSOL CONCLUSIONS

From 25-27 June 2002, Commonwealth Judicial Officers comprising Judges, Heads of Judiciary and Magistrates throughout the Commonwealth met in Limassol, Cyprus, at a Colloquium on "Combating Corruption Within the Judiciary".

The Colloquium welcomed the commitment of the Commonwealth Heads of Government to the Framework for Commonwealth Principles on Promoting Good Governance and Combating Corruption[7] and their intention to develop national strategies to promote good governance and eliminate corruption. The Limassol Conclusions can be regarded as one of the initiatives spearheaded by the Commonwealth Secretariat to eliminate corruption in one area where it ought not to be allowed to flourish, namely the Judiciary.

After extensive discussion in working groups on papers presented during the Colloquium by distinguished jurists, a variety of recommendations appropriately called the Limassol Conclusions were adopted. These conclusions are wide-ranging and multi-dimensional covering as they do guidelines on judicial ethics, anti-corruption programmes, strategies at eliminating corrupt practices within the Judiciary, recruiting persons of integrity and competence, to name a few.

With regard to judicial ethics formulation and adoption of a code was recommended to the judicial systems throughout the Commonwealth, and I would like to add here that such a code should not be confined to judges or magistrates only, but should be formulated for all support staff and personnel employed within the system. Training programmes were also recommended, and again these should be organised for the support staff as well. Such persons must be sensitised to the realisation that they are an integral part of the court system, and misconduct on their part reflects adversely on the entire administration of justice.

The recommendations embraced members of the legal profession as well with a suggestion that anti-corruption programmes for members of the Bar be promoted. This is very timely and necessary since in some jurisdictions support staff are particularly vulnerable to unscrupulous lawyers who dangle financial carrots and inducements before economically-deprived court employees in order to ensure their clients' acquittal or determination of cases in their favour.

With regard to the underpaid support staff one working group at Limassol recommended that such persons should be appointed to positions in the judicial system by the same body or commission which is responsible for appointing judicial officers in countries where such a commission exists. This commission should be independent and constitutionally established and protected. Judicial appointments should not be placed in the hands of the Executive or Head of Government which will clearly compromise the integrity of the Judiciary. Similarly, persons at lower levels in the judicial system need to be insulated from governmental pressure, and be paid salaries and emoluments commensurate with the positions they hold.

The Colloquium recognised that transparency assists in combating corruption, and suggested that judicial officers and court staff be encouraged to foster greater public awareness of the court's operations, role and function. For too long the court has been regarded as a mysterious organisation too complex for ordinary minds to comprehend, with its sombre attire, legal jargon and age-old traditions. Appearing before an austere personage dressed in peculiar black robes and looking down from on high can be a terrifying experience for the average person. Those who are responsible for the administration of justice need to make courts more user-friendly while at the same time preserving some of the traditions and certainly its dignity.

Regular visits to the courts in jurisdictions of the Commonwealth should be encouraged. Justice must not be regarded as a cloistered virtue; it must be patent and not obscure. The public must have free access to the courts and see the system at work. If this is denied inevitably adverse conclusions will be drawn based on hearsay and rumours which can only enure to the detriment of the administration of justice and an erosion of public confidence.

Overall, recommendations made at Limassol were directed to all stakeholders connected with the judicial system, namely, the Judiciary itself, the legal profession, and governments. Of course, the main stakeholder is the Judiciary and those charged with its administration.

The buck stops there, and the primary responsibility for eradicating corruption from the court system rests with the Judiciary and its administrators. However, the Judiciary does not operate in a vacuum, and it not self-sustaining. This leads me inevitably to a discussion of what is familiarly known as the Latimer House Guidelines[8], and now formally called the Commonwealth Principles. For ease of reference I shall utilise the familiar nomenclature.

LATIMER HOUSE GUIDELINES

These Guidelines were formally endorsed by the Commonwealth Heads of Government in 2003 at Abuja, Nigeria, and were principles on good practice governing relations between the Executive, Parliament and the Judiciary in the promotion of good government, the rule of law and human rights. The sections relevant to this presentation are Preserving Judicial Independence, Judicial Ethics, and Judicial Accountability.

In the section on Preserving Judicial Independence, the responsibility of providing sufficient and sustainable funding to enable the Judiciary to perform its functions to the highest standards rests on the government. Such funds once voted for the Judiciary by the Legislature should be protected from alienation and misuse. The allocation or withholding of funding should not be used as a means of exercising improper control over the Judiciary. Further, it was stated that appropriate salaries and benefits, supporting staff, resources and equipment are essential to the proper functioning of the Judiciary, and as a matter of principle judicial salaries and benefits should be set by an independent body and their value maintained.

The Judiciary's independence is severely compromised if it has to depend on the Executive for increases in its emoluments whenever that Executive sees it fit to grant an increase. This should be placed in the hands of a non-partisan body to review and recommend increases whenever necessary taking into account relevant factors.

As mentioned earlier in reference to the Limassol Conclusions the Guidelines in relation to Judicial Ethics stipulate that a code of conduct should be developed and adopted by each Judiciary as a means of ensuring the accountability of judges, and was in fact the basis for the recommendation in the Limassol Conclusions. Legitimate public criticism of judicial performance as a means of ensuring accountability was stressed in the Guidelines under this head.

The Colloquium at Limassol agreed that accountability was important if the Judiciary is to develop competence and remain impartial and independent, and it was imperative that a mechanism be devised for dealing with complaints against judges. It urged that such mechanism must be transparent in order to command public respect and acceptance. The Latimer House Guidelines, however, suggest that discipline of judges should be conducted by the chief judge and should not include public admonition. The thinking which informs this view is to avoid public humiliation and embarrassment thereby bringing the entire Judiciary into disrepute.

Another aspect of accountability which forms part of the Limassol Conclusions is the relationship between the Judiciary and the court staff to which I alluded earlier. The view was expressed that there should be a greater degree of judicial awareness of the work of the court staff, and liaison with the said staff should be encouraged in order to ensure the smooth operation of the judicial system.

In most jurisdictions members of the Judiciary are totally unaware of the functions which support staff perform except of those working in close collaboration with the judge. Members of the Judiciary need to climb down from their ivory towers and take an interest in what goes on around them. They need to be familiar with all aspects of the work of the courts and the persons who operate within the system. Every cog, no matter how small, is important if the wheels of justice are to turn smoothly. A greater degree of interaction is required in order to inspire confidence and trust between the Judiciary and its support staff. If a level of trust is developed this may lead inevitably to some degree of loyalty to the system, and perhaps reduce temptation which eventually leads to corruption of the entire judicial process.

As indicated earlier in this presentation corruption in its ordinary meaning connotes fraudulent conduct typically involving bribery or some financial advantage. However, there are other aspects of corruption which are equally reprehensible, and I refer specifically to corruption of one's mind which in relation to the Judiciary may be reflected in the delivery of perverse judgments based on a distortion of facts given at the behest of a relative or an acquaintance. This strikes at the very root of one's personal integrity, and unfortunately there are no easy solutions in this regard. Integrity is a virtue which inheres in an individual, and which cannot be learnt.

The need for judicial codes of ethics cannot be over-emphasised as they may indicate what is regarded as acceptable conduct. Sadly, one cannot always assume that everyone who aspires to or holds judicial office is aware of the components of correct judicial behaviour. Codes of ethics hopefully will point would-be aspirants in the right direction.

The methods used to eradicate corruption from the judicial system will vary within jurisdictions, but the aim should always be to sensitise judicial officers and support staff to the need for upholding the integrity of their offices within the court system. It is a goal which must be pursued resolutely in the quest for good governance within the administration of justice.

14th Commonwealth Law Conference
United Kingdom
September, 2005

Endnotes

1 Article 10.
2 Article 14 (1).
3 Communication No. 263/1987, M. Gonzalez del Rio-v-Peru (Views adopted on 28 October, 1992).
4 Framework for Commonwealth Principles on Promoting Good Governance and Combating Corruption approved by CHOGM in Durban, 1999.
5 General Assembly resolutions 40/32 of 29 November, 1985 and 40/146 of 13 December, 1985.
6 1997 – Findings, Conclusions and Recommendations.
7 Footnote 4 at p. 2.
8 Formulated at Latimer House, United Kingdom, in June 1998.

CHAPTER 5

THE CARIBBEAN COURT OF JUSTICE AND ITS RELATIONSHIP WITH THE CARICOM SINGLE MARKET

Before I commence discussion on the topic of this address, I wish to congratulate heartily the Barbados Public Workers' Cooperative Credit Union on the celebration of its 36th Anniversary, and on its outstanding success over the past years. I am extremely impressed with the progress made from a small savings society in 1970 with a capital of $1732 and operating out of a suitcase to assets of over $400M today. What an achievement! The progressive success of this outstanding institution is testimony to the dedication, unswerving commitment, loyalty and determination of its members. Special tribute must be paid to the Union's founding member, Sister Olive Trotman whose contribution was the cornerstone on which its present success was built. I am indeed honoured to have been asked to deliver this year's lecture in the Memorial Lecture Series honouring this outstanding lady, and also to be the first female to do so. My tribute to Olive Trotman is summed up in this phrase "Never underestimate the power of a dedicated woman".

I understand that the initial response and performance of the Civil Service Credit Union as it was then known was disappointing, and this makes the progressive development of the present credit union even more awesome, and continuous growth over the years overwhelming. From being referred to as "the poor man's bank" you are now a financial giant in the world of commercial banking.

The words of the Committee headed by Ralph Boyce and which was established in 1975 to make recommendations for the resuscitation of the credit union which had gone into a decline, were prophetic and indicative of the grit and determination that propelled you to your present position. That Committee determined that "the Credit Union would be transformed to a powerful economic grouping which will set the pattern for others to follow". You have proved that prophecy to be correct, and may have even surpassed all expectations.

Any organisation is as strong as its members and its leaders want it to be, and it is obvious that the collective leadership and membership of the Barbados Public Workers' Cooperative Credit Union have taken their responsibilities to their organisation and the Barbados public seriously.

The contribution of credit unions in the Caribbean Region is incalculable and significant as these unions provide financial and other support to the communities in which they operate. They contribute to the well-being of their members who in most instances would have been economically deprived of the means and the wherewithal to improve their financial positions.

The mission statement of the BPWCCU attests to this. It reads thus: "Our mission is to render excellence in service to our members while providing the means for enhancing their financial, economic and social well-being, in consonance with cooperative principles."

The continued growth of the credit union demonstrates that it is fulfilling its mission, and I am positive will continue to do so in the future.

I shall now embark on the subject of this lecture which is a discourse about the Caribbean Court of Justice.

THE CARIBBEAN COURT OF JUSTICE

The Caribbean Court of Justice is now a reality having been inaugurated on 16th April 2005. In spite of public awareness efforts by the CARICOM Secretariat several months before the inauguration, misconceptions about the Court abound in relation to its functions, independence and its relationship with the domestic courts of the Region. The Caribbean Court of Justice which I shall hereafter refer to as "the Court" exercises two jurisdictions – an appellate and an original. Even though the focus of this lecture will be on the original jurisdiction, with which the CARICOM Single Market will be concerned, I shall digress briefly to mention a few facts about the appellate jurisdiction.

For most of the English-speaking CARICOM countries, the Judicial Committee of the Privy Council was and still is the final court for appeals emanating from their domestic appellate courts. Since the inauguration of the Court, only two CARICOM states have elected to utilise the appellate jurisdiction – Barbados for whom the Privy Council was its final appellate court, and Guyana whose domestic court of appeal was its final court. Obstacles in the form of referenda in some and objections by opposition political parties to the passage of the required legislation in others have delayed the signing on to the appellate jurisdiction in these states.

The original jurisdiction, however, has the full support of all Member States of CARICOM. The Court in its original jurisdiction operates as an international tribunal adopting and applying international law in its interpretation of the Revised Treaty of Chaguaramas Establishing the Caribbean Community including the CARICOM Single Market and Economy, which in the preamble thereto affirmed that the original jurisdiction of the Court is essential for the successful operation of the Single Market and Economy. In 2001 the Agreement Establishing the Caribbean Court of Justice came into effect conferring on the Court exclusive jurisdiction to hear and deliver judgment on:

(a) disputes between Contracting Parties to the Agreement;
(b) disputes between any Contracting Parties to the Agreement and the Community;
(c) referrals from national courts or tribunals of Contracting Parties to the Agreement;
(d) applications by nationals in accordance with Article XXIV, concerning the interpretation and application of the Treaty.[1]

Both the Treaty and the Agreement recognise the sovereignty of the Member States of the Caribbean Community, and a natural consequence of this is that each Member State could interpret and apply the Treaty as it sees fit. Of necessity, this would lead to varied interpretations and differences of opinion. With the establishment of the Court certainty and uniformity of interpretation of the terms of the Treaty are guaranteed. It is beyond dispute that certainty of an important international instrument such as the Treaty is a *sine qua non* in attracting investment to the Region, and it follows that uncertainty and unpredictability of legal decisions on economic issues will become a disincentive to any commercial activity.

While preservation of the sovereignty of Member States is acknowledged and the desirability of entrenching the Court in their national constitutions is accepted, it was recognised that the original jurisdiction of the Court must be compulsory, ipso facto, without special agreement.[2] This means that there are no options if uniformity and certainty is to be achieved when applying and interpreting the Treaty. Hand in hand with this compulsory nature of the original jurisdiction is the dictate that judgments of the Court when handed down must be complied with promptly by Member States, organs, bodies and entities of the Community as well as by any persons to whom a judgment applies[3]. Enforceability of judgments of domestic courts is usually provided for by legislation enacted in Member States. In relation to enforcement of the judgments of the Court, Member States agree to take all necessary steps, including the enactment of legislation, to ensure that all authorities act in aid of the Court, and that any judgment, order, decree or sentence of the Court be enforced by all courts and authorities of a Member State in the same way as any judgment, order, decree or sentence of a superior domestic court of that State.[4] This provision applies to both jurisdictions of the Court as does Article III of the Agreement that the decisions of the Court shall be final.

In any court the doctrine of *stare decisis* or judicial precedent is important for its stability and predictability, and both the Treaty and the Agreement[5] address this by providing that judgments of the Court shall be legally binding precedents for parties in proceedings before the Court unless such judgments have been revised.

Even after a judgment has been delivered it may be revised within five years on an application based only upon discovery of some fact of such a nature as to be a decisive factor, and which was unknown to the Court and the party claiming the revision when the judgment was given.[6]

In exercising the exclusive jurisdiction conferred on the Court provision is made in the Treaty for the delivery of advisory opinions at the request of Member States to a dispute,[7] and referrals[8] which arise when a national court of a Member State being seised of an issue whose resolution involves a question concerning the interpretation or application of the Treaty, considers that a decision on the question is necessary to enable it to deliver judgment. That national court must refer the question to the Court for determination before delivering judgment in keeping with the desirability for uniformity of interpretation; no other court or tribunal of any Member State is vested with the power to interpret or apply the provisions of the Treaty which is the sole prerogative of the Court applying in this regard such rules of international law as may be applicable. In applying rules of international law the Court is obligated to make a finding and cannot remain silent because of obscurity of the law. All of this, however, is without prejudice to the Court's power to decide disputes on equitable principles if the parties so agree.[9]

Much reliance will be placed and assistance gleaned from international tribunals such as the European Court of Justice and the Court of Justice of the Common Market for Eastern and Southern Africa which are courts established with a similar function to interpret and apply relevant instruments.

Advisory opinions can be sought from the Court only by Member States or the Community itself on issues covered by the Treaty whenever necessary.

A question that may spring readily to the minds of citizens of the Region is whether individual persons have access to the Court in its original jurisdiction. As mentioned earlier the Court's jurisdiction includes hearing applications by nationals which include individual persons as well as legal persons such as companies. However, this is possible only with the special leave of the Court in proceedings where:

(a) the Court determines in any particular case that the Treaty intended that a right conferred by it on a Member State should enure for the benefit of its nationals;
(b) the persons concerned establish that they have been prejudiced in the enjoyment of that benefit;
(c) that the Member State which is entitled to espouse the claim in the proceedings before the Court either omitted or declined to do so or expressly agreed that the persons concerned may espouse the claim instead of the Member State; and
(d) the Court finds that the interest of justice requires that the persons be allowed to espouse the claim.[10]

Primarily the focus of the Court's jurisdiction will be in hearing and determining disputes between Member States and disputes between Member States and the Community. If the aforementioned conditions are satisfied persons (natural or legal) may have access to the Court in relation to issues which may arise under the Treaty. This may, for example, be claims of a commercial nature or of the free movement of skills, goods or services.

Apart from launching proceedings a national may apply to the Court to intervene in a proceeding before the Court if it is felt that such a person or entity has a substantial interest of a legal nature which may be affected by a decision of the Court.[11] This also applies to a Member State or the Community.

Universally, procedures for settlement of disputes usually form part of investment instruments in the commercial arena. The desire to promote the concept of alternative dispute resolution (in all forms) is recognised in both the Treaty and the Agreement[12] which urge Member States to the maximum extent possible, to encourage and facilitate the use of arbitration and other modes of alternative dispute resolution for the settlement of private international commercial disputes among nationals of the Community as well as among Community nationals and nationals of third States.

I reiterate here that the Court in exercising its original jurisdiction shall apply international law which is applicable to both civil law and common law jurisdictions thereby rendering it acceptable to the Member States of Suriname and Haiti with civil law jurisdictions.

At this stage I shall move on to discuss the relevance of the Court to the CARICOM Single Market, my knowledge of which is somewhat limited and for which I crave your indulgence.

CARICOM SINGLE MARKET

When the Revised Treaty of Chaguaramas establishing the Caribbean Community was signed it included the CARICOM Single Market and Economy. I am informed that only the Single Market has survived, and the "Economy" has been deferred hopefully for some opportune and auspicious time in the future.

Perforce one is compelled to ask what is meant by and envisaged as a "single market" within the Caribbean Community. I have gleaned much from an article by Mr. Ivor Carryl, Programme Manager for the Single Market and Economy in the CARICOM Secretariat, entitled "*Notes on the Operationalisation of the Single Market and Economy*".[13] He explained it thus:

> *The applied notion of the CSME includes the equal right or access to any market by natural and juridical persons whether as buyers or sellers, irrespective of nationality or the location of the good without*

reiteration except as authorised by or specified in the Treaty as negotiated by the contracting parties.

Mr. Carryl indicated certain basic criteria which have to be satisfied, namely,

(a) negotiating equal rights and terms of access of nationals from different states to supply goods and provide services and skills in particular markets; and
(b) enjoying these negotiated rights or access when the states making the commitments take action to remove restrictions that prevent entry and participation in the negotiated markets.

He went on to state that when all of the restrictions or discriminatory treatment that existed at the time of entry into force of the Treaty have been removed in all of the markets which were the subject of negotiation and agreement, the sum total of the markets against which measures were removed results in the creation of the Single Market and Economy. A court would have jurisdiction over the rights and terms of access and the commitments to grant them on or after the date when they fall due and none other; further, some markets may not be included in the Single Market at a particular point in time and would be outside the jurisdiction of courts.

I apprehend the CSME to be one large single economic zone within which people, markets, services and skills can move freely with minimum restriction. Inevitably problems will arise, for instance, with removal of restrictions that prevent entry and participation in the negotiated markets, and it is in this regard that the Court's original jurisdiction comes into operation in resolving disputes between Member States or applications by nationals.

There is another area covered by the Treaty in which the Court's jurisdiction will be employed. The Treaty establishes a competition policy the goal of which is to ensure that the benefits expected from the creation of the CSME are not frustrated by anti-competitive business conduct,[14] and for the purpose of implementing that policy provides for the establishment of a Competition Commission[15] with a variety of powers to deal with business conduct which prejudices trade or prevents competition within the CSME. The Treaty empowers the

Competition Commission to apply to the Court for relevant orders when conducting investigations and also for a party aggrieved by a determination of the Commission to apply to the Court for a review of the determination[16]. In addition, the Court may on an application of the Commission, review a decision of the Commission where the decision was induced by deceit or improper means.[17]

All of the foregoing indicates that the future of the CSM is heavily dependent on the Court and on its interpretations of the Treaty whenever it is called upon to make them. In this regard the Court while utilising all relevant aspects of international law and the experience of other international tribunals will over time build for itself a body of precedents relevant to our Region.

CONCLUSION

The way ahead for the Court as it exercises its original jurisdiction will present many challenges particularly in its interpretation and application of the provisions of the Treaty. The learned President of the Court, The Rt. Hon. Mr. Justice Michael de la Bastide, T.C., P.C., in a presentation at a conference[18] held here in Barbados last year on a similar topic indicated areas in which the Court will have to chart its own course, one being the extent to which effect should be given to provisions in the Treaty which are not expressly incorporated into domestic law or are inconsistent with local law. He posed as an example the question of how the freedom of movement of capital is to be reconciled with exchange control restrictions that have not been modified to accommodate it.

Reference was made at the beginning about several misconceptions which have plagued acceptance of the Court as part of the judicial systems of the Region; chief among these is that the Court will be controlled by the politicians and Governments. Let me explode this myth immediately by stating that unlike the judges of the European Court of Justice who are appointed by the Ministers of Government, the judges of our Court are appointed by an independent Regional and Legal Services Commission comprising:

(a) two representatives each of the Regional Bar Associations;
(b) two jurists nominated by the Regional universities and the Council of Legal Education;

(c) the Chairman of one of the Judicial Service Commissions of a Member State;
(d) the Chairman of one of the Public Service Commissions of a Member State;
(e) two persons from civil society nominated jointly by the Secretary General of CARICOM and the Director General of the OECS, and
(f) two persons nominated jointly by the Bar or Law Associations of the Member States.

The President of the Court is the Chairman of the Commission which in addition to appointing the judges of the Court also appoint officials and employees and determine their conditions of service. The only office to which the Commission does not make an appointment is that of the President of the Court who is appointed by the Heads of Government of the Region on a recommendation from the Commission. Applications for appointments to the Court are considered from qualified persons from all over the Commonwealth, and is not confined to persons from the Region. I can see no room for political interference or control in appointments of the judges, and to suggest that these persons can be influenced by politicians is an insult to the integrity of those who comprise the Court.

Another misconception surrounds the financing of the Court which popular opinion regards as being a burden on the Member State in which the Court is located. A Trust Fund has been established by all of the Member States with technical assistance from the Caribbean Development Bank which was also instrumental in raising the sum of US$100M from international financial markets for the purpose of financing the Court. This sum was lent to the Member States, and is repayable over a period of between fifteen (15) to twenty (20) years at low rates of interest so as not to impose an undue financial burden on them. The amount raised was paid over to the Trust Fund which is administered by a Board of Trustees comprising reputable persons, some skilled in business and others holding high judicial office. The object was to ensure that the finances of the Court are in safe hands.

Other misconceptions suggesting that the Court was established to enforce the death penalty, and that the judges will not be of equal intellectual calibre as those of the Privy Council are not worthy of comment, and I mention them only in passing.

Before concluding this lecture, I wish to correct an omission to mention that the Original Jurisdiction Rules 2005 have been finalised and are now available from the Court and accessible on the Court's website. These Rules were drafted in keeping with provisions in both the Treaty and the Agreement[19] and which empowered the President of the Court to establish Rules of Court for the exercise of the original jurisdiction. It is hoped that with the Rules in place the Court will be utilised fully in carrying out its mandate.

The Court is now a reality, and there is no turning back. We can only go forward and strive in the years ahead to craft a jurisprudence for the Caribbean Region of which we can all be truly proud. The time has come to throw off the last shackles of colonialism, and assume responsibility for dispensing justice to our own people in our own courts and according to our own customs and culture.

Thank you once again for inviting me to be part of your 36th Anniversary celebrations.

Congratulations and best wishes for the future!

36th Anniversary of Barbados Public Workers
Cooperative Credit Union
2005

Endnotes

1 Article X11.
2 Article 216 of the Treaty; Article XVI of the Agreement.
3 Article 215 of the Treaty; Article XV of the Agreement.
4 Article XXVI of the Agreement.
5 Article 221 of the Treaty; Article XXII of the Agreement.
6 Article 219 of the Treaty; Article XX of the Agreement.
7 Article 212; Article XIII of the Agreement.
8 Article 214; Article XIV of the Agreement.
9 Article XVII of the Agreement.
10 A summary of Article XXIV of the Agreement.
11 Article XVIII of the Agreement.
12 Article 223 of the Treaty; Article XXIII of the Agreement.
13 "Caribbean Court of Justice – Issues and Perspectives" (2001) Vol. 1.
14 Article 169.
15 Article 171.
16 Article 175.
17 Article 180.
18 Conference on the CARICOM Single Market and Economy: Toward CSME and Beyond, May 5, 2005.
19 Article 220 of the Treaty; Article XXI of the Agreement.

CHAPTER 6

FOSTERING A CULTURE OF RESPECT FOR HUMAN RIGHTS WITHIN THE JUDICIAL SYSTEMS OF THE COMMONWEALTH CARIBBEAN

The point of departure in any discourse on human rights will inevitably commence from the Universal Declaration of Human Rights[1] and on to the twin International Covenants on Civil and Political Rights[2] and Economic, Social and Cultural Rights[3] ratified or acceded to by member states of the United Nations which have undertaken to give effect to their laudable objectives. The independent states of the Commonwealth Caribbean[4] are no exception. In addition, a few of these states have also ratified the American Convention on Human Rights[5] with similar objectives.

Recognition of human rights and freedoms is invariably achieved by the ratifying of international treaties and conventions by states eager to be part of an international complying community. Of more importance, however, and in fact far more difficult to achieve is ensuring respect for these fundamental rights. This difficulty was recognised in the Preamble to the Universal Declaration of Human Rights which recites a pledge by member states to "achieve the promotion of universal respect for and observance of human rights and fundamental freedoms," "and strive by teaching and education to promote such respect." The Covenant on Civil and Political Rights, the American Convention on Human Rights, and the Convention on the Rights of the Child[6] specifically extract from states parties an undertaking to "respect and ensure" to all individuals the rights contained in those treaties.

In this regard one Caribbean state (Guyana) has expressly provided in its Constitution for the establishment of a Human Rights Commission, one of the primary functions being "to advocate and promote respect for, and an understanding of, human rights," and another being to "educate the public regarding the nature and content of such rights". Guyana has even expanded the human rights regime by providing for the establishment of individual rights commissions for women, children and indigenous peoples as well as a tribunal charged with the responsibility of dealing with violations and enforcement of rights covered by the specific commissions. It is expressly stated that every person contemplated by the respective international treaties to which that state has acceded is entitled to the human rights enshrined in the said treaties, and such rights shall be respected and upheld by the Executive, Legislature, Judiciary, organs and agencies of Government and all natural and legal persons.[7] This Constitution has incorporated unique provisions under the heading of "Guiding Principles and Objectives," which, *inter alia*, exhort courts to pay due regard to international law, conventions, covenants and charters bearing on human rights when interpreting the fundamental rights provisions.[8]

All of the constitutions of the Commonwealth Caribbean states have enshrined provisions for fundamental human rights and freedoms and the protection afforded to them which were influenced in large measure by the European Convention for the Protection of Human Rights and Fundamental Freedoms[9]. It is impossible due to the constraints of time and space to discuss in depth the wide range of these rights, so the paper will be restricted to a discussion of the right to life, protection from inhuman and degrading punishment, protection of the law, protection from discrimination and equality before the law.

RIGHT TO LIFE AND PROTECTION FROM INHUMAN AND DEGRADING PUNISHMENT

These rights common to all constitutions have given rise to more judicial precedents within the Commonwealth Caribbean than any other being inextricably linked to the death penalty which under the laws of all of the states is the ultimate sanction for a person convicted of the offences of murder and treason. Two constitutions specifically stipulate convictions for these two offences as being exceptions to the right to life.[10] Jamaica while retaining the death penalty has categorised the offence of murder into capital and non-capital offences.

The constitutionality of the death penalty has been challenged in domestic courts at all levels, and for those states which have ratified the American Convention on Human Rights[11] and accepted the jurisdiction of the Inter-American Court of Human Rights, petitions have been lodged with the Inter-American Commission seeking relief from the death penalty after conviction.

The judgments of the Judicial Committee of the Privy Council (hereinafter referred to as "the Privy Council") being the highest domestic court of last resort for all but two of the Commonwealth Caribbean states, have ebbed and flowed on the constitutionality of the death penalty deeming it unconstitutional in the case of *Watson v R*[12] (Jamaica) and constitutional in *Matthew v The State*[13] (Trinidad and Tobago) and *Boyce and Joseph v R*[14] (Barbados). The variance in the decisions depended on interpretations of the relevant constitutional provisions.

In *Watson*, the Jamaican Government sought to amend statutory provisions for the offence of murder by retaining the death penalty only for capital offences as mentioned earlier, no doubt in an attempt to alleviate the harsh effects of the death penalty which in some quarters could be regarded as cruel and inhuman punishment. Without delving into the intricacies of the arguments, this had the effect of rendering the amending legislation unconstitutional according to the reasoning of the Privy Council since it was not an existing law that had been saved when the Jamaican Constitution came into effect upon the grant of independence.

By contrast the relevant statutory provisions in *Matthew* (Trinidad and Tobago) and *Boyce* (Barbados) were held to be constitutional, being existing laws which were saved under the independence constitutions.

Those states which have ratified the international human rights treaties mentioned earlier, sometimes find themselves in a quandary in relation to their international obligations. It is ironic that Jamaica, which sought to modify the effect of its existing legislation by categorising the offence of murder, found that the effort was unconstitutional. Had it been deemed constitutional Jamaica would have succeeded in a limited way. The minority judgment of the Privy Council in *Watson*, which favoured a different interpretation of the relevant provisions of the Constitution, saw the attempt by Jamaica as a "bona-fide move in the direction of seeking to protect the human rights of individual defendants."

In the Caribbean, the difficulties encountered by a state in honouring its international obligations under treaties which it ratifies may be attributable to indolence or reluctance in incorporating these treaties into domestic law by enactment of specific parliamentary legislation.

If they are not, they remain unincorporated (though ratified) and are unenforceable on the domestic plane. Hence a state's international obligations under an unincorporated international treaty, particularly a human rights treaty ratified for the benefit of a state's nationals, cannot be enforced on the domestic plane, an inexplicable conundrum which individuals in monist jurisdictions find difficult to comprehend.

Invariably, a person convicted of the capital charge of murder, having exhausted all of the domestic remedies, seeks relief from the death penalty by having recourse as a last resort to the provisions of an international treaty which was ratified by the state for the benefit of its nationals. Although such a person can seek relief under that treaty, time may be unkind as the state is under no obligation to delay execution pending the result of an approach to the relevant body under the international treaty, the same not having been incorporated into the domestic law. This was addressed and discussed in the case of *Neville Lewis v Attorney General of Jamaica and Another*[15] where the Privy Council held that when a state acceded to international treaties even though unincorporated into domestic law, and allowed individuals to petition international human rights bodies, the protection of the law conferred by the constitution entitled a petitioner to complete that procedure and to obtain the reports of such bodies as well as a stay of execution until the reports are received and considered. The state, however, is not obliged or bound to accept the recommendations of the treaty body in determining the fate of the convicted person.

This issue arose recently in an appeal to the Caribbean Court of Justice.[16] Incidentally it was an appeal by the Attorney General of Barbados against Boyce and Joseph, the same persons referred to earlier who had appealed to the Privy Council a few years before challenging the constitutionality of the mandatory death penalty. In this case the State of Barbados appealed against a commutation of the sentence of death to one of life imprisonment imposed by the Barbados Court of Appeal. Other proceedings had been instituted after the decision of the Privy Council which gave rise to the appeal. The Caribbean Court of Justice was required to determine the effect of unincorporated human rights treaties on the execution of a death sentence, and the relationship between such treaties and domestic law in that regard. The State of Barbados had ratified the American Convention on Human Rights, but had not incorporated it into domestic law through its Parliament. The Convention permits every person condemned to death to apply for amnesty, pardon or commutation of sentence, and specifically provides that "capital punishment shall not be imposed while such a petition is pending decision by the competent authority".[17]

The domestic machinery established under the constitution to exercise the prerogative of mercy, after due consideration declined to do so in the petitioners' favour, and fixed dates for execution of the sentences of death while petitions before the Inter-American Commission on Human Rights were still pending. The question for consideration – should the State carry out the sentences bearing in mind the impact which undue delay in the execution of a sentence of death may have on a convicted person's protection from cruel, inhuman and degrading punishment guaranteed under the constitution?

The dilemma facing a State in these circumstances is that it has no control over the length of time which a treaty body may take to conclude its deliberations. The dilemma is further compounded by the guidelines issued by the Privy Council in *Pratt v Attorney General of Jamaica*[18] familiarly referred to as the Pratt & Morgan Guidelines to the effect that where execution is delayed for more than five years after a sentence of death has been pronounced there would be strong grounds for concluding that an execution after such a delay was an infringement of a condemned person's constitutional right against inhuman and degrading punishment.[19] Those Caribbean states for whom the Privy Council is the court of last resort are caught between striving to comply with the Guidelines on the domestic plane and seeking to permit their nationals to take advantage of the provisions for redress under an unincorporated international treaty which it has ratified on the international plane, placing them in a position akin to the mythological god Janus with two faces each looking in opposite directions, and which as one judgment of the Court aptly suggested as appearing to be schizophrenic.

The Caribbean Court of Justice after consideration of relevant case law on the issue drawn from several jurisdictions of the Commonwealth, reasoned that by ratifying an international treaty, in that case the American Convention on Human Rights, the State had thrown a condemned person a lifeline, and queried whether it was fair to yank it away by claiming that the unincorporated international treaty formed no part of the domestic claw, and he derived no right from the mere ratification. The Court ultimately based its conclusions on a legitimate expectation of the condemned persons fostered by the fact that it was the practice of the Government of Barbados to give an opportunity to condemned persons to have their petitions to international human rights bodies processed before proceeding to execution, and this was regarded as conduct complying with the state's treaty obligations on the domestic plane. In the Court's opinion "to deny the substantive benefit promised by the creation of the legitimate expectation here would not be proportionate having regard to the distress and possible detriment that will be unfairly occasioned to men who hope to be allowed a reasonable time to pursue their petitions and receive a favourable report from the international body. The substantive benefit the condemned men legitimately expect is actually as to *the procedure* that should be followed before their sentences are executed." This notwithstanding, the Court went on to state that protracted delay on the part of the international body in disposing of the proceedings initiated before it by a condemned person, could justify the State despite the existence of the condemned person's legitimate expectation, proceeding with the execution before completion of the international process.

At this juncture, it is of interest to mention the case of *Johnson (Errol) v Jamaica*[20] which involved a report of the United Nations Human Rights Committee on a communication from a Jamaican convicted of murder who having exhausted all of his domestic appeals petitioned the Committee for consideration based on the fact that Jamaica had ratified the Optional Protocol to the International Covenant on Civil and Political Rights. After reviewing the facts and relevant case law the Committee held by a majority, *inter alia*, that a delay of 51 months in hearing an appeal in a capital case, barring exceptional circumstances, was unreasonably long and was incompatible with article 14(3)(c) of the Optional Protocol; that the death penalty could only be imposed in accordance with the law and as the provisions of the Covenant had not been observed at the trial and could not be remedied on appeal, the requirements of a fair trial (Article 14 of the Covenant - right to a fair hearing) had not been satisfied and accordingly there had been a breach of Article 6 of the Covenant (the right to life).

PROTECTION OF THE LAW

This term lends itself to a wide, varied interpretation and definition, and can embrace a multitude of rights which demand protection under the laws of a particular state. The constitutions of the Commonwealth Caribbean enshrine provisions to secure protection of the law for persons charged with a criminal offence, for example, the presumption of innocence, the right to be informed of the nature of the offence, the right to defend oneself in person or by a legal representative, the right to a fair hearing within a reasonable time by an independent and impartial court or tribunal, and protection of all other rights connected therewith.

Effective protection of human rights depends on the availability at all times of access to competent, independent and impartial courts of law which administer justice fairly in keeping with constitutional provisions complying with the International Covenant on Civil and Political Rights[21] and the American Convention on Human Rights.[22] The concept of a fair trial which is an absolute right does not lend itself to a precise or specific definition, but involves several components.[23] Violation of the rights mentioned earlier may result in a trial being regarded as unfair. The presumption of innocence in relation to anyone charged with a criminal offence is the bedrock of the common law and the cornerstone on which the adversarial system in a criminal trial is built. No burden is placed on an accused person to prove his innocence. The accuser must prove all allegations beyond reasonable doubt although there may be circumstances when this burden shifts.

The right to defend oneself in person or by a legal representative of his own choice guaranteed under protection of the law provisions in Commonwealth Caribbean constitutions gave rise to comparison with the European Convention on Human Rights[24] when the Privy Council was required to consider the said provision in the constitution of Barbados in *Hinds v Attorney General of Barbados*[25]. One of the questions which arose for determination was whether the denial of free legal representation had breached the appellant's right to a fair hearing within the constitution. Although the European Convention and the Constitution of Barbados both provide for a person charged with a criminal offence to be permitted to be legally represented, the European Convention expanded this to provide that if such a person did not have the means to pay for legal representation it should be provided free when the interests of justice so require.

In Barbados legal aid was only automatically provided to persons charged with certain "scheduled" offences, and in complex cases a trial judge could procure the grant of legal aid where it was deemed to be necessary. The Privy Council held that "it was clear that while a defendant was not automatically entitled to legal aid, he was guaranteed a fair hearing", and the provision in the constitution permitting him to be legally represented did not undermine that right.

Another dimension of the constitutional right to legal representation when charged with a criminal offence is the additional right in some of the Commonwealth Caribbean constitutions to hold communication with one's legal representative, a right which the American Convention on Human Rights[26] guarantees, and which was considered in a case from Trinidad and Tobago, namely, *Mohamed (Allie) v The State*,[27] involving exclusion of a confession allegedly made by an accused person without communicating with his lawyer. It was held by the Privy Council, allowing the appeal, that although the right to communicate with a lawyer was fundamental, no absolute right existed as to the exclusion of a confession obtained in breach of that right; however, where disputed facts were established a judge was required to exercise a discretion so as to balance the interest in securing evidence to ensure that justice was done with the need to protect individuals from serious breaches of their constitutional rights. Reference to this was made in a similar case from The Bahamas with a similar constitutional provision – *Simmons v R*[28].

PROTECTION FROM DISCRIMINATION AND EQUALITY BEFORE THE LAW

I commence discussion on these two fundamental rights with a quotation from the United Nations Human Rights Committee to the effect that "non-discrimination, together with equality before the law and equal protection of the law without any discrimination, constitute a basic and general principle relating to the protection of human rights"[29].

The twin international covenants mentioned at the beginning protect both the right against discrimination and the right to equality before the law[30], but specific treaties address these two basic human rights affecting specific categories of persons - the Convention on the Elimination of All Forms of Racial Discrimination[31], the Convention on the Elimination of All Forms of Discrimination Against Women[32] and the Convention on the Rights of the Child, ratified by most of the Commonwealth Caribbean countries. The constitutions in large measure give effect to the provisions of these treaties in defining discrimination and discriminatory conduct; a few of them contain specific provisions guaranteeing equality before the law. Some may posit the view that the provision against discrimination impliedly ensures equality before the law when it defines discriminatory conduct as being "affording different treatment to different persons attributable wholly or mainly to their respective descriptions by race, place of origin, political opinions, colour or creed."[33] If one is treated differently from others in similar circumstances it follows that you are a victim of discrimination.

Over the years, the Judiciary in the collective jurisdictions of the Commonwealth Caribbean have been required to interpret and give effect to these constitutional provisions thereby ensuring a varied body of precedent on what constitutes discrimination within the meaning of the relevant statutes, and whether the principle of equality before the law was violated.

An example of a court's judgment on the discrimination provision in a Constitution is the case of *Neilsen v Barker and Another*[34] from Guyana which concerned the deportation of a Danish prohibited immigrant to his place of birth to face imprisonment for crimes committed there. On appeal from an order for his deportation he claimed that he had been discriminated against contrary to the discrimination provision in the Constitution in that he had been detained when no steps had been taken against others who had been convicted of offences committed abroad. The Court of Appeal in dismissing his appeal held that the constitutional protection against discrimination (Article 149) had to be construed strictly as being limited to protection against discrimination in relation to matters of race, place of origin, political opinions, colour and creed; the applicant had not shown that he had been discriminated against in respect of any such matters and accordingly, he could not claim a breach of his constitutional rights under Article 149. By an amendment to that provision of the constitution in 2003, the category of matters was enlarged,[35] and is an indication that the category ought never to be closed or restricted only to those matters enumerated in the provision.

In *Smith and Another v L.J. Williams Ltd*[36] the Court of Appeal of Trinidad and Tobago in interpreting the constitutional provision on the right to equality of treatment from a public authority held that in order for the respondent company to establish that it had suffered a breach of that right contrary to section 4(d) of the Constitution, it was not necessary to show that the breach fell within the introductory words of section 4 ("discrimination by reason of race, origin, colour, religion or sex").

The learned judge at first instance in the same case in discussing section 4(b) of the constitution relating to the right of the individual to equality before the law and the protection of the law expressed the view that the section guaranteed and intended to ensure that where parties are similarly placed under the law they are entitled to like treatment under that law. This right is breached when it can be shown that there was bad faith or hostile intention and a lack of even-handedness in the treatment of the applicant. This reasoning was followed in *Sumayyah Mohammed v Moraine and Another*[37] also a case from Trinidad and Tobago which concerned refusal of admission of an Islamic student to a secondary school on the ground that the "hijab" which the student insisted that she must wear due to firm religious beliefs was not part of the school's uniform. The trial judge found no contravention of that provision in the Constitution since it was not shown that there was any bad faith or hostile intention.

ENFORCEMENT OF PROTECTIVE PROVISIONS

All of the constitutions in some form seek to protect the fundamental rights and freedoms enshrined therein by expressly providing for their enforcement and remedies for their violations without which they would be meaningless, thereby rendering the rule of law a mockery. Enforcement and redress are entrusted to the courts acting within their original jurisdiction, and with a mandate to make such orders and give such directions as may be deemed appropriate if satisfied that no other form of redress is available under any other law.[38]

DEROGATION FROM PROTECTIVE PROVISIONS

International human rights treaties oft times prohibit derogation from certain provisions. The Covenant on Civil and Political Rights[39] and the American Convention on Human Rights[40] stipulate that there should be no derogation from such provisions as the right to life, the right to freedom from torture, cruel, inhuman and degrading punishment or treatment, *inter alia*, these being so basic to the inherent dignity of the human persona. At least one constitution of the states under discussion (Antigua and Barbuda) expressly prohibits derogations from any of the fundamental rights and freedoms recognised therein.[41]

Some derogation is nevertheless permissible during a period of public emergency which threatens the life of a nation and which is officially proclaimed. Such "public emergency" may include a state of war or the result of a natural disaster or other calamity, and is so defined in all of the constitutions. "Saving of existing law" provisions can be found in all of them to the effect that nothing contained in or done under the authority of any written law shall be held to be inconsistent with or in contravention of any of the fundamental rights and freedoms provisions. In some of the constitutions the right to life provisions and the freedom from inhuman or degrading punishment or treatment are excepted while in others there are no exceptions. This means that during a proclaimed period of public emergency some or all of the fundamental rights and freedoms may be suspended. However, even in times of public emergency there are certain inherent rights which ought not to be derogated from because of their fundamental character and indispensability, for example, the right to a fair trial and the right to be tried by an independent and impartial tribunal. Most of the constitutions expressly provide for preservation of these fundamental rights of persons detained during a state of public emergency. Of necessity, the permissible derogation from the enshrined fundamental rights can only prevail for the duration of the public emergency, and the proclamation declaring the state of such emergency may remain in force for specified periods of time provided in the constitution.

RESPONSIBILITIES OF THE JUDICIARY AND LEGAL PROFESSION

The executive and the legislative branches of a state exercise their mandate and discharge their responsibilities to the citizens of the state by ratifying treaties and enacting legislation to protect fundamental human rights and freedoms, but the Judiciary breathes life into the constitutional provisions and makes them effective and meaningful in keeping with the mandate entrusted to it under the original jurisdiction of the courts. In discharging this mandate, whenever competent to do so, the Judiciary should pay regard to the international covenants and relevant case law, and within permissible limits give purposive and liberal interpretations of legislation when granting relief for violations of human rights.

Equal responsibility for the development of a culture of respect for fundamental rights and freedoms rests on members of the legal profession who must be prepared to be the guardians and watchdogs of violations and breaches of the rights of the citizenry of a state. The profession must not allow such violations to go unredressed, even if it requires undertaking *pro bono* representations. A system of legal aid should be established by states to ensure that violations of rights are not overlooked and uncompensated based solely on a person's impecuniosity and financial inability to seek justice in our courts. This is an ever-present obstacle to redress in Caribbean states with low personal incomes and high costs of living. The legal profession in these states owes it to its citizens to ensure respect for rights guaranteed to them under the constitution, and it should spare no quarter in the quest to uphold and preserve these rights.

Fulfilling the commitments under international treaties which they ratify must be the foremost priority of all of the Commonwealth Caribbean states. This involves the formulation of education programmes geared towards raising awareness of and respect for human rights, and discouraging wanton disregard for their infringement.

I conclude this discourse as it began with reference to the Universal Declaration of Human Rights, particularly to one of the tenets found in the Preamble – reaffirmation of the faith of the peoples of the United Nations in fundamental human rights, in the dignity and worth of the human person and in the equal rights of men and women. If collectively the states of the Commonwealth Caribbean strive assiduously to foster a culture of respect for human rights the laudable objectives of the Declaration will be achieved and the hopes and aspirations of their people realised.

15th Commonwealth Law Conference
Nairobi, Kenya
9th -13th September, 2007

Endnotes

1 Adopted by the General Assembly of the United Nations on 10 December, 1948.
2 Adopted by the General Assembly of the United Nations in 1966.
3 Adopted by the General Assembly of the United Nations in 1966.
4 Antigua and Barbuda, The Bahamas, Barbados, Belize, Dominica, Grenada, Guyana, Jamaica, St. Christopher and Nevis, St Lucia, St Vincent and the Grenadines, Trinidad and Tobago.
5 Adopted by the Inter-American Conference on Human Rights on 22 November, 1969.
6 Adopted by the General Assembly of the United Nations in 1989.
7 Article 154A of Guyana Constitution.
8 Article 39(2).
9 Signed at Rome on 4 November, 1950
10 Section 4(1), Antigua and Barbuda; Section 4(1) St Christopher and Nevis.
11 Trinidad and Tobago suspended its ratification on 26 May, 1999 over the death penalty issue.
12 [2005] 1.AC 472.
13 [2004] UKPC 34.
14 [2004] UKPC 34.
15 [2001] 2 AC 50.
16 Attorney General et al v Jeffrey & Lennox Ricardo Boyce [CCJ Appeal No. CV 2 of 2005].
17 Article 4(6).
18 [1994] AC 1.
19 In 2002 Barbados amended this constitutional provision to avoid any infringement by providing that any delay in executing a sentence of death imposed on a person shall not be inconsistent with or in contravention of it.
20 (1996) 55 WIR 208.
21 Article 14.
22 Article 8.
23 See the recent decision of the Caribbean Court of Justice in *The Queen v Mitchell Lewis [2007] CCJ 3 (AJ).*
24 Article 6.
25 [2002]2 WLR 470.
26 Article 8(2) (d).
27 [1999] 2 AC 111.
28 [2006] UKPC 19.
29 General Comment No. 18, in United Nations Compilation of General Comments, p. 134, para. 1.
30 ICCPR, Articles 2(1) & 26; ICESCR, Articles 2 (2) & 3.
31 Adopted by the General Assembly of the United Nations in 1965.
32 Adopted by the General Assembly of the United Nations in 1979.
33 Descriptions by sex, gender, pregnancy, marital status, age, disability, religion have been included in some constitutions.
34 (1982) 32 WIR 254.
35 Now provides for "age, disability, marital status, sex, gender, language, birth, social class, pregnancy, religion, conscience, belief, culture".
36 (1982) 32 WIR 395.
37 (1994) 49 WIR 371.

38 This provision was removed from the Constitution of Guyana, and there is no longer a bar to seeking redress under any other law.

39 Article 4(2).

40 Article 27(2).

41 Section 19.

Judges of the Caribbean Court of Justice

Front row- sitting - left to right:
The Hon. Mr. Justice Nelson; The Right Hon. Mr. Justice de la Bastide TC, President, The Hon. Mr. Justice Duke Pollard.

Back row - standing – left to right:
The Hon. Mr. Justice Wit; The Hon. Mme. Justice Bernard, The Hon. Mr. Justice Saunders, The Hon. Mr. Justice Hayton.

CHAPTER 7

THE CARIBBEAN COURT OF JUSTICE: A NEW JUDICIAL EXPERIENCE

The inauguration of the Caribbean Court of Justice in April 2005 represented the culmination of aspirations in earlier years to establish a court of last resort for the Caribbean Region to replace the Judicial Committee of the Privy Council (The Privy Council) which was and still is for most Commonwealth Caribbean jurisdictions, the final court. These aspirations were endorsed by the legal profession through the Organisation of Commonwealth Caribbean Bar Associations (OCCBA) over thirty years ago, although the idea of such a court was not an original one having been contemplated early in the last century. The court was envisaged as a Caribbean Court of Appeal with an appellate jurisdiction hearing appeals from domestic appellate courts and an original jurisdiction to interpret regional treaties.

The year 1973 saw the emergence and adoption of the Treaty Establishing the Caribbean Community and Common Market, familiarly known as the Treaty of Chaguaramas[1]. A report from the West Indian Commission established in 1989 by the Caribbean Community (CARICOM) Heads of Government and comprising eminent persons of the Region recommended widening of the Caribbean Community and developing a Single Market and Economy (SME) as well as the establishment of a Caribbean Supreme Court with an original jurisdiction to adjudicate disputes among Member States pertaining to the economic integration together with an appellate jurisdiction hearing appeals from domestic appellate courts. The acceptance of these recommendations led to the signing of the Revised Treaty of Chaguaramas Establishing the Caribbean Community Including the CARICOM Single Market and Economy (The Treaty)[2], and provision for the establishment of a Caribbean Court of Justice (The Court). The Agreement Establishing the Court (The Agreement) preceded the Treaty[3] and provided for both an original and an appellate jurisdiction[4].

JUDICIAL SYSTEMS OF CARICOM MEMBER STATES

One of the legacies of British colonialism bequeathed to its former colonies is the judicial system based in its entirety in most instances on the English system with the same hierarchy of courts and their nomenclature. The Judicial Committee of the Privy Council in England was and still remains for all, except two[5] of those former British Caribbean colonies, the court of final resort for appeals from domestic appellate courts. Although the common law of England became the common law of these former colonies and essentially remains so, there are some exceptions, for example, the Roman-Dutch system of land ownership in Guyana, and the French Civil Code of St. Lucia, which has resulted in a "legal mix" of common law and civil law.

Suriname's membership of CARICOM with its civil law system exemplifies the diversity of the Community which over time may, at some future date include Cuba; prophetically the complexities which may arise will test the capabilities of the Court to deal with such a diversity of legal systems. Suriname's Court of Justice at present remains its court of last resort.

AGREEMENT ESTABLISHING THE COURT

The existence of a regional court, specifically with an appellate jurisdiction, is nothing new for the former British colonies of the Caribbean Region[6]. The achievement of independent status by the colonies led to the establishment of their own appellate courts, but with retention of the Privy Council as the final court of appeal. The Agreement Establishing the Court which preceded the signing of the Treaty represented the conviction of the Contracting Parties that the Court would have "a determinative role in the further development of Caribbean jurisprudence through the judicial process" and would be entrenched in their national constitutions; moreover, they were well aware that "the establishment of the Court was a further step in the deepening of the regional integration process."[7]

THE APPELLATE JURISDICTION

In this jurisdiction, the Court operates as a court of last resort for those Member States accepting it as such and being structurally placed at the end of the litigation process. The conceptualisers of the Court sought to fulfil two dreams for the Caribbean Region by uniting them in one judicial system – the long-sought need for a final appellate court to replace the Privy Council, a respected tribunal of colonial memory, and the establishment of an international court to ensure effective implementation of the Treaty.

In the exercise of its appellate jurisdiction the Court is a superior court of record with such jurisdiction and powers as are conferred on it by the Agreement.[8] Appeals lie to the Court as of right from final decisions of the courts of appeal of the Contracting Parties in the following cases:

(a) in civil proceedings where the matter in dispute is of the value of not less than $25,000E.C. or where the appeal involves property or a right of the said value;
(b) in proceedings for dissolution or nullity of marriage;
(c) in any civil or other proceedings which involve a question as to the interpretation of the constitution of the Contracting Party;
(d) in proceedings relating to redress for contravention of the provisions of the constitution of the Contracting Party;
(e) in proceedings relating to the exercise of a jurisdiction conferred expressly on a superior court under the constitution of the Contracting Party;
(f) such other cases as may be prescribed by any law of the Contracting Party.

Subject to the above, an appeal also lies to the Court with special leave of the Court in any civil or criminal matter. Apart from appeals to the Court as of right an appeal can be brought with leave from the court of appeal of a Contracting Party in final decisions in any civil proceedings where, in the opinion of the court of appeal, the question involved in the appeal is one of great general or public importance or otherwise and ought to be submitted to the Court; also, in other cases as may be prescribed by any law of the Contracting Party.

What is more than passing strange in relation to the appellate jurisdiction is that although the Agreement was signed by nearly all of the Member States of the Community, only two of those States (Barbados and Guyana) have enacted the required domestic legislation to accord access to the Court by their nationals. Since its inauguration these two States have been utilising the Court to its fullest. The inhibiting factor in relation to the other States is the requirement in some constitutions for a referendum to de-link from the English Privy Council and hesitancy in having this done or the need for involvement of opposition political parties in enacting relevant legislation, but which in some instances is not forthcoming at present. One can only hope that over time these hurdles will be surmounted, and all of the Member States will make the appellate jurisdiction accessible to their nationals.

The following sentiments expressed by Professor Francis Jacobs in the Journal of International Economic Law published on 14 February, 2008[9] are instructive:

> *A supreme court of high calibre has been established in the Caribbean which would be able to take account of local values and develop a modern Caribbean jurisprudence in an international context. It is regrettable that political difficulties have obstructed acceptance of its jurisdiction and that the outdated jurisdiction of the Judicial Committee of the Privy Council survives, in often bizarre detail, for many of those States. All possible steps should be taken to encourage the Caribbean States to accept the jurisdiction of their own supreme court.*

THE ORIGINAL JURISDICTION

The provisions of the Agreement governing the original jurisdiction of the Court are replicated in the Treaty in almost identical terms, exemplifying a synergetic relationship. Because of this, reference will be made to similar articles in both instruments when considering the relevant provisions.

My learned colleague and friend, Hon. Mr. Justice Duke Pollard, in his book, "The Caribbean Court of Justice: Closing the Circle of Independence", posited that "the Court is perceived as the institutional centrepiece of the CSME which aspires to the creation of a single economic space superimposed on autonomous political jurisdictions in order to approximate in fact, if not in law, a single economy from the economies of many Member States".

In its original jurisdiction, the Agreement, subject to the Treaty, confers on the Court exclusive jurisdiction to hear and deliver judgment on:

(a) disputes between Contracting Parties;
(b) disputes between any Contracting Parties and the Community;

(c) referrals from national courts or tribunals of Contracting Parties;
(d) applications by nationals concerning the interpretation and application of the Treaty.[10]

The Court's exclusive jurisdiction also embraces delivery of advisory opinions concerning the interpretation and application of the Treaty given only at the request of Member States parties to a dispute or the Community.[11]

Both instruments recognise the sovereignty of the dualist Member States of the Community, and a natural consequence of this is that each Member State could interpret and apply the Treaty as it sees fit. Of necessity, this would lead to varied interpretations and differences of opinion. With the establishment of the Court certainty and uniformity of interpretation of the terms of the Treaty are guaranteed, thereby avoiding fragmentation if left to individual domestic courts. It is beyond dispute that certainty of an important international instrument, such as the Treaty, is a *sine qua non* in attracting investment to the Region, and it follows that uncertainty and unpredictability of judicial decisions on economic issues will become a disincentive to potential investors.

As a consequence, when a national court or tribunal is seised of an issue involving interpretation or application of the Treaty, and which is necessary to enable it to deliver judgment, that court or tribunal must refer the question of such interpretation or application to the Court for determination;[12] this is the sole prerogative of the Court. Similar provisions are to be found in the instruments of the European Union, and were intended as those in our Treaty, to secure uniformity. It is expected that this provision will have a significant impact on the work of the Court with the referral procedure being utilised by domestic courts when faced with matters requiring interpretation of the Treaty.

It would be a futile exercise and totally meaningless to the parties involved if Member States, the organs and bodies of the Community as well as the Community itself were to ignore or refuse to comply with judgments of the Court, and for this reason both instruments provide that the Court's judgments must be complied with promptly by Member States and entities of the Community as well as any persons to whom a judgment applies.[13]

The original jurisdiction of the Court is recognised as being compulsory, *ipso facto*, and without special agreement[14], an important provision if the Court is to execute its functions effectively.

Being essential for the successful operation of the CSME whose birth reflected a "*commitment to deepen regional economic integration in order to achieve sustained economic development based on international competitiveness*", with objectives similar to the European Union, the Court as an international court is empowered under both instruments to apply such rules of international law as may be applicable, and may not decline to make a finding on the ground of obscurity of the law. These provisions, however, will not prejudice the power of the Court to decide a dispute *ex aequo et bono* if the parties so agree.[15]

Much reliance will be placed and assistance gleaned from international tribunals such as the European Court of Justice and the Court of Justice of the Common Market for Eastern and Southern Africa which are courts established with a similar function to interpret and apply the relevant instruments.

After proceedings are instituted before the Court either between Member States or between a national and another Member State, a third party may wish to intervene to protect an interest. In this regard the Agreement permits intervention if the intended intervener, whether Member State, the Community or a person, establishes that it has a substantial interest of a legal nature which may be affected by a decision of the Court.[16]

If circumstances arise after a judgment of the Court has been handed down and which may adversely affect the parties, a request for the judgment to be revised can be made. Such a request may be considered by the Court if an application is made within six months of the discovery of a fact which was not known at the date of the judgment and which may have been a decisive factor provided such an application is made not more than five years from the date of judgment.[17]

Queries have often been raised about the Court's powers in enforcing its judgments. Enforcement of judgments of domestic courts is usually provided for by legislation of the particular state. In like manner Contracting Parties (Member States) agree to take all necessary steps, including the enactment of legislation, to ensure that all authorities in the State act in aid of the Court, and that any judgment or order of the Court be enforced by all courts and authorities of a Contracting Party in the same way as any judgment or order of a superior domestic court of that State.[18] This provision applies to both jurisdictions of the Court as does Article III of the Agreement which provides that the decisions of the Court shall be final.

The perception of the average Caribbean citizen is that the Treaty came into being mainly for the regulation of trade and maintaining a sound economic environment for Member States, and only incidentally for the benefit of individuals. Nothing could be further from the truth. There are several provisions in the Treaty which have a direct bearing on the every day life of persons in the Caribbean Region, for example, the movement of skilled persons and of nationals without harassment, as well as the elimination of the requirement for passports, to name a few[19]. This is an important aspect of the Court's jurisdiction and provision is made for hearing and determining disputes involving persons or legal entities (such as companies) of a Contracting Party concerning interpretation or application of the Treaty.[20] It can only be invoked with special leave of the Court if it determines that the Treaty intended that a right or benefit conferred on a Contracting Party was to enure to the benefit of the persons or entities directly. In its application to the Court the persons or entities have to establish that they have been prejudiced in respect of the enjoyment of the right or benefit, and that the Contracting Party who is entitled to espouse the claim has omitted or declined to do so or has expressly agreed to the persons or entities doing so in its stead. The Court ultimately has to find that the interest of justice requires that the persons or entities be allowed to espouse the claim. The Court in its first case in the original jurisdiction is at present in the process of determining issues in relation to this provision of the Treaty in proceedings between two companies and a Member State.

In any court binding judicial precedent is desirable (the doctrine of *stare decisis*) if stability and predictability are to be maintained particularly in a court entrusted with the jurisdiction of interpretation of a treaty essential for the successful operation of a single market and economy aimed at attracting investment. Both the Agreement and the Treaty provide that judgments of the Court shall be legally binding precedents for parties in proceedings before it[21] taking into account revision of a judgment. It is acceptable that judgments of the Court should be legally binding precedents for parties involved in proceedings before the Court; what is yet to be decided by the Court is whether it will consider itself bound by its own decisions. The Privy Council has never regarded itself bound by its own decisions which sometimes has led to inconsistency and unpredictability particularly when the liberty of persons is involved. It is too early to forecast what course the Court will take having been in existence for a relatively short period of time with appeals in its appellate jurisdiction coming from only two Member States, and only now beginning to hear matters in its original jurisdiction.

One of the concerns of the Community reflected in the Treaty was that "*the benefits expected from the establishment of the CSME were not frustrated by anti-competitive business conduct*".[22] To avoid and monitor such practices provision is made for the establishment of a regional competition commission to be appointed by the Regional Judicial and Legal Services Commission[23] (functions of which will be discussed later). In carrying out its duties the Competition Commission may seek the Court's intervention when necessary, and any party aggrieved by a determination of the Commission may apply to the Court for a review of that determination.[24]

Anti-competitive business conduct may be prohibited by a Member State, and examples of such conduct are enumerated in the Treaty,[25] such as the direct or indirect fixing of purchase or selling prices or the artificial dividing up of markets or restriction of supply sources. Of course, the list is not exhaustive, and where a Member State is uncertain whether a particular business conduct is prohibited under the Treaty, the State may apply to the Commission for a ruling on the matter. The Court's jurisdiction may also be invoked by the Commission to review its own decision if it is found or felt that such a decision was induced by deceit or improper means.[26]

Notwithstanding the compulsory and exclusive jurisdiction accorded to the Court to hear and determine disputes between Member States concerning the interpretation and application of the Treaty, elaborate provisions are stipulated in the Treaty for the settlement of disputes without recourse to the Court[27], for example, where allegations arise that an actual or proposed measure of a Member State is or would be inconsistent with the objectives of the Community or there are allegations that the purpose or object of the Treaty is being frustrated or prejudiced. A perusal of the relevant articles of the Treaty suggests that every effort should be made and all procedures exhausted in settling disputes between Member States and between organs and bodies of the Community before the jurisdiction of the Court is invoked in contentious proceedings. Alternative disputes settlements are to be encouraged by Member States to the maximum extent possible in relation to private commercial disputes among Community nationals as well as among Community nationals and nationals of third States.[28] The Agreement also enjoins Contracting Parties to do the same.[29] This being so, proceedings instituted by private persons and entities may be the vehicle to drive the Court forward in making an impact as "*the institutional centrepiece of the CSME*."

JUDGMENTS OF THE COURT

Since its inauguration in April 2005, and until very recently the Court's judgments have been handed down exclusively in its appellate jurisdiction in mainly civil matters with a few criminal and family law appeals. To date over forty (40) matters have been filed in the Court, with only two in the original jurisdiction. Within the appellate jurisdiction several applications for special leave to appeal as a poor person were granted. These applications vindicate the establishment of the Court as providing access to justice to those who cannot afford the expense of legal representation to the Privy Council located thousands of miles away from the Region; similarly, the frequent use of audio-conferencing which further reduces travelling costs to litigants. Following are a few of the Court's judgments.

The landmark judgment of the Court in *Attorney General of Barbados v Joseph & Boyce*[30] defined the Court's jurisprudence on the effect of an unincorporated human rights treaty ratified by the Executive on the international plane and sought to be enforced on the domestic plane in death penalty cases. Several other issues fell to be determined with judgments written by all of the Judges of the Court. This case was the first major test of the Court on the deeply-sensitive issue of the death penalty particularly as it was perceived within the Caribbean Region and predicted to be a "hanging court", based on the false assumption that the Judges would comply with the wishes of the political directorate who in some instances had been dissatisfied with judgments of the Privy Council allowing appeals of persons convicted of murder.

Following is a short summary of the facts of the case. Two men were convicted of the offence of murder by the courts in Barbados, and exhausted all of their remedies up to the Privy Council. Death warrants were read to them by decision of the local Privy Council (a committee on the prerogative of mercy) while awaiting hearing of their petitions to the Inter American Commission on Human Rights based on Barbados' ratification of the Inter American Convention on Human Rights which had not been incorporated into the domestic law by legislation. The condemned men sought unsuccessfully to postpone their executions by instituting proceedings in the High Court, and later appealed to the local Court of Appeal which commuted their sentences to life imprisonment. The Attorney General appealed to the Caribbean Court of Justice.

As mentioned earlier several other issues arose which time does not permit to mention, but with regard to the effect of unincorporated international treaties on a condemned person's right to the protection of the law, the Court held that the respondents had a legitimate expectation that they would be allowed a reasonable time within which to complete the process initiated by petitioning the Inter American Commission on Human Rights, and for the State to attempt to execute them before that process was completed was a denial of their right to the protection of the law. Legitimate expectation, simpliciter, was expressed to be procedural, and vulnerable to frustration by a change of official conduct according to one of the Judges who posited that international acts by the Executive must be accompanied by "treaty-compliant" conduct on the municipal plane in dualist jurisdictions in order to engender such an expectation to which municipal courts may accord protection. The conduct in this case regarded as being compliant with the Treaty was the Barbados Government's stated position that it was its practice to permit condemned persons an opportunity to have petitions to international human rights bodies processed before execution of their sentences in keeping with its commitment to honour its international obligations. This was the main factor giving rise to a legitimate expectation, and one queries whether, absent such conduct, an unincorporated treaty ratified by the Executive on the international plane can provide an effective remedy for a national on the domestic plane.

What makes this issue in the judgment interesting is the judgment of one of the Judges from a civil law jurisdiction with its monist approach to the incorporation of international treaties into domestic law. He opined that the strongest concept underlying the doctrine of unenforceability of ratified treaties was the separation of powers, and expressed the view that although this may be sufficient reason for the existence of the doctrine in the unwritten English Constitution it was unsuitable for the Commonwealth Caribbean with written Constitutions. An in-depth analysis of the judgments is recommended to appreciate the advantages of diversity of opinion in the Court's quest to create a Caribbean jurisprudence.

Another appeal of interest is the case of *The Queen v Mitchell Ken O'Neal Lewis*[31] concerned primarily with issues of procedure under Section 6(c) of the Caribbean Court of Justice Act of Barbados. The Section provides for an appeal to lie to the Court from decisions of the Court of Appeal as of right in any civil or criminal proceedings which involve a question as to the interpretation of the Constitution. The preliminary issue which fell to be determined was whether the Crown can appeal as of right to the Court by virtue of Section 6(c). This arose in circumstances where an accused was convicted of murder and sentenced to death. On appeal to the Court of Appeal the conviction was quashed and a new trial ordered on the ground that prejudicial material had been introduced in the presence of the jury and this rendered the trial unfair. The Crown through the Director of Public Prosecutions submitted that the Court of Appeal's conclusion was based on an erroneous interpretation of the "fair hearing" provision in the Constitution of Barbados which is the usual provision found in all constitutions based on the Westminster model – a fair hearing within a reasonable time by an independent and impartial court, and for this reason the Crown had an appeal as of right to the Court.

All of the judges of the Court agreed that the right of appeal created by Section 6(c) of the Caribbean Court of Justice Act of Barbados is available to the Crown provided that the case involves a question concerning the interpretation of the Constitution, and the question whether in this case the accused received a fair hearing was a question not of interpretation of the relevant section of the Constitution, but of the application of it to the facts, and accordingly the Crown was not entitled in this case to appeal as of right to the Court. The appeal was dismissed, but the order for a retrial was left intact.

One of the judges delivered a judgment on the susceptibility of the term "fair hearing" to judicial interpretation, which has the effect of enhancing the rich pool of judicial opinions available from the Court.

The whole concept of adverse possession of immovable property was discussed in the recent Guyanese appeal of *Toolsie Persaud Ltd. v*

Andrew James Investments Ltd. And Others[32] which concerned certain lands originally owned by two of the respondents, but compulsorily acquired by the Government of Guyana and later sold to the appellant who went into possession under the agreement of sale. Several years later upon a constitutional motion filed in court by the first respondent the compulsory acquisition orders were declared null and void. The appellant company while still in possession of the lands later applied to the court for prescriptive title. Three issues arose for consideration – (a) did the State have the necessary intention for its possession to be adverse when that possession was based on the belief that it was the owner under a compulsory acquisition order subsequently declared to be invalid, (b) was it possible for the State to acquire land by adverse possession, and (c) did a landowner's right of action to recover land acquired from him by the State under an invalid compulsory acquisition order only arise when the order was declared to be invalid by a court upon a constitutional motion brought by the landowner?

In relation to (a) the Court held that physical occupation and use of land with the intention and effect of excluding everyone else, amounts to adverse possession, whether the occupier acts in good faith believing himself to be the owner, or in bad faith knowing that someone else is the owner. With regard to (b) the Court held that a landowner's constitutional right to prevent the State from positively taking his land from him against his will, was completely consistent with a landowner losing his title if for twelve years he failed to take any action against someone who was occupying his land and excluding him from it. In answer to (c) the Court held that a landowner's right of action to recover his land arises as soon as he can bring an action in which he can claim recovery of title and possession; thereafter time runs against him. Passing of possession from the State to the appellant was seamless, and possession pursuant to a contractual right could be added to the State's earlier adverse possession.

As mentioned earlier in this presentation Guyana's law of immovable property is based in large measure on the Roman-Dutch system of land ownership, and this arose for consideration in a recent appeal from the Court of Appeal of Guyana in the case of *Harrinauth Ramdass v Salim Jairam and Others*[33] which originated from an agreement of sale of land between the appellant and his sister, who was deceased at the date of hearing of an action brought by the appellant against her. After the appellant entered into possession of the land in accordance with the agreement, the sister later sold and passed title for the said portion of land to another purchaser at a higher price. The appellant filed proceedings against the vendor and the new purchaser for specific performance of the agreement and revocation of the title of the purchaser.

The appellant alleged in his pleadings that the vendor and the purchaser had conspired to defraud him of the property, but gave no particulars of the alleged fraud and the allegation was later withdrawn. However, he sought to persuade the court that he acquired an equitable interest in the land. The trial judge held that equitable interests in immovable property are not recognized in Guyana, and refused the order for specific performance as well as the claim for the revocation of the purchaser's title.

An appeal to the Court of Appeal of Guyana was dismissed. In an appeal to the Caribbean Court of Justice the main issue concerned the ongoing debate of whether equitable interests in land in Guyana are recognized or can be acquired having regard to the development of the law of immovable property in Guyana inherited from the Roman Dutch system, particularly in relation to a purchaser who is put in possession under an agreement of sale. The majority view reflected in Guyanese cases and the independent analysis of the Court indicate an acceptance of the conclusion that equitable interests in land are not recognized in Guyana although statutory provisions permit the application of equitable remedies. Accordingly, the appellant acquired no equitable interest in the land purchased from his sister. He, however, was entitled to seek from her an order for specific performance of the agreement of sale which in fact he sought, but only after she had passed title to the other purchaser who acquired an indefeasible title subject only to a possibility of it being declared void for fraud which was abandoned at the hearing of the action in the lower court.

In relation to the grant of leave to appeal as a poor person the case of *Elizabeth Ross v Coreen Sinclair*[34] exemplifies the Court's efforts to afford access to justice by all. Leave to appeal as a poor person had been refused by the Court of Appeal of Guyana, and the applicant was ordered to lodge security for costs in the sum of $100,000G within ninety (90) days failing which the appeal would stand dismissed. She sought leave from the CCJ to appeal as a poor person being blind and virtually penniless. The case involved ownership of a condominium in which she had resided for several years as a tenant of a deceased resident, but owned by a housing authority. The administratrix of the deceased resident, who is the respondent was in no better financial position. The appeal involved issues about the rightful owner of the condominium, and which the Court considered had reasonable prospects of success.

The main issue, however, centred around the procedural point of whether the Court could grant leave to appeal as a poor person when such leave had been refused by the Court of Appeal which under the Appellate Jurisdiction Rules of the CCJ was the Court empowered to grant such leave; this would have the effect of reversing the decision of the court below and the appearance of the Court sitting as a court of review. The Rules make no provision for this. After hearing arguments, both written and oral from Counsel for the parties who appeared *pro bono*, the Court granted leave to the applicant to appeal as a poor person by utilising Rule 1.3 of the CCJ Rules which defines the overriding objective as being "to enable the Court to deal with cases fairly and expeditiously so as to ensure a just result." The reasoning was that the fact that the Rules conferred on the Court of Appeal the power to grant leave to appeal as a poor person, does not mean that a refusal of such leave disables the Court if it considers that the interest of justice so requires, from making an order of its own granting such leave, particularly if the appeal is considered to have merit.[35]

As stated earlier two cases have been filed recently in the original jurisdiction, and are in the process of hearing. It is hoped that now that the ice has been broken there will be a steady flow particularly from natural and juridical persons within the Region.

ADMINISTRATION

(a) Appointment of Judges

The unique feature of the Court is not confined only to its peculiar dual jurisdiction. Being an international court with jurisdiction to apply and interpret a Treaty subscribed to by Member States of an economic union, one would expect that appointment of the judges of the Court would be influenced by the Member States who may field candidates for appointment either in an individual capacity or as representing a State. This form of judicial appointment to international courts and tribunals is frequently the norm, for example, appointments to the European Court of Justice (ECJ) on which member states of the European Union are represented, the International Court of Justice (ICJ), and other international tribunals appointments to which are made by the United Nations states parties. In contrast the Judges of the Caribbean Court are appointed by a Regional Judicial and Legal Services Commission (RJLSC)[36] comprising representatives of regional bar associations, civil society and academic institutions, totally independent of political influence and of which the President of the Court is the Chairman. The establishment of this Commission sought to allay deep-seated fears (real or perceived) within the Caribbean Region about political interference in the judgments of the Court due to some alleged unfortunate instances of perceived interference within the domestic courts of the Region.

In a recent work titled "The International Judge", the authors[37] expressed the view that "*in general one cannot apply to become an international judge*"[38], and that "*national governments have total control over who will be put forward for an international judicial position and who will not*". To avoid such a situation the appointment procedure for the Court involved advertisements in the media and online, which attracted applications both from the Caribbean Region and the international community. Interviews followed and short lists compiled from which the final six judges were selected with no consideration being given to equitable geographical distribution; judges were chosen solely for their individual expertise. Incidentally two of the Judges appointed do not belong to any CARICOM Member State. The Agreement provides for the composition of the Court to be the President and nine other Judges.[39]

The Judges of the Court are chosen and appointed solely by the Commission. The Agreement provides for the appointment of the President to be made by the qualified majority vote of three-quarters of the Contracting Parties.[40] However, this can only be done on an affirmative recommendation of the Commission.

Criteria for appointment as a Judge of the Court laid down in the Agreement include judicial experience for a period of not less than five years in a common law or civil law jurisdiction or engagement in the practice or teaching of law for a period of not less than fifteen years. Regard will also be had to high moral character, intellectual and analytical ability, sound judgment, integrity and understanding of people and society.[41] With such criteria the Judges of Court will be assessed ultimately by the quality of the judgments emanating from the Court.

TENURE OF OFFICE OF THE JUDGES

The majority of judges serving on international courts do so for specified term limits, seven or nine years, and because they are elected they can be re-elected for a further specified term. In relation to the Court the Agreement provides for length of tenure tied to the attainment of a fixed age of retirement rather than a term limit. The Agreement stipulates a retirement age of seventy-two years[42] with a discretion recently given to the RJLSC to grant an extension of an additional three years upon request and if the services of the Judge are deemed necessary for the work of the Court. The President is mandated to serve as President for a non-renewable term of seven years.

Concerns have surfaced that the Judges of the Court do not enjoy the same security of tenure as judges of domestic courts whose appointments are entrenched in the domestic constitutions of Member States; in fact this issue was litigated in the Jamaican courts all the way to the Privy Council[43] which held that the Judges of the Court did not enjoy the same security of tenure under the Constitution as the Judges of the higher Jamaican domestic court, and deemed the legislation which sought to implement the Court to be unconstitutional. To ensure security of tenure of the judges of the Court Member States must honour not only the undertaking enshrined in the Treaty to employ their best endeavours in completing the constitutional and legislative procedures required for their participation in establishing the Court,[44] but also the desirability of entrenching the Court in their national constitutions in accordance with the Preamble to the Agreement; to this one may add entrenchment on the same terms as the judges of their domestic courts.

With regard to removal of a judge from office, this can only be achieved by inability to perform the functions of the office, whether due to illness or for misbehaviour, with a procedure for such removal being invoked by the RJLSC.[45] Accountability of the holders of judicial office is essential in inspiring public confidence, and in this regard self-regulation of judicial conduct must be a priority. To ensure this a code of judicial conduct has been formulated.

(a) Financial Provisions

One incidence of judicial independence is that the Judiciary considered to be the third branch of a State, must be provided with sufficient and sustainable funding by the other two branches – the Executive and the Legislature – for the performance of its functions to the highest standards. This is one of the Guidelines for preserving judicial independence reflected in the "Commonwealth Principles on the Accountability of and the Relationship between the Three Branches of Government".[46] In this regard the expenses associated with the Court including maintenance of the seat of the Court (based in Trinidad and Tobago) under the Agreement are to be borne by the Contracting Parties.[47]

Based on past experiences of States' tardiness in honouring regional financial commitments and in order to guarantee the Court some measure of financial autonomy from regional governments, a Trust Fund was created by the Member States with capital of US$100 million which was raised through international financial markets by the Caribbean Development Bank. The said sum was transferred to a Board of Trustees of reputable persons with the requisite skills who are responsible for its management and disbursement to the administrators of the Court for its management. It was lent to the Member States at low rates of interest and repayable over a period of fifteen to twenty years.

This arrangement for financing an international court has been commended by experts knowledgeable about the operations of international courts. It is certainly a novel arrangement, and again another feature of the Court's uniqueness.

POTENTIAL ISSUES FOR THE COURT'S DETERMINATION

With the birth of the CSME in 2001 the Court in its original jurisdiction was regarded as being essential for its successful operation. To date only the "Single Market" aspect has been implemented with the "Economy" being deferred to some opportune future date. In the present dispensation Member States resolve "*to establish conditions to facilitate access by their nationals to the collective resources of the Region on a non-discriminatory basis,*"[48] and which is reflected in the Treaty.[49] It provides that "*within the scope of application of the Treaty and without prejudice to any special provisions . . . any discrimination on grounds of nationality only shall be prohibited.*"

I posit that this Article of the Treaty is fundamental to the success of the Single Market involving as it does persons (natural and juridical) of the Region. It is the people of the Region from the collective Member States who will ensure success; divisiveness will ensure failure. In this regard the Court's role will be pivotal in resolving issues that will inevitably arise among nationals of one Member State residing or employed in another Member State amid allegations of perceived discrimination. Being cognisant of the tendency of nationals of one Member State to view those born in another Member State as foreigners, it is expected that allegations of discriminatory treatment will lead to recourse to the Court for an interpretation of the Treaty.

Another aspect of the Treaty with which the Court will have to grapple is the prohibition of new restrictions by Member States relating to the right of establishment of nationals of other Member States save as otherwise provided in the Treaty.[50] The right of establishment within the meaning of that part of the Treaty includes the right to engage in any non-wage-earning activities of a commercial, industrial, agricultural, professional or artisanal nature, or to create and manage economic enterprises which include any type of organisation for the production of or trade in goods or the provision of services. Again, because of the same perceptions of nationals of one Member State against others, the Court will play a decisive role in determining issues concerning the right of establishment.

Laudably, Member States undertake to: "*take all appropriate measures, whether general or particular, to ensure the carrying out of obligations arising out of the Treaty or resulting from decisions taken by the Organs and Bodies of the Community,*" and to "*facilitate the objectives of the Community*" as well as "*abstain from any measures which could jeopardise the attainment of the Treaty.*"[51]

The question arises – will the Court ever be called upon to interpret or apply this important provision of the Treaty? Maybe, the answer lies in the hands of the peoples of the Caribbean Region.

International Association of Law Libraries
San Juan, Puerto Rico
2008

Endnotes

1 Signed at Chaguaramas, Trinidad and Tobago, on 4 July, 1973.
2 Signed at Nassau, The Bahamas, on 5 July, 2001.
3 Came into force on 14 February, 2001.
4 Article III of the Agreement.
5 Barbados and Guyana.
6 See the Federal Supreme Court of 1950's, the British Caribbean Court of Appeal of 1960's and the present Eastern Caribbean Supreme Court with both original and appellate jurisdictions comprising Anguilla, Antigua & Barbuda, British Virgin Islands, Dominica, Grenada, Montserrat, St. Kitts & Nevis, St Lucia, St. Vincent and the Grenadines.
7 Preamble to the Agreement.
8 Article XXV.
9 Extracted from Professor Jacobs' book, "The Sovereignty of Law: the European Way (Cambridge; Cambridge University Press, 2007. Professor Jacobs is Professor of Law, King's College, London, and former Advocate General of the European Court of Justice.
10 Article XII of the Agreement, Article 211 of the Treaty.
11 Article XIII of the Agreement, Article 212 of the Treaty.
12 Article XIV of the Agreement, Article 214 of the Treaty.
13 Article XV of the Agreement, Article 215 of the Treaty.
14 Article XVI of the Agreement, Article 216 of the Treaty.
15 Article XVII of the Agreement; Article 217 of the Treaty.
15 16 Article XVIII; there is no similar provision in the Treaty.
16 17 Article XX of the Agreement, Article 219 of the Treaty.
17 Article XX of the Agreement, Article 219 of the Treaty.
18 Article XXVI of the Agreement.
19 Article 46.
20 Article XXIV of the Agreement, Article 222 of the Treaty.
21 Article XXII of the Agreement; Article 221 of the Treaty.
22 Preamble to the Treaty.
23 Article 172.
24 Article 175.
25 Article 171.
26 Article 180.
27 Articles 187 - 210.
28 Article 223.
29 Article XXIII.
30 (2006) 69 WIR 106.
31 (2007) 79 WIR, 75.
32 CCJ Appeal No. CV 1 of 2007.
33 CCJ Appeal No. CV 3 of 2006.
34 CCJ Appeal No. CV 13 of 2007
35 The full texts of all of the judgments can be accessed by visiting the Court's website at www.caribbeancourtofjustice.org.
36 Article V of the Agreement.
37 Daniel Terris, Cesare P.R. Romano, Leigh Swigart, Brandeis University Press 2007.

38 The footnote to this was that a notable exception is the Caribbean Court of Justice; whether or not governments put forward suggestions for candidates, it should be noted that the CCJ has recently accepted applications from all interested parties regardless of origin.
39 Article IV.
40 Article IV(6).
41 Article IV(II).
42 Article IX.
43 Independent Jamaica Council for Human Rights Ltd –v- Hon. Syringa Marshall-Burnett & Attorney General. of Jamaica (2005) PC 3; 65 WIR 268.
44 Article 224.
45 Article IX of the Agreement.
46 Agreed by Law Ministers and endorsed by the Commonwealth Heads of Government Meeting, Abuja, Nigeria 2003.
47 Article XXVIII of the Agreement.
48 Preamble to the Treaty.
49 Article 7.
50 Article 32.
51 Article 9.

CHAPTER 8

THE ROLE OF THE APPELLATE COURT

The topic of this address is multi-jurisdictional and multi-dimensional. As such it involves discussion of court systems which are jurisdictionally different even among countries which share a common law history. Primarily appellate courts are courts of review of the decisions of lower courts, and may be intermediate courts or courts of last resort with a power of review only on points of law where the leave of such a court is obtained or courts whose sole function is review of decisions concerning a country's constitution or basic law.[1]

Discussion of the appellate courts of a few selected Commonwealth countries (England and Wales, Canada, Australia, India, South Africa, New Zealand and the Caribbean) will form the basis of this paper, with some comparative reference to the United States Supreme Court. One of the enduring legacies of British colonialism being the court and judicial systems, it is appropriate to commence our journey with a historical tour of the systems of England and Wales.

From the earliest years of trial by ordeal, the passage of the Judicature Act 1873 was transformational in the judicial system of England and Wales merging as it did the common law and equity, and establishing the High Court and the Court of Appeal. The Criminal Appeal Act 1907 brought into being the Court of Criminal Appeal, the jurisdiction of which later passed to the Court of Appeal under the Criminal Appeal Act 1966.

The House of Lords in addition to its legislative function, was vested with a judicial function as a court of last resort, its jurisdiction being regulated by the Appellate Jurisdiction Act 1874 and later Acts; its original jurisdiction is confined to peerage claims. The Court's appellate jurisdiction covers appeals from the Court of Appeal of England and Wales and Northern Ireland, civil appeals from the

Court of Session of Scotland, appeals directly from the High Court of England and Wales and Northern Ireland "leapfrogging" the Court of Appeal, and appeals from the Court Martial Appeal Court. An appeal from a lower court is accepted only with leave of that court or of the House of Lords except an appeal from the Court of Session of Scotland which requires only to be certified that there are reasonable grounds for the appeal.

With the new Supreme Court (formerly the House of Lords) at the apex of the hierarchy of the English court system, the Divisions of the High Court (Queen's Bench, Family and Chancery) exercise appellate jurisdiction as administrative and divisional courts hearing appeals from crown courts, county courts, magistrates' courts and tribunals.

DOCTRINE OF PRECEDENT

Inevitably any discussion on appellate courts involves the applicability of the doctrine of precedent which in one sense depends on the hierarchy of courts, and in another on whether an appellate court is bound by its own decisions known as "*stare decisis*." The hierarchy of courts dictates that the decisions of higher courts are binding on courts of lower jurisdiction, for example, decisions of the Supreme Court, Court of Appeal and High Courts bind the magistrates, crown and county courts in England and Wales. An appellate court such as the Court of Appeal may also be bound by its own decisions as was first decided in *Young v Bristol Aeroplane Co. Ltd.*[2] In that case the Court of Appeal held that it was bound to follow its own decisions and those of courts of co-ordinate jurisdiction, the only exceptions being (1) to decide which of two conflicting decisions of its own it will follow, (2) to refuse to follow a decision of its own which, though not expressly overruled, cannot, in its opinion, stand with a decision of the House of Lords , and (3) not to follow a decision of its own if it is satisfied that the decision was given *per incuriam.*[3] A fourth exception where a law was assumed to exist in a previous case, but did not, was established in *R (on the application of Kadhim) v Brent London Borough Housing Benefit Review Board.*[4] *Lord Denning*, that illustrious and renowned jurist of revered memory and who acquired the reputation of being the great dissenter while in the Court of Appeal (and also while in the House of Lords), expressed strong views against rigidly following

Young, and found ways of getting around a previous decision if he felt that it was wrongly decided, sometimes by distinguishing it either on the facts or the law.

Unusually, the Criminal Division is not bound by its previous decisions, no doubt placing the need to be fair and just above the need to be certain and rigid.

Prior to 1966, the House of Lords like the Court of Appeal was bound by its own decisions; in fact as far back as 1898 in *London Street Tramways Company Ltd v The London County Council*[5] the House held that a decision upon a question of law is conclusive and binds the House in subsequent cases. *The Earl of Halsbury, L.C.* reasoned that although cases of individual hardship may arise after a judgment is given and which the profession may find to be erroneous, greater inconvenience would ensue in having each question subject to being reargued and "the dealings of mankind rendered doubtful by reason of different decisions so that in truth and in fact there would be no real final Court of Appeal."

This continued to be the position until 1966 when a Practice Statement (Judicial Precedent)[6] was issued in which the learned Law Lords recognised that "too rigid adherence to precedent may lead to injustice in a particular case and also unduly restrict the proper development of the law." They reserved the right to depart from a previous decision whenever it appeared right to do so.[7] This did not affect the value of precedent in cases in lower courts, and all other courts that recognised the House of Lords as the court of last resort. So far the position seems to be the same in relation to the new Supreme Court of England and Wales.

Before leaving the discussion on precedent mention should be made of the European Court of Justice in relation to the House of Lords and its successor, the new Supreme Court. This Court, now part of the English legal system by virtue of the European Communities Act 1972, and established under the Treaty of Rome 1957, is clothed with jurisdiction to determine questions of law pertaining to any Community instrument, and as such can overrule all other national courts including the Supreme Court (and former House of Lords) on matters of Community law. Only in this regard does the Supreme Court yield to any other court as the final arbiter of issues affecting nationals of England and Wales.

THE JUDICIAL COMMITTEE OF THE PRIVY COUNCIL

The Privy Council as it is familiarly known (and will hereafter be so described) can be said to be the most multi-faceted court in the judicial system of the United Kingdom since its establishment by the Judicial Committee Act 1833. Besides being one of the highest courts in the United Kingdom it is also the court of last resort for several Commonwealth countries which were former colonies of Great Britain. In addition to jurisdiction in some domestic matters, the Government may refer any issue to the Committee for "consideration and report." Additionally, it is the court of final resort for the Church of England.

Precedent

Judgments of the Privy Council in cases from overseas Commonwealth jurisdictions are only persuasive in courts of the United Kingdom, but are binding precedent in the lower courts of the jurisdiction from which they emanate.

Not unlike the former House of Lords the Privy Council never regarded itself bound by its own decision, and this was held to be so in three cases from the Caribbean.[8] *Lord Hoffman*, however, in one instance was of the opinion that the fact that the Board has the power to depart from earlier decisions does not mean that there are no principles which should guide it in deciding whether to do so. He went on to state that: "*if the Board feels able to depart from a previous decision simply because its members on a given occasion have a doctrinal disposition 'to come out differently,' the rule of law itself will be damaged and there will be no stability in the administration of justice ...*

Further reference will be made later about the impact of the judgments of the Privy Council when discussing the appellate courts in the selected jurisdictions.

CANADA

Within the hierarchy of the Canadian judicial system the Supreme Court of Canada which came into being in 1875 by an Act of Parliament, and is now governed by the Supreme Court Act, stands at the apex of a structure which is multi-dimensional. It comprises both federal and provincial court systems as well as military courts and tribunals. The Federal Court of Appeal hears and determines appeals from the federal court trial division and federal administrative tribunals, and the

Provincial Courts of Appeal function as appellate courts for provincial, superior courts and provincial administrative tribunals. The Supreme Court is the ultimate court of appeal for all of these courts including the military courts.

Leave to appeal to the Supreme Court is given if the case involves issues of law or a question of great public importance that warrants consideration. In addition, the Court can hear references from the Governor in Council for opinions on the constitutionality or interpretation of federal or provincial legislation.

The early beginnings of the Supreme Court did not augur well for its future. Its first case in April 1876 was a reference sent from the Senate requesting the Court's opinion on a private bill; it was not until one year after its first sitting that the Court began to sit regularly.

Despite the creation of the Supreme Court in 1875 the Privy Council continued to be the court of last resort for Canada until 1933 for criminal appeals, and 1949 for civil appeals.

Precedent

Shortly after appeals to the Privy Council were abolished, the Supreme Court's approach to decisions emanating from the House of Lords began to change, and their relevance to Canadian jurisprudence was called into question. Illustrative of this is the case of *Fleming v Atkinson*[9] involving a collision between a motor car and cattle on the municipal highway and consideration of the right of an adjoining landowner to permit cows to run at large on the highway. The question arose whether an English common law rule was applicable. It was held by a majority of the Supreme Court that the injured motorist was entitled to succeed. Reference was made to an English case of *Searle v Wallbank*[10] that the English common law rule was to the effect that highways in England having come into existence by dedication rather than by governmental action there was formerly no real risk of damage from the presence of straying animals, hence no duty of care to users of the highway. This had been followed in one case in Ontario of *Noble v Calder*[11] in which the English common law position as defined in *Searle v Wallbank* (*supra*) had been applied. *Judson, J* writing the majority judgment reasoned that the historical basis for the rule in *Searle* was dependent upon the peculiarities of highway dedication in England which had never existed in Ontario; the public right of passage on the highways of Ontario was never subject to the risk of stray animals as the highways were created by the province and vests in the province. He concluded that this alone was sufficient to distinguish the law of Ontario from the law of England and to render the principle stated in *Searle* inapplicable to Ontario.

Later in *Ares v Venner*[12] the issue of the admissibility of hospital records and exceptions to the hearsay rule arose for consideration and involved discussion of the House of Lords decision in *Myers v Director of Public Prosecutions*[13] and whether extension of the exceptions to the hearsay rule should involve a legislative or judicial solution. *Hall, J* in delivering the judgment of the Court adopted and followed the minority views of *Lords Donovan and Pearce* in *Myers* which supported a judicial solution rather than a legislative one. *Lord Donovan* had expressed the view that: *"the common law is moulded by the judges and it is still their province to adapt it from time to time so as to make it serve the interests of those it binds."* The opposite view was taken by *Lord Reid* who posited that: *"the most powerful argument of those who support the strict doctrine of precedent is that if it is relaxed judges will be tempted to encroach on the proper field of the legislature."*

Hall, J's opinion was that the Court (the Supreme Court) should adopt and follow the minority view rather than resort to saying in effect: *"This judge-made law needs to be restated to meet modern conditions, but we must leave it to Parliament and the ten legislatures to do the job."* This indicated a pragmatic and less rigid approach to precedent commensurate with modern conditions.

The scope of the Canadian Bill of Rights enacted in 1960 as a federal statute was limited, and rarely were such statutes deemed to be inoperative by the Supreme Court. In *R. v Drybones,*[14] a landmark decision, the Court, however, held that Section 94(b) of the Indian Act which prohibited Indians from being intoxicated off a reserve, was inoperative being in violation of Section 1 of the Bill of Rights which recognised the enjoyment of certain rights without discrimination based on race, colour or national origin.

In *Attorney General of Canada v Lavell*[15] the Court held that the enfranchisement of Indian women for marrying a non-Indian as provided under Section 12(1)(b) of the Indian Act did not violate the respondent's right to equality before the law under Section 1 (b) of the Bill of Rights and so the impugned Section of the Indian Act was not inoperative.

Dissatisfaction with the Bill of Rights eventually led to the adoption in 1982 of the Canadian Charter of Rights and Freedoms which was entrenched in the constitution of Canada. It broadened the scope of the fundamental rights and freedoms with wide powers of interpretation and enforcement being given to the courts, the Supreme Court of Canada being the ultimate authority. This mandate was utilised by the Supreme Court in several cases, two of them being foremost in mind – *R v Morgantaler*[16] (involving abortion rights) when the Court found that Section 251 of the Criminal Code violated a woman's right to security of the person under Section 7 of the Charter. The other was *Vriend v Alberta*[17] in which the Supreme Court held that a legislative omission regarding sexual orientation in the Alberta Individual Rights Protection Act violated Section 15 of the Charter.

AUSTRALIA

Provision in Section 71 of the Constitution of Australia led to the establishment in 1901 of an appellate court known as the High Court of Australia with its first sitting taking place in 1903 and comprising jurists from the newly created Commonwealth of Australia with a jurisdiction embracing the state supreme courts. In *Dalgarno v Hannah*[18] (among the first cases decided by the High Court on appeal from the Supreme Court of New South Wales) the Court expressly stated that Section 73 of the constitution "provides that the High Court shall have jurisdiction, with such exceptions and subject to such regulations as the Parliament prescribes to hear and determine appeals from all judgments, decrees, orders and sentences of any federal court, or court exercising federal jurisdiction, or of the Supreme Court of a state." Defying critics who at the time feared that the Court would be a tribunal with no real status, the Court spoke through its judgments and over the years gained a reputation for judicial excellence.

The High Court stands at the pinnacle in the hierarchy of courts in Australia with two streams – the superior courts which comprise the supreme courts in each state and territory and which normally hear appeals from inferior courts in their area, and federal courts which are superior courts with jurisdiction over laws made by the federal Parliament, and from the family court. Appeals to the High Court are by special leave only; hence for most cases the appellate divisions of the supreme courts of each state and the federal court are the ultimate appellate courts. The Full Court of the High Court is now the court of last resort for the whole of Australia.

THE HIGH COURT AND THE PRIVY COUNCIL

Section 74 of the Constitution prohibited appeals to the Privy Council on constitutional matters involving disputes about the limits of Commonwealth or state powers except where the High Court certified the appeal which occurred only once. In *Kirmani v Captain Cook Cruises Pty Ltd* (No.2)[19] the High Court explained the reason for this to be that it rigorously insisted on maintaining its ultimate constitutional responsibility to decide conflicts between the Commonwealth and the states without the intervention of Her Majesty in Council; in fact, the Court felt that by granting a certificate for the appeal it would be abdicating its responsibility to decide finally questions concerning the limits of Commonwealth and state powers, questions which had a peculiarly Australian character and were of fundamental concern to the Australian people.

In 1968 by the Privy Council (Limitation of Appeals) Act all appeals to the Privy Council involving federal legislation were discontinued, and in 1975 the Privy Council (Appeals from the High Court) Act closed the door on all appeals to the Privy Council. In 1986 with the passage of the Australia Acts all appeals from state supreme courts to the Privy Council were finally terminated, leaving the High Court as the only court of last resort for all Australian courts.

Precedent

The question whether the High Court should be bound by its own decisions (*stare decisis*) was decided as far back as 1913 when, in *Australian Agricultural Company v Federated Engine-Drivers*[20] *Isaacs, J* reasoned that "*where the prior decision is manifestly wrong, then, irrespective of consequences, it is the paramount and sworn duty of the Court to declare the law truly.*" This liberal approach to precedent preceded the House of Lords Practice Statement (Judicial Precedent) by thirty-three years, and is consistent with the approach of the Australian courts to eschew rigidity in interpretation of the law in favour of pragmatism and practicality.

With the severing of ties to the Privy Council in 1968 and 1975 *Gibbs, J* in *Viro v R*[21] articulated the view that: "*The Court was not bound by decisions of the Privy Council, which no longer occupied a position above the High Court in the judicial hierarchy. As such it was for the High Court to assess the needs of Australian society and to expound and develop the law for Australia in the light of that assessment."*

Similar sentiments indicative of the Australian High Court's intention to create a jurisprudence relevant to the needs of its people and the development of the law in Australia were expressed by *Barwick, C.J.* in the said case, and repeated twenty-five years later by *Kirby, J* in *Barns v Barns.*[22] The High Court over the years has indeed fulfilled its mandate and continues to do so.

INDIA

The Supreme Court of India which was inaugurated on 28 January 1950 as the highest court in the judicial system has a tri-partite jurisdiction – original, appellate and advisory. The exclusive original jurisdiction relates to disputes between Government and one or more states or between states involving any question on the existence or extent of legal rights or the enforcement of fundamental rights. The appellate jurisdiction covers judgments of one or more of the twenty-one high courts in civil and criminal cases, and the special advisory jurisdiction may be invoked by the President of India by specific referral to it according to the constitution.

One unique feature of the Supreme Court's jurisdiction is the somewhat recent innovation of entertaining and deciding matters of public interest sent to it by members of the public either by writ petition or a simple letter addressed to the Chief Justice of the Court. This "public interest litigation" has led to several landmark cases being decided by the Court.

Lower down the hierarchy in the judicial system are the high courts of each state, and below them subordinate district courts all dealing with civil, criminal and family litigation. The high courts serve primarily as appellate courts hearing appeals from lower courts although they have an original jurisdiction in civil and criminal matters specifically conferred on them by a state or under federal law. Constitutionally all inferior courts including the high courts are bound by the decisions of the Supreme Court.

The relationship between the executive and judicial arms of the State has not been without some degree of conflict since the establishment of the Supreme Court. One area of law which gave rise to a confrontation was the executive's attempt to abridge the fundamental rights provisions in the constitution by the passage of amendments to implement land distribution and which affected one's right to property. In *Golaknath and others v The State of Punjab*[23] the Court held that fundamental rights could not be abridged or taken away by amending legislation. In the course of one of the judgments the learned Justices opined that fundamental rights are the primordial rights necessary for the development of human personality, and were rights which enabled a man "to chalk out his own life in the manner he likes best."

Similarly, in *Kesavananda Bharati v The State of Kerala*[24] the learned Chief Justice in his judgment emphasised the importance of the preservation of the freedom of the individual which could not be amended out of existence; therefore the fundamental rights conferred by the constitution cannot be abrogated, though a reasonable abridgement of those rights could be effected in the public interest. The judgments of the other Justices reflected the same opinion that amendments to the constitution could be made providing the basic structure remains intact. The fallout from this decision was that during a state of emergency in 1975 an amendment to the constitution was passed which nullified the effect of the decision. A few years after the emergency, however, the Supreme Court reaffirmed its power of judicial review in another case.

Precedent

For the Supreme Court of India like other final appellate courts *stare decisis* arose for determination in the case of *The Bengal Immunity Co. Ltd v The State of Bihar and others.*[25] In doing so reference was made to decisions of the English and Australian courts as well as the Supreme Court of the United States of America. In the course of his judgment *Das, CJ* (ag.) concluded that there was nothing in the Indian constitution which prevented the Supreme Court from departing from a previous decision if it was convinced of its error and baneful effect on the general interests of the public. He articulated the view that in considering the applicability of English decisions it should be borne in mind that those decisions may well have been influenced by considerations which could no longer apply to the circumstances then prevailing in India.

Bhagwati, J., another member of the Court, adopted the reasoning of other final courts that the only safeguard which should be put on the exercise of the power of reconsideration of earlier decisions was that the earlier decision should be manifestly wrong or erroneous particularly when the court is concerned with the construction of provisions of a constitution (as was the case before them) which cannot be easily amended. The Court ultimately decided to review an earlier decision in order to rectify an erroneous interpretation of the constitution which had resulted in considerable inconvenience and hardship.

On this issue the dissenting opinion of *Ramaswami, J.* in *Golaknath and others v The State of Punjab* (*supra*) was that even though the constitution is an organic document intended to serve as a guide to the solution of changing problems which the Court may have to face from time to time, the Court must be reluctant to accede to the suggestion that its earlier decisions should be frequently reviewed or departed from. He opined that in such a case the test should be what is the nature of the error alleged in the earlier decision and its impact on the public good; further, it is also a relevant factor that the earlier decision had been followed in a large number of cases and multitude of rights and obligations had been created.

SOUTH AFRICA

With the establishment of the Constitutional Court in 1994, South Africa now boasts of two courts of last resort in its judicial system, the other being the Supreme Court of Appeal. The Constitutional Court, however, is regarded as the highest court, and is the final court for appeals relating to the constitution. In this regard its decisions are binding on all other courts, and it has exclusive jurisdiction to declare any Act of Parliament invalid or unconstitutional.

The Supreme Court of Appeal formerly referred to as "The Appellate Division" which was first established in 1910 when the Union of South Africa was created, had a change of name under the constitution of 1996. It is the final court of appeal in all matters from the high courts and lower courts except those concerning the constitution when it gives way to the Constitutional Court.

In addition to its function as an appellate court in civil and criminal matters from the high courts, there is a special procedure for referrals to be made to the Supreme Court of Appeal by the Minister for Justice and Constitutional Development whenever there is any doubt as to the correctness of a high court decision in a criminal case on a question of law or where such a decision is in conflict with a decision given by another high court. The Supreme Court of Appeal may hear arguments in order to determine the issue for future guidance of all of the courts. Similar referrals may be made by the Minister to the Supreme Court after consultation with the South African Law Reform Commission where there are conflicting decisions in civil matters from different high courts.

In relation to constitutional matters, although the Supreme Court of Appeal may make orders upholding the validity of Acts of Parliament or concerning conduct of the President, an order of constitutional invalidity has no force unless confirmed by the Constitutional Court. The importance and ultimate authority of the Constitutional Court as the final arbiter on all issues pertaining to the constitution was emphasised in the judgment of *Chaskalson, P,* in *Pharmaceutical Manufacturers Association of South Africa and Another: In re Ex Parte President of the Republic of South Africa*[26] which raised the question whether a court has the power to review and set aside a decision made by the President of South Africa to bring an Act of Parliament into force. The Transvaal High Court was requested to review and set aside the President's decision to bring a 1998 Act into operation in order to govern the registration and control of medicines for human and animal use. The High Court declared the decision of the President null and void, and referred it to the Constitutional Court for confirmation of its order. The Constitutional Court confirmed the order of the High Court but for different reasons raising the issue of whether the High Court's order setting aside the President's decision was a finding of constitutional invalidity that required confirmation by the Constitutional Court under section 172(2)(a) of the constitution.

In the course of his judgment *Chaskalson, P* stated that the Constitutional Court occupies a special place in the new constitutional order, and was established as part of that order as a new court to be the highest court in respect of all constitutional matters, and as such, the guardian of the constitution; it has exclusive jurisdiction in respect of certain constitutional matters, and makes the final decision on those constitutional matters that are also within the jurisdiction of other courts. He went on to say that that was the context within which Section 172(2)(a) provides that an order made by the Supreme Court of Appeal, a high court or a court of similar status concerning the constitutional validity of an Act of Parliament, a provincial Act or any conduct of the President has no force unless confirmed by the Constitutional Court.

The constitution of South Africa has been regarded within legal circles as one of the most progressive within recent times particularly with regard to the protection of fundamental rights and freedoms, formulated as it was to correct the harsh abuses of the apartheid system. In this regard the role of the Constitutional Court was defined as protector and enforcer of the Bill of Rights embodied in the Interim Constitution of 1994. That Bill of Rights applied to all law, and Section 173 of the Constitution gives to all higher courts (the Constitutional Court, the Supreme Court of Appeal and the high courts) "the inherent power to protect and regulate their own process, and to develop the common law, taking into account the interests of justice."

A very interesting case which exemplifies the Constitutional Court's obligation to develop the common law in order to promote the objects of the Bill of Rights is *Alix Jean Carmichele v The Minister for Safety and Security and Another.*[27] The applicant sued the respondents for damages arising out of an attack on her by a man who was awaiting trial for attempted rape on another woman, and who was granted bail despite his history of sexual violence. Both the High Court and the Supreme Court of Appeal dismissed her claim on the ground that she had failed to establish a legal duty specifically owed to her by the police and prosecutor who could not therefore be liable to her for damages. In a unanimous decision, the constitutional Court upheld an appeal against the decisions of the lower courts. In the course of a most enlightening judgment *Ackerman & Goldstone, JJ* remarked that under the constitution of South Africa the duty cast upon judges is different in degree to that which the Canadian Charter of Rights casts upon Canadian judges. The South African constitution brought into operation, "in one fell swoop," a completely new and different set of rights imposing on all of the courts a general duty to develop the common law where it deviates from the spirit, purport and objects of the Bill of Rights. This duty upon the judges arises in respect of both the civil and criminal law whether or not the parties in any particular case request the court to develop the common law.

The Constitutional Court remains unswerving in its mandate to uphold the law and the constitution of South Africa.

NEW ZEALAND

The Supreme Court of New Zealand (like the Caribbean Court of Justice) is one of the newest courts of final resort among other such courts having come into existence on 1st January 2004 by virtue of the Supreme Court Act 2003 replacing the Privy Council as New Zealand's final appellate court. Appeals to the Supreme Court in civil matters only are by leave of the court if it is satisfied that it is in the interests of justice to give such leave, and in the criminal matters specifically authorised by statute. Generally, appeals are heard from the Court of Appeal only, but in exceptional circumstances the court may give leave to appeal from a decision of a lower court.

Prior to the establishment of the Supreme Court, the Court of Appeal of New Zealand had existed since 1862 hearing appeals from the High Court, then called the Supreme Court.

Precedent

A discussion on precedent in the court system of New Zealand should centre mainly around the decisions of the Court of Appeal having regard to its long existence and the more recent establishment of the Supreme Court which is now the final appellate court.

After the English decision in *Young v Bristol Aeroplane Co. Ltd* (*supra*) in which the Court of Appeal held that it was bound by its own decisions, the Court of Appeal of New Zealand in *Re Rayner (deceased), Daniell and Others v Rayner and Others*[28] in a majority decision held that: "*the Court of Appeal is free to overrule a judgment of that Court which is contrary to the current of New Zealand authority theretofore existing, or which, though not expressly overruled, is, in principle, in conflict with a decision of the House of Lords or the Privy Council or inconsistent with a judgment of the High Court of Australia.*"

The issue of *stare decisis* arose on several occasions after *Rayner* but with no definitive position taken.[29] In *Collector of Customs v Lawrence Publishing Co. Ltd.*,[30] *Richardson, J*, concluded that while the Court had not pronounced in any definite way on the circumstances in which it would reconsider an earlier decision the practice of the Court indicated a cautious willingness to review earlier decisions in perceived appropriate cases, and a reluctance to be completely fettered by its own past decisions. He conceded that adherence to past decisions promotes certainty and stability, but concluded that the Court had the final responsibility within New Zealand for the administration of the laws of New Zealand, and while its decisions are subject to review by the Privy Council few litigants who are unsuccessful in the Court of Appeal feel able to follow that path; hence he thought it unwise to formulate any absolute rule.

Finlay, J in *Rayner* (*supra*) had stated in his judgment that: "*the Court of Appeal in New Zealand occupied a position in the judicial hierarchy which differed very materially from that of the Court of Appeal in England, and it followed consequently that the Court of Appeal was in effect, in nearly all cases, the final court of New Zealand.*"

This was based on the fact of the final court (the Privy Council) being thousands of miles away. With the establishment of the Supreme Court of New Zealand this is no longer the position, and in light of this a more definitive position of the effect of *stare decisis* on the Court of Appeal inevitably will change if it has not done so already. The focus of the doctrine now shifts to the Supreme Court.

THE PRIVY COUNCIL AND NEW ZEALAND

This can best be addressed by reference to a speech given by Chief Justice Dame Sian Elias to the 13th Commonwealth Law Conference held in Melbourne, Australia, in April, 2003 before the establishment of the new Supreme Court.[31] While agreeing that the real benefit obtained by New Zealand's legal system from appeals to the Privy Council was the benefit of a second appeal, albeit in a tiny number of cases, Dame Elias posited the view that in some cases where the New Zealand Court of Appeal was rightly reversed, the same result would have been achieved on further appeal within New Zealand. She went on to state that the main reason that there were so few landmark decisions on appeal from New Zealand was that in the common law world such decisions were landmarks for all countries in that the common law tradition tended to pull all countries together in most cases. This meant that the landmark decisions of the House of Lords, or the High Court of Australia, or the Supreme Court of Canada generally gained acceptance in New Zealand and throughout the common law world as much as or even more than those of the Privy Council.

Dame Elias observed that the Privy Council had increasingly accepted that local conditions justify different treatment. Two cases amply exemplify this point of view. In *Invercargill City Council v Hamlin*[32] the Privy Council held that although inheriting English common law, it did not follow that New Zealand common law would develop identically. The Court of Appeal should not be deflected from developing New Zealand common law merely because the House of Lords had not regarded an identical development as appropriate in England. Accordingly, the Court of Appeal was entitled consciously to depart from English case law on the ground that conditions in New Zealand were different.

Similarly, in *Lange v Atkinson*[33] the Board noted that for some years it had recognised the limitations on its role as an appellate tribunal in cases where the decision depends upon considerations of local public policy. It concluded that the courts of New Zealand were much better placed to assess the requirements of the public interest in New Zealand than the Board, and accordingly on the particular issue it would not substitute its own views, if different, from those of the New Zealand Court of Appeal.

Since its establishment the Supreme Court decisions have covered a varied spectrum of issues. In *Ngan v R.*[34] the Court had to consider the scope and application of Section 21 of the New Zealand Bill of Rights Act 1990 regarding the right to be free of unreasonable search and seizure, and held that evidence of a crime discovered incidental to an inventory search of a car involved in an accident was admissible in court. The Court found that the Act did not make the search of *Ngan's* property unlawful.

Another decision of the Supreme Court delivered recently in the case of *Jeffries v The Privacy Commissioner*[35] involved the question of whether privilege is capable of applying to unsolicited communications and information, and whether the identity of the informant is capable of being within the scope of the privilege.

The Supreme Court of New Zealand seems well on its way to developing its own jurisprudence and carving a niche for itself among the final appellate courts both within and outside of the Commonwealth.

CARIBBEAN APPELLATE COURTS

The grant of independence to the former British colonies of the Caribbean led to the establishment of appellate courts within their jurisdictions with the Privy Council retaining its status as the court of last resort for all except one.[36] The inauguration of the Caribbean

Court of Justice in April 2005 has seen three Caribbean states, Barbados, Guyana and recently Belize, accepting this Court as their final appellate court.[37]

The appellate courts in the Caribbean[38] hear and determine appeals from their domestic courts, and have over the years sought to develop a jurisprudence which reflects the mores and customs of their societies while applying the common law which for all former colonies has been the common law of England. This was preserved legislatively after the attainment of independence, for example, in Trinidad and Tobago[39] and Guyana.[40]

In some instances, however, the common law did not always square with local circumstances and situations. *Crane, J.A.* sitting in the Court of Appeal of Guyana in the case of *Peter Persaud and Others v Pln. Versailles & Schoon Ord Ltd*[41] expressed strong views that despite the fact that statute stipulated that the common law of the (then) Colony was to be the common law of England, this in no way fettered the jurisdiction of the Guyana Court from itself developing and expanding the common law to meet the justice of the case when necessary.

EFFECT OF DECISIONS OF THE PRIVY COUNCIL IN THE CARIBBEAN

Apart from a few dependencies and small colonies in world-wide geographical locations the Privy Council's greatest remaining influence is felt within the Commonwealth Caribbean region comprising in some instances states that have shed the colonial mantle for over forty years. Being the court of final jurisdiction for these states their courts are bound by decisions emanating from the Privy Council with results which are oft times baffling and bewildering to citizens and which run counter to accepted norms in their societies.

The Trinidadian case of *Kizza Sealey and Marvin Headley v The State*[42] provides an apt illustration. The two appellants who were charged and convicted of murder appealed to the Court of Appeal of Trinidad and Tobago who dismissed the appeal whereupon they appealed to the Privy Council. The prosecution's case rested mainly on the testimony and positive identification of the appellants at the scene by an off-duty corporal of police who knew both of them from childhood and lived in the same neighbourhood; in fact one of the appellants under cross-examination at the trial admitted that he knew the police corporal who lived next to him. Their Lordships of the Privy Council at the hearing recognised that the case against the two appellants was a very strong one and that from a reading of the transcript the alibi evidence appeared unimpressive. However, allowing the appeal, a majority of the Board concluded that there was an omission of a good character direction by the trial judge which was a defect in the conduct of the trial despite the fact that the omission was not attributable to the trial judge, but the fault of defence counsel who did not raise it in evidence. They reasoned that whilst it appeared probable that the jury would have convicted they were unable to conclude that the jury would inevitably have convicted. Both the majority and the minority of the Board agreed that the alibi evidence was in reality very weak as against the strength of the evidence of the police corporal. In the opinion of the minority the appellants had had the benefit of the usual directions on the presumption of innocence and of the approach which must be taken to defence evidence; also it was stretching imagination too far to suppose that a good character direction would have made any difference to the result of the case.

The acquittal of the appellants still remains inexplicable to the average citizen of Trinidad and Tobago who cannot comprehend that two men who were positively identified by a reliable witness were freed despite the failure of their defence counsel to lead evidence of their good character. Such are the vagaries of the law.

There have been instances when the Law Lords of the Privy Council have conceded that judges of the domestic courts are in a better position to determine certain issues based on their knowledge of local conditions and their experience as happened in *Peter Seepersad v Theophilus Persad & Capital Insurance Co. Ltd*[43] when the Board expressed the view that the amount determined by the Trinidad and Tobago Court of Appeal as damages for pain and suffering in an accident claim was the product of the views of appellate judges on a topic peculiarly within their own experience and their Lordships were not disposed to amend it. A similar approach was take in *Basdeo Panday v Kenneth Gordon*[44], a libel suit, when the Board opined that how words of the alleged character would be understood and what effect such words would have on those who heard them are matters on which local courts are far better placed than their Lordships.[45]

CARIBBEAN COURT OF JUSTICE

For the past five years since its inauguration on April 16, 2005 the Caribbean Court of Justice has sought as its mission to foster the development of an indigenous Caribbean jurisprudence, and visualises an accessible, innovative and impartial justice system reflective of the Region's history, values and traditions. This Court is regarded as being unique in that it seeks to combine in twin jurisdictions, appellate and original, the Caribbean Region's need for a court of last resort for domestic appellate courts as well as an international court with a mandate to interpret and apply, where necessary, provisions of a regional economic treaty.

Within one year of its inauguration the Caribbean Court was required to decide an appeal from a decision of the Court of Appeal of Barbados[46] on a constitutional motion involving, *inter alia,* whether, and in what manner unincorporated international human rights treaties which give a right of access to international tribunals affect the rights and status of a person convicted of murder and sentenced to a mandatory death penalty. The Court of Appeal of Barbados relied on a decision of the Privy Council in *Neville Lewis v The Attorney General*[47] (an appeal from Jamaica) by which it was bound, the Privy Council being at that time its final appellate court. The Caribbean Court felt obliged to determine whether *Lewis* should or should not continue to be the law of Barbados, and this required a re-examination of other judgments of the Privy Council. The Court was mindful of the fact that its establishment has given rise to speculation concerning its approach to judgments of the Privy Council. In deciding what this approach ought to be one has to bear in mind the stated mission of the Court which is to foster the development of an indigenous Caribbean jurisprudence. In pursuing this goal the Court in *Joseph and Boyce* postulated the view that it will consider the opinions of the final courts of other Commonwealth countries and particularly the judgments of the Privy Council which determine the law for those Caribbean states that accept the Privy Council as their final appellate court. It stated further that in this connection it accepted that decisions made by the Privy Council in appeals from other Caribbean countries while it was still the final appellate court for Barbados were binding in Barbados in the absence of any material difference between the written law of the respective countries from which the appeals emanated and the written law of Barbados. Further the Caribbean Court stipulated that these decisions continue to be binding in Barbados notwithstanding the replacement of the Privy Council unless and until they are overruled by the Caribbean Court.

After extensive consideration and deliberation of the case law drawn from several jurisdictions on the issue mentioned earlier the Caribbean Court concluded that the result which it arrived at was not dissimilar to that reached by the Privy Council in *Lewis*, albeit by a different route, and saw no reason to disagree with the Board's conclusions.

Over the past five years of the Court's existence several other cases provided the opportunity to elucidate and interpret some troubling points of law particularly in cases concerning title to land in Guyana. In *Harrinauth Ramdass v Salim Jairam*[48] an appeal from the Court of Appeal of Guyana, the issues related to the ongoing debate of whether equitable interests in land are recognised in Guyana having regard to the development of the law governing immovable property and its Roman-Dutch history. A review and analysis of the relevant case law led to a final conclusion that equitable interests in land are not recognisable in Guyana. This was followed by another Guyanese appeal, *Jassoda Ramkishun v Conrad Ashford Fung-Kee-Fung*[49] concerning the concept of fraud in relation to immovable property, the relevance of South African case law as well as the position of heirs as volunteer transferees and the grant of specific performance against a volunteer both in English law and Roman-Dutch law, issues which are of extreme importance to the development of land law in Guyana.

The Caribbean Court is still in its infancy when compared with other appellate courts with a final jurisdiction; hence it may be too early for it to decide whether it will be bound by its own decisions, which though it may result in certainty and stability may give rise to rigidity and inflexibility when later cases require the Court to revise its thinking on a particular precedent. Nevertheless, a final court's review of its earlier decisions ought not to be undertaken whimsically or fancifully, but must be taken after careful consideration and a conviction that the earlier decision was completely erroneous.[50] A change in the composition of the court ought not to be good reason to depart from an earlier decision. In *Charles Mathew v The State*[51], however, the Privy Council with an enlarged Board overruled *Balkissoon Roodal v The*

State[52] (both cases from the Court of Appeal of Trinidad and Tobago), the purpose being to decide whether *Roodal* should be followed not only in Trinidad and Tobago but also in other Caribbean states which have similar constitutions and a right of appeal to the Privy Council. Their Lordships considered that: "*it would be impossible to apply it to other countries merely for conformity with Trinidad and Tobago but equally impossible to declare that it was not the law in other countries but still formed part of the law of Trinidad and Tobago.*"

These are situations with which the Caribbean Court of Justice will have to grapple in the years ahead as it strives to develop its own jurisprudence.

SUPREME COURT OF THE UNITED STATES OF AMERICA

Although this paper is directed mainly at the role of appellate courts of Commonwealth jurisdictions, it can only be enhanced by a comparison with the court of final jurisdiction of the United States of America where there are more similarities than differences, the common law being the *fons et origo* of both jurisdictions.

Like any court newly constituted the Supreme Court established in 1789 in its early era heard few cases, the first being *West v Barnes*[53] argued in 1791 before the Jay Court (Chief Justice John Jay), two years later. It involved a procedural issue where the Court was required to overrule a Rhode Island state statute. *Marbury v Madison,* [54], however, is regarded as the landmark case (Marshall Court) which formed the basis for the exercise of judicial review in the United States under Article 111 of the constitution, and which declared the Court to be the supreme arbiter of the constitution.

The Supreme Court's main jurisdiction is appellate although it may exercise an original jurisdiction involving disputes between two or more states much like the Caribbean Court of Justice, but which it rarely exercises.

The United States court structure comprises courts of appeals which are intermediate appellate courts of the federal court system. These courts hear appeals from district courts within the federal judicial circuit, and review decisions serving as the final court in most federal cases. This is primarily due to the fact that fewer than 100 cases are heard annually by the Supreme Court which stands at the apex of the federal court system. On matters concerning interpretation of federal law and statutes, including the U.S. constitution, decisions of the Supreme Court are binding on all lower courts even on state courts which are not part of the federal system.

The Supreme Court has to its credit several important decisions handed down over the years during the tenure of various Chief Justices, the most notable being by the Warren Court (1953 - 1969) in *Brown v Board of Education of Topeka*[55] when it held segregation in public schools to be unconstitutional, and the Burger Court (1969-1986) in *Roe v Wade*[56] which ruled that the constitution protected a woman's right to privacy and control over her body thereby removing bans on abortion.

Precedent

With jurisdiction of courts within the United States judicial system comprising state and federal courts the doctrine of precedent follows the same pattern. As is generally accepted courts of lower jurisdiction are bound by the decisions of courts of higher jurisdiction, with the decisions of courts of last resort normally binding all courts within a court system. Within the states court systems, decisions of state appellate courts bind only courts of lower jurisdiction within that state, but not those of other states. Within the federal system higher federal courts bind lower federal courts within their jurisdiction. Conflicting decisions within federal courts as to the meaning of federal laws are usually resolved by the Supreme Court whose decision is binding on all courts.

What will now be considered is the Supreme Court's approach to precedent in relation to its own decisions. In *Burnet v Coronado Oil & Gas Co.*[57] *Brandeis, J* in a dissenting opinion expressed the view that: "*stare decisis is usually the wise policy because in most matters it is more important that the applicable rule of law be settled than that it be settled right... But in cases involving the Federal Constitution, where correction through legislative action is practically impossible, this Court has often overruled its earlier decisions.*"

He went on to say that: "*the reasons why this Court should refuse to follow an earlier constitutional decision which it deems erroneous are particularly strong where the question presented is one of applying, as distinguished from what may accurately be called interpreting the Constitution.*"

One can conclude that in constitutional matters the Supreme Court exercises more flexibility in applying the doctrine of *stare decisis*. In *Smith v Allwright*[58] the Court postulated that when convinced of former error it has never felt constrained to follow precedent, and where constitutional questions were concerned with corrections depending upon amendment rather than upon legislative action, the Court throughout its history has freely exercised its power to re-examine the basis of its constitutional decisions. There have been opinions expressed which indicate that while adherence to precedent is not to be applied rigidly in constitutional matters, any departure from the doctrine of *stare decisis* demands special justification. This was the view of *O'Connor, J* in *Arizona v Rumsey*.[59] Later in *Planned Parenthood of Southern Pa. v Casey*[60] together with *Kennedy and Souter, JJ, O'Connor, J* reiterated that view when seeking to uphold the earlier decision in *Roe v Wade* (*supra*) to the effect that: "*only the most convincing justification under accepted standards of precedent could suffice to demonstrate that a later decision overruling the first was anything but a surrender to political pressure and an unjustified repudiation of the principle on which the Court staked its authority in the first instance.*"

CONCLUSION

An assessment of the role of appellate courts in the jurisdictional hierarchy of any court system indicates that even though they are mainly courts of review of decisions of lower courts, in discharging this mandate one of the main objectives is ensuring stability in and conformity with the law even though not always resolutely adhering to consistency in their decisions. The waning influence of the House of Lords and the Privy Council on former colonies was aptly demonstrated when a majority of these independent states (former colonies) unapologetically indicated that the development of the law in their countries depended solely on the crafting of their own jurisprudence and not on one moulded in the traditions of their former masters. Unfortunately, this approach has not been adopted by all of the newly independent states.

One feature common to all appellate courts in whatever jurisdiction is the doctrine of *stare decisis* which has been discussed. While its binding force affects lower courts in a judicial hierarchy, and is generally immutable, courts of last resort enjoy much more flexibility and freedom to effect change in their decisions. This sometimes depends on the composition of a final appellate court or the need for review if circumstances of a later case require that the relevant law be elucidated. One commendable aspect of a final court's decision not to be bound by its own decisions is that it is utilised sparingly and with special justification bearing in mind that such courts should be perceived as fulfilling their objectives of achieving judicial consistency and certainty in their decisions without making them the sacrificial lambs on the altar of expediency. This will always be the role of an appellate court in every jurisdiction where the common law is applied in whatever form peculiar to the needs and traditions of the people of that jurisdiction.

With the establishment of indigenous final appellate courts in most of the former colonies of Great Britain the judgments of these courts are often cited as persuasive authority in judgments of fellow appellate courts, and even in judgments of the House of Lords and Privy Council. This cross - fertilisation can only enhance and enrich the development of jurisprudence based on the common law across borders and continents within the Commonwealth.

I shall end this presentation by making reference to a lecture given by Sir Shridath Ramphal, former Commonwealth Secretary General, in 2009 entitled "*A Commonwealth of Laws: At 60 and Beyond*" and reported in the CMJA Commonwealth Judicial Journal of 3 June, 2010 which most of, if not all of us must have read. During the course of the lecture he made reference to the fact that strange as it may seem now, the issue of a Commonwealth Court of Appeal as a final court of appeal for all Commonwealth countries, including Britain, was prominently addressed at 1965 Commonwealth and Empire Law Conference held in Sydney, Australia. Sir Shridath quoted from a background paper prepared by Lord Gardiner, then Britain's Lord Chancellor, when he was silk together with R. Graham Page, who put the case for a Supreme Court of the Commonwealth in terms which he said may surprise us today. One paragraph urged that with such a court Commonwealth countries would influence each other in the development of Commonwealth law. All countries submitting to the jurisdiction would in every way be treated on an equal basis, subordinating their own final courts of appeal to the overriding appellate jurisdiction of the Supreme Court of the Commonwealth.

Sir Shridath's opinion was that it was too late, and for all its merits, he believed it still is, at least today. He expressed the hope that if the Commonwealth itself prospers, some such collective judicial forum may one day become more generally acceptable. This may seem an impossible dream as we gather here today discussing the role of appellate courts in our various jurisdictions, but we can at least revel in the dream that at some distant futuristic day that dream may somehow become a reality. We can dream, can't we?

Commonwealth Magistrates and Judges' Association Conference
Brighton, United Kingdom
13th – 16th September, 2010

Endnotes

1 See the Constitutional Court of South Africa which will be discussed in greater detail later.
2 [1944] K.B., 718.
3 Re-affirmed By *Lord Diplock* in *Davis v Johnson* [1978] UKHL 1, [1979] AC 264.
4 [2001] QB 955.
5 [1898] A.C. 375.
6 [1966] 1 WLR 1234.
7 [Lord Reid stated in *R v National Insurance Commissioner, Exp Hudson* [1972] AC 944 "the practice will be used "sparingly" when the previous wrong decision is thought to be impeding the proper development of the law or to have led to results which were unjust or contrary to public policy." Some examples where previous decisions of the House were overruled are *Conway v Rimmer* [1968] AC 910 overruling *Duncan v Cammell Laird* [1942] AC 624, *Milangos v George Frank (Textiles) Ltd* [1976] AC 443 overruling *In Re United Railways of Havana and Regla Warehouse Ltd* [1961] AC 1007. In the criminal jurisdiction *R v Howe* [1987] AC 417 overruling *DPP for Northern Ireland v Lynch* [1975] AC 653.
8 *Neville Lewis v Attorney General of Jamaica* (2000) 57 WIR 275; [2000] UKPC 35C; *Charles Matthew v The State* (2003) 64 WIR 270; [2004] UKPC 33C; *Lemuel Gibson v The Government of the United States of America (The Bahamas)* 70 WIR 34; [2007] UKPC 52.
9 [1959] 18 DLR (2d) 81.
10 [1947] A.C. 341.
11 [1952] 3 DLR 651.
12 [1970] SCR 608.
13 [1965] A.C. 1001.
14 [1970] SCR. 282.
15 [1973]SCR 1349.
16 [1988] 1 SCR 30.
17 [1998] 1 SCR 493.
18 [1903] HCA 1, [1903] 1 CLR 1.
19 [1985] HCA 27, 159 CLR 461.
20 [1913] 17 CLR 261.
21 [1978] 141 CLR 88.
22 [2003] CLR 169: "Although this Court continues to pay respect to the judicial reasons of the Privy Council, especially in respect of Australian appeals at a time when the Privy Council was a court within the Australian judicial hierarchy, we are not bound by such reasons." See also similar views of *Crane J.A.* in the Court of Appeal of Guyana in *Peter Persaud and Others v Pln. Versailles & Schoon Ord Ltd* (1971) WIR 107 at 132 to this effect: "It is my considered opinion that consequent on the removal of the Privy Council as our final court of appeal, the doctrine of *stare decisis* ... is a dead letter with us; its former judgments are now only of persuasive authority. Of course, we shall continue to cite, apply and to follow them, and when we do so, they will thereafter speak with our authority."
23 [1967] AIR 1643.
24 [1973] 4SCC, 225.
25 [1955] AIR, SC 661.

26 [2000] ZACC 1.
27 [2001] CCT 48/00.
28 [1948] NZLR 455.
29 See *Preston v Preston* [1955] NZLR 1251; *Re Manson* [1964] NZLR 257; *Mc Farlane v Sharp* [1972] NZLR 838.
30 [30] [1986] NZLR 404.
31 Parliamentary Library -background information service for members of Parliament 2003/02 8 May 2003.
32 [1996] NZLR 513.
33 [2000] NZLR 257.
34 [2007] NZSC 105.
35 [2010] NZSC 99.
36 Guyana severed ties with the Privy Council in 1970.
37 Antigua & Barbuda, The Bahamas, Dominica, Grenada, Jamaica, St Christopher & St. Nevis, St Lucia, St Vincent & The Grenadines, Trinidad and Tobago have still retained the Privy Council as their final appellate court.
38 The Bahamas, Barbados, Belize, Guyana, Jamaica, Trinidad and Tobago, and the Eastern Caribbean Court of Appeal for Anguilla, Antigua & Barbuda, British Virgin Islands, Dominica, Grenada, Montserrat, St. Christopher & Nevis, St Lucia, and St Vincent & the Grenadines.
39 See Section 12 of Trinidad and Tobago Supreme Court of Judicature Act, Chap. 4:01.
40 See Section 3(b) of the Civil Law of Guyana Act, Cap. 6:01 in relation to immovable property.
41 (1970) 17 WIR 107.
42 (2002) 61 WIR 491; [2002] UKPC 52.
43 (2004) 64 WIR 378; [2004] UKPC 19.
44 (2005) 67 WIR 290; [2005] UKPC 36.
45 Similar approach adopted in New Zealand cases of *Invercargill City Council v Hamlin (supra)* and *Lange v Atkinson (supra).*
46 *Attorney General and Others v Jeffrey Joseph and Lennox Ricardo Boyce* (2006) 69 WIR 104.
47 (1999) 57 WIR 275, [2001] 2 AC 50.
48 (2008) 72 WIR 270.
49 CCJ Appeal CV 14/2007.
50 See *The Bengal Immunity Co. Ltd v State of Bihar* [1954] INSC 120; *Queensland v Commonwealth* [1977] 139 CLR 585.
51 (2004) 64 WIR 412; [2004] 33 JCPC.
52 (2003) 64 WIR 270; [2003] 78 JCPC.
53 2 US 401 (1791).
54 5 US (1 Cranch) 137 (1803).
55 347 US 483 (1954).
56 410 US 113 (1973).
57 285 US 393 (1932) [1].
58 321 US 649 (1944).
59 467 U.S. 203 (1984).
60 505 U.S. 833 (1992).

CHAPTER 9

THE CARIBBEAN COURT OF JUSTICE: ITS INSTITUTIONAL UNDERPINNINGS

In addressing this topic, I can do no better than commence with a quotation from a publication commemorating the 5th Anniversary of the Caribbean Court of Justice (the Court) which is to this effect – "When a new Court is being created in a nation, it has the walls of a traditional policy and operative framework. When a new Court is being created without the traditional framework provided by single nationhood it is being created on a clean canvas…."

The Court's creation being on a clean canvas required decisions on an assortment of issues without any traditional framework. Through the ingenuity and perspicacity of forward looking thinkers and strategists charged with the responsibility of establishing an operational framework, traditions for the new emerging Court were formulated which sought to reflect an ethos uniquely Caribbean.

In pursuit of its laudable objectives the Court's stated mission is:

> *to perform to the highest standards as the supreme judicial organ in the Caribbean Community ensuring in its original jurisdiction uniform interpretation and application of the Revised Treaty of Chaguaramas, thereby underpinning and advancing the CARICOM Single Market and Economy, and as the final court of appeal for member states of the Caribbean Community to foster the development of an indigenous Caribbean jurisprudence.*

This complements the Court's stated vision "to provide for the Caribbean Community an accessible, fair, efficient, innovative and impartial justice system built on a jurisprudence reflective of our history, value and traditions while maintaining an inspirational, independent institution worthy of emulation by the courts of the region and the trust and confidence of the people."

INSTITUTIONAL UNDERPINNINGS

Several institutional linchpins initially ensured the Court's secure foundation, and these will be discussed individually.

Finance

The coming into force of the Agreement Establishing the Court, signed by the Heads of Government of the Caribbean Community on 14th February, 2001, was fostered by the conviction of the Contracting Parties that the Court would have a determinative role in the further development of Caribbean jurisprudence through the judicial process, and with the awareness that the establishment of the Court was a further step in the deepening of the regional integration process. These were very laudable sentiments and objectives, but I am sure underlying them was the problem of securing the requisite financial means to make the Court a reality. Article XXV11 of the Agreement provided for the expenses associated with the Court to be borne by the Member States (the Contracting Parties). Prompt payment of financial commitments by States may have presented challenges based on experience in other regional areas. The problem was solved with the investment of US$100,000,000 raised by the Caribbean Development Bank on international markets and secured by the establishment of a trust fund administered by a Board of Trustees drawn from regional institutions. The said sum is to be repaid by the governments of the Region over a period of years at low interest rates.

The purpose of this original and impressive method of funding a judicial institution with twin jurisdictions and which has attracted international attention, achieved two major objectives. First, it relieved the governments of providing annual financial disbursements for maintenance of the Court, and secondly, of greater importance, it ensured the complete independence of the Court and insulation from perceived political interference which was one of the major concerns of some persons in the Region.

The Board of Trustees was clothed with responsibility for directing the operations of the Fund with functions which range from evaluation of the Fund's performance, establishing financial regulations and authorising the provision of resources required for the biennial capital and operating budget of the Court and the Regional Judicial and Legal Services Commission.

The Preamble of the Revised Agreement Establishing the CCJ Trust Fund signed in January 2004, recognised the importance of adequate and secure funding to the sustainability, independence and credibility of the Court, and since its inception the Board of Trustees sought to give effect to its philosophy that "the fund will be invested prudently with a long term investment horizon in a wide range of tax-efficient international instruments so as to produce an optimal gross rate of return with reasonable security of its capital." In light of this the Board developed Investment Guidelines for the Fund approved by the Heads of Government. The year 2008, however, proved to be a challenging one due in no small measure to the unfavourable world-wide investment climate, but by the close of the year 2009 the Fund had rebounded and now shows a healthy net rate of return.

Appointments

The Court has been commended repeatedly by international observers for its unique method of appointment of judges to a court which is simultaneously an appellate court and an international one with an original jurisdiction. Unlike the majority of international courts, e.g., the International Court of Justice and the European Court of Justice, appointments are not made or influenced by member states, and the judges are appointed to serve in their individual capacities and not as representatives of the state of which [s]he is a national. Judicial and personnel appointments are the responsibility of an independent Commission comprising representatives of regional bodies (public service commissions, bar associations, universities and civil society) mainly outside the pale of politicians, and chaired by the President of the Court. The Commission ensures the independence of judicial appointments from State intervention which was a major concern of critics opposed to the establishment of the Court.

The recruitment net for the appointment of judges is cast beyond the Caribbean region and embraces applicants worldwide who satisfy the requisite criteria of being a judge of high moral character, intellectual and analytical ability with at least five years' experience in a court of unlimited jurisdiction within the Commonwealth or from a state with a civil law jurisdiction; similarly someone engaged in the practice or teaching of law for a period of not less than fifteen years within the Commonwealth or from a civil law jurisdiction.

Significantly appointment of the President of the Court is the only appointment which rests in the hands of the Heads of Government of the Contracting Parties by a majority three-fourth vote and based on a recommendation of the Commission. The judges aside, appointments to the other offices within the Court's administration are also the responsibility of the Commission including the determination of terms and conditions of service and termination of such appointments.

Privileges & Immunities

In recognition of the fact that independence of any court is essential for its operational capabilities and protection of its impartiality and dignity, the Agreement provided in Article XXX for the formulation of a protocol on privileges and immunities to be enjoyed by judges and officers of the Court as well as the Commission which is charged with the responsibility of appointing judges and other personnel. The protocol operates to protect both the property and assets of the Court from search and confiscation, and grants a wide range of immunities to the judges and members of the Commission, for example, exemption from immigration restrictions and personal arrest or detention.

At this stage mention must be made of a protocol entitled "Interfacing and Interaction of the Regional Judicial and Legal Services Commission, the Caribbean Court of Justice and the Caribbean Court of Justice Trust Fund." This Protocol signed on 25th January, 2007 recognised the importance of preserving judicial independence, including, including its administrative independence, and the need for a process of consultation between the respective entities in respect of the requisitioning and disbursement of monies of the Trust Fund for the operations of the Court and the Commission. It also established procedures to be followed.

Administration

The administration of the Court without doubt is the engine which propels the whole vehicle forward. It is the bedrock and main underpinning of the Court; if the administration is weak the whole institution will collapse. We are, however, fortunate and proud to have a Court Administrative Unit headed by a Court Executive Administrator which is strong, dependable, and progressive. It comprises the following divisions:

- Court Registry
- Court Library Services
- Information and Communications Technology
- Court Security
- Court Finance and Accounting
- Court Facilities, Assets and Office Management
- Court Protocol and Information
- Public Education and Communications

A discussion of the work of each of these departments will highlight their functions and effect on the efficiency of the Court.

Court Registry

Critical to the work of the Court in its adjudicative capacity is the Court Registry and its staff which includes the Sub Registries of the courts of all of the Contracting Parties within the Community.

It is self-evident that the Registry of any Court is the gateway to the judicial process. Apart from being the repository of all legal documents it oversees strict compliance with established rules of procedure and monitors the filing process until the hearing. With a dual jurisdiction, the work of the Registry is varied, one such variant being the Registry's responsibility for service of documents in the original jurisdiction. Also, vital to the efficient functioning of the Registry is its communication and close relationship with the Sub Registries which are in fact the Registries of the national courts of the Contracting Parties. These Sub Registries act on behalf of the Court's Registry in respect of service and filing of documents.

Court Library Services

No less crucial to the Court's success is the Library Services and also the Research Assistants who facilitate the work of the Judges of the Court particularly in the area of research. For a newly established court of last resort the Library has succeeded largely in providing and equipping the Court with current legal material and ready access to recent judgments emanating from other courts. It is recognised by the Administration that the value of a library depends on the quality of its collection as well as the expertise of its staff to locate quickly and accurately required information. This has led to exposure to and interaction with the work of other law libraries. The Court's last Annual Report indicates that the library continues to enhance its archival collection which consists of out of print material and rare books which may still be relevant to our jurisprudence, for example, Roman-Dutch law on which Guyana's law of immovable property is based as well as the Civil Code of St. Lucia. Further, to satisfy an increasing demand for non-legal material a special collection of titles on CARICOM and other prominent leaders of the Region has been developed.

Recognising that achieving a balance between print and electronic resources is critical to developing a dynamic library collection, the Library has access to well-known online databases such as Westlaw and LexisNexis. Escalating costs for printed legal material has resulted in increased use of online services which in the electronic world is assuming large proportions. Gifts from overseas sources such as the High Court of Australia has also enhanced the quality of the Library's collection.

In the last Annual Report the Library identified certain goals which it intends to achieve in the years ahead some of these being:

- continuing development of its collection through both print and electronic sources in order to meet the research needs of the Court;
- developing new services and programmes;
- increasing generated publications and research tools;
- developing in-house databases of legislation on CCJ and other materials.

Information and Communications Technology

Since its inauguration, the Court has attracted much attention for its impressive courtroom technology and facilities which are ranked as the best in the Caribbean Region and comparable to any in the developed world. The arrangements are such that spectators are afforded the opportunity of following the arguments in a case from screens in the courtroom with the Judges utilising all available technology in the recording of the proceedings. Maintaining the technological capabilities of the Court, research and providing training for new technology remains the main focus of this Unit in pursuit of its mission of ensuring access to justice.

Included in the Court's technology is the invaluable asset of court reporting which which provides for instantaneous video recording of the Court's proceedings. These transcripts are made available to the Judges and Counsel appearing in the proceedings at the end of a day's hearing. Hard copies of transcripts of all proceedings are stored as permanent records of the Court.

Court Security:

The security of the Court has never been taken for granted since its inauguration, and the Court Security Unit continues to build on its mission to maintain excellence in its security services including initiation of occupational health and safety standards.

The formulation of a policy document entitled "Excellence in Security Services" outlined the concepts of excellence and service, the effectiveness of which depends on training, the provision of relevant equipment, and the commitment and dedication of staff members. In this regard efforts have been and continue to be made to upgrade the skills and spontaneous reaction of the Unit to emergencies which may arise.

Court Facilities, Assets and Office Management:

The overarching vision of this Unit is to provide a safe, accessible and convenient facility worthy of emulation. The goals identified in pursuit of this vision range from seeking proactive solutions to emerging challenges and efficient maintenance of the physical environment and assets to ensuring satisfaction of both internal and external users of the Court's facilities by providing a safe and functional work environment. Overall, there is the realisation that achievement of the Unit's goals depends to a considerable extent on the training of its staff followed by critical review of its policies. In this regard training is geared specifically to the effective management of Court facilities including implementation of a computerised maintenance management system.

Court Protocol and Information:

Attracting public trust and confidence is the bedrock of any court as it seeks to administer justice between citizen and citizen and citizen and the State. The role of the Court Protocol and Information Division in this regard is vital, and is the principal organ in the meaningful exchange of information emanating from the Court. It seeks to provide a service which is courteous, efficient and easily accessible. Listing among its strategic objectives is the dissemination of information through an integrated public education and information programme aimed at local, regional and international consumers through audio visual media and outreach services.

Over the years of its existence the Court has attracted and facilitated a wide range of visitors with varying interests but with one focus on ascertaining the achievements of the Court in the management of its two jurisdictions. The Court's main outreach vehicle, however, continues to be its Public Education and Information Programme, and research undertaken by the Court Protocol and Information Officer revealed that the Court needs to "market" itself in order to gain a degree of acceptance particularly within the Caribbean Region due to "ignorance and uncertainty about its existence". He also opined that "in spite of disinformation put about on the Court, there is a tier of unplumbed public goodwill towards the Court that can and must be nurtured." I find favour with these sentiments and wholeheartedly endorse them.

It is self-evident that the Registry of any Court is the gateway to the judicial process. Apart from being the repository of all legal documents it oversees strict compliance with established rules of procedure and monitors the filing process until the hearing. With a dual jurisdiction the work of the Registry is varied, one such variant being the Registry's responsibility for service of documents in the original jurisdiction. Also vital to the efficient functioning of the Registry is its communication and close relationship with the sub-Registries which are in fact the Registries of the national courts of the Contracting Parties. These sub-Registries act on behalf of the Court's Registry in respect of service and filing of documents.

Court Finance and Accounting:

Management and control of the funds of the Court is the responsibility of this Division which works in close collaboration with the Trustees of the Trust Fund to which earlier reference has been made. Part of this responsibility includes timely submission and preparation of financial reports reflecting disbursement of funds by way of salaries and other Court expenditure. The heavy responsibility of managing the finances of any institution requires development of accounting performance standards and policies which can bear strict scrutiny, and the staff of the division keep abreast of current accounting procedures by attendance at international training seminars and workshops.

The Court's Pension Plan provides a defined benefit contribution for Judges and staff, and with systems and procedures in place the Division maintains and monitors important databases; typical work activities include updating pension scheme member records, and, *inter alia*, liaising with other departments to ensure compliance with legal and regulatory aspects of pensions administration.

The Court has benefitted from financial assistance from international institutions, chief among these being the result of a Financing Agreement between the European Union and the Caribbean Forum of ACP States (CARIFORUM) signed in 2008 and reflected in a European Development Fund Grant of 1,315,000 Euros for the Court's development. The main objective of the Grant is to enhance and improve the Court in its original jurisdiction pertinent to its role as an international court, and continues to be utilised in strengthening the Library facilities, procuring appropriate technology in facilitating multilingual users, and disseminating information about the Court through seminars and conferences including interaction with the European Court of Justice.

Public Education and Communication:

The mantra of this Division formed in June 2008 underscores the Court's commitment to public education, by "supporting access to justice, building public trust and confidence and assisting the Court's accountability." Its main objectives to educate and inform users of the Court on a regional and international level about the Court's work, and to build and develop relationships with various sectors of the regional diaspora have led to the utilisation of certain tools such as public education visits in the Caribbean Region and opening the Court to visits from various interest groups including students of schools at all levels.

It will not be immodest to state that one such regional visit to Belize in June 2008 may have contributed in no small measure to that country's decision to sign on to the appellate jurisdiction of the Court in 2010. Apart from meetings with Government officials, there was interfacing with tertiary level students and teachers in Belize City, an exercise which we hope was productive.

Of great delight, have been visits to the Court by students from secondary schools within Trinidad and Tobago, and I venture to suggest, the Court's most successful example of public education and awareness of the Court's functions. Hopefully, the interaction with the public at all levels will ensure that the Court's stated vision becomes a reality.

CONCLUSION

I trust that the exposition of the various components which underpin the Court and its work has been instructive and enlightening. In fulfilment of its mission to perform to the highest standards as the supreme judicial organ of the Caribbean Community, commitment and dedication will be its mantra. I posit, however, that the Court's most challenging task and its most crucial will be attracting public confidence and convincing naysayers of its competence and independence with assurance that the quality of its judgments can bear international comparison. Without public confidence and trust the Court's vision will fail and its mission frustrated. The Court's goal must be to earn that trust and confidence of the peoples of the Caribbean Region.

Caribbean Academy for Law & Court Administration
Caribbean Court of Justice
Trinidad and Tobago
December 6th – 10th, 2010

CHAPTER 10

STRENGTHENING DIVERSITY IN THE JUDICIAL SYSTEM

Seven decades ago the idea of a woman dispensing justice in a court of law would have been unheard of. Much has been done since then to bring women into the judicial system. I can attest to this personally having been persuaded thirty-two years ago to join the judiciary in my country, Guyana, the first woman to be appointed to such a post. When invited to do so I confess to having serious misgivings. My first concern was whether I was up to the task, the next was how would my male colleagues react to having a woman in their midst. Would I encounter antagonism or resentment? How would the members of the Bar accept rulings and judgments from a woman?

Thirty-two (32) years later I admit that all my doubts and fears were misconceived. I encountered no bias or prejudice from either Bench or Bar. Since my appointment in October 1980, other women have been appointed to the Judiciary, and such appointments have ceased to be of any significance, and have become the norm.

In the Commonwealth Caribbean region, steps toward greater gender diversity within the Judiciary have been slow, but steady. Today, although women are still under-represented in the Judiciary, the progress taking place gives reason for some optimism.

First, let me to say a few words about the importance of strengthening gender diversity in the Judiciary.

To preserve and enhance the administration of justice, it is vital to maintain public trust and confidence in the justice system. The make-up of the Judiciary should reflect that of society. There is evidence that a lack of gender diversity impairs public confidence in the Judiciary.[1] This can create a psychological barrier to access to justice in the minds of women who perceive that the Judiciary does not represent or understand them. At a time when too many crimes against women go unreported, this perception can serve as a further deterrence to the justice system.

It is imperative that there are no institutional and structural barriers to capable female candidates for the Bench. The justice system will clearly benefit from the contributions of the most brilliant legal minds and the eradication of such barriers will also improve confidence in the system by exhibiting fairness, merit, and equality of opportunity.

It has been propounded that female Judges bring a different perspective which would enrich the Bench through its realistic insight and understanding of other women. Of course, all women may not share the same perspective on a given case, and there may be differences in understanding among women from different racial, economic or religious backgrounds. I would suggest, however, that female Judges are more likely to be familiar with the experiences and views of other women than male Judges would be, and therefore may be better equipped to deal with those views in their rulings.[2] All this ensures that the justice that is rendered is aware rather than oblivious.

Within the Caribbean Region diversity takes on a meaning not only pertaining to gender, but includes ethnicity. In selecting and appointing judges in some jurisdictions of the Caribbean ethnic balance is oft-times taken into account to reflect the ethnic composition of the particular state. Over the years, the gender component has been mainly addressed in all jurisdictions throughout the hierarchy of courts. This includes lower courts where magistrates hear summary matters in both civil and criminal jurisdictions as well as preliminary inquiries in criminal matters, akin to grand juries in the American legal system where the prosecution seeks to determine whether a prima facie case has been made out against a defendant. In Guyana, women form the majority of magistrates at this lower level, and indeed it may be so in other jurisdictions of the Caribbean region. Within recent years, however, and certainly since my appointment, the number of women sitting as judges in the next tier within the hierarchy of courts, that is, in what we term as "high courts" (which is a step below our Courts of Appeal) has increased, as well as women sitting in the Courts of Appeal.

Of great significance is the fact that at present in the Caribbean Region in both common law and civil law jurisdictions there are at least three female Chief Justices presiding in the jurisdictions of Jamaica, the Eastern Caribbean and Suriname. The President of the Court of Appeal of the Bahamas is also female, and is the second woman to be appointed to that position. In Barbados, there has never been a female

Chief Justice; but currently six out of the eight High Court Judges are women and one out of five Court of Appeal Judges is female. Other than the Chief Justice, there is one other female serving on the Court of Appeal of the Eastern Caribbean Supreme Court, totalling two out of five Justices of Appeal. In addition, seven of the seventeen High Court Judges in the Eastern Caribbean are women.

These statistics suggest that there is some gender diversity being promoted in the Commonwealth Caribbean. Overall, there is still room for improvement if the Bench is to be truly reflective of the make-up of our society.

The high profile of judges in every society raises expectations of honesty, fairness and independence, not to mention our ability to find acceptable solutions to the myriad problems with which we are confronted on a daily basis. Inherent in the qualities expected of a judge, and in fact a fundamental right of every citizen of a state, is fairness - the right to receive equal treatment by those constitutionally entrusted with the duty to hold the scales of justice evenly. Judges in our jurisdiction upon assumption of office swear to administer justice according to law without fear or favour, affection or ill-will. Of course, judges come in all sizes, shapes, backgrounds, genders and ethnicities. We also bring with us personal beliefs, prejudices and opinions on a variety of issues which affect society. All of this may have an impact (positive or negative) on matters which fall to be determined by us. Judges are expected to be objective, not subjective. Our personal prejudices must be subsumed in striving to be just and impartial. It is an ideal to which every judge aspires and is expected to achieve.

We must continue to actively encourage and strengthen diversity in the Judiciary if we value increased access to justice for all members of society, enhanced public trust and confidence, and the preservation of the proper administration of justice.

International Association of Women Judges
"Women & The Rule of Law"
Washington DC
26th - 27th February, 2013

Endnotes

1 Dermot Feenan, "Women Judges: Gendering Judging, Justifying Diversity", Vol. 35: Issue 4 (December 2008) *Journal of Law and Society*, p. 494.

2 Joy Milligan, "Pluralism in America: Why Judicial Diversity Improves Legal Decisions About Public Morality", Vol. 81: Issue 3 (2006) *New York University Law Review*, pp. 1229-1230.

CHAPTER 11

DISPUTE RESOLUTION: THE REVISED TREATY OF CHAGUARAMAS AND THE CARIBBEAN COURT OF JUSTICE COMPATIBILITY OR CONTROVERSY?

The collapse of the West Indian Federation in the early 1960s seemed then to have sounded the death knell to the dreams of the Caribbean Region for a united political and economic powerhouse hopefully achieving collectively what may have seemed impossible individually for small states with fragile economies based mainly on tourism, sugar and banana production controlled by the former colonial masters. All, however, was not lost when the political leaders of the day once again endeavoured to promote the economic development of the Region by establishing the Caribbean Free Trade Association (hereinafter referred to as "CARIFTA") in 1965[1] with objectives to increase and expand trade between Member States thereby fostering harmonious development and liberalisation, and ensuring fair competition.

This tentative attempt at regional economic cooperation matured with the establishment of the Treaty of Chaguaramas Establishing the Caribbean Community and Common Market signed on July 4, 1973 by all Member States of the Region.[2] The vision of the signatories went beyond trade, and embraced the optimum utilisation of available human and natural resources of the Region by co-ordinated and sustained economic development. The Community's objectives embraced economic integration, coordination of foreign policies and functional cooperation with the Annex to the Treaty establishing the Common Market Council on which each Member State was represented. The Council's responsibilities can be summarised as being administrative (ensuring the efficient operation and development of the Common Market), supervisory (making proposals for the progressive development of the Common Market), adjudicatory (receiving and considering alleged breaches of obligations arising under the Annex and deciding thereon), and exercising such powers and performing such duties as were conferred upon it.

The response to the global economic challenges of the late 1980s which the Heads of Governments of the Caribbean Community anticipated would impact significantly on their fragile economies, together with a commitment to deepen regional integration, resulted in the Declaration of Grande Anse in 1989 establishing an independent Commission under the Chairmanship of Sir Shridath Ramphal, later Secretary General of the Commonwealth. This Commission produced in 1992 a report intituled appropriately "Time for Action" and embracing wide-ranging recommendations, among them being rapid development of a Single Market and Economy. This led ultimately in 2001 to the signing and adoption of the Revised Treaty of Chaguaramas Establishing the Caribbean Community Including the CARICOM Single Market and Economy[3] (hereinafter referred to as the "RTC").

What will forever be regarded as a recommendation of outstanding significance coming out of that Commission led eventually to the establishment of the Caribbean Court of Justice (hereinafter referred to as the "CCJ"), a regional court which had been contemplated in several forms and by several regional groups over a considerable period of time. The Regional Heads of Government as Contracting Parties being "convinced that the Caribbean Court of Justice will have a determinative role in the further development of Caribbean jurisprudence through the judicial process," brought into force an Agreement Establishing the Caribbean Court of Justice[4] (hereinafter referred to as "the CCJ Agreement") which provided for two jurisdictions – original and appellate.

Upon signing the RTC the States Parties affirmed that the original jurisdiction of the Court was essential for the successful operation of the Single Market and Economy, and provision was made in the RTC for the Court to have compulsory and exclusive jurisdiction to hear and determine disputes concerning the application and interpretation of the RTC[5]. Further, and of significant importance is the fact that the Member States agree that they recognise as compulsory, *ipso facto* and without special agreement, the Court's original jurisdiction (See Article 216). Each Member State also undertook to employ its best endeavours to complete as soon as possible the constitutional and legislative procedures required for its participation in the regime establishing the Court (See Article 224).

Separate and apart from the exclusive jurisdiction conferred on the CCJ under the RTC, both Treaties of 1973 and 2001 established procedures for settlement of disputes between Member States wherever these arose. Even before these treaties their forerunner, the CARIFTA Agreement of 1965 established a procedure for settlement of disputes between the three States which had signed that Agreement. This is a convenient point of departure to initiate a discussion on settlement of disputes between States as provided for in the Treaties.

AGREEMENT ESTABLISHING THE CARIBBEAN FREE TRADE ASSOCIATION

This Agreement signed on 15th December, 1965 by the Governments of Antigua and Barbuda, Barbados and Guyana (then British Guiana), sought, *inter alia*, to promote the expansion and diversification of trade within the areas of the Member Territories, collectively called the Caribbean Free Trade Area. This was based on the recognition that they shared a common determination to fulfil the hopes and aspirations of the peoples of the Caribbean for full employment and improved living standards; also, an awareness that the broadening of domestic markets through the elimination of barriers to trade between the Territories was a prerequisite of development.[6]

The Agreement's Complaints Procedure[7] provided for referral of disagreements or complaints by Member Territories to a Council comprising the institution and organs of the Association with power to make arrangements for examining the matter, and in so doing to have regard to whether it had been established that an obligation under the Agreement had not been fulfilled or any objective of the Association was being frustrated. The arrangements referred to included a reference to an examining committee comprising persons of competence and integrity, and appointed on such terms and conditions as were to be decided by the majority vote of the Council.

The responsibilities of the Council embraced exercising such powers and functions as were conferred upon it by the Agreement, supervising the application of the Agreement and keeping its operation under review, as well as considering any further action by Member Territories to promote the attainment of the objectives of the Association.[8] In exercising its responsibility under the Complaints Procedure, the Council was empowered to take decisions and make recommendations which bound all Member Territories.

TREATY ESTABLISHING THE CARIBBEAN COMMUNITY AND COMMON MARKET

By 1973 when the Caribbean Common Market was established membership had expanded to twelve independent Caribbean States and Montserrat.[9]

This Treaty with similar aspirations as CARIFTA, provided for disputes concerning the interpretation or application of the Treaty to be determined by the Conference, one of the principal organs of the Community unless otherwise provided for.[10]

The Disputes Procedure within the Common Market as set out in the Annex[11] adopted criteria similar to Article 26 of the CARIFTA Agreement, for the referral of disputes to the Common Market Council,[12] the other organ of the Community, where a Member State considered that any benefit conferred upon it by the Annex or any objective of the Common Market was being or may be frustrated with no satisfactory settlement having been reached between the Member States concerned.

Among the powers exercisable by the Council was referral to an *ad hoc* Tribunal constituted in accordance with Article 12 of the Annex and comprising qualified jurists as arbitrators drawn from a list maintained by the Secretary General, and to which every Member State was invited to nominate two persons. If either the Council or the Tribunal found that any benefit conferred on a Member State or any objective of the Common Market was being or may have been frustrated, the Council could by majority vote make appropriate recommendations to the Member State concerned. Failure or inability to comply with such recommendations could result in the Council by majority vote authorising any Member State to suspend its obligations to the offending State as the Council considered appropriate. Provision was made for any Member State at any time while any matter is under consideration to request the Council to authorise interim measures to safeguard its position.

Sheldon McDonald in his literary work, "CARICOM and the New Millennium: Dispute Settlement Put Right" (An analysis of the Dispute Settlement Regimes in the Revised Treaty of Chaguaramas Establishing the Caribbean Community Including the CARICOM Single Market And Economy within the Context of General International Law and International Trade Law particularly Regional Integration Law), emphasised the fact that after such an involved procedure the only sanction was a non-binding recommendation, and unlike the Treaty proper, the Member State was under no duty to explain its failure to comply with the recommendation; further, whereas all decisions and recommendations under the Treaty required unanimity, this recommendation was by majority vote.

Mr. Mc Donald further commented on the fact that Member States did not assume the automatic right to refer disputes to the Tribunal; instead this rested with the Council with the possibility that the majority could frustrate a request for such a reference even though legitimate.

THE REVISED TREATY OF CHAGUARAMAS (RTC)

The States Parties to the RTC[13] having committed themselves to deepening regional economic integration through the establishment of the CARICOM Single Market and Economy (CSME) in order to achieve sustained economic development, and being mindful that disputes among States could affect adversely the desired goals, affirmed in the Preamble to the RTC that "the employment of internationally accepted modes of disputes settlement in the Community will facilitate the achievement of the objectives of the Treaty." They also considered that "an efficient, transparent, and authoritative system of disputes settlement in the Community will enhance the economic, social and other forms of activity in the CSME ... " The scope of this system is considerably wider than the Treaty of 1973. Whereas resolutions of disputes concerning the interpretation or application of the 1973 Treaty was the sole responsibility of the Heads of Government,[14] and its mandate was to consider whether "any benefit conferred on a Member State or any objective of the Common Market was being or may be frustrated if no satisfactory settlement is reached between the Member States," the scope of the RTC disputes settlement was widened to include, *inter alia*, allegations that an actual or proposed measure of another Member State is or would be inconsistent with the objectives of the Community.

Although the RTC's disputes settlement regime is addressed extensively in Chapter 9, the Conference of Heads of Government still retains the right to consider and resolve disputes between Member States[15] in much the same way as it did under the 1973 Treaty.

With the commitment to deepen regional economic integration by avoidance of disputes among Member States, the RTC advocates recourse to several internationally accepted modes of dispute settlement, namely, good offices, mediation, consultations, conciliation, arbitration and adjudication.[16] Any of these modes of settlement may be utilised by Member States to resolve disputes without prejudice to the exclusive and compulsory jurisdiction of the CCJ in the interpretation and application of the RTC.

The mandate of the CCJ in the exercise of its exclusive jurisdiction is not confined to hearing and determining disputes between Member States or between Member States and the Community, but includes determining referrals from national courts of Member States (Article 214 of the RTC and Article XIV of the CCJ Agreement), and of immeasurable importance, hearing applications by private persons, whether natural or juridical, who may be allowed with special leave by the Court, to appear as parties in proceedings before the Court subject to specific conditions being satisfied.[17]

The delivery of advisory opinions concerning the interpretation and application of the RTC also falls within the remit of the CCJ's exclusive jurisdiction, the opinions being delivered only at the request of Member States parties to a dispute or at the request of the Community, possibly through the Secretary General. (See Article 212 of the RTC; Article XIII of the CCJ Agreement).

In spite of the Court's compulsory and exclusive jurisdiction to determine disputes between Member States, alternative dispute resolution remains the primary objective of Member States of the Community.

The desirability of employing and exhausting all avenues for dispute resolution between Member States is emphasised in the mandatory language of the RTC which enjoins Member States to proceed expeditiously on agreement for modes of settlement and implementation of such settlements.[18] In fact, Chapter 9 addresses Disputes Settlement in Articles 187 through 223 including those Articles relative to the CCJ.[19] Significantly, in relation to the settlement of private commercial disputes among Community nationals as well as among Community nationals and nationals of third states, Article 223 of the RTC obligates Member States to encourage and facilitate the use of arbitration and other modes of alternative disputes settlement "to the maximum extent possible", and so does Article XXIII of the CCJ Agreement which specifically refers to the settlement of international commercial disputes. Additionally, the mandatory nature of Article 223.2 of the RTC ensures that each Member State provides appropriate legislative procedures to ensure observance of arbitration agreements, and for the recognition and enforcement of arbitral awards in such disputes.

THE BASSETERRE TREATY

The Treaty Establishing the Organisation of Eastern Caribbean States (the Basseterre Treaty) must also be considered. It was signed into force on 18th June, 1981 by the Heads of Government of the Eastern Caribbean States, (See Antigua & Barbuda, Dominica, Grenada, Montserrat, St. Kitts-Nevis-Anguilla, St. Lucia, St. Vincent & the Grenadines) the main goal being cooperation in strengthening links by unified efforts and resources. The principal institution, "the Authority" comprises the Heads of Government of the Member States. In the relevant provision of the Treaty on the settlement of disputes arising between Member States, if such disputes cannot be resolved amicably by direct agreement, the Treaty mandates that they be submitted to a Conciliation Commission by either party upon an undertaking to accept the conciliation procedure. Any recommendation of the Conciliation Commission is final and binding in sharp contrast to the relevant provisions of the RTC. Of interest, all Member States of this Treaty are now Member States of the RTC thereby creating an overlap situation giving rise to the availability of two options.

Although the main thrust of this paper is the dispute resolution regime of the RTC, other issues connected with the CCJ in its principal role of interpreting and applying the RTC will be addressed.

It is convenient at this juncture to discuss the compulsory and exclusive jurisdiction of the CCJ. Member States under Article 216 of the RTC (Article XVI of the CCJ Agreement) agree to recognise as compulsory, *ipso facto* and without special agreement, the original jurisdiction of the Court. (See judgment of the CCJ in *Trinidad Cement Ltd. v The Caribbean Community* [2009] CCJ2 (OJ)) and comment that "by signing and ratifying the Revised Treaty and thereby conferring on this Court *ipso facto* a compulsory and exclusive jurisdiction to hear and determine disputes concerning the interpretation and application of the Revised Treaty, the Member States transformed the erstwhile voluntary arrangements in CARICOM into a rule-based system, thus creating and accepting a regional system under the rule of law.") In the exercise of its original jurisdiction, Article 217 (See Article XVII of the CCJ Agreement) enjoins the Court to apply such rules of international law as may be applicable, and under Article 221 (See Article XXII of the CCJ Agreement) the judgments of the Court shall constitute legally binding precedents for parties who appear before it unless such judgments have been revised in accordance with Article 219 (See Article XX of the CCJ Agreement). It is apposite at this point to raise the following question. *Is the jurisdiction of the CCJ really exclusive?*

The late Professor Ralph Carnegie, History Graduate of the University College of the West Indies and Rhodes Scholar, who graduated with First Class Honours in Jurisprudence from Oxford University, in a learned presentation at a Faculty Workshop Series of the Faculty of Law of the University of the West Indies on November 25, 2009, posed the question – "How Exclusive is 'Exclusive' in Relation to the Original Jurisdiction of the Caribbean Court of Justice?" Several very interesting and thought-provoking opinions were expressed by him, a few of which will be advanced post mortem and attempts at answers given.

Article 211 of the RTC having conferred on the CCJ compulsory and exclusive jurisdiction to hear and determine disputes concerning the interpretation and application of the RTC limited that jurisdiction by the opening words of the Article "Subject to this Treaty", and which is circumscribed similarly in Article XII of the CCJ Agreement. Many opinions have been profered as to the import of these words. Justice Duke Pollard, former Judge of the CCJ, posited the view that the said circumscription has extremely important implications for the interpretation of the RTC, and opined that the phrase "subject to" introduces a dominant provision followed by one or more subservient provisions as lawyers familiar with the elementary principles of drafting (as he is) must appreciate. (*See Presentation at the ACP-EU International Conference on 21st May, 2008 in Brussels, Belgium).* The conclusion he arrived at was that consequently the compulsory and exclusive jurisdiction of the CCJ cannot be construed to take precedence over other relevant treaty provisions, for example, the wide-ranging disputes settlement regime of Chapter 9 of the RTC, particularly Article 193.1 which imposes what may be regarded as a mandatory obligation on Member States in a dispute to enter into consultations. This is concluded by the use of the word "shall" in the Article instead of "may". Realistically only failure of the consultative process permits Member States in a dispute to resort to arbitration or adjudication.

The exclusivity of the CCJ's jurisdiction under Article 211 of the RTC (Article XII of the CCJ Agreement) becomes more complex from Professor Carnegie's point of view. In his discourse referred to earlier his reasoning raised the following queries about what he termed "the non-curial" modes of dispute settlement being those distinguishable from the CCJ's adjudication:

> If the non-curial modes in Chapter 9 RTC are among the intended reference of the qualification 'subject to this Treaty' in Article 211 RTC, there is a problem in that recourse to those modes is not only also stated by Article 188.1 RTC to be 'subject to the provisions of this Treaty', but additionally, is under Article 188.4 RTC '[w]ithout prejudice to the exclusive and compulsory jurisdiction of the Court in the interpretation and application of this Treaty under Article 211.' So, the Chapter 9 non-curial modes are not modes which prevail over the exclusive jurisdiction by virtue of the 'subject to the treaty' qualification in Article 211.1 RTC. How then can the non-curial modes have any application at all, if the CCJ's jurisdiction is exclusive and, by virtue of the 'without prejudice' phrase, overriding also?"

An analysis of Professor Carnegie's queries seems to suggest that since the non-curial modes of dispute settlement in Chapter 9 of the RTC are themselves circumscribed under Article 188.1 which begins "Subject to the provisions of the Treaty", and additionally under Article 188.4 are "without prejudice to the exclusive and compulsory jurisdiction of the Court" they can be overridden, and are not modes which prevail over the CCJ's exclusive jurisdiction; hence the jurisdiction of the Court is not circumscribed by the use of the words "Subject to this Treaty".

Professor Carnegie theorised that the text excludes one hypothetical possibility, this being, that the other modes of settlement are only available if the CCJ consents to their operation. He enlarged his theory by stating that the choice to use one or more of the non-curial modes lies with the parties to a dispute, and when a Member State has recourse to a dispute settlement against another Member State, Article 189(a) mandates that they proceed expeditiously to an exchange of views. Professor Carnegie, however, suggests such a requirement seems superfluous if a non-CCJ mode is available only at the option of the CCJ. In support of this theory he drew attention to the fact that there is no reference in the RTC text to an exchange of views being required when a private sector party (meaning a private individual or a private corporate entity) brings a claim before the CCJ under Article 222 of the RTC or when CARICOM is a party to the case. He alluded to the fact that no reference was made in any of the cases decided by the CCJ in its original jurisdiction to any obligation on any of the parties to initiate an exchange of views. He concluded that this is arguably *sub silentio* confirmation that the exchange of views requirement does not apply to an Article 222 matter. In response, it is suggested that consideration must be given to the fact that although no provision for this has been made to date in the Original Jurisdiction Rules, parties are not prohibited after a court proceeding is launched to engage in an exchange of views without prejudice to its continuation provided such a course is accepted by the Court.

Article 187 of the RTC gives rise to an interesting array of reasons for non-curial modes of dispute settlement concerning the interpretation and application of the RTC. While Article 187(a) refers to allegations that an actual or proposed measure of another Member State is, or would be, inconsistent with the objectives of the Community, and hence can be invoked only by a Member State, the other allegations may be invoked by private parties, for example, by natural or juridical persons under Article 222 or any other entity, (See *TCL v. CARICOM* [2009] CCJ4 (OJ)) and not excluding a Member State.

As mentioned earlier Article 188.1 lists the array of options for settlement of disputes available to any party. Article 188.2, however, provides that where the dispute is not settled either party may have recourse to another mode except arbitration or adjudication which can be regarded as rule-binding procedures. One may hazard a guess that the reason for excepting these two modes is that parties should endeavour to exhaust fully during the early stages of dispute resolution non-contentious modes of settlement before resort to the modes of arbitration or adjudication which could sometimes be contentious. Professor Carnegie posits the view, which is arguable, that the utilisation of the non-curial modes may be treated as preliminary procedures only and which may be followed by later reference to the CCJ at the option of any of the parties.

It is interesting, however, to analyse Articles 188.3 & 4. Article 188.3 permits the parties to a dispute to agree on recourse to good offices, mediation or conciliation while a settlement is pending subject to the procedural rules applicable in respect of arbitration or adjudication. One possibility that suggests itself is that even after parties to a dispute have resorted to arbitration or adjudication a settlement may be envisaged, and recourse may still be had to the non-contentious modes of settlement. Needless to say, this depends on whether the procedural rules applicable to arbitration or adjudication permit such a course.

Support for this opinion can be found in Sheldon McDonald's treatise when he expressed the view with reference to Article 188.3 that it permits free choice, and allows parties to have negotiations even on the margins of the two exceptions of arbitration and adjudication; if the recourse to the other modes resolves the matter report to the arbitration panel or the Court could be sanctioned and reflect a binding resolution of the dispute.

Article 188.4 makes specific reference to the CCJ's exclusive and compulsory jurisdiction under Article 211, and without prejudice to it, permits parties (by use of the word "may") to utilise any of the voluntary modes of settlement giving rise to the query whether the jurisdiction of the CCJ can be utilised as a first or last resort.

Significantly by virtue of Article 12.8 of the RTC the Conference being the supreme Organ of the Community, may consider and resolve disputes between Member States, the language of which suggests that this may be another option available to Member States, and must be read in conjunction with Article 189 which mandates Member States to proceed expeditiously to an exchange of views on agreement on a mode of settlement.

Of some importance as well is Article 13 of the RTC concerning the Community Council of Ministers which consists of Ministers responsible for Community Affairs and any other Minister designated by the Member States in their absolute discretion. The duties of the Council are defined in Article 13.4 of the RTC, and "without prejudice to the generality of the foregoing provisions", include, *inter alia*, to "ensure the efficient operation and orderly development of the

CSME, particularly by seeking to resolve problems arising out of its functioning, taking into account the work and decisions of COTED" (Article 13.4(f)), and to "receive and consider allegations of breaches of obligations arising under this Treaty, including disputes between Organs of the Community"(Article 13.4(g).

When one considers the options for the settlement of disputes arising between Member States the choice of good offices, mediation or conciliation seem to be unrestricted although subject to expeditious resolution. Where, however, a requesting Member State alleges that the action taken by the requested Member State constitutes a breach of obligations arising from or under the provisions of the RTC consultations seem to be mandatory under Article 193, and such consultations must take place within 14 days of the request. This seems to indicate the serious nature of breaches of Treaty obligations whether by Member States against other Member States or against individuals or entities of Member States as reflected in Article 187 of the RTC.

Justice Pollard in reference to Article 193 in his treatise mentioned earlier, opined that the requirement to settle a dispute concerning the RTC by consultation where both disputants so prefer would operate to displace the jurisdiction of the CCJ, and it hearkens back to the traditional and preferred mode of resolving disputes by states entities; in fact he concluded that since Member States are free to employ the broad range of other disputes settlement modes, it is a moot point how compulsory and exclusive is the jurisdiction of the CCJ in interpreting and applying the RTC. It may be that, consultations apart, in disputes between Member States concerning allegations of breaches of obligations under the RTC, Article 12.8 (the Conference option) may be utilised notwithstanding the other options.

Professor Carnegie adverted to the fact that the CCJ has not had so far to address any issues pertaining to the dispute settlement function of the Conference, and opined that should this arise, it may perhaps be expected that "taking its cue from Article 12.8 RTC, the CCJ would show the kind of deference to the Conference that the International Court of Justice showed to the Security Council in the *Lockerbie* case" (See *Libyan Arab Jamahiriya v. United States of America*). He explained that in that case the ICJ held that invocation by the Security Council of its powers under Chapter VII of the United Nations Charter prevailed over other obligations of the parties to the case under other international agreements. In the hypothetical instance before the CCJ, the express provision of Article 12.8 of the RTC makes the recommended deference easy to justify without reference to any overriding of treaty law.

Some concerns were raised by Professor Carnegie in relation to the Competition Commission, the establishment, composition, functions and powers of which are defined in Articles 171-174 of the RTC. He described disputes which may arise between a Member State and the Commission as a "turf dispute" which under Article 176.6 may be referred to the CCJ by the Member State concerned. He observed that the CCJ Rules do not refer to this procedure, and wondered where guidance on the procedure is to be found. He pondered whether it may perhaps be inferred from the CCJ's decision in *Johnson v. CARICAD* (See [2009] CCJ3 (OJ)) that such proceedings would have to be treated as an action against the Community. No doubt Professor Carnegie's conclusions were based on the assumption that the Competition Commission was an Organ or at most an Institution of the Community. For this reason, it is necessary to examine the functions of the Competition Commission and clarify some misconceptions.

The functions of the Competition Commission comprising seven members, a Chairman being one such member, include, *inter alia,* applying the rules of competition in respect of anti-competitive cross-border business conduct, promoting and protecting competition in the Community and co-ordinating the implementation of the Community Competition Policy. In determining anti-competitive business conduct which is addressed in Article 175 of the RTC, provision is made under sub-paragraphs 11 and 12 for recourse to the CCJ by the Commission (11), and (12) by a party aggrieved by a determination of the Commission under exercise of its powers granted in Article 174.4. Similarly, negative Clearance Rulings made by the Commission under Article 180 of the RTC are reviewable by the CCJ on an application by the Commission.

The relationship between the Competition Commission and the CCJ was defined and determined in the recent case of *Trinidad Cement Ltd. v. The Competition Commission* (See [2012] CCJ4 (OJ)) where the Court held that the Commission enjoys full juridical personality making reference to the Agreement entered into between the Community, the Government of Suriname as the seat of the Commission and the Commission itself that the Commission "shall have full juridical personality". (See Article XV of the Agreement signed in St. Vincent & the Grenadines on 13th February, 2007). The Court, in considering its competence to review the decisions of the Commission, concluded that there was no conduct or exercise of power on the part of a Treaty-created institution which could escape its judicial scrutiny due to the CCJ's compulsory and exclusive jurisdiction to adjudicate disputes concerning the interpretation and application of the RTC as well as the Treaty's normative structure geared at transforming the CSME into "a regional system under the rule of law".

This may have provided answers to some of the queries raised by Professor Carnegie in his paper concerning the Competition Commission. It is an exercise in superfluity to emphasise that the Competition Commission is not an Organ of the Community, its powers and functions having been defined in Articles 173 & 174. The Commission can carry out investigations and hold inquiries to determine anti-competitive business conduct by an enterprise. Article 175.11 empowers the Commission to apply to the CCJ for an order when an enterprise fails to take corrective action which the Commission had ordered. Similarly, a party aggrieved by a decision of the Commission can under Article 175.12 apply for a review of that decision to the CCJ; in fact, the Commission itself can invoke the jurisdiction of the CCJ for a review of its own decision on an application for a negative clearance ruling when that decision was obtained by deceit or improper means. (See Article 180.3).

All of the above indicates that the Competition Commission enjoys full juridical personality, and has no "Organic" status within the Community. The Commission has formulated its own rules of procedure, and in the Original Jurisdiction Rules of the CCJ procedural rules have been formulated in relation to matters concerning the Commission; these include provision for service of documents on persons and organs within the Community, including COTED which may be affected or were involved.

In relation to Article 175.12 Professor Carnegie queried whether this provision permitting a party aggrieved by the Competition Commission's determination of anti-competitive business conduct to apply to the CCJ for a review suggests inconsistency with the Court's jurisdiction being original, and can be regarded as being more akin to a supervisory jurisdiction by way of judicial review. Again, the answer to this contention lies in the aforementioned dicta in the judgment of the Court which emphasised the exclusivity of the CCJ's jurisdiction to scrutinise the conduct or exercise of power of any Treaty-created institution. This case was decided after Professor Carnegie's death, and one can only surmise whether had it been decided in his lifetime it may have influenced his conclusions.

Although not directly connected to the RTC's disputes settlement regime, it may be apposite to make reference to the referral provisions of the CCJ's compulsory and exclusive jurisdiction (See (Articles 211.1(c) & 214 of the RTC; Articles XII (c) & XIV of the CCJ Agreement) and the delivery of advisory opinions (See Article 212 of the RTC; Article XIII of the CCJ Agreement) referred to earlier. Neither of these has been utilised since the inauguration of the CCJ in 2005 so there is no precedent for their utilisation. The national courts of the Member States to the RTC whenever seised of matters which may concern the application or interpretation of the RTC are enjoined to stay completion of the matter until a ruling from the CCJ on the issue has been obtained. National courts were reminded of this in a recent case before the CCJ. (See *Humming Bird Rice Mills Ltd. v. Suriname & The Caribbean Community* [2012] CCJ1 (OJ) para. [26]). Hypothetically, assuming a claim is brought by a private individual or entity against a Member State which involves some provision of the RTC and a settlement is envisaged, it is suggested that wisdom should dictate that the proposed settlement be deferred until a definitive ruling on the interpretation and application of the RTC is obtained from the CCJ. In like manner, Member States involved in a dispute which can be resolved by mediation or consultation may seek an advisory opinion from the CCJ on the application or interpretation of any provision of the RTC before settlement of the dispute. This may be advisable in order to test the legality of the proposed settlement.

Such an approach is discussed by Sheldon McDonald in his literary work (p. 42) where he stated positively that it is permissible for parties by prior action emanating from consultations to agree to be bound by such an opinion. He went on to state that in this way the parties may avoid contentious court proceedings, and as a corollary it may be an invaluable contribution to the building up of Community Law. Having regard to the fact that the CCJ has not as yet been utilised in this regard this may be a long way off in becoming a reality.

More detailed consideration will now be given to settlement of disputes by arbitration. Mention had been made earlier to Article 223 of the RTC and Article XXIII of the CCJ Agreement which by mandatory language suggest that arbitration be utilised as one of the primary modes of dispute settlement particularly those concerning private commercial transactions. Despite the fact that Article 204 of the RTC indicates arbitration as an option, the elaborate provisions in Articles 205 – 210 and 223 indicate that parties particularly where private commercial activity is involved should adopt this as their main form of settlement even above court adjudication. Provision is made for Third Party Intervention by a Member State who is not a party to a dispute (Article 208).

The importance attached to this mode of settlement is further highlighted by the mandate to each Member State to provide appropriate procedures in its legislation to ensure observance of arbitration agreements and the recognition and enforcement of arbitral awards (Article 223.2). Credit is even given under Article 223.3 to a Member State which has implemented the 1958 United Nations Convention on the Recognition and Enforcement of Foreign Arbitral Awards or the Arbitration Rules of the United Nations Commission on International Trade Law as having complied with Article 223.2.

One can presume with some degree of certainty that the motivation for urging the timely settlement of private commercial disputes, whether regional or international, is to avoid the adverse effects which protracted delays in resolution of such disputes could have on the fragile economies of Member States as well as the resultant serious impact on the enhancement of the CSME; all of this is separate and apart from the drastic loss of confidence in the investment climate of the Region.

COMPARISONS AND CONTRASTS BETWEEN THE CCJ AND THE ECJ

An assessment of these two international courts may indicate that the Caribbean Court of Justice is likely to be to the Caribbean Community what the European Court of Justice is to the European Union particularly in relation to the creation of a Single Market among Member States. In this regard, certain provisions of the CCJ's original jurisdiction mirror those of the ECJ. The role of both Courts is a supervisory one charged with the responsibility of monitoring the application and implementation of economic treaties.

Justice Pollard, in a comparison between the two courts made the comment that the CCJ which in the exercise of its original jurisdiction as an international tribunal is considered in some quarters as the institutional centrepiece of the CSME, but unlike the ECJ it has no supranational competence, and is not integrated as an organ in the institutional arrangements of the Caribbean Community. He posited the view that this was due in large measure to the dual status of the CCJ as a municipal court of last resort for most but not all members of the Community, and as an international tribunal for all members of the Community. (See "The CSME and the CCJ" a paper largely based on an article entitled The CSME, CCJ and the Private Sector which appeared in The Caribbean Integration Process: A People Centred Approach edited by K. Hall and M. Chuck-A-Sang, Ian Randle Publishers, Kingston, 2007, pp 24-47).

The issue of referrals from Member States is common to both Courts, but with different applicability. The import of Article 214 of the RTC is similar to Article 234 of the Maastricht Treaty which brought into being the European Court of Justice. In like manner if the issue of interpretation of the Treaty is raised before any court of a Member State, it may request the ECJ to give a ruling thereon. Although at first blush the provisions may appear to be similar, there are some crucial differences. Whereas the language used in Article 214 of the RTC appears to be mandatory in that where a court or tribunal of a Member State when seised of an issue involving the interpretation or application of the RTC shall refer the question to the CCJ for determination, a court or tribunal similarly placed with interpretation of the Maastricht Treaty may, if it considers that a decision on the question is necessary to enable it to deliver judgment, request the ECJ to give a ruling thereon. Article 234 extends this further to provide for situations where there is a case pending before a national court of a Member State against whose decisions there is no judicial remedy under national law, that court or tribunal may bring the matter before the Court of Justice.

Justice Pollard remarked on the difference between the two provisions by pointing to the fact that unlike the ECJ, the CCJ in cases of referrals from national courts or the tribunals is competent to interpret and apply the RTC. Article 234 of the Maastricht Treaty provides only for an interpretation by the ECJ. Justice Pollard went on to point out that despite obvious differences in the formulation of the referral provisions in the two regimes, their essential thrust is similar, namely, to ensure certainty and uniformity in the applicable law.

He theorised that in much the same way that the provision of Article 234 was credited with promoting social and economic cohesion in the European Union by allowing the ECJ to insinuate itself in the domestic law of participating states, such a role may be of even greater importance within the Caribbean Community where the prevalence of dualism and the non-applicability of the principle of direct effect aggravates the problem of establishing a uniform legal infrastructure in CARICOM.

Continuing the discussion on referrals or references to the ECJ by national courts or tribunals, the case of *Julia Schnorbus v Land Hessen* (See Case C-79/99, judgment given on 7/12/2000) illustrates the basis on which a reference to the Court can be made when it noted that the Court has consistently held that it is solely for the national court to determine, in the light of the particular circumstances of the case, the need for a preliminary ruling in order to enable it to give its judgment, and consequently if questions submitted to the Court concern the interpretation of Community law, the Court, is in principle, obliged to give a ruling. Unfortunately, to date the CCJ has not had the opportunity to make any ruling on referrals, but optimistically this may change in the near future.

The RTC in Article 221 (Article XXII of the CCJ Agreement) sought to ensure consistency in the judgments of the CCJ by providing that they shall constitute legally binding precedents for parties in proceedings before the Court unless such judgments have been revised in accordance with Article 219. Consistency and uniformity in the application and interpretation of an economic treaty is a *sine qua non* for the development of confidence in tribunals and courts under whose mandate such interpretation fall. National courts of the European Union have accepted the supremacy of European law affirmed by the ECJ to a large extent in certain areas of dispute, for example, sex discrimination. In *Costa v ENEL* (See ECJ Case 6/64) the ECJ established the principle of supremacy of Community law, a consequential result being that precedence must always be given to Community law over conflicting national law.

The CCJ in the recent case of *Shanique Myrie v The State of Barbados* (See [2013] CCJ 3 (OJ)) availed itself of the opportunity to define the supremacy of Community law when it upheld the validity and applicability of a 2007 Conference Decision of Member States permitting the right of entry of nationals of one Member State into another for a period of six months, this being an implementable decision at Community level, and therefore binding on all Member States without the need to be enacted domestically. The Court went on to hold that if binding regional decisions can be invalidated at the Community level by the failure of a Member State to incorporate those decisions domestically, the efficacy of the entire CARICOM regime would be jeopardised; further, the certainty, predictability and uniformity of Community law would be destroyed.

THE RTC AND THE WTO (World Trade Organisation)

Dispute settlement is regarded by the WTO which came into force in 1995 as the central pillar of international and multilateral trade, governed essentially by agreed procedures under the Dispute Settlement Understanding agreed to by member states of the WTO.

Part Three of the RTC on SUBSIDIES embracing Articles 96 – 116 covers every aspect of the imposition of subsidies under the remit of COTED, one of the Organs of the RTC, but Article 116.6 specifically provides that no Member State shall impose countervailing duties other than provisional countervailing duties without prior authorisation from COTED, and the determination and imposition of definitive countervailing duties shall be governed by the relevant provisions of the WTO Agreement on Subsidies and Countervailing Measures. COTED's authority seems to be limited to authorising only provisional countervailing duties.

The WTO Agreement on Subsidies and Countervailing Measures (the SCM Agreement) concerns multilateral disciplines regulating the provision of subsidies and the use of countervailing measures to offset injury caused by subsidised imports, an Agreement to which all member states of the WTO are expected to adhere. There is as a consequence a WTO dispute settlement mechanism which doubtless is utilised whenever the need arises.

It can be logically concluded that Article 116.6 was drafted in compliance with the WTO mechanism in mind and which may bind all CARICOM Member States as members of the WTO. One can well understand why such disputes may not fall under the jurisdiction of the CCJ.

CONCLUSIONS

The Preamble to the CCJ Agreement indicates that the Contracting Parties were "convinced that the Caribbean Court of Justice will have a determinative role in the further development of Caribbean jurisprudence through the judicial process" with its establishment being "a further step in the deepening of the regional integration process". The Preamble to the RTC affirming that "the original jurisdiction of the Caribbean Court of Justice is essential for the successful operation of the CSME", The Regional leaders of the Community thereby carved a niche for the CCJ in giving effect to the traditions and mores of the people of the Caribbean Region through its judgments primarily in its appellate jurisdiction though not exclusively so, and through its original jurisdiction. In doing so it will blaze a trail through virgin territory of interpreting and applying a Treaty with the laudable objectives of enhancing "the participation of their peoples, particularly the social partners in the integration movement". It will also establish conditions which "would facilitate access by their nationals to the collective resources of the Region on a non-discriminatory basis".

In the short and exhilarating experience of the Court the collective conclusion and prediction suggests that the jurisprudence deriving from its original jurisdiction will be advanced and developed primarily through disputes between natural and juridical persons and Member States of the Community rather than between the Member States themselves. This is due in large measure to the detailed Disputes Settlement Regime of Chapter Nine of the RTC, which suggests exhaustion of the listed options of resolution before energetic recourse to the CCJ when disputes arise between Member States. One can only surmise whether this was the intention of the crafters of the RTC; only time will tell.

THE CCJ AS A CATALYST FOR CHANGE

The CCJ in both its original and appellate jurisdictions has an obligation to foster and encourage the implementation and fashioning of alternative means of dispute resolution within the Region. The continuity of an overwhelming backlog of cases hampering the efficiency and ability of national courts to deliver justice in a timely manner must be the compelling motivator for the regional establishment of centres providing alternative means of case disposal if the maxim "justice delayed is justice denied" is to be relegated to the dump-heap of history in a forgotten past.

Progress has been made in the Region as most national courts have embarked on some form of alternative dispute resolution. It is predicted that these small steps will develop exponentially throughout our Region in the short term as we stride resolutely forward in improving delivery of justice to the people of our Member States.

Thesis as 2013 Research Fellow
Institute of Advanced Legal Studies
Inns of Court, London

Endnotes

1 Founded by Antigua & Barbuda, Barbados and Guyana on 15 December, 1965, with the signing of the Dickenson Bay Agreement, and later joined by Trinidad and Tobago, Dominica, Grenada, St. Kitts-Nevis-Anguilla, St. Lucia, St Vincent and the Grenadines, Montserrat, Jamaica and Belize.
2 Signed at Chaguaramas, Trinidad and Tobago by Antigua and Barbuda, Bahamas, Barbados, Belize, Dominica, Grenada, Guyana, Jamaica, Montserrat, St. Kitts-Nevis-Anguilla, St. Lucia, St. Vincent, Trinidad and Tobago.
3 Signed on July 5, 2001 in Nassau, Bahamas by Heads of Government of the Community.
4 Signed on February 14, 2001 in Barbados.
5 Article 211.
6 Preamble of the Agreement and Article 2.
7 Article 26.
8 Article 28.
9 Membership was also open to any other state of the Caribbean Region that is, in the opinion of the Conference of the Community able and willing to exercise the rights and assume the obligations of membership in accordance with Article 29 of the Treaty.
10 Article 19.
11 Article 11.
12 Article 5 of the Annex.
13 Signed in Nassau, The Bahamas, on 5 July, 2001.
14 Article 19 of 1973 Treaty.
15 Article 12(8).
16 Article 188.
17 Article 222 of the Treaty; Article XXIV of the Agreement.
18 Article 189.
19 Articles 211–222.

CHAPTER 12

THE INDEPENDENT JUDICIAL MIND

I chose this topic for my address this evening as I consider it necessary and important for the public to be made aware about what informs the judicial mind in arriving at decisions, and in the official and personal conduct on and off the Bench.

Three important and historic international gatherings of Heads and Representatives of Judiciaries worldwide resulted in recommendations and conclusions which have had a significant impact on the conduct and ethics of judicial officers wherever located.

The first of these conferences took place in the United Kingdom in 1998 from which emerged what was known originally as the Latimer House Guidelines and later as the Commonwealth Principles on the Accountability of and Relationship Between the Three Branches of Government.

The second was held in Bangalore, India, in 2002 when the Bangalore Principles of Judicial Conduct were formulated and adopted, the impact of which has been far-reaching and has given rise to acceptance of codes of judicial conduct in various forms.

Also in 2002, Commonwealth Judicial Officers including myself as Chancellor of the Judiciary of Guyana, met in Limassol, Cyprus, at a Colloquium from which emanated the Limassol Conclusions.

The Bangalore Principles, however, have had the most significant effect on judiciaries as they have formed the basis for judicial codes of conduct which embrace the Values of Independence, Impartiality, Integrity, Equality, Propriety, Competence and Diligence, and Accountability.

As Chancellor of the Judiciary, I considered it necessary to formulate a Code of Conduct for our Judiciary and Magistracy with similar Principles and Values. After consultations such a Code was adopted, and came into effect in November 2003. A copy was given to each judge and magistrate upon elevation to office. Commendably our present Chancellor, Hon. Mr. Justice Carl Singh, has continued the practice. When the Caribbean Court of Justice was inaugurated a draft Code was available, but not yet accepted. The current President of the Court assigned me the task of bringing it into operation; after a series of monthly meetings the Code was adopted by the Judges of the Court in 2013 based on the Bangalore Principles.

I have chosen for discussion three of the Principles and Values which I feel are relevant to the topic of this address. They are Independence, Integrity and Propriety.

THE PRINCIPLE OF INDEPENDENCE

The Bangalore Principles define this principle as a "prerequisite to the rule of law and a fundamental guarantee of a fair trial". A judge shall therefore uphold and exemplify judicial independence in both its individual and institutional aspects.

The institutional aspect of the Principle of Independence of the Judiciary is stressed and emphasised far more frequently and attracts more comment whenever discussion of the role of the Judiciary in any society arises. An independent Judiciary is regarded as the hallmark of good governance and exemplifies the sought-after goal of separation of powers of a state. One of the values in support of this Principle and which is reflected in any judicial code of conduct (including ours) exhorts a judge to exercise the judicial function independently on the basis of the judge's assessment of the facts and in accordance with a conscientious understanding of the law; this must be free of any extraneous influences, inducements or pressure from any quarter or for any reason. In this address I am more concerned with the independence of the judicial mind. All requirements may be in place to conform with the ideal of separation of judicial powers from the other branches of a state, but ultimately the independence of the judicial mind is paramount.

THE PRINCIPLE OF INTEGRITY

An integral aspect of the Principle of Independence is the important and precious value of integrity which is essential to the proper discharge of the judicial office.

The Bangalore Commentary on this value defines integrity as "the attribute of rectitude and righteousness". Its components have been identified as honesty and judicial morality. There are no degrees of integrity. One either has it or not. In relation to the Judiciary it is more than a virtue; it is an absolute requirement.

It is sometimes difficult to explain integrity in specific terms, but it is recognizable when one assesses the actions and character of an individual. One of the rules of the Principle of Integrity in the Guyana Code of Conduct is that a judge shall ensure that her/his conduct is above reproach both in public as well as private life in the view of a reasonable observer. This may seem to impose severe restrictions on the life of a judge, but it is one of the burdens of judicial office. It may oft times require restraint on a judge's interaction with members of the public and on her/his private life. An example of this is considering what social invitations one should accept, and places of entertainment one should frequent. It is never easy to make such decisions, but in striking the right balance a judge should consider whether in the eyes of a reasonable, fair-minded member of the public, the conduct is likely to call into question the judge's integrity or lead to diminished respect.

This, however, in no way suggests that a judge should live in an ivory tower or in isolation from society. Interaction with the public at all levels is an important component of judicial life. It enables one to keep a finger on the pulse of a nation, and assists immeasurably in carrying out a judge's primary function of determining what is just and fair in particular circumstances. The caveat, however, is caution and the realisation that as a judge you are the subject of constant public scrutiny and comment.

THE PRINCIPLE OF PROPRIETY

This Principle is intertwined with and is often indistinguishable from the principle of integrity. It is addressed at length in most codes of conduct including ours, the reason being that it can cover several situations that may confront a judge. It must be realised, however, that it is not possible to embrace every situation which a judge may encounter; it is very often left to the judge's own personal code of values and innate sense of what is appropriate conduct in a given situation to determine which path one should take.

Both integrity and propriety are based on public perception. Propriety can be summed up as being how it might look in the eyes of the public. The Commentary on the Bangalore Principles stipulates that what matters most is not what a judge does or does not do, but what others think the judge has done or might do. It is all about perception. An example is given where a judge who speaks privately and at length with a litigant in a pending case will appear to be giving that party an advantage even if in fact the conversation is completely unrelated to the case. It goes on to state that since the public expects a high standard from a judge, she or he must when in doubt about attending an event or receiving a gift, however small, ask the question, "how might this look in the eyes of the public?", and will it create in the mind of a reasonable observer the perception that the judge's ability to carry out the functions of office has been impaired.

This test can sometimes impose unnecessary strain on a judge in her/his interaction with friends and even relatives. The reality may differ considerably from the perception. It is never easy for a judge to assess a situation and determine how one's actions will be perceived in the eyes of the public. It may give rise to doubts in one's mind, and if such doubts do arise, the best decision may be to withdraw from the situation or discontinue further contact or involvement in the activity.

No one ever promised that the life of a judge would be easy. To a very large extent it depends as mentioned earlier on the judge's own moral code which inheres in every person and which is based on one's parental and religious upbringing as well as one's socialisation. For those brought up in a crucible where certain traditional values were inculcated there is no difficulty; you will be acting in accordance with your nurturing and upbringing. One, however, has to be cognisant of the fact that some values have undergone metamorphoses within modern times; nevertheless, the core values of honesty, integrity and a keen sense of what constitutes right and wrong never change despite the fact that our younger members of society see everything through the crucible of being right, and nothing is ever wrong. We often hear the question asked: "What is wrong with that? It is my right to act as I think fit". Sad to say, this is not a luxury which the Judiciary can enjoy.

We are bound by the traditions of dispensing justice and invoking precedent of what conduct is right or wrong within the parameters of the law, and in doing so our own moral codes of conduct must be the ones we can invoke when faced with certain situations in our private lives. The values of honesty, integrity and propriety are the cornerstones on which judicial conduct is built, and every aspirant to judicial office must respect and be mindful of them.

One of the Commentaries of the Bangalore Principles on the Value of Independence advises that public awareness of judicial independence should be encouraged, and suggests that judges should in view of the public's own interest, take advantage of appropriate opportunities to help the public understand the fundamental importance of judicial independence.

As mentioned at the beginning of my address, and which I repeat, it is important for the public to be aware of what informs or should inform the judicial mind either when dispensing justice or in the day to day interaction with members of the public. The ultimate objective of any Judiciary is to inspire confidence in the administration of justice.

In this regard, I conclude this presentation with a quotation of Justice Frankfurter of the United States Supreme Court, and which I utilised at the end of the Preface of the Guyana Code of Conduct:

> *The Court has neither the purse nor the sword; its authority rests on substantial public confidence in its moral sanctions.*

Guyana Transparency Institute Anniversary Dinner
Georgetown, Guyana
9th December, 2014

CHAPTER 13

BEING A JUDGE IN THE MODERN WORLD

In addressing this topic, the first question to be answered is what is meant by the modern world and from whose perspective. A modern world depends on a period of time and also stages of development and economic growth in a particular country. One has to have regard to the fact that there are varying degrees of modernity between developed and developing societies.

Invariably one associates modernity with development and the availability of modern conveniences, goods and services. We tend to forget or overlook the fact that the vast majority of the world is under-developed or not developed at all.

However, for the purpose of this discussion we can accept the modern world from the perspective of development with functioning democratic institutions and accessibility to required services for comfortable living, and since the topic concerns judging in a modern world, we can assume that we mean judging in the 21st century and possibly in the latter part of the 20th century.

I speak mainly from a personal perspective, and in doing so I have to cast my mind back to the time when I became a judge in my homeland of Guyana which although geographically located in South America and bordered by Brazil, Venezuela and Suriname, was the only British colony in that continent. As a result, our ties culturally and traditionally have been with the English-speaking Caribbean. Being a former colony within the British Empire we inherited the British legal system and the common law. Our procedural rules and legislation were copied wholesale from the British system sometimes producing peculiar results; in fact, some procedures and legislation which have been repealed here are still on our statute books and followed without regard to changing circumstances.

We also inherited judicial wear and courtesies which continued and still continue even after independence. One aspect of judicial wear which was abolished in 1970 was the use of wigs which, however, is still used in some Caribbean countries. Along with the wigs Guyana abolished appeals to the Judicial Committee of the Privy Council, and maintained our Court of Appeal as our final court until 2005 when we joined the Caribbean Court of Justice. The rest of the Caribbean has been slow in replacing the Privy Council as the court of last resort, and so far, only two others apart from Guyana have accepted the Caribbean Court of Justice as their final court – Barbados and Belize. The reason for this has more to do with politics in some instances than with a reluctance to sever the umbilical cord.

I shall at this point speak briefly about the Caribbean Court of Justice which was inaugurated in April 2005 with seven judges and two jurisdictions – original and appellate. The main purpose for establishing the Court was to interpret and implement an economic treaty entered into by members of the Caribbean Community – the Revised Treaty of Chaguaramas – in much the same way as the European Court of Justice and the European Union. The Caribbean Community comprises states of the English-speaking Caribbean together with Suriname and Haiti. The original jurisdiction of the Court is devoted to hearing disputes concerning the Treaty brought by member states against each other or by private individuals or entities against the member states. The appellate jurisdiction covers appeals from the national courts of appeal and operates as the court of last resort as mentioned earlier for three of the member states.

Membership of the Court is open to any judge or academic with a common law background, and a civil law one with qualifications in international law. Judges sit in their individual capacities and not as representatives of one's country of birth – hence we have at present an English and a Dutch judge.

I now return to the topic of this evening's discussion. As stated earlier Guyana and the other former colonies of the Caribbean have adopted the English procedure and legislation, but although much reliance is placed on English cases as precedents the Caribbean courts as a whole are endeavouring to develop their own jurisprudence based on Caribbean customs and traditions, and wherever appropriate local decisions are cited with approval.

With regard to the topic there are some new and emerging issues with which a judge in the world today may be confronted and which never arose for judicial consideration 30 – 40 years ago. One such issue is computer crime which is increasing exponentially having regard to the fact that the electronic industry is developing at such a rapid rate that what is new today is likely to be out of date within a few weeks. An increasing number of computer crimes are being committed both domestically and internationally. A personal computer connected to the internet may be infected with malicious software within a very short space of time. There are different types of attacks on computers some in an attempt to access stored information which may have a saleable value, e.g. corporate espionage, or seeking to control a computer to be used to send spam or host illegal content.

Here, in England I am informed that legislation has been enacted to control these crimes, and of necessity cases have been brought with persons being charged which requires judicial personnel to be involved and to be familiar with the details of such crimes in order to impose penalties where necessary. This type of crime presents new challenges for current judges with the advent of the world-wide web. In my part of the world legislation has not as yet been passed to combat computer crime, but I am sure that in the near future this will become necessary.

The subject of surrogacy is another new issue which judges here now have to adjudicate upon. This arises when a woman carries a baby for another who is unable to do so or to conceive. Several legal issues could arise apart from the medical ones, and these could be monumental leading possibly to extensive litigation when disagreements arise. Rights of custody, visitation, inheritance, adoption, emotional attachments, are only few of the problems which may flow from surrogacy, if not properly addressed at the initial stages of this new form of parenting. Judges have to be sensitive to the issues involved and make decisions which are fair and within the boundaries of the law being at all times mindful that the welfare of the child or children involved is the paramount consideration.

I have been advised that under English law the mother of a child born through surrogacy is always the surrogate mother, as the law regards the woman who gives birth to a child as the lawful mother. There are also issues which may arise through international surrogacy, that is, mothers giving birth to children through surrogacy arrangements with foreign women or couples or vice versa. Laws may also be broken by advertising surrogacy. All of these impose obligations on modern day judges.

Of even greater significance is the issue of same-sex marriages and all of the legal problems which can arise from such unions, although these may be capable of easier resolution as the same laws applicable to other marital unions may apply., e.g. adoption and custody of children, maintenance and division of marital assets, the parties being the only difference. So far in my part of the world we have not as yet had to deal with this issue, but I am certain that we shall have to do so within the not too distant future. In like manner, the issue of surrogacy. We have to be prepared to deal with them when they arise.

We now live in a world which has shrunk in terms of travel and the access to information easily obtained through the internet and social networking. This has made the commission of criminal offences much easier to perpetrate and slower to detect. Although crimes such as trafficking in persons were committed in the past, the number of victims smuggled across borders and forced into prostitution and other sexual crimes has increased world-wide. Human trafficking has become a problem for both developed and developing countries. Caribbean countries have not escaped the international network, and our courts of necessity are grappling with the ever-increasing incidents of minors being forcefully abducted from their homelands.

Moving away from new criminal offences and other world-changing issues, positively the delivery of justice has been expedited in developed and some developing countries. The filing of court documents and all of the procedures connected with hearing of cases have been made considerably easier and faster. Whereas in the past hearings of cases were delayed by cumbersome recording of evidence often being handwritten or translated by shorthand reporters, such evidence can be made available instantly and transcripts delivered immediately. The work of judges has been made much easier including the research required for the delivery of judgments. One just has to enter the name of a relevant case into a computer and the answer is at your fingertips. Our Court is the beneficiary of modern technology for which we are indeed grateful, and for which we have been commended repeatedly.

Of course, all of this leads back to my opening remarks about the developed and developing world. We have to be cognizant of the fact that there are parts of the world where modern technology is still a distant dream, and courts and judicial personnel (including magistrates) continue to dispense justice without the trappings of modern technology. Justice must be administered whether the evidence is recorded by hand or by a machine, and whether the research is obtained through legal tomes or through a search engine. It is conceded that the lack of advanced technology reduces the capacity of courts to deliver justice in a timely manner, and developing countries continue to be plagued by ever-increasing backlogs of cases. In some countries with weak economies the choice between improving the judicial system and constructing a hospital or school is easy to make with the judicial system being relegated to the bottom of the list of priorities.

Another development within the Judiciary at this point in time is the large number of women who are entering the legal profession compared with the numbers several years ago. Within the Caribbean women are graduating from the law schools in considerably higher percentages than men. I am sure this is not confined to the Caribbean and may be so in other jurisdictions. It will certainly have implications for women joining the Judiciary eventually although at present we see them at the lower end of the judicial spectrum, e.g. as magistrates. The number of female judges particularly in the higher echelons of the judicial system is still much lower than men, myself included being the only female judge among six males. Hopefully the tide will change as women ascend the ladder and break the proverbial glass ceiling.

One important aspect of being a judge in today's world is transparency. Judicial decisions and the reasoning which informed the making of those decisions are more publicly scrutinized than in an earlier era. Formerly judges tended to work with greater privacy and virtually no accountability; they did not feel obliged to disclose their thought processes in arriving at decisions except through published law reports; in fact, judges never interacted with the press. Today in some jurisdictions through an active press and other media, the Judiciary has come under a microscope with detailed inquiries being made of circumstances which informed their rulings. Although judicial interaction with the media is still restricted to some extent, it is less rigid, and some jurisdictions have public relations personnel attached to the courts thereby shielding the Judiciary from media exposure. Nevertheless, the whole aspect of judicial accountability has assumed importance, and some current views reveal that the Judiciary should no longer be cloistered, but more transparent particularly in relation to decisions that arouse public interest and the effects of which may have implications for a significant majority of citizens.

Similarly, judicial conduct attracts far more media attention than it did in past decades. Of course, we now live in a very open society where privacy is limited and one's actions come under severe public scrutiny.

In these circumstances the adoption of judicial codes of conduct has become necessary with guidelines on how judges should conduct themselves. This was unheard of years ago. No one would have thought that there was need to lay out rules on how judges ought to comport themselves. Sadly today, this is necessary, and the Bangalore Principles of Judicial Conduct first discussed in Bangalore, India, early in this century and later adopted by Chief Justices and senior judicial officers from around the world, promulgated such principles as integrity, impartiality, equality, propriety, independence, competence and diligence. These principles have been accepted by Judiciaries of the Commonwealth and elsewhere and have given rise to the acceptance of codes of conduct for judges and magistrates. In most instances these codes are merely advisory rather than punitive, operating as guidelines on the types of conduct that is expected from the holders of offices of trust, and from whom the public demands higher standards of behaviour.

A recent addition to codes of judicial conduct in some countries is advice on dealing with social networking and placing of information on these web sites which may have an adverse effect on matters before the courts. This is certainly a new phenomenon which has implications for the Judiciary if not handled carefully. Discretion and caution in deciding what a judge posts on social network sites are important factors to be considered in order to preserve the integrity of judges, and to avoid compromising the administration of justice generally.

Several examples of abuse of the process have surfaced with judges being utilized as pawns in contested cases either by unwittingly accepting social invitations from persons or friends involved in proceedings before them or contacts being made through their relatives, friends and sometimes judicial staff. Judges have to be on their guard constantly when interacting socially or accepting invitations which appear ostensibly innocuous. This is particularly so in small jurisdictions where judicial personnel is well known. The problem may not be so acute in large jurisdictions where it is easier for judges to be anonymous with such anonymity being a blessing in disguise.

What has become a world-wide concern within recent times is preservation and protection of the environment with legislative measures being taken to avoid its pollution and destruction. Judges may now find that their dockets include cases concerning restraint on destruction and excavation of heritage sites and forests mainly for mining and other forms of development. It cannot be denied that destruction and exploitation of our natural resources has been and continues to be effected in the name of rapid and aggressive modernization thereby creating imbalances within our eco-systems. Some jurisdictions have established environmental agencies and courts to handle the plethora of cases concerning destruction of the environment which in former years was not as extensive or which was overlooked in the name of progress.

I end by referring to the most significant issue which has arisen during this century and which a judge in these modern times may have to confront in the future. It is the new and developing concept of cloning, that is, producing an identical clone of another animal or maybe futuristically another human being. Cloning has started with animals, and some time in years ahead the skill may be perfected to produce a human clone. The legal issues which may arise from this concept are mind-boggling, and laws will have to be formulated to deal with the problems from this experiment with nature if and when it becomes a reality. Let us hope that we are well prepared to deal with it if it ever arises.

These are just a few issues which from my perspective a judge in the present state of world events and advancement may have to confront in the day-to-day administration of justice. I am certain there are several others which may arise depending on the jurisdiction within which a judge is required to serve and the level of attention which is given by governments to these issues either as priorities or issues which depending on their economies do not require urgent attention and could be deferred to some futuristic date.

Delivered at lecture series by Diversity & Development Team
Judicial College
Judiciary of England & Wales
Royal Courts of Justice
25th November, 2013

CHAPTER 14

CAPITAL PUNISHMENT: TO ABOLISH OR NOT TO ABOLISH, THAT IS THE QUESTION

The abolition of capital punishment and the removal of the death penalty from the statutes of countries which still retain it has given rise to extensive discussion and controversy whenever and wherever it is mentioned.

My presentation today will be in support of its abolition. I begin by referring to a comment attributed to the Secretary General of the United Nations, Mr. Ban Ki Moon, in New York on 3 July, 2012 and reported in an Amnesty International article on the Death Penalty in the Caribbean – A Human Rights Issue, which is to this effect:

> "The right to life is the most fundamental of all human rights.... The taking of life is too absolute, too irreversible, for one human being to inflict it on another even when backed by Legal process."

Within the Caribbean Region all of the English-speaking countries which inherited the English legal system in colonial times provide in their criminal statutes for the imposition of the death penalty as punishment upon conviction for the offence of murder and treason.

Significantly although sentences of death continue to be passed in some of these countries executions have not been carried out for several years. The following table indicates the year when the last execution took place:

Antigua & Barbuda:	1991
Bahamas:	2000
Barbados:	1984
Belize:	1985
Grenada:	1978

Guyana:	1997
Jamaica:	1985
St. Kitts/Nevis:	2008
St. Lucia:	1995

Article 3 of the Universal Declaration of Human Rights which is generally regarded as the cornerstone of the protection of human rights and was accepted by the General Assembly of the United Nations on 10th December, 1948, provides that everyone has the right to life, liberty and the security of person.

Its later offsprings, were the twin treaties – the International Covenant on Civil and Political Rights and the International Covenant on Economic, Social and Cultural Rights - both adopted by the United Nations in 1966. Article 6 of the ICCPR gave rise to two Protocols, the second being directly pertinent to the death penalty, and adopted by the United Nations on 15th December, 1989. Article 1 of that Protocol provides that no one within the jurisdiction of a state party shall be executed, and each state party shall take all necessary measures to abolish the death penalty within its jurisdiction. This Protocol is the only international treaty aiming to provide for total abolition of the death penalty, but three others have regional scope, for example, the Protocol to the American Convention on Human Rights to Abolish the Death Penalty which was adopted by the General Assembly of the Organisation of American States in 1990, and which has relevance for states within the Caribbean Region. Five states have ratified the Convention; none has signed or ratified the Protocol.

Article 4(6) of the Convention gives a person sentenced to death the right to apply for amnesty, pardon or commutation of sentence, and specifies that capital punishment shall not be imposed while a petition is pending. The petition is not admissible unless all local remedies under domestic law have been exhausted, and is filed within six months from the date of dismissal of the petitioner's final domestic appeal.

MANDATORY DEATH PENALTY

A significant feature of capital punishment is its mandatory nature and irreversible effect. Judges or officials who impose the penalty have no discretion to be lenient. There are no mitigating factors which can be considered; it is final and irrevocable except where applications can be made in some countries to a committee on the prerogative of mercy which is empowered to commute the penalty to life imprisonment when all appeals against sentence have been exhausted.

The mandatory nature of the death penalty has been challenged both before regional courts and international fora. In 2002 the Inter-American Commission on Human Rights in the case of *Hilaire Constantine & Benjamin v Trinidad & Tobago* held that the mandatory imposition of the death penalty constituted an arbitrary deprivation of the right to life in violation of the American Convention on Human Rights. Regional appellate courts have also held that the mandatory death penalty in domestic constitutions was inhumane and degrading.

The last person executed by hanging in the English-speaking Caribbean was Charles Elroy Laplace of St. Kitts/Nevis on 19th December, 2008 for the murder of his wife. Mr. Laplace's case illustrates the challenges that retentionist countries face in ensuring adequate legal representation for persons facing a death sentence. The United Nations Human Rights Committee comments that capital defendants should be provided with counsel "at all stages of the proceedings". Yet it appears that Laplace lacked the needed legal representation throughout critical stages of his post-conviction case. The Eastern Caribbean Supreme Court dismissed his appeal on the grounds that he filed it past the deadline and although he could have made a final appeal to the Judicial Committee of the Privy Council he did not do so. It appeared likely that the Government did not provide him with the necessary legal representation to assist him in filing an appeal. Amnesty International calls attention to the question of whether Laplace's right to apply for an amnesty, pardon or commutation would have been upheld.

Progress has been made within the English-speaking Caribbean during the last decade due in large measure to the judgments of the aforementioned courts and tribunals. Below is the present position in the Caribbean states:

Antigua & Barbuda:	now discretionary; retained only for aggravated murder
Bahamas:	retained only for certain types of murder
Barbados:	legislation proposed, not yet enacted
Belize:	no longer mandatory

Dominica:	no longer mandatory; no legislation as yet
Grenada:	no longer mandatory, discretionary for aggravated murder
Guyana:	no longer mandatory under legislation
Jamaica:	no longer mandatory
St. Kitts/Nevis:	no longer mandatory
St. Lucia:	no longer mandatory
St. Vincent:	no longer mandatory
Trinidad & Tobago:	still mandatory

Although according to Amnesty International over 140 countries have abolished the death penalty in law or in practice, and over 97 had removed it from their statutes, the English-speaking Caribbean states continue to retain it. This could be attributed to the ever-increasing rise in violent crime resulting in death particularly when one considers the size and population of these states. Popular opinion regards the death penalty as a deterrent and solution to the problem although studies and statistics do not always support this view. Politicians are somewhat hesitant to abolish it lest they seem to be soft on serious crime. A sentence of life imprisonment for murder would be regarded as being light by a populace nurtured in the expectation of hanging being the penalty for taking someone's life unlawfully.

As mentioned at the beginning of this presentation executions have not been carried out for several years in the English-speaking Caribbean states. This may be due in large measure to the judgment of the English Judicial Committee of the Privy Council in the case of *Pratt & Morgan v Attorney General of Jamaica* (1994) 2A.C. 1; (1993) 43 WIR, 340 which held that it was unconstitutional to execute the Appellants who had been on death row for nearly 14 years. Because the Constitution of Jamaica prohibits inhuman and degrading punishment, excessive delays ought not to occur between sentencing and execution of the punishment. In cases of such excessive delay, the death sentence should be commuted to life imprisonment. The JCPC further held that any delay of more than five years between sentencing and execution was evidence that carrying out the sentence would constitute inhuman and degrading punishment.

The constitutions of most, if not all, of the former colonies of Great Britain contain similar provisions, and the JCPC was until 2005 for some of the states, the court of final resort, and therefore binding. Since its inauguration in 2005 the Caribbean Court of Justice is now the final appellate court for Barbados, Guyana, Belize and Dominica. The effect of this development and how earlier precedents of the JCPC would be regarded was discussed in the case of *Attorney General of Barbados et al v Jeffrey Joseph & Lennox Ricardo Boyce* (2006) 69 WIR,104. It was agreed that decisions of the JCPC handed down while it was still the final court of appeal for the states which now have the Caribbean Court of Justice as its final court would be binding and continue to be so in the absence of any material difference between the written law of the respective countries from which the appeals emanated and the written law of the case before the Court, in this case Barbados, unless they are overruled by the CCJ.

I commend to you all of the five judgments in this case which deals with the various aspects of the death penalty and its execution. The following excerpt from the joint judgment of *Michael de la Bastide, P, and Saunders, J* is both interesting and informative:

> With the exception of the British Dependent territories, the laws of all the countries of the Commonwealth Caribbean make provision for capital punishment. We recognise that the death penalty is a constitutionally sanctioned punishment for murder and falls within internationally accepted conduct on the part of civilised States. The death penalty, however, should not be carried out without scrupulous care being taken to ensure that there is procedural propriety and that in the process fundamental human rights are not violated. Death is a punishment which is irrevocable. Amidst deep and continuing controversy over the death penalty, it must be acknowledged that several court decisions in the Caribbean over the last two or three decades have done much to humanise the law and to improve the administration of justice in this area.

The judgment of It, J in the same case summarised the substance of the decision in in this way:

> A State that wishes to retain capital punishment must accept the responsibility of ensuring that execution follows as swiftly as practicable after sentence, allowing a reasonable time for appeal and consideration of reprieve. It is part of the human condition

> that a condemned man will take every opportunity to save his life through use of the appellate procedure. If the appellate procedure enables the prisoner to prolong the appellate hearings over a period of years, the fault is to be attributed to the appellate system that permits such delay and not to the prisoner who takes advantage of it."

This echoes dicta of Lord Griffiths who delivered the judgment of the JCPC, and should be regarded as a realistic approach to the issue of whether capital punishment should be abolished. If governments wish to retain the death penalty, it behoves them to ensure that the domestic appellate process is accelerated. Admittedly they may have no control over the international appellate process, but these bodies should be persuaded to conclude their decisions within a period of at least eighteen months as suggested by in his judgment in the CCJ Barbados case of referred to earlier. The prisoner is entitled to utilise every available process and cannot be blamed if this segment of the appellate process usurps an inordinately long period of time.

The prospect of having the death penalty and capital punishment removed from the statutes of the English-speaking Caribbean states is encouraging, even though progress may be slow due to a rising murder rate in states such as Trinidad & Tobago where the death penalty is perceived to be the solution for reducing it. Preserving the status quo is the easy way; re-educating the populace is much more difficult. Introducing life imprisonment will be regarded as being soft on crimes involving death. It is reported recently that Guyana is considering discussion on the issue, and a referendum may be contemplated.

If the replacement for the death penalty is life imprisonment, discussion will arise as to whether such imprisonment will be interpreted literally or continue to be a specified period of years as it is in some countries at present. Deprivation of one's liberty for as long as you live may be worse than execution.

That is the question!

Commonwealth Magistrates & Judges Conference
Georgetown, Guyana
September, 2016

PART II

LEGAL PROFESSION

Court of Appeal of Guyana

Left to right:— The Hon. Mme. Justice Desiree Bernard, The Hon. Mr. Justice Aubrey Bishop, The Hon. Chancellor, Mr. Justice Kenneth George, The Hon. Mr. Justice Maurice Churaman and The Hon. Mr. Justice Lennox Perry.

CHAPTER 15

THE IMPACT OF THE ENGLISH COMMON LAW ON CARIBBEAN SOCIETY

Of necessity, any discussion of the topic I have chosen must commence with a definition of the term "Common Law". What is the Common Law of England? Its origin in medieval times was undoubtedly customary. Principles were developed which never had their genesis in any written form of words.

Blackstone in his Commentaries[1] described these principles which are said to be customary as "general customs, which are the universal rule of the whole kingdom, and form the common law, in its stricter and more usual signification". A further illustration of this was given by *Sir Frederick Pollock*[2]:

> *leges et consuetudines regni [laws and customs of the realm] has been a regular collective name of English law since the latter half of the twelfth century at latest, in other words, ever since our law has had any terminology of its own; in the fourteenth century 'lex et consuetudo regni nostri' was so well established as meaning the Common Law that it could be seriously argued (though without success) that it was bad pleading to apply the term to law made by a statute. The very name Common Law seems to imply some kind of reference to general usage and acceptance as being the ultimate claim of the law upon the individual citizen's allegiance. In short, the Common Law is a customary law if, in the course of about six centuries, the undoubting belief and uniform language of everybody who had occasion to consider the matter were able to make it so.*

Accepting that the Common Law derived principally from custom, over the years a body of law developed based on judicial interpretation of the popular sentiment. Thus precedent was born and became the life blood of the common law being a guide to future conduct. Judges developed the doctrine of *stare decisis* adopting the same course in cases as was taken previously leading to stability in decisions, and regarding them as binding on future courts.

ADVENT OF THE ENGLISH COMMON LAW IN THE CARIBBEAN

In the 17th and 18th centuries Britain continued its quest for more lands to conquer, and sought to extend its influence to the far-flung corners of the earth with the boast that the sun did not ever set on the British Empire. As Britain expanded she took to her colonies all of her institutions – social, financial, religious and legal, *inter alia,* and established them along identical lines with those in the mother country. With regard to the legal system, the Common Law of England became the Common Law of the particular colony, and the structure of the court system in large measure mirrored that of England with no regard to relevance or suitability to local conditions.

(1) Preservation of the Common Law

Some of the Caribbean islands and the mainland territory of Guyana conquered by the British were no exception. They inherited all of the institutions and the legal system of England. In some of the English-speaking territories of the Caribbean certain aspects of the Common Law of England were expressly preserved as the law of the colony by legislation. In Guyana, for example, the Civil Law of Guyana Act, Cap. 6:01[3] passed on 1st January, 1917 was intituled "An Act to codify certain portions of the Roman-Dutch Law of the State and in other matters to substitute the English Common Law and Principles of Equity, along with certain English Statutory Provisions for the Roman-Dutch Law". Section 3(b) provides as follows:

> the common law of Guyana shall be the common law of England as at the date aforesaid including therewith the doctrines of equity as then administered or at any time hereafter administered by the courts of justice in England, and the High Court shall administer the doctrines of equity in the same manner as the High Court of Justice in England administers them at the date aforesaid or at any time hereafter.

This Act was passed to codify certain portions of the Roman-Dutch Law which was applied in Guyana in relation to immovable property. I shall refer to this more specifically later in the presentation.

The island of St. Lucia in like manner expressly provided for the common law of England to apply to certain aspects of the law of the then colony. Article 917A of the Civil Code of St. Lucia, Cap. 242 is to this effect:

> (1) Subject to the provisions of this article, from and after the coming into operation of this article the Law of England for the time being relating to contracts, quasi-contracts and torts shall *mutatis mutandis* extend to this colony.

This was applied in the case of *Mendes v. Philbert*[4] when the Court of Appeal of the West Indies Associated States held that the effect of Art. 917A of the Civil Code was to make the English common law doctrine of *scienter* part of the law of St. Lucia, and since this point was not raised at the trial where a respondent sued for damages for personal injuries arising from an attack from dogs, the magistrate's order awarding the respondent damages was erroneous and would be set aside.

(2) Structure of the Court System

The English court structure in most instances was transported *in toto* into the Caribbean territories without reference to relevance, cultural patterns or size of the particular island or state. Provision was made for magistrates' courts, district courts and high courts. All appeals from the high courts or supreme courts of the Caribbean territories went to the Judicial Committee of the Privy Council in England (hereinafter referred to as the Privy Council), and in most cases this is still so. In the middle of this century there was established an intermediary court of appeal with a varied nomenclature-first the West Indian Court of Appeal, then with an attempt at federation, the Federal Supreme Court, and lastly the British Caribbean Court of Appeal. With the advent of independence most of the states established their own courts of appeal, but with the exception of Guyana, retained appeals to the Privy Council.

There have been, still and will continue to be arguments for and against the retention of the Privy Council as the final court of appeal of the Caribbean region, and I shall return to this topic later in the presentation.

In some instances, certain states of the Caribbean have established special courts to meet special needs in the particular society. One example of this was the establishment of the Gun Court in Jamaica in the early 1970s to deal with the alarming rise in crimes involving the use of firearms. Family Courts have also been established in some Caribbean territories to adjudicate on all matters pertaining to the family. Of course, there have been for several years in some territories, for instance, in Guyana, Juvenile Courts which were established to handle all matters affecting juveniles, and were presided over by a magistrate who held the hearings of criminal offences committed by juveniles in camera. Probation officers were utilised to carry out investigations of the juvenile's family background with a view to determining punishment which invariably involved committal to a correctional and rehabilitation centre.

In Guyana there was also established a Land Court with jurisdiction to adjudicate on petitions for declarations of title to land having regard to the Roman-Dutch system of conveyancing.

In the colonial era nearly if not all of the courts of the Caribbean colonies were presided over by English magistrates and judges mainly with little or no knowledge of local customs and cultural traditions. They applied the English rules and laws rigidly and uncompromisingly sometimes with ridiculous results, e.g. there was provision in the laws of some states for deeming someone found wandering "a rogue and vagabond", and imposing a term of imprisonment when all that he may have been guilty of was not having a home or a family.

The Caribbean courts during this period in our history also followed the rules of procedure of the English courts. The English Rules of the Supreme Court formed the base upon which the rules of court of the colonies were founded. In most instances these rules were taken verbatim from the English rules. In some instances, however, procedural rules were formulated to meet local conditions, e.g. in Guyana there are rules regulating the procedure for entering oppositions to the passing of conveyances for land which is based on the Roman-Dutch system, and is peculiar to Guyana. Also, peculiar to Guyana and some other Caribbean territories were the rules permitting barristers-at-law to act as solicitors prior to the fusion of the profession. Section 10(2) of the Legal Practitioners Act, Cap. 4:01[5] is to this effect:

> A barrister who practises as a solicitor shall, in so far as he so practises, be deemed to be a solicitor. Any question arising under this subsection as to what constitutes practising as a solicitor shall, subject to any enactment for the time being in force, be decided by the Court.

EXAMPLES OF JUDICIAL ADAPTATION OF ENGLISH COMMON LAW TO LOCAL SITUATIONS

(a) Family Law

As in other areas of the law the English matrimonial rules were applied inflexibly with sometimes catastrophic results. The case of *Henry v. Henry*[6] which is a decision of the Supreme Court of Trinidad & Tobago Appellate Jurisdiction is an excellent example of the impact of the English common law on society in the Caribbean and the effects it can have on the lives of its people. In that case a wife lawfully married under the provisions of the Muslim Marriage and Divorce Registration Ordinance, Cap. 29, No. 4, brought a complaint against her husband under the Separation and Maintenance Ordinance, Cap. 5, No. 15, s. 3, for maintenance on the grounds of his wilful neglect to maintain her. The magistrate found the complaint proved and made an order. The husband appealed. At the hearing of the appeal further evidence was received from an expert witness in Islamic law and custom, which established that Muslim marriages are potentially polygamous. It was held:

(i) that the only kind of marriage that entitled the parties thereto to the remedies, adjudication and relief of the matrimonial law of England upon which the Trinidad and Tobago general law relating to marriage is based, is a marriage that is monogamous in the Christian sense of the term, and
(ii) that a Muslim marriage not being monogamous in the Christian sense of the term, the magistrate had no jurisdiction to make an order for maintenance in this case.

Gomes, C.J. in the course of the judgment made this comment:

> *It is a well-established principle of law that the only kind of marriage that entitled the parties thereto to the remedies, adjudication or*

relief of the matrimonial law of England (which is the basis of our general law relating to marriage) is a marriage that is monogamous in the Christian sense of the term.

He went on to refer to the oft-quoted dictum of *Lord Penzance* in the case of *Hyde v. Hyde*[7] to the effect that marriage as understood in Christendom was defined as the voluntary union for life of one man and one woman to the exclusion of all others.

The decision turned mainly on the wording of the Muslim Marriage and Divorce Registration Ordinance which provided for the registration of Muslim marriages and divorces, but did not stipulate (unlike the Hindu Marriage Ordinance) that a marriage solemnised between persons professing the Muslim faith shall be valid as if it had been solemnised in conformity with the provisions of the Marriage Ordinance which related to marriages between persons of the Christian religion.

It must have seemed incredible to nationals of a country whose marriage had been registered in accordance with the law to discover that that marriage was regarded as polygamous and not recognised because it did not conform with the Christian and English concept of marriage and was "repugnant to local matrimonial law" (a quotation of Counsel for the appellant).

A court of similar jurisdiction in Trinidad and Tobago in the later case of *Mohamed v. Mohamed*[8] did not depart from this position where on an application by a wife of a marriage registered under the same Muslim Marriage and Divorce Registration Ordinance for an order against her husband for maintenance for the children of the said marriage, it was held that even though, as for herself, the wife is not entitled to the remedies, adjudication and relief afforded by the matrimonial law applicable to monogamous unions in the Christian sense of the term, she nevertheless enjoyed a legally married status by the laws of Trinidad and Tobago, and the legitimation of the children of her marriage by statute had the effect of clothing her with the status of a mother within the meaning of the Infants Ordinance.

The anomaly thus created had the effect of denying a wife married under the Muslim faith the right to sue her husband for maintenance for herself not being regarded as a married woman within the meaning of such a term according to the English concept of marriage, but permitting her to sue her husband for maintenance for their children who were regarded as legitimate under the same Muslim Marriage and Divorce Registration Ordinance.

Thus was the impact of the English common law on Caribbean society, and a clear example of discrimination against a section of people born within our Region and entitled to the protection of our laws. Of course, we must be mindful of the fact that these cases were decided during colonial times and in the pre-Independence era of the Caribbean, and may have been decided differently now with legislation which would have sought to correct the anomaly.

In most of the Caribbean territories English matrimonial law was applied, and the grounds for the dissolution of a marriage were the same as those in England with the exception of Guyana where there exists the Roman-Dutch concept of malicious desertion which is desertion proceeding *ex malitia*, i.e., from design or pre-meditated determination. The *ratio decidendi* in the case of *Siebs v. Siebs*[9] indicates the influence of the concepts of English law on a Roman-Dutch concept when the Court of Appeal held that there was no difference in the state of mind required to found malicious desertion and that of the English doctrine of constructive desertion. *Persaud, J.A.* in the course of his judgment made this comment:

> *For my part, I can find no difference between the state of mind required to found malicious desertion and that which must exist in the spouse whose conduct leads the other spouse to depart from the matrimonial home. The object is the same; the mode of achieving that object is different.*

Guyana still remains the only country in the Region which has retained this peculiar concept of malicious desertion, and is at present no more than a nomenclature for the concept of desertion. In the very near future it may fade into history when the sole ground for dissolution of a marriage will be its irretrievable breakdown based on a separation for a specified period.

(A) Law of Movable and Immovable Property

As mentioned earlier the Civil Law of Guyana Act, Cap. 6:01[10] sought to codify certain portions of the Roman-Dutch Law in relation to immovable property. Section 3(c) expressly provided that the English common law of real property shall not apply to immovable property in Guyana and Section 3(d) is to this effect:

> There shall be as heretofore one common law for both immovable and movable property, and all questions relating to immovable property within Guyana and to movable property subject to the law of Guyana shall be adjudged, determined, construed and enforced, as far as possible, according to the principles of the common law of England applicable to personal property: with certain provisos.

The effect of this was that all English principles concerning personalty were now to be applied to immovable and movable property alike in Guyana. This came up for consideration before the Court of Appeal in the case of *Lambert v. Caldeira*[11] particularly in the judgment of *Crane, J.*, as he then was, who held that in relation to a registered deed of gift of immovable property executed by a donor who bound herself "to hold the same unto and to the use of the donee in fee simple and absolutely and beneficially free from any resulting trust in favour of the grantor", in view of the provisions of the Civil Law Ordinance, Cap. 2 (as it then was), it appeared that the general rule in the transfer of chattels was relevant to the situation, and if the deed was valid and enforceable, then the property would be in the nature of an *inter vivos* donation of movable property that had been duly executed, proved and filed as of record.

The concept of the "chattel house" unknown to English law is a peculiar phenomenon of Caribbean society and most territories have given it statutory recognition. Under Section 2 of the Summary Ejectment Ordinance, Cap. 27, No. 17 of Trinidad and Tobago as quoted by *Fraser, J.* in the case of *Mitchell v. Forde & Cowie*[12] "premises" means "lands, houses or other corporeal hereditaments, and includes chattel or movable houses". The learned judge stated in his judgment that "the manner of its statutory insertion indicates that the chattel house had become a part of the common law of Trinidad and Tobago, [and] it seems appropriate, therefore, to apply the principles developed by the courts in England to this locally important, if novel, off-shoot in the law of real property". He held in that case, *inter alia,* that the house (the subject matter of the dispute) was a type of fixture which attracted a relaxation of the general rule as to annexation of chattels to the soil and was consequently removable as a tenant's fixture at the end of or during the term of the tenancy.

At page 414 he made this comment:

> *It is this right to remove which can be sold or assigned. The article itself cannot be sold. What I have stated are the incidents peculiar to fixtures in England, and in the absence of any evidence of local custom or of restraining judicial authority I feel myself constrained by the provisions of S. 5 of the Landlord and Tenant Ordinance (T) to apply them to fixtures in Trinidad and Tobago. I therefore construe the legal interest in a tenant's fixture in Trinidad & Tobago to be a combination of a power to remove the fixture at the end of the term coupled with an interest in a tenancy of the land.*

He also expressed the view that the concept of the chattel house having become a part of the legal system of Trinidad and Tobago, and the extent to which it is used fully justified statutory treatment as a distinct entity.

With regard to fixtures annexed to land demised by a tenant legislation in territories of the Region followed the laws of England, e.g. Section 5 of the Landlord and Tenant Ordinance, Cap. 27, No. 16 of Trinidad and Tobago (*supra*) provided that:

> whenever any question shall arise touching the right of the lessee or tenant of any land to remove any fixtures annexed or affixed to the land demised during the continuance of the lease, or touching the liabilities of any lessee, his heirs, successors, etc. every such question shall be determined according to the law of England.

Under English law a tenant's fixtures annexed or affixed to the land became part of the land demised, and was removable at the end of the term only if it had been affixed for the purpose of trade, the general rule being that whatever is annexed to the realty became part of it – *quicquid solo plantatur, solo cedit* – a maxim and doctrine derived from Roman law.

Some territories of the Region, however, enacted legislation abolishing this doctrine, e.g. in Guyana, Section 15 of the Landlord and Tenant Act, passed in 1947 provided that the doctrine of the common law (*quicquid solo plantatur, solo cedit*) shall have no application to tenant's fixtures of any kind, and all such fixtures affixed to a tenement by a tenant and any building erected by him thereon shall be his property and be removable by him before or after the termination of the tenancy.

The doctrine was also abolished in Barbados under Section 163(1) of the Property Act, 1979 which provides as follows:

> Any chattel, engine, machinery, fencing or other fixture, or any building, erected on or affixed to the demised premises by the lessee at his sole expense, for any purpose of residence, trade, manufacture or agriculture, or for ornament or for the domestic convenience of the lessee in the occupation of the demised premises, but not so erected or affixed in accordance with any obligation or in violation of any agreement in that behalf, may be removed by the lessee at any time during the continuance of the lease.

Trinidad and Tobago retained the doctrine under Section 5 of the Landlord and Tenant Act, Cap. 27, No. 16 passed on 2nd March, 1846 and as set out earlier. This may have been changed in a Landlord and Tenant Act of 1981, but it could not have been ascertained at the time of preparation of this presentation.

I am reliably informed that St. Lucia has also expressly retained the doctrine under Article 369 of the Civil Code which stipulates that "ownership of the soil carries with it ownership of what is above and what is below it".

(c) Doctrine of Unjust Enrichment

I pass now to a doctrine in the English common law over which opinions are divided, and in fact *Lord Porter* in the English case of *Reading v. Attorney General*[13] expressed the firm view that the law of unjust enrichment formed no part of the law of England. Our legal systems based as they are on the English legal system, and the Common Law of England being the Common Law of our territories, have *ipso facto*, adopted a similar position.

The doctrine of unjust enrichment came up for consideration before the Court of Appeal of Guyana in 1970 in the case of *Peter Persaud and others v. Pln. Versailles & Schoon Ord. Ltd.*,[14] and as happened in England there were divergent views. *Cummings, J.A.* expressed grave doubt as to whether the law of unjust enrichment is part of the law of Guyana, and *Crane, J.A.* (as he then was) felt that there was no impediment to the application of the doctrine as the jurisdiction of the High Court of Guyana is not fettered from itself developing and expanding the common law with the aid of the principles of equity in fitting cases. *Bollers, C.J.* shared his view and he made this comment at page 118 of the judgment:

> *It is clear that controversy exists amongst the Judges in England as to whether the principle of unjust benefit or unjust enrichment exists in the English law or not, and whether this principle which was derived from the genius of Lord Mansfield, as set forth by him in the case of Moses v. Macferlan [1760] 97 E.R. 676, should find its place in English jurisprudence. But whether this is so or not, as I said on another occasion, as this country has now achieved the status of complete independence, we judges will no longer consider ourselves hidebound by English decisions, but with mature judgment in appropriate cases will strike out on our own and mould the common law to suit the needs of our ever-changing society.*

This case concerned the deductions from their wages of amounts due by employees, the appellants, for food and drink consumed by them as members of a staff club, and payment for which they had authorised their employers, the respondents, to deduct from their wages. The club was later closed, but the employers continued to make the deductions for outstanding amounts due by the employees to creditors of the club. The appellants launched proceedings to recover the amounts thereby deducted. *Crane, J.A.* in the course of his judgment at page 130 had this to say:

> *Underlying the law of restitution is the conception that no one should unjustly enrich himself at the expense of his neighbour. As I see it, I must march with those in the vanguard of progress and try to develop the law by means of the application of equitable remedies in the dualism of common law and equity which is sanctioned by and built into our legal system – see S. 3 (B) of the Civil Law of Guyana Ord. Cap. 2.*

I hope that I shall be pardoned for setting out a bit extensively portions of the judgments in this case, but they illustrate far more graphically than I can the desirability of our courts to be less influenced by the pronouncements and decisions of the courts of England.

One can never over-emphasise the urgency for the courts of our Region to develop a jurisprudence of our own by modifying or expanding the common law to meet local situations and the justice of a particular case.

(d) Criminal Law

As in the civil jurisdiction of our courts the influence of the English law and precedent has been no less pervasive in the criminal law. We inherited all of the offences, defences, and the jury system. We have been throughout the years guided by their decisions, e.g. Section 3 of the Criminal Law (Offences) Act, Cap. 8:01 of Guyana[15] first passed in 1894 provides as follows:

> *Subject to the provisions of this Act and of any other statute for the time being in force all the rules and principles of the common law relating to indictable offences and other criminal matters shall, as far as they are applicable to the circumstances of Guyana, be in force therein.*

Section 16 of the Criminal Law (Procedure) Act, Cap. 10:02[16] also first passed in 1894 in like manner provided that the practice and procedure in criminal causes and matters shall be the same as that in the High Court of Justice and the courts of assize and of gaol delivery in England. However, within recent times in England most criminal offences have become statutory offences differing in some respects from ours and sometimes not relevant to our behavioural patterns. There may be occasions when we find ourselves unable to follow judgments of the English courts which we feel were wrongly decided. This view was expressed by *Haynes, J.A.* as he then was, sitting as a member of the Court of Appeal of Guyana in the case of *The State v. Sookraj Evans*[17] where he held that the Guyana Court of Appeal should act on the principle that although for obvious reasons it will be predisposed to accept and normally will accept a judgment of the House of Lords on a point of English common law as correct and as our law, it has jurisdictional freedom and a constitutional judicial duty to hold differently if the Court is convinced fully on just grounds that the principle or rule laid down in it or the declaration of what is not the common law, is misconceived and wrong.

This case involved circumstantial evidence, and *Haynes, J.A.* discussed extensively the correctness of the decision of the House of Lords in the English case of *Mc Greevy v. D.P.P.*[18] that there is not and never was legal requirement for a special direction to be given by a trial judge, and the House of Lords was not prepared to make a new rule to that effect. He queried whether this decision should be followed in Independent Commonwealth countries. He discussed the position of the Canadian, New Zealand and Australian courts in relation to judgments of the House of Lords and the trend of Australian courts not to follow slavishly English judgments which are patently incorrect. Within our Region, he referred to the case of *Johnson v. R.*[19] decided by the Court of Appeal of Trinidad and Tobago, and the judgment of *Wooding, C.J.* That case was one of murder, and the objective and subjective tests in relation to justifiable homicide as laid down in the English case of *D.P.P. v. Smith*[20], fell to be determined. *Wooding, C.J.* at page 415 of the judgment felt:

> *In view of the provisions of S. 3 of the Offences Against the Person Ordinance, and of S. 12 of the Supreme Court of Judicature Act which incorporates as part of our law the common law of England, and since any decision of the House of Lords must be regarded as the prevailing law and, in so far as it interprets the common law of England, we must, whatever our own view, accept its judgment in Smith as declaratory of the law here.*

In *D.P.P. v. Smith* (*supra*) *Lord Kilmuir* had laid down the objective test, but in spite of the above opinion expressed by *Wooding, C.J.* the Court of Appeal of Trinidad and Tobago in fact advised trial judges in that territory to direct on the subjective test, and expressed the view that the objective test may be an aid and no more, indicating that unless there is nothing to the contrary to be found in the evidence, it should never be wholly decisive.

I now return to *Haynes, J. A.* in *The State v. Sookraj Evans (supra)* who made this point after reviewing cases from other Commonwealth jurisdictions:

> Strictly speaking, subject to what is said below, that would be declaratory of the state of our common law when the appellant was

> put on trial. Accordingly, the failure to give this special direction to the jury then would be no misdirection. If, however, a common law rule or practice had developed differently in Guyana and it could be said that there was then a well-settled compulsory practice or rule here to give the special direction in terms or effect, this would raise the question of … the exercise of a judicial choice by this court as to whether or not *Mc Greevy* compelled a change.

The totality of all of this is that courts of the Commonwealth must feel free to develop and interpret common law principles as they seem fit having regard to local conditions and whether they consider particular decisions of the English courts wrongly decided, without being obliged to follow them because of statutory compulsion or to preserve judicial uniformity.

Three years before *The State v. Sookraj Evans (supra)* the Court of Appeal of Jamaica in the case of *R .v. Martin Wright*[21] held that the respective opinions expressed by the Judicial Committee of the Privy Council in two earlier cases concerning sentencing of accused who were under 17 years at the date of commission of the offence but over that age at date of conviction, were in conflict and could not be reconciled and, further, the opinion given in relation to one of the cases was given *per incuriam* and did not, therefore bind the court.

(e) Administration of Oaths to Witnesses

Oaths taken by witnesses have throughout the history of the English common law followed prescribed forms, and have been administered in conformity with Christian principles. There have been, however, cases decided in the English courts where witnesses have been permitted to swear to oaths in accordance with what is binding on their conscience (see *Omychund v. Barker*[22]).

In the Caribbean, our courts have followed the format of and manner in which oaths are administered in England and which are based on the Christian religion. With the advent of the Rastafarian religion in the Caribbean the Jamaican courts were called upon to determine whether the refusal of a trial judge to permit an accused to be sworn in a form which he considered binding on his conscience and which was not in the prescribed form, was wrong. It arose in the case of *R. v. Hines and King*[23] when an accused declined to be sworn in the form prescribed by S. 3 of the Oaths Law, Cap 264 of Jamaica which was identical in format with S, 2 of the Oaths Act 1909 of England, and began "I swear by Almighty God ...." His reason for refusing to be so sworn was that he professed the Rastafarian faith and would only consider himself bound by an oath in the form commencing "I swear by Almighty God, King Rastafari...." as he and other members of that faith regarded and worshipped the Emperor of Ethiopia as "the true and living God that sits on the throne of David". The trial judge refused to permit Hines to be sworn in a form other than that prescribed by S. 3 of the Oaths Law, Cap. 264 stating that as far as he knew an oath taken in the form in which Hines wished to take it was not lawful. Hines rested his case, and was convicted. On appeal, it was held that the trial judge erred in refusing to permit Hines to be sworn in a form which Hines declared to be binding on his conscience and in so doing deprived the accused of his right to give sworn testimony in his defence and his convictions therefore could not stand.

Luckhoo, J.A. in the course of his judgment made reference to S. 21(5) of the Constitution of Jamaica which reads "No person shall be compelled to take any oath which is contrary to his religion or belief or to take any oath in a manner which is contrary to his religion or belief."

S. 3 of the Oaths Law, Cap. 264 of Jamaica, however, as stated earlier was based on and was identical in content to the English Oaths Act. *Luckhoo, J.A.* remarked that as far as those statutory enactments went the position in England and Jamaica appeared to be the same, but posed the question whether the prescribed statutory form and manner for the administration and taking of an oath was compulsory or permissive. He observed that having regard to the multitude of different religious beliefs which exist in the world it is to be expected that an oath under the common law would take some of very many forms. He traced the history of the present Jamaican statutory provision based throughout on English legislation, and concluded that there is nothing in the enactments which have been traced – English or Jamaican – which would have the effect of rendering invalid an oath administered or taken in a form and manner permissible under the common law. He summed up his conclusions in relation to the appellant *Hines* in this way:

> *... However misguided one may think Hines to be in his professed belief as a member of the Rastafarian sect that the Emperor of Ethiopia*

is a Divine Being, the fact remains that such is his professed belief and indeed the professed belief of the sect to which he belongs. The form in which Hines wished to take the oath was consistent with that professed belief and declared by him to be binding on his conscience ....

This case exemplifies the impact of the English common law on local custom and religion not always negatively, but sometimes positively ensuring the development of our mores and the ethos of our own jurisprudence.

ABOLITION OF APPEALS TO THE JUDICIAL COMMITTEE OF THE PRIVY COUNCIL AND ESTABLISHMENT OF A REGIONAL COURT OF APPEAL

It is apposite at this point to consider the desirability of developing a jurisprudence peculiar to our needs, culture, traditions and regional objectives. I think it is imperative that we pause and reflect on how appropriate certain aspects of the English common law and legal systems are to our Region, and not follow the tried and beaten path of English precedent. Inextricably tied to this laudable goal is the compunction to establish our own final court of appeal. We have taken our own political, economic and social destinies into our own hands with the assumption of independent status in all but one or two of the Caribbean islands and the establishment of the Commonwealth Caribbean Community. Several years before these events we became a force to be reckoned with in the field of cricket being invincible against our former colonial masters, yet we cling tenaciously to a court thousands of miles away established in colonial times to consider and determine appeals from its colonies.

Without detracting from the excellence and soundness of the decisions handed down by the Judicial Committee of the Privy Council over time I make bold to state that it is a court whose swan song must be sung. Several of England's former colonies have severed the umbilical cord and established final courts of their own, but we in the Caribbean along with one or two other Commonwealth territories seem reluctant to leave the nest and fly with our own wings.

Our failure so far to have established our own final court demonstrates our lack of faith and confidence in our jurists and legal academics. The Region has produced a coterie of legal luminaries in the past and continues to do so –men and women who have equalled if not surpassed in some instances their English counterparts if one can judge from the quality of the decisions emanating from those courts in recent times. We must also come to terms with the fact that we may have overstayed our welcome, and our host may be relieved to have us take our leave. Who better can judge whether a chattel house on blocks in the gap in St. Lawrence, Barbados, belongs to the tenant or the owner of the land or whether a member of the Rastafarian religion in Kingston, Jamaica or Kingstown, St. Vincent, ought to swear by Jah or the Emperor of Ethiopia rather than by Jesus Christ, or the financial implications of holding a box hand in Guyana or sou-sou as it is called in Trinidad and Tobago?

This fact was highlighted by the Privy Council in the case of *John and Others v. Director of Public Prosecutions for Dominica*[24] when it held, *inter alia*, that questions of the evaluation of evidence are essentially matters for a local appellate court and are not matters upon which, generally speaking, the Judicial Committee of the Privy Council would presume to differ from that court, whatever view their Lordships might have been disposed to take had the appeal in question initially come before them.

Within recent times the political leaders of the Region have revived discussion on the establishment of a final regional court of appeal and the abolition of appeals to the Privy Council giving rise to the possibility that such a court may become a reality hopefully in the not-too-distant future. There are, however, compromises to be made and hurdles to overcome, cost being one of the main considerations as well as the location and jurisdiction. Although Guyana has long since abolished appeals to the Privy Council, and now commends the establishment of a final regional court, but without committing itself fully to participation, it is hoped that eventually all of the Caribbean territories will arrive at a consensus, however remote that possibility may seem at present. We shall have failed in our duty to ourselves and to the future generations of Caribbean people if we do not establish our own judicial institutions and develop our own jurisprudence thereby bequeathing to those yet unborn a heritage of which they can be justly proud.

JUDICIAL ACTIVISM

Within recent years the issue of human rights has become the focus of peoples everywhere, and all have been hastily climbing on the bandwagon. It has attracted international attention with the adoption and ratification of several declarations and conventions, and the creation of commissions and groups to monitor their implementation. All of these treaties guarantee non-discrimination on the grounds of race, sex, colour, religion or political beliefs, and most countries ratify them out of a sense of diplomatic duty rather than a genuine commitment to the principles embodied in the particular treaty. Invariably enforceability and implementation of all international human rights norms depend on the particular state enacting legislation making them enforceable in the courts or ensuring their nationals effective remedies for violations of their human rights enshrined in the treaties.

Much depends, however, on the willingness of the Judiciary in a particular state to give effect and meaning to these enshrined rights and freedoms. It is the responsibility of the Judiciary to interpret laws and safeguard the rights of citizens regardless of the consequences to a particular government. The time has come for judges to interpret international treaties in domestic courts in order to provide remedies for the wrongs suffered by citizens.

Apart from international treaties and human rights issues, judges also ought to give more liberal interpretations to certain aspects of the common law, and not be hidebound by earlier rigid and conservative views expressed by judges who lived in a different era. To illustrate this point I quote from a presentation of the *Rt. Hon. Sir Robin Cooke*, President of the Court of Appeal of New Zealand, entitled "The Dynamics of the Common Law":[25]

> The achievements of the common law are often instinctively and greatly overrated by those who have been nurtured in it. Certainly, clarity of principle, intellectual honesty, a confidence that in the general run of cases the basic rules will produce results – these might be thought to be prime goals of any worthwhile and mature legal system. Yet one has only to look at some of the most elementary and every day subjects of the common law to find that they are not attained.

> The consequence is that the general character of the common law is very much what each hierarchy of national Courts, and each generation of Judges and Practitioners therein, make it. As already suggested, a common perception of the current English Judicial mood is that it is unadventurous.

Within recent times, however, judicial developments have been moving apace. There has been in England frequent Mareva injunctions and Anton Piller orders, powers of search conferred on officers of the Inland Revenue Administration to combat a rise in tax frauds, the claim of investigative journalists to confidentiality of their sources, computer frauds and the new body of law which must inevitably build up around cases brought by victims of HIV/AIDS against those who infected them. Judges have to prepare themselves in the next century to deal with these new and modernistic problems, and to depart from the old restrictive interpretations of the common law. They have to strike out and blaze new trails in dealing with new issues in a changing world.

The issues that affect us most in the Caribbean are the increasing incidence of drug use and abuse and the insidious rise in the number of HIV/AIDS cases. Are we prepared to deal with the legal aspects of these problems? Are heavy custodial sentences the answer to the drug problem? Should we consider rehabilitation rather than punishment? As far as I am aware we have not had to confront the HIV/AIDS issue in our courts as yet, but are we prepared for it when it does surface? We have to begin to confront these issues and find solutions for them as well as the myriad human rights abuses which occur daily in our individual societies.

CONCLUSION

Whatever the shortcomings and deficiencies of the common law it was an invaluable legacy inherited by Britain's former colonies, and has been a unifying force among countries that share the same legal system. Its influence may be waning even in the motherland that gave it birth as time and again it has yielded to statute which threatens to obliterate it completely. English law is fast becoming codified as the legislature seeks the medium of a statute to correct defects which surface in the common law and to provide remedies where none existed before.

The influence of Britain on her former colonies is strong, and despite their independent status many countries of the Commonwealth very often follow *verbatim* the wording of English statutes in drafting their own. In spite of and maybe because of the varied mosaic of cultures, traditions and customs of the countries which share the same history of English colonialism, the common law and the body of precedent built up around it has been enriched in its development, and made strong and dynamic. May it always remain so even in a world which is changing rapidly and moving inexorably into a new century.

Tortola, British Virgin Islands,
September, 1991

Endnotes

1 Blackstone's Commentaries I.
2 First Book of Jurisprudence by Sir Frederick Pollock.
3 Laws of Guyana, Vol. II.
4 (1971) 16 WIR, 255.
5 Laws of Guyana, Vol. II.
6 (1959) 1 WIR, 149.
7 [1866] L.R. 1 P & D, 133.
8 (1960) 3 WIR, 202.
9 (1969) 14 WIR, 72.
10 Laws of Guyana, Vol. II.
11 (1970) 18 WIR, 15.
12 (1963) 5 WIR, 409.
13 [1951] 1 AER, 617.
14 (1970) 17 WIR, 107.
15 Laws of Guyana, Vol. II.
16 Laws of Guyana, Vol. II.
17 (1975) 23 WIR, 189.
18 [1973] 1 AER, 503.
19 (1966) 10 WIR, 402.
20 [1961] A.C., 290.
21 (1972) 18 WIR, 302.
22 [1744] 1 Atk, 21; 26 ER, 15.
23 (1971) 17 WIR, 326.
24 (1985) 32 WIR, 230.
25 9th Commonwealth Law Conference, Auckland, New Zealand.

CHAPTER 16

THE STATE OF THE LEGAL PROFESSION: THE WAY FORWARD

The legal profession historically has been the most maligned of all professions, and has been the butt of much criticism and witticism many of them negative, such as, "Some lawyers are just the opposite of laundrymen; they lose your suit and then take you to the cleaners", or "A lawyer is a glib-tongued fellow who defends your property from an enemy in order to save it for himself".

Be that as it may, the legal profession has endured for centuries ensuring that the rights of persons are protected and enforced, and guarding against excesses committed by or against other individuals or by or against the State.

We in the countries of the Caribbean being former colonies inherited the English legal system from the mother country Great Britain. The common law of England became the common law of the colonies, and the structure of the court system reflected in large measure the English court system without regard to relevance or suitability to local conditions. In like manner, we inherited all of the traditions of the English Bar particularly court dress – wigs (full-bottoms and all), gowns, bibs, three-piece suits of ancient vintage – and endured the discomfort of such attire in sweltering heat with pride and dignity reflective of a true English barrister. In this regard time has brought about change in some of the territories of the Caribbean particularly here in Guyana. Wigs and bibs were abolished in 1970 when we achieved Republican status, and appeals to the Privy Council went the same way. I shall comment on this in greater detail later.

COURT PROCEDURE AND NEW TECHNOLOGY

Although time has eroded some of the time-honoured English traditions we in this part of the world have still basically retained the conservatism and in some instances rigidity of the English court procedure of the recent past. I say recent past because within the last two years we have witnessed a complete overhaul of the rules of civil procedure in the United Kingdom. The objective is to make access to justice simple and uncomplicated for the average citizen unfettered by rigid rules the adherence to which sometimes works injustice to a litigant who is often hard-pressed to understand why he lost his case on a procedural point when all of the evidence dictated that he should have won.

We, however, still cling slavishly to the old rules which were lifted verbatim from the English rules nearly fifty years ago, and which in some instances are anachronistic and archaic in a world of the 21st century. The existing rules of court which govern our civil procedure were adopted in 1955 and have not been revised over the last forty-five years. A body of precedent has been built up over the years around these rules, and this is commendable. Nevertheless, the time has come for us to think seriously of revising and amending these rules as well as other relevant legislative enactments to provide for modern-day situations, e.g. the reception of photo copies, facsimiles, computer printouts, and whenever it comes to Guyana, DNA evidence.

I note that one of the issues targeted for discussion at this Conference is improvement to the Evidence Act and the use of technology in the recording of court proceedings. This is in keeping with what I just mentioned. Members of the public are often dismayed to learn that a judge and magistrate still record all evidence in manuscript which is laborious and time-consuming. Our court records too are still handwritten and held together by paper clips which leads inevitably to pleadings being misplaced or misfiled. It is time that the Supreme Court Registry be computerised so that records of cases and their status and location can be readily ascertained. Every judge should have at his/her disposal a computer terminal to assist in legal research and to be kept informed about recent developments in all aspects of the law as well as facilitate the speedy preparation of rulings and decisions. We need to move swiftly from the 20th into the 21st century as we are lagging far behind our counterparts in the Caribbean not to mention the rest of the western world.

LAW REPORTING

Collaterally, action must be directed at bringing our law reports from way back in the last quarter of the last century into the new century.

It is nothing short of disgraceful that the last published report is 1975, and for this we must be grateful to former Chancellor Bishop and his team of young editors together with financial assistance from the Lions and Rotary Clubs. This is by no means an easy task which requires commitment, dedication and finance. In spite of the enormity of the task efforts must be made and resources identified to continue the exercise. The legal profession must be responsible for publishing reports of cases decided in our courts. We owe it not only to ourselves but also to students and young practitioners who are entering the profession in large numbers every year, and who need guidance and every assistance if they are to make a contribution to the development of our own jurisprudence. This is a challenge which I now throw out to your association, and which I hope will be taken up.

INDEPENDENCE OF THE JUDICIARY

One of the topics slated for discussion later this morning is "The Independence of the Judiciary". This is a phrase which has been bandied about frequently, and lip service paid to it by judges and governments everywhere. The acceptable understanding of judicial independence is that a judge must be free from pressures, real or perceived, in arriving at decisions made according to law regardless of the identity of the litigants. The learned judge must operate in an environment which conduces to the dispensation of justice without fear or favour, affection or ill-will consistent with the oath taken upon appointment.

Judicial independence is fragile and can be easily destroyed or compromised. Therefore, no effort must be spared to preserve and cherish it. With this as one of its primary objectives from 15th to 19th June, 1998 legal personnel from the Commonwealth and invited by the Commonwealth Parliamentary Association, the Commonwealth Magistrates' and Judges' Association, the Commonwealth Lawyers' Association and the Commonwealth Legal Education Association, met at Latimer House in the United Kingdom where they hammered out and adopted what has come to be known as the Latimer House Guidelines. These Guidelines cover such topics as Parliament and the Judiciary, Preserving Judicial Independence, Preserving the Independence of Parliamentarians, Women in Parliament, Judicial and Parliamentary Ethics and Accountability Mechanisms among others. I shall focus solely on the guidelines on Preserving Judicial

Independence as this is pertinent to the topic which you will be discussing later this morning.

Under this subject Judicial Autonomy, Funding and Training are discussed. The recommendations under Judicial Autonomy include provisions for judicial appointments to be made on merit by a judicial services commission, such appointments to be normally permanent; the judicial services commission should be established by the Constitution or by statute with a majority of members drawn from the senior Judiciary; appointments to all levels of the Judiciary should have, as an objective, the achievement of equality between women and men; judicial vacancies should be advertised; recommendations for appointment should come from the commission.

In relation to Funding the Guidelines recommend that sufficient funding be provided to enable the Judiciary to perform its functions to the highest standards as appropriate salaries, supporting staff, resources and equipment are essential to the proper functioning of the Judiciary; further, as a matter of principle, judicial salaries and benefits should be set by an independent commission and should be maintained; also the administration of monies allocated to the Judiciary should be under the control of the Judiciary.

On the issue of Training a culture of judicial education should be developed. Training should be organised, systematic and ongoing and under the control of an adequately funded judicial body; also, courses in judicial education should be offered to practising lawyers as part of their ongoing professional development training.

On Judicial Ethics it is recommended that a Code of Ethics and Conduct be developed and adopted by the Judiciary as a means of ensuring the accountability of judges. This accountability is dealt with under two heads – discipline and public criticism. With regard to discipline it was felt that in cases where a judge is at risk of removal, the judge must have the right to be fully informed of the charges, to be represented at a hearing, to make a full defence, and to be judged by an independent and impartial tribunal. Grounds for removal of a judge should be limited to inability to perform judicial duties and serious misconduct; in all other matters the process should be conducted by the chief judge of the courts. A further recommendation which sparked some in-depth discussion at a meeting of Chief Justices during the Commonwealth Magistrates' and Judges' Association Conference held in Edinburgh, Scotland, in September 2000, was that disciplinary procedures should not include the public admonition of judges, and any admonition should be delivered in private by the chief judge. There were views for and against private admonition, and I daresay that it will continue to be on such a sensitive issue.

This is also tied to the question of public criticism of the Judiciary. The Guidelines proffer that legitimate public criticism of judicial performance is a means of ensuring accountability, and that the criminal law and contempt proceedings are not appropriate mechanisms for restricting legitimate criticism of the courts. We live in an age where accountability is expected from persons who hold public office, and many feel that the Judiciary ought not to be exempted, and should not utilise the weapon of contempt of court or threat of criminal prosecution for perceived disrespect of judicial office. David Pannick, Q.C. of the English Bar, in his book titled "Judges" under the Chapter where he discussed Criticism, illustrated this change of approach by the following story:

> In 1527 Serjeant Roo, a great lawyer of that time, more eager to show his wit than to be made a judge, composed a satire on the abuses of the law for which Lord Chancellor Wolsey was responsible. The satire was delivered in the presence of the King. Roo was summarily dispatched to prison. Nowadays a more tolerant attitude is taken towards critics of the Judiciary. Nevertheless, lawyers and non-lawyers remain reluctant to emulate the critical approach of Serjeant Roo.

David Pannick also made the point that although criticising judges out of court may now be less dangerous, contempt of court still has its penalties for those who are unable to control their emotions in court. This, however, is not a lecture on contempt of court so I shall not comment any further.

In relation to Executive Accountability the Latimer House Guidelines make reference to the process of judicial review and recommended that Commonwealth governments endorse and implement the principles of judicial review enshrined in the Lusaka Statement on Government under the Law. Most countries in the Commonwealth are moving towards implementing judicial review, and the Caribbean is no exception. This is discussed by Professor Albert Fiadjoe in his book "Commonwealth Caribbean Public Law", and we have the pleasure of having him here with us today. I shall leave further discussion on this topic in his capable hands when he addresses this Conference later.

My final comment on the Latimer House Guidelines is that they are just that – Guidelines. They have not as yet been adopted by the Heads of Government of the Commonwealth, and at the end of the meeting at Latimer House it was decided that they should be forwarded to the Commonwealth Secretariat for consideration by the Law Ministers and Heads of Government. It was also decided that if they are adopted an effective monitoring procedure should be devised, e.g. a Standing Committee under which all Commonwealth jurisdictions accept an obligation to report on their compliance with the Guidelines. The Guidelines were unanimously endorsed by Chief Justices of the Commonwealth who attended the CMJA Conference in September 2000 in Edinburgh, Scotland.

CARIBBEAN COURT OF JUSTICE

In relation to the Caribbean Court of Justice for the past twenty-five years an ongoing debate has taken place throughout the territories of the Caribbean about the desirability of establishing a final court of appeal within the Region. Of necessity hand in hand with this has been discussion on the wisdom of abolishing appeals to the Judicial Committee of the Privy Council. On a personal note, I have been involved in these debates and discussions with lawyers in the Region when I had the honour of being President of OCCBA (the Organisation of Commonwealth Caribbean Bar Associations) some years ago. For this length of time we have argued, disagreed and debated the pros and cons of the establishment of a final court, and, sad to say, we are no closer to achieving this dream than we were twenty-five years ago. During these years, several states in the Caribbean have achieved political independence from the Mother country with their own flags and national anthems, but still cling tenaciously to a court thousands of miles away which was established in colonial times to hear and determine appeals from the colonies of the British Empire. The territories of the Caribbean have taken their destinies into their own hands in every aspect of life except in the establishment of a final appellate court about which many have doubts, preferring to retain a court far removed from the place where the tort or crime was committed. One is forced to pose the question – who better can judge whether a chattel house on blocks in the gap in St. Lawrence, Barbados, belongs to the tenant or the owner of the land, or whether a member of the Rastafarian religion in Kingston, Jamaica, or Kingstown, St. Vincent, ought to swear by Jah or the Emperor of Ethiopia rather than by Jesus Christ or the financial implications of a box hand in Guyana or sou-sou as it is called in Trinidad and Tobago?

The fundamental problem in achieving a consensus on the establishment of a final appellate court in the Region seems to me to be doubts that those responsible for its establishment will be able to attract persons with the requisite judicial competence and ability who can deliver judgments of the same quality and standard of those delivered by members of the Board of the Judicial Committee of the Privy Council. There is also grave doubt about the independence of the court, and fears that Governments of the Region will seek to compromise that independence or influence the appointments of persons to the court.

In life there are never absolute guarantees; much, if not everything, rests on the integrity of the persons who hold positions of eminence. It is a sad indictment of our Region that it is felt that we cannot identify persons of high moral character and legal scholarship to adjudicate and deliver justice to our own people. It also indicates basic distrust of our leaders maybe born of experience, but if we are to move forward and control all aspects of our development we must make the first step. The task of establishing a Caribbean Court of Justice is fraught with difficulties, not the least of which is finance. Ways and means, however, must be found to make the Court a reality. Let us hope that it does not take another twenty-five years to achieve this dream and sever the ties which still bind us to our colonial past. We are a collection of fledgling nations with a very short history of independence. Of necessity mistakes will be made, maybe very grave ones with far-reaching effects, but it is only out of these mistakes that we can build a strong court and develop a jurisprudence which is truly ours. It is an immense challenge, but the longest journey begins with the first step, and we must be bold and courageous to take that step.

HUMAN RIGHTS

My brief comment on the subject of human rights is that all treaties and conventions ratified and acceded to by our Government must be incorporated into our Constitution and made justiciable in our courts. At present these human rights treaties depend on the passage of domestic legislation consistent with the articles of the treaties for enforceability, e.g. the Convention on the Elimination of All Forms of Discrimination Against Women or the Covenant on Civil and Political Rights are not enforceable in our courts *per se* even though the articles of these treaties may be reflected in legislative provisions.

I note that another burning issue to be discussed over the next two days is Police Violence, and this falls under the topic of human rights. Within recent times there have been repeated allegations of police brutality, and some way must be found to bridge the ever-widening gap between the police and citizens with the police arraigned against the very public which they are expected to protect. It is hoped that this stand-off will be resolved by dialogue instead of confrontation.

GENDER BIAS IN THE LAW

Having inherited the English common law and laws we also inherited all of its discriminatory practices and gender stereotypes, e.g. the old concept of a wife pledging her husband's credit for necessaries or a husband maintaining an action for interference with his consortium. Although these concepts are no longer with us we now live in an age of increasing violence against women. This is of particular relevance at the moment as we observe United Nations Day Against Violence Against Women. I make mention of this in the context of women who are frequently charged with murder of their male partners following prolonged physical abuse which cannot be raised as a defence at their trial. A woman in this situation can only raise the usual defence of self-defence if it arises and she can satisfy a court that she did act in self-defence. Women throughout the world have raised their voices against this denial of justice which has resulted in some countries admitting evidence of what is called "battered woman's syndrome".

I am mindful of the fact that this is not a gathering which is exclusively female, and I am not here to advocate the rights of women. I am sure that you will hear much more of this topic in the presentation of Ms. Tracy Robinson, an attorney from Jamaica. Nevertheless cognisant of the fact that this is not a profession exclusively for men it behoves us all to address the scourge of violence in our midst particularly directed at women, and find solutions for the myriad problems which confront us as a result of it.

CONCLUSION

I wish to congratulate the Guyana Bar Association for organising this Conference which is timely and absolutely necessary particularly for our young attorneys. The wide-ranging agenda is impressive and provides an opportunity to discuss and debate issues of concern to both Bench and Bar as well as the public at large. I wish you a very stimulating and productive Conference, and I am sure that the deliberations and resulting conclusions emanating therefrom will enure to the benefit of all who are involved in the administration of justice in Guyana. The theme of the Conference indicates the forward thrust of your Association, and the commitment to confront new challenges as we enter a new century.

I shall end as I began with a touch of humour:

> Two attorneys were having a conference trying to negotiate a settlement in a case. After getting nowhere one said to the other, "Look, let us be honest with each other". "Okay, you first", replied the other. And that was the end of the discussion.

And this also is the end of my address. Best wishes for a successful Conference.

Guyana Bar Association Conference
25th November, 2000

CHAPTER 17

LAW IN A CHANGING SOCIETY

Today must, in the minds of all of you, rank as the most important and memorable day of your lives. You are embarking on a voyage of discovery and a new beginning. You are now qualified professionals. You have seen the culmination of your dreams and aspirations. You have made the transition from student to lawyer and advocate. The long and tiring years of study and sacrifice have ended, you have won the prize. You have earned the right to be called an "attorney-at-law". You, your parents, guardians, spouses and other relatives are justifiably proud.

However, in the midst of the euphoria which surrounds this moment is the reality that you are about to enter a highly competitive profession where your skills and talents will be sorely tested, where you will soon discover that the ideals of student life are a far cry from the realities of practice at the Bar. You will learn that sometimes even though the law may favour your client he/she may yet lose because of poor advocacy or false testimony of a witness. You will find that some of your colleagues have perfected the art of theatrics to distract or win sympathy for a client or to change the direction in which the case is proceeding. Alan Dershowitz, a well-known American defence attorney, in his book "Reversal of Fortune", related how his son, a professional magician, regarded his father's exploits in Court – "You and I both do the same thing – sleight of hand – making things appear to be what they're not".

Having attempted to prepare you for the realities of life as a practitioner and having pricked your bubble of idealism, I have to assure you that you are on the threshold of the most exciting adventure in your lives and entering the noblest and most self-satisfying profession of all – the practice of law. This inevitably leads me to ask what is the purpose of law? Some may define it as the preservation of a stable environment governed by rules enacted for the protection of citizens of a State with sanctions imposed for breach of these rules. Law has also been defined as rules laid down for the guidance of persons by persons having power over them.

Whatever the definition the law reflects the values and mores of a society. It should also reflect the evolving dynamic changes and expectations of the people for whom it was established. Sad to say, in many instances the law does not always keep step with society, particularly in a fast-moving, ever-changing world. Oft times it is difficult to balance this need for change with the desirability for stability and certainty in the law around which a large body of precedent is built. Cases are decided every day in our courts on various aspects of the law. In these cases, earlier decisions on a particular point are often cited as authorities in support of Counsel's contentions. This is based largely on a presumption that if a court had interpreted the law in a particular way on facts and circumstances similar to the matter in hand, then a later court ought to follow the precedent and decide similarly. Persons who come before our courts must expect their cases to be decided in a certain way, and this certainty in the law is expected and taken for granted; if the doctrine of "*stare decisis*" was not applied there would be chaos and confusion. The outcome of a case would depend on the whims and caprices of the particular judge hearing it.

Having said this one very often has to breathe new life into the law, and not be hide bound by precedent which results in rigidity and suffocation of initiative in doing justice between citizen and citizen and citizen and the State. That great jurist of revered memory, *Lord Denning*, well known for his dissenting judgments, in his book, "*The Discipline of Law*", expressed the view that some lawyers may interpret the doctrine of "*stare decisis*" to mean "Stand by your decisions and the decisions of your predecessors, however wrong they are and whatever injustice they inflict." In dissenting from this view, he had this to say:

> I take leave to point out that, so interpreted, the doctrine of precedent does nothing to broaden the basis of freedom, rather to narrow it. If lawyers hold to their precedents too closely, forgetful of the fundamental principles of truth and justice which they should serve, they may find the whole edifice comes tumbling down about them.

Of course, the binding nature of the doctrine of precedent depends on the relative status of the courts concerned. Decisions of higher courts are binding on lower courts, and hitherto higher courts were also bound by their own decisions. In England, the case most often cited as having finally established that the House of Lords was bound by its past decisions is *London Tramways v London County Council* [1898] A.C., 375, although it was virtually settled in 1861 in *Beamish v Beamish* 9HLC, 274. This continued to be the position until 1966 when a Practice Statement was issued in which the learned Law Lords recognised that "too rigid adherence to precedent may lead to injustice in a particular case and also unduly restrict the proper development of the law." They modified the existing practice, and reserved the right to depart from a previous decision whenever it appeared right to do so.

Of more relevance to us in this part of the world is the fact that the Judicial Committee of the Privy Council has never felt itself bound by its own decisions as was decided as far back as 1892 in *Read v Bishop of Lincoln* [1892] A.C.,644, and in 1950 in *Gideon Nkambule v The King of Swaziland* [1950] UKPC.

Even within the same jurisdiction some courts have held that they are not bound by their previous decisions, e.g. *The Bengal Immunity Co. Ltd. v The State of Bihar, 2SCR, 603* held that there was nothing in the Constitution of India which prevented the Supreme Court from departing from a previous decision of its own if the court was satisfied of its error and its baneful effect on the general interests of the public.

Within our jurisdictions of the Caribbean there are cases where our courts have departed from the doctrine of "*stare decisis*". In 1964 the Court of Appeal of Jamaica in *Hanover Agencies Ltd. v Income Tax Commissioner* (1964)7WIR,300, did not consider itself bound by a decision of the former Court of Appeal. The Court of Appeal of Guyana in a criminal case of *The State v Oswald Gobin and Boniface Griffith* (1976)23WIR,256, held that the principle underlying "*stare decisis*" in the Court of Appeal is not the same for criminal as for civil cases, and in criminal cases it is less rigid; jurisdiction of the court to overrule previously decided cases is a continuing one, and the court will exercise judicial review whenever there is to be determined "some broad issue of justice, public policy or question of legal principle". In a criminal cause or matter which is plainly wrong and manifestly unjust the court will overrule it without hesitation.

That same court earlier in a civil case of *Glen v Sampson* (1972)19WIR,237 held that it had jurisdiction to overrule former judgments of the British Caribbean Court of Appeal, and to refuse to follow those of the Privy Council. More specifically in the same year in *Walter Seepersaud v Port Mourant Ltd.* (1972)19WIR,393, the same Court held that where the court has given a previous decision which it is satisfied was wrong, it is the court's duty to depart from that decision when it appears right to do so.

These are just a few examples of courts not being rigidly bound to former precedents which later courts found to be palpably wrong or unjust only for the sake of stability and certainty.

Evolutionary changes have taken place in several aspects of the law within the last quarter of a century. In the field of intestate succession in most jurisdictions in the Region children born out of wedlock can now share equally in the estate of a deceased father with children born within wedlock. The distinction between legitimate and illegitimate children has been removed, and the word "bastard" has been expunged from the statute books. This is indeed a major change from the accepted earlier position when a child born out of wedlock was regarded as less than normal, and was discriminated against in every sphere of life. How humiliating and degrading particularly when that child was not responsible for the nature of his/her birth. Society's approach to such children has certainly undergone a metamorphosis in the same way as society's acceptance of single motherhood.

An example of progressive trends in society leaving the law behind is the archaic provision of a wife pledging her husband's credit for necessaries. This is an anachronism of the distant past when wives had no independent means and were completely dependent on their husbands for financial support. Even though never utilised and abolished in most jurisdictions the provision remains on the statute books in others, e.g. in Guyana. The same can be said for the ludicrous claim for damages from a co-respondent or adulterer. Fortunately, nearly all jurisdictions have revoked these anachronistic laws in the light of changing and progressive attitudes of the modern world.

In this Region our courts have not been oblivious to the winds of change blowing through our communities, and commendably have been swift to adapt and adjust to them. In the case of *R v Hines & King* (1971)17WIR,326, the Court of Appeal of Jamaica held that a trial judge erred when he refused to permit a defendant, a Rastafarian, to be sworn in a form which he declared to be binding on his conscience but which did not conform with the prescribed Christian oath laid down by statute; by so doing the trial judge had deprived the defendant of his right to give sworn testimony in his defence, and his conviction therefore could not stand. Oaths taken by witnesses throughout the history of the English common law followed prescribed forms in conformity with Christian principles, and one of the learned justices expressed the view that however misguided one may think the defendant to be in his professed belief as a member of the Rastafarian sect that the Emperor of Ethiopia is a Divine Being, the fact remains that such is his professed belief, and the form in which he wished to take the oath was consistent with that belief and declared by him to be binding on his conscience.

Within recent years there has been a more liberal and pragmatic approach to interpretation of the law, and in England there have been revolutionary changes in civil procedure. All of the old rules to which some of us in this part of the world still cling tenaciously and hold sacrosanct have been relegated to the dung heap of history. The trend seems to be towards making courts more accessible to ordinary citizens, and also ensuring a speedier and simpler resolution of disputes. Judicial personnel now look at fairness and achieving justice rather than enforcing strict compliance with rules.

The focus of recent decisions emanating from the Privy Council seems to be on what is reasonable and just, and in this regard the State is held to account in the same way as any individual. This was illustrated by the decision in *Jennifer Gairy v Attorney General of Grenada* (P.C. Appeal No.29/2000) when *Lord Bingham of Cornhill* who delivered the judgment of the Board expressed the view that to deny the appellant the remedy sought to enforce his constitutional rights would run counter to the Board's constitutional decision-making exemplified by the cases of *Maharaj v The Attorney General of Trinidad & Tobago* (No.2)[1979]A.C. 385, *Observer Publications Ltd. v Campbell "Mickey" Matthew and Others* [2001]UKPC,11, and *The Bahamas District of the Methodist Church in the Caribbean and the Americas and Others v The Hon. Vernon J. Symonette, M.P., Speaker of the House of Assembly and 7 Others* (unreported, 26 July, 2000). It would also run counter to the trend of constitutional decision-making elsewhere.

Lord Bingham also made reference to the case of *Levesque v Attorney General of Canada et al* [1985])25DLR(4th),184 in which a serving prisoner claimed and sought to enforce a right to vote, and it was held that he had such a right. There arose the question whether an order of mandamus could issue to enforce it, and *Rouleau, J.* held that "if the Canadian Charter of Rights and Freedoms, which is part of the Constitution of Canada, is the supreme law of the country, it applies to everyone, including the Crown or a Minister.... Accordingly, *a fortiori* the Crown or one of its representatives cannot take refuge in any kind of declinatory exception or rule of immunity derived from the common law so as to avoid giving effect to the Charter."

It seems that orders of mandamus can now be made against the Crown in Canada, and the trend in other jurisdictions seems to suggest that it is regarded as being unfair and unjust for a citizen to be without a remedy where his constitutional rights have been affected by an officer of the State. These sentiments were expressed by *R.M. Sahai, J.*in the Indian case of *N. Nagendra Rao and Co. v State of A.P.,* AIR 1994 S.C.2663 and were referred to by *Lord Bingham* in *Gairy. Sahai, J* went on to say:

> ...The modern social thinking of progressive societies and the judicial approach is to do away with archaic State protection and place the State or the Government at par with any other juristic legal entity.

This is indeed revolutionary and in keeping with the modern trend of fairness pervading all common law jurisdictions; it reflects liberal and practical thinking in ensuring that justice is available to all citizens and unfettered by conservatism and rigidity.

The world around us has changed dramatically. We now live in an age where information on any subject imaginable can be accessed at the click of a button. Research is made considerably easier than it was over twenty years ago. Gone are the days when lawyers spent hours poring over heavy tomes in cluttered libraries, and decisions on important points of law were not available for several months after they were decided; now they can be obtained within hours of being handed down.

We also live in a world where crimes can be solved and paternity of children established by DNA evidence. Our laws must keep abreast with and provide for these changes. We certainly live in exciting times, and it calls for mental adjustment and acuity to cope with these changes which are swirling around us or run the risk of being left behind. You are fortunate to be entering the legal profession at this point in time, and are in a position to be in the vanguard of change. Grasp the opportunities that are offered and blaze a trail to further development.

Amidst all of the change within society which has resulted in new thinking and re-assessment of our value system, the lawyer's abiding duty to represent his client's interests to the best of his ability and within the boundaries of the law remains constant. This never changes, and is in keeping with the oath taken upon admission to practise. Clients who brief Counsel are entitled to expect to be represented in a professional manner and to rely on Counsel's loyalty to his cause. Advocacy is an indispensable tool in a lawyer's arsenal; the essential principles of advocacy include a duty to act for any client irrespective of the merits of the cause, and to speak out on your client's behalf without fear or favour.

In the course of your practice you may encounter clients who are difficult and demanding. It requires an enormous degree of patience and firmness in relating to such a client. Your obligation is to give to a client the best advice you can based on the facts of the case and the law applicable to those facts. Your advice may not always be accepted, but it is a duty you should never shirk regardless of the consequences. Clients are not always able to focus on what is at issue, and this may be a major obstacle to the successful presentation of his case. Invariably some details of a case may loom large in the opinion of the client, but may not be central to the main issue involved; on the other hand, he may overlook or omit to mention a fact seemingly unimportant to him which may tilt the balance in his favour. These are some of the hazards which may confront you in the course of your practice, and which have to be resolved. No lecture can prepare you for these, and solutions for which come only with experience.

Apart from a duty to your client there is also a duty to the court – a duty to be frank and honest in the presentation of a client's case. This includes giving to the court all help and assistance by making available all authorities pertinent to the issue to be decided including those which may be against your client, but which may assist in elucidating complex points of law.

The obligations to a client and the duty to the court are immutable and never change even in a fast-moving society where the time-honoured virtues of honesty and integrity are fast becoming distant dreams; they still hold good today and always will in spite of the rapid decline of traditional standards.

Graduates, as you bask in the sunshine of your success and dream of the financial prospects about to unfold, spare a moment to remember that the future of the Caribbean Region rests in your hands. The mantle of judicial leadership will be placed on your shoulders within the next decade or sooner. You have to be prepared and well-equipped to accept it. We are on the verge of establishing a Caribbean Court of Justice after more than twenty-five years of talking about it. There is at present very vocal opposition by many who express the view that we do not have within the Region persons of comparable ability and judicial stature to those who sit on the Judicial Committee of the Privy Council. This is regrettable, and a serious indictment against our judicial and legal personages in the Region.

Whatever shortcomings there are, and I am sure there are many, we have to complete our independence by controlling our entire legal system and administration of justice. There is a Chinese proverb to the effect that the longest journey begins with the first step. We must be bold and confident enough to take that first step. We owe it to you and to future generations. You, the graduates of 2001 must dedicate yourselves to raising standards of conduct and professionalism in whatever field of practice you engage in. We have to build confidence in our legal systems, and it has to start with you. You can do it, you must do it. Go forward confidently, and may all your efforts be crowned with success. May God bless you all as you stride bravely into your new careers in a new century.

Heartiest Congratulations and best wishes for the future!

Graduation Address
Hugh Wooding Law School
6th October, 2001

CHAPTER 18

LAUNCHING OF BOOK ENTITLED *"JUDICIAL REVIEW IN THE COMMONWEALTH CARIBBEAN"* AUTHORED BY DR. RAJENDRA RAMLOGAN

I wish to extend to Dr. Rajendra Ramlogan my heartfelt congratulations on producing another literary work – *"Judicial Review in the Commonwealth Caribbean"*, the first being *"Commonwealth Caribbean Business Law"* produced jointly with Natalie Persadie.

These literary works form part of the Commonwealth Caribbean Law Series published by Routledge-Cavendish, and include a range of subjects from Public Law, Tort, Property Law, Civil Procedure, Law and Legal Systems to Criminal Practice and Procedure by outstanding academics and legal scholars within the Caribbean Region. I am informed that collectively they are now required reading for students at the faculties of law and law schools within the Region.

Dr. Ramlogan's "Judicial Review" will, I predict, become required reading not only for law students, but also for members of the judiciary and legal practitioners, being launched at a time when judicial review constitutes a large portion of the case load of at least two countries of the Region – Guyana and Trinidad and Tobago.

Within this jurisdiction, that is, Trinidad and Tobago, such proceedings are regulated by the Judicial Review Act of 2000. Barbados, as far back as 1980 regulated judicial review by the Administrative Justice Act, and may have been the first country within the Region to do so by legislative means. Others, for example, Jamaica and the Eastern Caribbean, have made provision in their civil procedure rules for judicial review of administrative actions. Guyana, the jurisdiction with which I am most familiar, is the only one where the old English prerogative writs of certiorari, prohibition and mandamus are utilised for the review of administrative acts. It is hoped that this will soon change when the new civil procedure rules come into force in the near future.

However, whatever form is utilised whether by statute, procedural rules or the prerogative writs, the acts of public administrative bodies are frequently subject to review by the courts. Checks and balances are essential in the realm of public administration to avoid excesses which wittingly or unwittingly may be committed by those exercising authority. Judicial review ensures that the process by which a decision is arrived at is fair, open and impartial, although not being a review of the actual decision. However, if the process is flawed, it may result in the whole decision being tainted as several legal authorities have decided, and the tribunal or body will be found to have acted outside of its jurisdiction.

Dr. Ramlogan has drawn upon the rich experience of the courts within our Region with a plethora of cases from Trinidad and Tobago, Guyana, Barbados, Jamaica, the Eastern Caribbean and Belize, defining the parameters of judicial review and country perspectives on the subject with a wide range of opinions. In discussing the grounds which give rise to judicial review a reader of this legal literary work will encounter an interesting mix of cases illustrating illegality, irrationality, and procedural impropriety on the part of authorities such as the customs, immigration, medical associations, police and teaching service commissions, and even judicial officers, to name a few. Other grounds discussed include error of law and failure to adhere to the principles of natural justice.

The issue of standing, that is, the right of a person or body of persons to seek prerogative orders, underwent change when judicial review was introduced in England in 1977. A more liberal approach developed moving from someone with a sufficient interest and who is personally aggrieved to one who is adversely affected or in situations where the application is justifiable in the public interest. This is a far cry from the approach taken by the Judiciary in earlier times who were reluctant to extend the parameters of standing for fear of swamping the courts with litigation. Some at present may express the view that that fear has materialised; a perusal of the cases discussed in Dr. Ramlogan's work, however, indicates the range of interests which applicants seek to protect.

Of interest is the brief mention of the recent doctrine of proportionality, which is of European origin and seems to be creeping into English Law via the European Communities Act and the Human

Rights Act. It has been adopted by the European Court of Justice and the European Court of Human Rights; in administrative law the principle underlying it is that administrative measures must not be more drastic than or disproportionate to the mischief it is intended to cure. The doctrine has not as yet found a firm footing in English jurisprudence, but will certainly in the near future.

This was predicted as far back as 1984 when *Lord Diplock* in the case of *Council of Civil Service Unions v. Minister for the Civil Service* (1985) A.C., 374 while expatiating on his three principles of illegality, irrationality and procedural impropriety as grounds for judicial review, posited that in the course of time further grounds may be added on a case by case basis, and made reference to the possible adoption in the future of the principle of proportionality influenced by the European Economic Community.

The House of Lords in 1991 in *R v. Home Secretary, ex parte Brind* (1991) 1 AC, 696, declined to accept Counsel's invitation to apply the doctrine having regard to the circumstances of that case. Later cases, particularly after the Human Rights Act of 1998 have utilised the principle in matters of judicial review as in the case of *Ahmed Saeed Ahmet Murkarkar v. The Secretary of State for the Home Department* (2006), EWCA, concerning a Yemeni appellant who was a visitor seeking to remain indefinitely in the United Kingdom contrary to the immigration laws at a time when he became ill and wholly dependent on his relatives who had permanent resident status. What was in issue was proportionality which compliance with the immigration laws bore to a deterioration in the appellant's health and personal circumstances necessitating his continued residence with his relatives.

The principle is not restricted solely to review of administrative action, but can be applied in other areas to achieve the goal of fairness in competing claims. In a recent judgment of the Caribbean Court of Justice – *Barbados Rediffusion Services Ltd. v. Asha Mirchandani and others* (No. CV 1/2005)- which involved failure to comply with the terms of an "unless" order in a civil claim for damages for libel which resulted in the Defence of the appellants being struck out, the President of the Court concluded that neither the Judge at first instance nor the Court of Appeal attempted to "carry out any sort of balancing exercise". He expressed the view that "had they done so, they would inevitably have come to the conclusion that to strike out the whole of the Amended Defence and order judgment to be entered for the respondents for damages and costs, was wholly disproportionate in the circumstances of this case; it was not either by considerations of fairness to the respondents or other litigants a response to defiance of an order of the Court that was so egregious that it demanded nothing less." For those reasons, the exercise of the Judge's discretion was found to be "fatally flawed and plainly wrong".

I commend this case to you, but as was pointed out in the English immigration case mentioned earlier different approaches to normal circumstances have to be applied on a case by case basis, and the House of Lords in an earlier immigration decision declined to lay down a more precise legal test. This just indicates the incipient introduction of the principle of proportionality into the English case law. The judgment of the Caribbean Court of Justice can be regarded in like manner, and I posit the view that we took a bold step and "tested the waters" in arriving at a decision that was fair and just in the circumstances of that particular case.

In closing I once again wish to congratulate Dr. Ramlogan on his recent literary work, and commend it to all here present and the wider regional legal community, universities and law schools.

Thank you very much, Dr. Ramlogan, for conferring on me the honour of launching your latest literary work.

Best wishes for the future!

Faculty of Social Sciences Lounge
University of the West Indies
St. Augustine, Trinidad and Tobago
December 11th, 2006

CHAPTER 19

GRADUATION ADDRESS AT THE EUGENE DUPUCH LAW SCHOOL

I have always regarded an invitation to deliver an address to the graduating class of any law school as a signal honour, and one which I am always delighted to accept. Hence when asked by the Chairman to address this august gathering my affirmative answer was inevitable. However, there was an added reason for the alacrity with which I accepted the invitation. I was informed that the year 2011 will mark the 40th anniversary of the establishment of the Council of Legal Education, and I recall with nostalgia the heady days of meetings of the Council in which I participated as a young representative of the Bar of Guyana in the 1970s. The anticipation of being on the verge of embarking on the training and shaping of legal minds within our Caribbean Region leading inexorably to the development of our own indigenous jurisprudence was exciting and exhilarating. Many had mixed feelings about the future and longevity of the Council, particularly, in light of the fact that our track record with regard to regional institutions had not been good, for example, the failure of the Federation and other aborted attempts at Caribbean unity; the only lasting edifices are the University of the West Indies and our cricket team which also now seems to be in tatters. History has proved the Council to be one of the more enduring of our institutions which in the near forty years of its existence has been responsible for launching the legal careers of hundreds of young men and women, and a few older ones too. A significant number has emerged as Prime Ministers, Ministers of Government, Attorneys General as well as Chief Justices, Heads of Judiciary, and Judges in both lower and appellate courts, including the Caribbean Court of Justice; similarly, in the field of academia as principals of the law schools and heads of universities. All of this is overwhelming testimony to the continuing excellence of the Council of Legal Education and its dedicated members and staff. My sole wish is that, God willing, I shall be around to participate in the Council's 50th year of contributing to the development of the law in the English-speaking Caribbean.

Now, for the main reason for my being here. Today, Graduates, marks the culmination of years of study leading up to your being entitled to be referred to as an attorney-at-law. I am sure it represents for some of you the fulfilment of a life's dream, for others a career choice which you were persuaded to embark upon. Whatever the reason, you are about to enter a profession of venerable antiquity characterised by such virtues as dignity, honour and integrity. These are enduring legacies and bequests which you have inherited as lawyers of the future, and which you are expected to preserve and nurture as members of this noble profession. I think it incumbent on me to offer some advice and guidance as you carry out the mandate entrusted to you.

In some of our Caribbean jurisdictions codes of professional conduct have been formulated by Bar Associations as guides as to what are acceptable behavioural norms in the day-to-day interaction of lawyers with their clients, colleagues and the Judiciary. As young prospective attorneys-at-law, it is important for you to know what will be expected of you.

INTEGRITY

The bedrock of one's professional life is and always should be the virtue of integrity defined as the quality of being honest and possessing strong moral principles. It is fundamental to the discharge of a lawyer's duty to his/her clients, to the court and fellow members of the profession. Without this quality, regardless of your competence, it avails you nothing; its absence can lead to a tarnished reputation for dishonesty and unreliability resulting invariably in disciplinary action and possible disbarment. The lawyer-client relationship is based primarily on trust. A client places his life and property in your hands, and confides in you his innermost fears and weaknesses expecting solutions to his problems. It is an awesome responsibility even though you may be adequately compensated financially.

The honesty to which I have alluded is not confined to monetary matters only; it includes being candid when proffering advice and giving opinions based on an assessment of the facts and applicable legal principles. The advice must reflect what you honestly consider to be the positive or negative aspects and probable result of any contemplated litigation, and not what you think the client may wish to hear. The advice and opinion should reflect both sides of an argument so that the client can weigh the pros and cons.

You will also be the repository of confidences revealed to you as a client's legal representative concerning, perhaps, that client's business affairs or maybe the commission of a criminal offence, information which remains confidential for the duration of the lawyer–client relationship. Such confidential information should not be divulged except expressly or impliedly authorised by the client, or exceptionally, in the interest of public safety.

RESPECT AND COURTESY

The practice of law can be and invariably is fascinating and mentally stimulating. The cut and thrust between lawyer and judge or magistrate should be cordial and courteous, never acrimonious. In spite of differences of opinion one golden thread which knits together the relationship between Bench and Bar is respect. This flows in both directions. The same respect that is expected from the Bar is also expected from the Bench. With regard to the Bar, a lawyer as an advocate has a responsibility to represent his/her client resolutely and vigorously; the disputative nature of litigation requires this. It is regarded as being "no tea party." The argumentation, however, must be conducted without rancour and ill-will with Counsel displaying respect and courtesy to the Bench and each other at all times. I concede that this sometimes may be difficult to sustain when Counsel regards a judge's interruptions or questions as being irritating or against his client's interest, but which oft times may be necessary either to protect a witness or elucidate facts. Avoid being overly aggressive or antagonistic in your presentations; they are never traits which are conducive to effective advocacy.

In their interactions with the Judiciary lawyers must always be mindful of the fact that judges have an important weapon in their arsenal – the weapon of contempt of court – which in fact is used very sparingly, but which when used can have a devastating effect on the career of a lawyer. It should be utilised only in extreme cases of unbearably rude and insulting behaviour to the Bench. No lawyer should ever have to be at the receiving end of a judge's resort to this procedure.

In preparing this address I gained much assistance from the Code of Professional Conduct of the Canadian Bar Association. The Preamble to the heading "Principles of Civility for Advocates" is applicable to lawyers in all jurisdictions. It indicates that "civility amongst those entrusted with the administration of justice is central to its effectiveness and to the public's confidence in that system. Civility ensures matters before the Court are resolved in an orderly way and helps preserve the role of Counsel in the justice system as an honourable one."

The actions of lawyers and judges within a courtroom can dictate the public's attitude towards the judicial system in which both members of the legal profession and the Judiciary are involved. Disrespect within the courtroom breeds disrespect outside in the court of public opinion. Judicial institutions cannot perform their primary objective to dispense justice unless they command the respect of the public, and the burden of achieving this objective rests on the shoulders of both Bench and Bar. Oft times the Bar is usually in a better position to gauge the reactions of the public to decisions emanating from the Bench and to defects in the judicial system. In this regard lawyers must assume the role of advocates for change wherever they consider this necessary. Bar Associations must be active and militant in ensuring that the administration of justice remains unpolluted by threats to its integrity. They must be forever watchful.

COMPETENCE

From an individual perspective self-development should be foremost on your agenda for future advancement. Do not rest on your laurels and conclude that the certificate which you received tonight represents the end of the road as far as preparation and long hours of reading are concerned. On the contrary, the certificate only verifies that you are now entitled to advise an unsuspecting public on the intricacies of the law. The practice of law in any area is a continuous learning experience; it never ends until you cease that practice or retire. The law is not static, but is in a constant state of change particularly in times in which we live when technology is moving at a frenetic pace; what is new and exciting today may be out of date months later. Lawyers now have to grapple with such new legal issues as crimes committed via the internet, environmental law, entertainment law, and the complications which may arise in family litigation through surrogate parenting. Crimes are solved by DNA evidence which can vindicate convicted persons sometimes years later. When I embarked on my legal career years ago these issues never arose and were never envisaged. In this environment lawyers who fail to keep abreast of developments in the law do a great disservice not only to their clients but also to themselves and to the profession as a whole. A lawyer who fails to prepare, prepares to fail.

The law develops through precedent. The success or failure of a client's case may rest on a precedent where judgment was rendered recently on similar or identical facts and circumstances. The law reports must become your constant companion and source of information. Knowledge of recent developments in the law may make a big difference between your being an outstanding competent lawyer or a mediocre practitioner only interested in receiving fees rather than earning them. Do not depend on theatrics or court craft to achieve success. Invariably it requires much more than that.

In similar circumstances when addressing the graduating class at Hugh Wooding Law School in 2001 I made reference to an excerpt from the book "Reversal of Fortune" by Alan Dershowitz, a well-known American jurist and defence appellate attorney; it bears repeating. He related how his son, a professional magician, regarded his father's exploits in Court as being akin to his by concluding "You and I both do the same thing – sleight of hand – making things appear to be what they're not." The popular belief is that lawyers are masters in the art of obfuscation resulting in witnesses becoming confused or entertaining doubts about the veracity of what they saw or did. This can be an asset, but must be accompanied with a sound knowledge of legal principles.

THE LAWYER IN PUBLIC OFFICE

So far my remarks have been directed mainly to those of you who intend to embark on a career at the private Bar. Most of what I mentioned applies in equal measure to those of you who intend to pursue employment in the public legal service. Your clients will not be private individuals, but the Government as public prosecutors or State Counsel in the Attorney General's chambers. The basic tenets of courtesy, dignity and respect never change regardless of the clientele which you serve.

A lawyer who holds public office may in the execution of his/her duties, encounter situations where a conflict of interest arises –

your public duty may clash with your personal or private interests or relationships. This can sometimes present you with a dilemma. As a public prosecutor you may be called upon to tender advice or institute proceedings against friends and acquaintances. Ultimately, such a conflict of interest can be resolved only by you weighing your obligations to the public and the State against personal considerations. If you conclude that you cannot resolve the conflict, the best course may be to request that you be relieved of that particular matter and recuse yourself.

INDEPENDENCE OF THE BAR

The legal profession is one institution which is regarded as being independent of government control and is self-governing. This is true at least of the profession in democratic western societies. The Canadian Bar Association Code of Professional Conduct in discussing this aspect of the Code made reference to a passage from a unanimous judgment of the Supreme Court of Canada in the case of *Canada (Attorney General) v Law Society* (*British Columbia*) [1982] 2 SCR 307, and because of its relevance to our society, I make reference to it:

> The independence of the bar from the State in all its pervasive manifestations is one of the hallmarks of a free society. Consequently, regulation of these members of the law profession by the State must, so far as by human ingenuity it can be so designed, be free from State interference, in the political sense, with the delivery of services to the individual citizens of the State, particularly in fields of public and criminal law. The public interest in a free society knows no area more sensitive than the independence, impartiality and availability to the general public of the members of the bar and through those members, legal advice and services generally.

If lawyers are to protect the rights of their clients particularly rights involving alleged violations by the State, independence of the Bar must be preserved. A lawyer's primary responsibility is to vindicate and protect the interests of his client, and this he must do fearlessly and honestly. Independence of thought particularly must always be protected whether that of the Bench or the Bar. We must all strive to preserve it.

CONCLUSION

The ordeal of sitting through a graduation address is not relished by any graduating class suffering from lecture fatigue. Your ordeal is about to come to an end except for one last bit of advice. You may regard yourselves as being hitherto overworked and deprived, but soon to be among the privileged. Indeed you are privileged having joined the professional class of citizens. Because of this much is expected of you. An old adage states that to whom much is given, much is expected. Membership of the privileged class which you are about to join carries with it responsibilities, one of which is to make your services available to those less fortunate without expectation of financial reward. In other words, to be involved in giving aid to the indigent and those in need of legal assistance. I am not suggesting that this be done as soon as you embark on your practice, but it is something which in the course of your legal career must be foremost in your mind. The acquisition of wealth must not be your sole objective. That wealth must be shared with those less fortunate. Violations of the rights of the poor invariably go unredressed because of inability to brief lawyers to vindicate these rights in a court of law.

Bear this in mind as you climb the ladder of success. A final bit of advice which I have always given when speaking to graduates. Let excellence be the mantra which guides you throughout your life. Never settle for mediocrity. Best wishes for the future. May God bless you in all of your undertakings.

Heartiest congratulations!

Graduation Address
Nassau, The Bahamas
19th September, 2009

CHAPTER 20

THE LAW AS A PROFESSION

The word "law" is an all-embracing, multi-faceted word used in a variety of ways by a variety of persons affected or involved in countless situations which arise throughout our universe. From time immemorial mankind living in communities has found it necessary to regulate conduct and interaction between persons. Experience has shown that unregulated conduct results in chaos and mayhem, war and destruction. All religions are founded on rules and laws which guide and direct their followers and believers in the search for order and discipline in their daily lives, and can be found in the holy books such as the Bible, the Koran and the Bhagavad Gita, to name a few. The law whether religious or secular, symbolises order, peace, good governance and stability in any society. It should also reflect evolving changes and expectations of the people for whom it was intended.

Inevitably, however, there will be breaches of the law. We do not live in an utopian world, and on a daily basis we witness examples of man's inhumanity to man. Laws are broken with impunity and reckless abandonment of principles of right and wrong. Both religious and secular laws impose sanctions for breaches with varying degrees of punishment depending on the nature of the breaches committed by individuals. Procedures were formulated and tribunals established to deal with infractions of the law and to impose penalties. In some societies patriarchs and elders in the community are entrusted with resolving disputes and dispensing justice. This sometimes necessitated the parties or accused to be advised or represented by a friend or one with knowledge of legal procedures. We call these knowledgeable personages lawyers – experts versed in the art of advocacy and members of a profession steeped in tradition. As colonies we inherited the English common law and practice which in some instances has no relevance to our customs and culture. Unfortunately, we sometimes cling tenaciously and hold sacrosanct outmoded laws based on English moral codes even after they have outlived their usefulness in a world which is changing rapidly.

Evolving changes have already taken place in several aspects of the law over the last two decades. In the field of intestate succession in most jurisdictions in the Caribbean Region children born out of wedlock now share equally in the estate of a deceased father with those born within wedlock, and the derogatory word "bastard" has been expunged from the statute books. Other anachronistic laws have been revoked in the light of progressive approaches and changes taking place throughout the world, although some of them still remain in our legislation. This indicates an urgent and dire need for law reform to cope with new developmental trends emerging at a frenetic pace in our world today.

I now wish to discuss the qualities which one should possess as you enter a profession steeped in tradition and regulated by codes of ethics. I am sure that all of you embarked on the study of law for a variety of reasons - fascination with legal principles, an opportunity to hone your oratorical skills, the gateway to a lucrative financial dream, or just an academic career path. Whatever this may be, I hope you have found the various interstices of the law intellectually stimulating.

There may be some of you who do not intend to embark on the practice of law, but may utilise your legal knowledge in other spheres of employment. However, for those of you who intend to become future attorneys-at-law, certain codes of conduct need to be considered.

An essential component of a lawyer's professional success, in fact in any profession, is the virtue of integrity defined as the quality of being honest and straightforward as well as possessing strong moral principles. Without this quality, regardless of your competence, your actions will always be suspect and your reputation and reliability compromised. The honesty to which I have alluded includes being candid when proffering advice and giving opinions to clients based on an assessment of the facts and relevant legal principles. It also includes being honest with the court before whom you are appearing, and not seeking to conceal legal authorities which may adversely affect your client's case. In relation to your client the advice you tender must reflect what you honestly consider to be the probable result of any contemplated litigation, and not what you think the client may wish to hear. Failure to do so may result in your client being saddled with an enormous bill for costs or a long term of imprisonment and your reputation for reliability shattered.

As a practising attorney-at-law you may be the repository of confidences revealed to you by your client, maybe concerning his business affairs or the commission of a criminal offence. Such information remains confidential for the duration of the lawyer-client relationship, and should not be divulged except expressly or impliedly authorised by the client or, exceptionally, in the interest of public safety.

The cut and thrust between lawyer and judge or magistrate in the daily practice in our courts is inevitable, but this must at all times be cordial and courteous, never acrimonious. In spite of differences of opinion respect should always be the guiding principle in that relationship. Of course, this flows in both directions. The same respect that is expected from the Bar is also expected from the Bench. It is an accepted norm that a lawyer has a responsibility to represent his/her client resolutely and vigorously, but this responsibility must never be carried out with rancour and ill-will which results in disrespect to both your colleagues and the Bench. Avoid being overly aggressive or antagonistic; these are never traits which are conducive to effective advocacy.

In their interactions with the Judiciary lawyers must always be mindful of the fact that judges have an important weapon in their arsenal – the weapon of contempt of court – which in fact is used infrequently, but which when used can have a devastating effect on the career of a lawyer. It should be utilised only in extreme cases of unbearably rude and insulting behaviour to the Bench. No lawyer should ever have to be at the receiving end of a judge's resort to this procedure.

The actions of lawyers and judges within a courtroom can dictate the public's attitude towards the judicial system. Disrespect within the court room breeds disrespect outside in the court of public opinion. Judicial institutions cannot perform their primary objective to dispense justice unless they command the respect of the public, and the burden of achieving this objective rests on the shoulders of both Bench and Bar. Oft times the Bar is usually in a better position to gauge the reaction of the public to defects in the judicial system, and in this regard must assume the role of advocates for change whenever this is necessary.

While integrity is an essential component of success, competence ranks equally in the list of qualities which a lawyer must possess. This involves being the best you can ever be by not being satisfied with a performance that is mediocre and far below acceptable standards. This seems to be norm today with persons putting into any area of endeavour just enough to scrape by and fulfil their lifelong ambitions. The practice of law demands more than mediocrity; it demands excellence if you are to provide your clients with the required expertise in solving their legal problems. The law is not static, and is in a constant state of change and development as mentioned earlier. Lawyers now have to grapple with such new legal issues as internet fraud, environment law, and the complications which may arise from surrogate parenting, not to mention DNA evidence which can vindicate persons convicted wrongfully of crimes committed years earlier.

When I embarked on my legal career several years ago these did not exist and were never envisaged. At present a body of precedent can develop over such issues, and you as students and future lawyers have to keep abreast with them.

So far I have discussed what is required of attorneys who opt to be part of the private Bar. However, some or a majority of you may seek employment in the public legal service, such as the Attorney General's Chambers or the Chambers of the Director of Public Prosecutions. Your client will not be private individuals, but the Government as public prosecutors or State Counsel. The basic tenets of courtesy, dignity and respect never change regardless of the clientele which you serve, so all that I have said earlier applies in equal measure to lawyers in the public sector.

A lawyer who holds public office may in the execution of his/her duties, encounter situations where a conflict of interest arises, for instance, your public duty may clash with your personal or private interests or relationships. This can sometimes present you with a dilemma. As a public prosecutor you may be called upon to tender advice or institute proceedings against friends and acquaintances. Ultimately, such a conflict of interest can be resolved only by you weighing your obligations to the public and the State against your personal affiliations. If you conclude that you cannot resolve the conflict, the best course may be to request that you be relieved of that particular matter and recuse yourself.

Now a word about inter-personal relationships when interacting with those around you. These are not skills which one learns in a classroom. They are acquired through experience. Wherever your chosen field of employment takes you never assume that you are the fount of all knowledge because you have joined the ranks of a profession. You have to make the mental adjustment to cope with situations where experience trumps qualifications. Avoid being arrogant even though a certain amount of intellectual arrogance can be an asset particularly in the practice of law. However, avoid lording it over others who have not had the opportunity or good fortune to pursue higher learning. Practical common sense is an asset on which you can draw in solving problems which may arise on a day to day basis. It is the knack of seeing things as they are, and doing things as they ought to be done. You will find that you will need to draw on this reservoir of common sense more than your academic ability in interacting with colleagues and clients when seeking to solve problems which may rise on a daily basis.

I return to the important goal of excellence which must become your mantra throughout life. Never see the glass as being half empty or half full, but always full and running over. The world is now a global village of which we are a part, and this being so you must be prepared to compete on an equal footing with the best in the world in your chosen fields of work. You have to drag yourselves out of complacency and cease being satisfied with second-best. This can never be repeated too often.

I must thank you for asking me to address you tonight, and I close by expressing my best wishes to all of you as you strive valiantly in the pursuit of your goals as future advocates vindicating the rights of our citizens and upholding the rule of law in our beloved country.

University of Guyana Law Society
Pegasus Hotel
13th March, 2010

CHAPTER 21

DUTIES OF THE ADVOCATE TO THE COURT

Discussion of this topic – Duties of the Advocate to the Court – has necessarily to be considered in the context of the inherent right of every citizen to a fair trial, particularly in criminal cases. This is a cardinal requirement of the rule of law as expressed by Lord Bingham, former Senior Law Lord, in his treatise entitled "The Rule of Law".[1] He posited the view that "scarcely less important than an independent Judiciary is an independent legal profession, fearless in its representation of those who cannot represent themselves, however, unpopular or distasteful their case may be". This has resonance in relation to an advocate's duty to his client, a point which will be developed under separate heads.

In relation to the advocate's duties to the court, reference to an article by Hon. Mr. Justice David Ipp, a renowned judge of the Supreme Court of Western Australia,[2] provides an excellent point of departure. The learned judge categorised a lawyer's duty to the court under four general heads:

(1) a duty of disclosure owed to the court,
(2) a duty not to abuse the court's process,
(3) a duty not to corrupt the administration of justice, and
(4) a duty to conduct cases efficiently and expeditiously.

This categorisation will form the basis of discussion under separate heads.

DUTY OF DISCLOSURE

Prosecuting Counsel:

It cannot be over-emphasised that the purpose of a criminal prosecution is not to obtain a conviction; it is to lay before a jury what the Crown considers to be credible evidence relevant to what is alleged to be a crime. Counsel have a duty to see that all available legal proof of the facts is presented. The role of prosecutor excludes any notion of winning or losing; his function is a matter of public duty.

If jurors determine that they are not completely satisfied as to the guilt of an accused and return a verdict leading to an acquittal, the prosecutor will have performed his/her primary duty.

The duty of disclosure placed on prosecuting counsel mandates that he/she disclose or make available to defence counsel statements of credible witnesses which could assist the case for the defence. This extends also to disclosing the names of witnesses who may not be credible, but could be of assistance to the defence. This obligation of disclosure by prosecuting counsel was discussed extensively in *R v. Stinchombe*[3] where *Sopinka, J* of the Supreme Court of Canada in concluding that the Crown has a legal duty to disclose all relevant information to the defence, postulated the view that "the fruits of the investigation which are in its possession are not the property of the Crown for use in securing a conviction but the property of the public to be used to ensure that justice is done." The learned judge was endorsing similar views of *Rand, J* in *Boucher* referred to above.

In fact, *Sopinka, J* extended the duty of disclosure to other information such as notes where there are no statements, and where there are no notes, all information in the prosecution's possession relating to any relevant evidence that persons can give (emphasis added).

In *Regina v. Leyland Justices, Ex parte Hawthorn*[4] the applicant was charged with driving without due care and attention, and two witnesses gave statements to the police, but the statements were not disclosed to him nor were they called to give evidence. The applicant was convicted. Later on in the hearing of an application for an order of *certiorari* to quash the conviction, the court found that the prosecution had erred by failing to observe the rules of natural justice, and the defendant had been deprived of the elementary right to be notified of material witnesses known to the police.

Prosecuting counsel's duty to the court extends even to withdrawal of a prosecution if there is no credible evidence or insufficient evidence against a defendant to sustain a conviction. In *Abbot v. Refuge Assurance Co. Ltd.*[5] *Ormorod, J* in his judgment made reference to the opinion of the trial judge, *Salmond, J*, to the effect that "it is a long established practice that if counsel in charge of a prosecution at any stage is convinced that there is no evidence against the defendant, or so little evidence that it would not be safe to leave the case to the jury, it is then the duty of counsel to acquaint the court with his views and to ask for leave to withdraw the prosecution."

Admittedly, what will now be discussed is not a duty of disclosure, but what forms part of the duties of prosecuting counsel and which bears consideration.

Prosecutors also have imposed on them a duty not to depart from good practices which may render a trial unfair or undermine its integrity. This duty was discussed in *Randall (Barry) v. R*[6] and reflected in the speech of *Lord Bingham* who delivered the advice of the Judicial Committee of the Privy Council to the effect that prosecuting counsel had conducted himself as no Minister of Justice should conduct himself. He expressed the view that "while the duty of counsel may require a strong and direct challenge to the evidence of a witness, and strong criticism may properly be made of a witness or a defendant, so long as that criticism is based on evidence or the absence of evidence before the court, there can never be any justification for bullying, intimidation, personal vilification or insult or for the exchange of insults between counsel."

The Judicial Committee of the Privy Council concluded that there had been such departures from good practice in the course of the trial as to deny the accused the substance of a fair trial. This included the trial judge's failure to exert the authority vested in him to control the proceedings and to enforce proper standards of behaviour. Cumulatively, this resulted in the convictions of the accused being quashed.

In April 2012, the Office of the Director of Public Prosecutions of Jamaica formulated a Protocol[7] to guide prosecutors whenever a decision to launch a prosecution is being considered, the objective being to be seen to operate in a transparent way on behalf of the public which it serves. The methodology and processes which should be employed by prosecutors in exercise of their functions are outlined in the Protocol, and applies when a decision is made to commence, continue or discontinue a criminal prosecution.

The prosecutor's ethical approach to criminal proceedings is addressed, the point being made that a decision to prosecute or not ought to be taken seriously in light of the fact that such a decision has the potential to undermine public confidence in the criminal process.

Reference is made to the cases of *Boucher* and *Randall* mentioned earlier, and in particular the dicta of *Rand, J* in *Boucher* to the effect that the function of a prosecutor is a matter of public duty to be performed "with an ingrained sense of the dignity, the seriousness and the justness of judicial proceedings". It is suggested that this includes the prosecutor inviting the court to stop proceedings if a prosecutor concludes that there is no longer a reasonable prospect of conviction.

The Protocol stipulates specifically that an important aspect of a prosecutor's duty is to ensure that a prosecution is not allowed to commence or continue, if to do so, would be seen by the courts as oppressive or unfair and amount to an abuse of the process of the court as a matter of law.

This Protocol can be regarded as a guide and best practice for prosecutors in the judicial systems of the Commonwealth Caribbean, and its adoption is recommended highly.

Defence Counsel:

The duty of disclosure expected of defence counsel could be more complex. Two duties may collide, that is, the overriding duty not to mislead the court, and the duty to defend a client to the best of his/her ability.

The dilemma was addressed aptly by *Lord Reid* in *Rondel v. Worsley*[8] in this way:

> *Every counsel has a duty to his client fearlessly to raise every issue, advance every argument, and ask every question, however distasteful, which he thinks will help his client's case. As an officer of the court concerned in the administration of justice, he has an overriding duty to the court, to the standards of his profession, and to the public, which may and often does lead to a conflict with his client's wishes or with what the client thinks are his personal interests. Counsel must not mislead the court, he must not lend himself to casting aspersions on the other party or witnesses for which there is no sufficient basis in the information in his possession, he must not withhold authorities or documents which may tell against his clients but which the law or the standards of his profession require him to produce.*
>
> *It encapsulates ideally an advocate's duty to the court which when circumstances dictate overrides the duty to clients.*

Interestingly, *Lord Diplock* in reference to a criminal trial in *Saif Ali v. Sydney Mitchell & Co (a firm) and others, P (third party)*[9] although postulating the view that "a barrister must not wilfully mislead the court as to the law nor may he actively mislead the court as to the facts," went on to say that "consistently with the rule that the prosecution must prove its case he may passively stand by and watch the court being misled by reason of its [the prosecution's] failure to ascertain facts that are within the barrister's knowledge." *Lord Diplock* seems to be suggesting that although an advocate owes a duty to the court to act in a particular manner, circumstances may arise when the duty to a client must be taken into account as long as it stays within the boundaries of respect for the court, and counsel refrains from personally misleading a presiding judge about the facts or the law. Court strategy and tactics in an adversarial system of practice may be permissible if not utilised deliberately to deceive or mislead.

Differences of judicial opinion, however, have arisen with regard to counsel neglecting to draw a judge's attention to omissions or errors of law when summing up to a jury in a criminal trial. In *R v. Southgate,*[10] *Edmund-Davies, J* commended defence counsel for bringing to the trial judge's attention an error in his summing up.

A different approach, though, was taken in *R v. Eugene George Cocks*[11] where the trial judge after the jury had retired to consider the verdict then sought to ascertain from both counsel whether he had omitted anything in the summing up, and was so informed, but did not recall the jury for further instructions. The Court of Appeal was firm in its conclusion that save in the most exceptional circumstances a judge should not embark upon discussion of the law with counsel once the summing-up is concluded. The Court opined that the practice adopted may cause embarrassment as defence counsel owes a duty to the client, and it is not counsel's duty to correct the judge if he/she has gone wrong. The Court, however, felt that prosecuting counsel has a right if it is thought that there was some misdirection of fact, to raise the matter with the judge <u>before</u> the jury retires (emphasis added). One can conclude that the difference in approach by the Court of Appeal between defence and prosecuting counsel stems from the fact that prosecuting counsel has an obligation to ensure that justice is done and that an accused has a fair trial, whereas defence counsel having a duty to the client to raise fearlessly every issue may have to weigh options depending on the defect or omission in the judge's summing up and the effect it may have on a favourable verdict for the client.

The case of *R v. Nicholas Webb Edwards,*[12] however, is instructive. It concerned the failure of a trial judge to direct the jury on the standard of proof in the summing-up in a trial of the accused for rape, and which the Court of Appeal regarded as a serious defect. The Court, however, applied the proviso to Section 2(1) of the Criminal Appeal Act 1968 for the reason that the evidence against the appellant was so overwhelming that a reasonable jury, properly directed on the standard of proof, inevitably would have convicted him. The Court, in dismissing the appeal, *per curiam*, considered it to be inconceivable that defence counsel, acting in the best interests of their client, could have failed to draw that serious omission in the summing-up to the attention of the judge. Their failure to do so deprived their client of the benefit of the jury hearing the direction on the standard of proof from the lips of the judge himself. The Court indicated that this could have been drawn to the judge's attention by defence counsel with the utmost discretion.

The duty of disclosure to the court is of particular importance when counsel seeks to obtain a court order on an *ex parte* application which by its very nature defies the maxim "*audi alteram partem.*" A judge of necessity is forced to rely on the *bona fides*, honesty and veracity of counsel seeking an *ex parte* order. These orders are invariably sought for injunctive relief to prohibit or restrain the infringement of some right or to enforce entitlement to a right, performance of which is being threatened or violated. In these circumstances counsel has an unqualified duty to make full disclosure to the court in any affidavit which ought to include all material facts relevant to the issue, and which are within counsel's knowledge or could have been ascertained upon proper inquiry. A plethora of cases over the years has adumbrated the principle of full disclosure being made in affidavits supporting requests for injunctions.[13] *Donaldson, J* in the Court of Appeal in *Bank Mellat v. Nikpour*[14] summarised it admirably in relation to the grant of a *Mareva* injunction when he said:

> *The rule requiring full disclosure seems to me to be one of the most fundamental importance, particularly in the context of the draconian remedy of the Mareva injunction. It is in effect, together with the Anton Piller order, one of the law's two nuclear weapons. If*

access to such a weapon is obtained without the fullest and frankest disclosure, I have no doubt at all that it should be revoked.

Donaldson, J was echoing similar sentiments expressed several years earlier by *Warrington, L.J* in *R v. Kensington Income Tax Commissioners ex parte Princess Edmond de Polignac.*[15]

Counsel sometimes may encounter a client whose instructions on the relevant facts were later found to be inaccurate or untrue or about which reservations arise. In these situations, if after unsuccessfully seeking confirmation of the veracity of the facts from the client, counsel's only recourse may be to withdraw from representing the client. The House of Lords in *Myers v. Elman*[16] held that a solicitor "cannot simply allow the client to make whatever affidavit or document he thinks fit, nor can he escape the responsibility of careful investigation or supervision. If the client will not give him the information which he is entitled to require, or if the client insists on swearing an affidavit which the solicitor knows to be imperfect, the solicitor's duty is to withdraw from the case."

In the opinion of *Viscount Maugham* even where a solicitor places innocently on a file an affidavit by his client which he discovers subsequently to be false, he owes it to the Court "to put the matter right at the earliest date if he continues to act as solicitor upon the record, and the duty of the client is equally plain." He rejected emphatically the notion that it was justifiable in such a case to keep silence and to wait until the plaintiff succeeds, if he can, in obtaining an order for a further and better affidavit. To do so is to obstruct the interests of justice and delay the hearing of the action even if disclosure is ultimately obtained.

In the Guyanese case of *In re a Legal Practitioner*,[17] the Full Court held that for a barrister or solicitor knowingly and deliberately to submit a false document intending it to be acted upon is grossly improper conduct and dishonourable both to himself and his profession.

DUTY NOT TO ABUSE THE COURT PROCESS

Frivolous or vexatious conduct:

Any conduct designed to injure the effectiveness of the business of a court is an abuse of the court process. This could include unsubstantiated allegations of misconduct against either counsel, litigants or witnesses involved in court proceedings. Unfounded allegations may be proffered by a client to embarrass an opponent, and it is counsel's duty to refrain from presenting these allegations to a court unless proved to be valid. If the client insists, counsel should withdraw his/her appearance, the paramount duty being to the court.

In *Clyne v. New South Wales Bar Association*[18] the High Court of Australia in commenting on the conduct of a barrister introducing damaging irrelevant matter into a proceeding, opined that "the barrister's privilege may be abused grossly if counsel, in opening a case, makes statements which may have ruinous consequences for the person attacked, and which he cannot substantiate or justify by evidence."

Unmeritorious Claims:

An advocate should refrain from initiating or continuing legal proceedings that have absolutely no prospect of success and are bound to fail and which may result in a court issuing an order for costs in favour of the opposing party, possibly to be paid by the offending counsel personally.

In *R v. Weisz*[19] a solicitor was instructed by a client to bring an action against bookmakers for money alleged to be owing by them to the client on bets, a claim which the client knew was not maintainable in law, but in the hope that the threat of publicity would induce the bookmakers to pay. *Lord Goddard, CJ* held that putting forward a feigned issue in a fictitious cause of action was a contempt and if it were successful could lead to an interference with or a distortion of the course of justice.

Lord Bingham as Master of the Rolls in *Ridehalgh v. Horsefield*[20] had this to say in relation to abusing the process of the court:

> *It is one thing for a legal representative to present, on instructions, a case which he regards is bound to fail; it is quite another to lend his assistance to proceedings which are an abuse of the process of the court. Whether instructed or not, a legal representative is not entitled to use litigious procedures for purposes for which they were not intended, as by issuing or pursuing proceedings for reasons unconnected with success in the litigation or pursuing a case known to be dishonest, nor is he entitled to evade rules intended to safeguard the interests of justice as by knowingly failing to make full disclosure on an ex parte application or knowingly conniving at incomplete disclosure of documents.*

Filing manifestly hopeless notices of appeal merely for the purpose of buying time also constitutes an abuse of process.[21] In some jurisdictions this may lead to protracted delays in having an appeal heard with the result that a successful litigant may, out of frustration, choose to accept a settlement rather than await a hearing of the appeal.

It is apposite at this juncture to refer to counsel submitting to a court unmeritorious points of law. This was discussed in *Abraham v. Jutsun*[22] where *Lord Denning, M.R.* expressed the view that it is the duty of an advocate to take any point which he believes to be fairly arguable on behalf of his client, and it is not for him to determine what shall be the effect of the legal argument; he is not guilty of misconduct simply because he takes a point which the tribunal holds to be bad, and only becomes guilty of misconduct if he is dishonest, that is, by knowingly taking a bad point and thereby deceiving the court. In the circumstances of this case an order for the solicitor to pay costs personally for taking an unmeritorious point was set aside on appeal for failure to give the solicitor an opportunity to be heard.

Undertakings:

Whether given to the court or to opposing counsel in proceedings, an undertaking has been described as being equivalent to an injunction with similar consequences for its breach.[23] This suggests that an undertaking must be honoured and taken seriously whether given orally or in writing. Apart from being oral or written an undertaking can be implied from circumstances surrounding litigation.

In *Harman v. Secretary of State for the Home Department*[24] the House of Lords held that a solicitor who in the course of discovery in litigation obtained possession of copies of documents belonging to his client's adversary gave an implied undertaking to the court not to use the copies nor to allow them to be used for any purpose other than the proper conduct of the action on behalf of his client, and breach of it was a civil contempt of court.

Disobedience to Orders of Court:

Lord Denning in his book "The Due Process of Law"[25] assessed the power of a court to give orders as being one of its most important, and indeed so it is. It is one of the powers utilised by courts, *inter alia*, to determine the rights of parties in litigation or to grant or restrain certain acts pending outcome of litigation.

Disobedience to orders of court attracts sanctions, and in relation to breach of injunctions *Lord Nicholls* in *Attorney General v. Punch Ltd*[26] concluded that "without sanctions an injunction would be a paper tiger," and went on to state that "if the rule of law is to be meaningful, the decisions of the court on how, and to what extent, the *status quo* should be maintained pending the trial must be respected."

This leads inevitably to a discussion on the nature of contempt of court which could be either civil or criminal. Civil contempt usually attracts less severe punishment, and is utilised when orders of court or undertakings are disobeyed.

Contempt of Court:

This very important weapon in a court's armoury is utilised for preserving and upholding its dignity and ensuring respect for its orders whether made in relation to undertakings, injunctions or in final determination of matters over which a judge adjudicates.

Referring again to Lord Denning's "The Due Process of Law," in discussing the topic of Contempt of Court, he made this comment:

> *There is not one stream of justice. There are many streams. Whatever obstructs their courses or muddies the waters of any of those streams is punishable under the single cognomen of 'Contempt of Court'.*

Disobedience to court orders constitutes civil contempt, and very often does not attract a term of imprisonment, although it could. A client ought not to be encouraged directly or impliedly to disobey any order which a court makes even though counsel may regard it as being harsh, unjust or unconscionable. The remedy lies in appealing against the order or requesting a stay or review of it.

An undertaking given to a court being equivalent to an injunction, its breach may be punished in the same way. In relation to an injunction a court can commit for contempt any person who, although not a party to an action, but one who knowing of the injunction or order of court, aids and abets a defendant in committing a breach of it or does some act which has the effect of interfering with the order. In *Jockey Club v. Buffham*,[27] however, it was held that this applied only to interlocutory orders and not to final orders since the essence of the contempt consisted in the interference with the course of justice in the proceeding in which the order was made.

Another aspect of a court's power to commit for contempt may arise in situations leading to disturbances in court which can include hurling insults at a judge, that is, either contempt in the face of the court or "scandalising the court." This form of misconduct could attract immediate censure by committal for a term of imprisonment if the required procedure is followed. *Lord Denning, M.R* in *Morris v. Crown Office*[28] described this form of contempt in this manner:

> *The phrase 'contempt in the face of the court' has a quaint old-fashioned ring about it; but the importance of it is this: of all the places where law and order must be maintained, it is here in these courts. The course of justice must not be deflected or interfered with. Those who strike at it strike at the very foundations of our society. To maintain law and order, the judges have, and must have, power at once to deal with those who offend against it. It is a great power – a power instantly to imprison a person without trial – but it is a necessary power.*

The opinion of *Salmon, L.J.* expressed in the same case was that "the sole purpose of proceedings for contempt is to give our courts the power effectively to protect the rights of the public by ensuring that the administration of justice shall not be obstructed or prevented."

The required procedure before committal for any contempt involves informing the contemnor of the nature of the contempt and requesting that cause be shown why he/she should not be committed. These essential requirements were considered and decided upon in several cases.[29]

Although contempt "in the face of the court" suggests a contempt committed in the presence of a judge in keeping with its historical development,[30] *Lord Denning, M.R.* in *Balogh v. St. Albans Crown Court*[31] referred to situations where contempt was committed within a courtroom but not seen by a judge or at some distance from the court. *Stephenson, L.J.* concurred when he said that he was satisfied that it was not limited to occurrences in the face of the court, but also any interference with the administration of justice.

DUTY NOT TO CORRUPT THE ADMINISTRATION OF JUSTICE

This duty in some instances may not be distinguishable from the duty not to abuse the court process in that abuse of the court process may have the effect of corrupting the administration of justice. The duty includes using every possible means to ensure that the "streams of justice" remain pure and unpolluted. This includes, *inter alia*, not participating either explicitly or impliedly in unseemly acts designed to thwart the judicial process. A hypothetical scenario may illustrate effectively corruption of the judicial system:

> *A security guard is charged with the theft of computers from a company where he is employed. He instructs his lawyer that he was on leave at the time when the theft occurred, and was nowhere near the scene. However, the prosecution case is based mainly on a statement from a friend of the accused in which he admits that the computers were "hot stuff" and he had "got rid of them for good money." On the day before the trial the accused, overcome with guilt, hands over to his lawyer a DVD with footage from a camera at the company's premises which shows him removing the computers in a van along with an address book containing names of buyers and the amount of money paid for the stolen items. The lawyer makes no disclosure of the footage and address book in conducting his defence of the accused. The accused is acquitted. Later prosecuting counsel discovers the cover-up by defence counsel. The question arises – what action should be taken against him?*

There is no doubt that there was corruption of the administration of justice for which defence counsel must be held accountable. At least, he should face disciplinary charges for obstructing the course of justice with possible suspension or disbarment being an officer of the court who is expected to ensure that the streams of justice are kept pure and unpolluted.

The Codes of Ethics of most common law jurisdictions provide guidelines for members of the legal profession in their interactions with clients, colleagues and the courts and the manner in which they are expected to conduct themselves as officers of the court. Upon admission to practise an attorney-at-law is expected to adhere to the principles of the Code, chief of these being to maintain the integrity, honour and dignity of the legal profession.

Although these Codes enjoin lawyers to represent their clients vigorously by fair and honourable means, they urge specifically avoidance of all sharp practices. The Disciplinary Procedures of the Legal Profession Act of Trinidad and Tobago[32] divide breaches of the Code of Ethics into two parts – those which may constitute professional misconduct (Part A), and those which shall constitute professional misconduct (Part B), (emphasis added), these being Mandatory Provisions and Specific Prohibitions which are also found in the codes of other Caribbean jurisdictions.[33] Among the mandatory provisions is the admonition that "an attorney-at-law shall not withhold facts or secrete witnesses in order to establish the guilt or innocence of the accused." Violation of these provisions constitutes professional misconduct.

The lawyer in our hypothetical case withheld vital evidence which, if revealed may have led to the conviction of his client. It was clear that secreting the incriminating DVD and address book was indulging in a sharp practice in defending his client, and which constituted professional misconduct.

The next question to be decided is what prosecuting counsel should do with the information which he/she discovered. The Legal Profession Acts of most Caribbean jurisdictions provide for establishment of Disciplinary Committees responsible for investigation of breaches of the Code of Ethics and for imposing sanctions, if necessary. Complaints may be made by aggrieved clients, and most Acts impose on a fellow attorney-at-law the duty to report to the Committee any improper or unprofessional conduct by colleagues except where the information obtained is received in confidence.[34]

Prosecuting counsel therefore is duty bound to report the conduct of defence counsel to the Disciplinary Committee for action and mandatory punishment which may include a fine or reprimand. If the Committee is of the opinion that the misconduct justifies more severe punishment, such as suspension or disbarment, it may forward a copy of the proceedings to the Chief Justice or Head of the Judiciary and to the Attorney General; in some jurisdictions the Committee has powers of suspension or disbarment.[35]

Apart from disciplinary action under the relevant Legal Profession legislation, defence counsel may have committed an offence under relevant criminal statutes, for example, perverting the course of justice.

If this is so prosecuting counsel may exercise the option of reporting the conduct of defence counsel to the relevant authorities, such as the Director of Public Prosecutions.

Intended Perjury by a Client

This could sometimes present counsel with a dilemma as mentioned earlier when discussing defence counsel's duty to a client. Reference was made to dicta of *Lord Reid* in *Rondel v. Worsley* to the effect that although counsel has a duty to defend a client fearlessly, he/she has an overriding duty to the court and the public which may often lead to conflict with a client's wishes or personal interest.

By the very nature of the lawyer/client relationship, lawyers are privy to confidences which clients will not share with other persons. This may include admissions of guilt to offences with which they are charged. The relationship of a lawyer to a client is based on confidence and trust, and counsel's duty is to defend the client whether he/she believes in the client's guilt or innocence, and even if a confession of guilt is revealed before a trial. If counsel continues to act he/she is duty bound to advise on a course of action which is consistent with his/her duty to the court. If the client enters a plea of "not guilty" at the trial counsel ought to advise about appropriate options open to the client after the prosecution has proved its case. Where the confession is made during the trial complications may arise. It is up to counsel to decide whether to withdraw appearance or advise the client on options consistent with an admission of guilt. Leave of the court to withdraw should be sought without compromising either the client's position or counsel's.

The case of *Sankar v. State of Trinidad & Tobago*[36] demonstrates the dilemma of counsel in advising a client on the alternative courses which may be adopted in relation to a defence on a charge of murder. The Judicial Committee of the Privy Council allowing the appeal held that if an advocate was embarrassed in the conduct of the defence by what he was told by the client he had a duty to explain the situation and inform his client of the options which arose, including the advocate's withdrawal from the trial if the course chosen was inconsistent with the advocate's duty to the court.

Connivance at Client's Improper Conduct

Counsel corrupts the administration of justice by turning a blind eye to a client's improper and dishonest conduct. The only recourse when such conduct is discovered is to withdraw appearance from any proceedings in which counsel represents a client. It is otiose to stress that for an advocate actively to encourage a client to misrepresent the truth either orally or in any written document, is reprehensible and unprofessional, to say the least. This warrants severe censure, if not disbarment.

The Canadian case of *R v. Sweezey*[37] is a classic example. Counsel advised his client to be evasive and forgetful to the police about his connection with the murder of certain persons, admission of which would have jeopardised his chances of securing a firearms certificate. The lawyer was charged and found guilty of obstructing the course of justice, and upon appeal against his sentence of eighteen months, *Mahoney J.A.* in upholding the sentence in a dissent had this to say which is applicable to an advocate in any jurisdiction:

> *The Canadian justice system relies on the honesty and integrity of counsel who practise within it. To that end, every lawyer is made an officer of the Courts in which he will practise. Cases before such Courts are in pursuit of justice through truthful evidence. A lawyer who attempts to obstruct justice by wilfully counselling evasive evidence not only commits an offence contrary to Section 127 of the Criminal Code but also breaches his solemn duty as an officer of the Court. Behaviour of this kind in a professional person trained in the law is all the more offensive because it defeats the very course of justice he has sworn to uphold.*

Attempting to Influence the Court

It is beyond doubt that any attempt by an advocate to discuss a pending case with a presiding judge is not only corrupting the administration of justice but a grave breach of professional ethics. Some Professional Codes provide specifically that attorneys-at-law refrain from this form of behaviour for which they can be disciplined.[38] This also includes attempting to influence members of a jury in any criminal trial in which an advocate is appearing for either the prosecution or the defence and either directly or indirectly.

DUTY TO CONDUCT CASES EFFICIENTLY AND EXPEDITIOUSLY

When a client retains a lawyer for representation in an action to be heard in a court of law, that client is entitled to assume that the lawyer is competent and knowledgeable in the intricacies of the particular law applicable to the case. A client is also entitled to assume that the retained lawyer will perform his/her duties efficiently and particularly without undue delay being cognisant of the maxim "justice delayed is justice denied." Breach of the duty to act efficiently and expeditiously could attract an action for negligence. This was held to be so in the Guyanese case of *Padmey v. Radhia*[39] in which *De Freitas, C.J.* concluded that "where a solicitor holds himself out to his clients as possessing adequate skill, knowledge and learning for the purpose of properly conducting all business that he undertakes whether contentious or non-contentious, and causes loss or damage to his client owing to the want of such knowledge as he ought to possess or the want of such care as he ought to exercise, he is guilty of negligence giving rise to an action for damages by his client."

James, L.J. in *Mc Fadden & Others*[40] described the duty which counsel owes to the court and to the public as including the clear presentation of the issues in a case and the avoidance of waste of time, repetition and prolixity, and in the conduct of every case counsel must be mindful of a responsibility to the public.

The Trinidadian case of *Young v. Morales*[41] added another dimension to the advocate's duty to conduct cases efficiently when *Hamel-Smith, J. A.* advised that "it is the duty of an attorney, when referring to any authority in support of his case, to ensure that the decision relied upon has not been overruled by a superior court." This may result in a court being misled, hopefully unintentionally.

Whether counsel conducted a client's case efficiently may arise for consideration by a court if a dissatisfied client files a suit for negligence in the conduct of the case which was lost. In the Australian case of *Giannarelli v. Wraith*[42] the High Court held that at common law a barrister cannot be sued by his client for negligence in the conduct of a case in court or in work out of court which leads to a decision affecting the conduct of a case in court. *Mason, C. J.* in the course of his judgment expressed the view that the performance of counsel of his paramount duty to the court will require him to act in a variety of ways sometimes to the possible disadvantage of a client. He explained that a barrister's duty to the court epitomises the fact that the course of litigation depends on the exercise by counsel of an independent discretion or judgment in the conduct and management of a case in which he has an eye, not only to his client's success, but also to the speedy and efficient administration of justice; the lawyer not being a mere agent for the litigant, exercises that independent judgment in the interests of the court, and if counsel were exposed to liability in negligence there would be a real risk that it would influence the exercise of his independent judgment. The litmus test is always whether counsel carried out his duty to his client efficiently and competently.

The criteria by which the competence of an advocate is measured ought not to be the length of his/her submissions or the number of cases cited in support of any point of law. The soundness and relevance of the arguments being advanced are the main criteria. Prolixity of pleadings and submissions may impress the client, but not always the judge. *Lord Templeman* in *Ashmore and Others v. Corporation of Lloyd's*[43] in pellucid language expressed his views on the matter:

> *The parties and particularly their legal advisers in any litigation are under a duty to cooperate with the court by chronological, brief and consistent pleadings which define the issues and leave the judge to draw his own conclusions about the merits when he hears the case. It is the duty of counsel to assist the judge by simplification and concentration and not to advance a multitude of ingenious arguments in the hope that out of 10 bad points the judge will be capable of fashioning a winner. In nearly all cases the correct procedure works perfectly well. But there has been a tendency in some cases for legal advisers, pressed by their clients, to make every point conceivable and inconceivable without judgment or discrimination.*

Before concluding this discussion, it may be appropriate to examine the issue of paramountcy of an advocate's duty to the court.

It is accepted that irreconcilable differences may arise between an advocate's duty to his client and duty to the court, both being of utmost importance to the efficient administration of justice within an adversarial common law system. Earlier, reference was made to dicta of *Lord Reid* in *Rondel v. Worsley* indicating that it is the duty of counsel to raise without fear every issue, advance every argument and ask every distasteful question which may assist the client's case. He, however, pointed to the fact that counsel as an officer of the court concerned in the administration of justice has an overriding duty to the court and to the public.

Mason, C.J in *Giannarelli v. Wraith* expressed definitively the view that counsel's duty to the court was paramount and must be performed even if the client gives instructions to the contrary. *Lord Denning* sitting in the Court of Appeal in *Rondel v. Worsley*[44] had posited a similar view in this way:

> *[The advocate] has a duty to the court which is paramount. It is a mistake to suppose that he is the mouthpiece of his client to say what he wants: or his tool to do what he directs.*

One can conclude from perusal of dicta in English cases of historic vintage which were accepted and followed in Australian cases, that the rationale for supremacy of the advocate's duty to the court was the overriding element of public interest and the goal of inspiring confidence in the administration of justice.

Contrastingly, in the United States justice system the duty to the client supersedes the advocate's duty to the court, the client being entitled to "zealous representation," which is regarded as the lawyer's primary duty.

In this regard, it is apposite to set out the relevant part of Canon 15 of the American Bar Association Canons of Professional Ethics[45] which reads as follows:

> *The lawyer owes entire devotion to the interest of the client, warm zeal in the maintenance and defence of his rights and the exertion of his utmost learning and ability, to the end that nothing be taken or be withheld from him, save by the rules of law, legally applied. No fear of judicial disfavour or public unpopularity should restrain him from the full discharge of his duty. In the judicial forum the client is entitled to the benefit of any and every remedy and defence that is authorised by the law of the land, and he may expect his lawyer to assert every such remedy or defence. But it is steadfastly to be borne in mind that the great trust of the lawyer is to be performed within*

and not without the bounds of the law. The office of attorney does not permit, much less does it demand of him for any client violation of law or any manner of fraud or chicane. He must obey his own conscience and not that of his client.

The use of phrases such as "entire devotion" and "warm zeal" indicates the high priority which is given to the lawyer's duty to his client, and when coupled with the fact that he is expected to exert "his utmost learning and ability to the end that nothing be taken or be withheld from him, save by the rules of law" emphasises in no uncertain terms the supremacy of the lawyer's duty to his client over any other duty. Not even the "fear of judicial disfavour or public unpopularity" should restrain him from the full discharge of his duty. There can be no higher threshold.

In Canada the two duties are given equal prominence which Gavin Mackenzie, author of "The Ethics of Advocacy,"[46] indicates may make ethical choices in advocacy more difficult. In an adversarial system, however, lawyers are expected to represent their clients fearlessly and vigorously, but within the boundaries of courtesy and respect laid down in relevant codes of ethics as well as uphold the principles expected from an officer of the court.

Canada's position was also discussed in "A Lawyer's Duty to the Court" by Robert Bell and Caroline Abela,[47] where reference was made to the case of *Schreiber v. Mulroney*[48] and dicta from the judgment of *Newbould J.* to the effect that it had never been clear to him which duty took precedence when a solicitor's duty to his client conflicted with a duty owed to other counsel and to the court, but concluded that "a lawyer cannot rely on a client's instructions as a defence if the lawyer has acted in a manner inconsistent with the goals of the judicial system; he must decline to follow instructions that would constitute misconduct."

This reflected the opinions expressed in the earlier case of *Meek v. Fleming*[49] where *per curiam* the Court found that the decision of leading counsel to conceal facts was wrong, and resulted in his duty to the court being subordinated unwarrantably to his duty to his client.

An assessment of the aforementioned views and opinions as well as perusal of professional codes of conduct indicates that advocates in their representation of clients are expected to do so skilfully, efficiently and with a high degree of professionalism. Needless to say, the interests of the client must be foremost, but not paramount to the duty owed to the court as the fountainhead of the administration of justice, and in which the public has a vested interest. This interest embraces safeguarding virtues of fairness and integrity, as well as ensuring that the judicial system remains pure, untainted and unsullied.

In the Australian case of *Council of the Queensland Law Society Inc. v. Wright*[50] the Court in reference to the advocate's duty to the court concluded that "the duty of candour and fairness is quintessential to the lawyer's role as officer of the court" and both "the court and the public expect and rely upon it."

United Kingdom
September, 2015

Endnotes

1 Penguin Books, London – 2011.
2 "Lawyers' Duties to the Court" reported in the Law Quarterly Review 1998 114(Jan) 63-107.
3 [1991] 3 S.C.R. 3-26.
4 [1979] 1 Q.B. 283.
5 [1962] 1 Q.B. 432 at 451.
6 (2002) 60 WIR 103.
7 See "The Decision to Prosecute: A Jamaican Protocol".
8 [1967] 3 All ER 993 at 998F.
9 [1978] 3 All ER 1033 at 1042 h, 1043a.
10 [1963] 2 All ER 833.
11 (1976) 63 Cr App. R 79.
12 [1983] 77 Cr. App. R.5.
13 See for example, Thomas A Edison Ltd. v. Bullock [1912] 15 CLR, 679, Siporex Trade S.A. v. Comdel Commodities Ltd [1986] 2 Lloyd's L.R., 428.
14 [1985] Fleet Street Reports 87 at 92.
15 [1917] 1 KB 486 at 509.
16 [1940] A.C. 282. See also In re a Legal Practitioner (1959) LRBG 13 (Guyana).
17 [1959] LRBG 13.
18 [1960] 104 CLR 186.
19 [1951] 2 K.B. 611.
20 [1994] Ch. 205 at p. 234.
21 See Chamberlain and Edwards v. Agard & Superintendent of Prisons of St. Catherine District (1979) 16 JLR 403 (Jamaica).

22 [1963] 2 All E.R. 402.
23 See Roberts v. Roberts [1990] 2 FLR 111, Butler-Sloss L J at 113 D-E.
24 [1983] 1 AC 280.
25 See page 36.
26 [2003] 1 A.C. 1046.
27 [2003] QB 462.
28 [1970] 2 QB 114 at 122 B-C.
29 See Re Pershadsingh (1960) 2 WIR 340; Maharaj v. Attorney General for Trinidad and Tobago [1977] 1 All ER 411; Eric Frater v. R (1981) 18 JLR 381; Bayley v. Blackman (1989) 24 Barbados Law Reports 285.
30 See Blackstone's Commentaries (1st edn. 1769) Vol.3 p.332 where it was aptly explained as … "when the fact, from its nature, must be evident to the court either from ocular or other irrefutable proof, then the law departs from its usual resort, the verdict of twelve men, and relies on the judgment of the court alone."
31 [1975]1Q.B. 73.
32 Cap. 90:03 Act 21 of 1986.
33 See Legal Profession Acts and Code of Ethics of Antigua and Barbuda, Barbados, Bahamas, Jamaica, Grenada, St. Lucia.
34 See Code of Ethics of Antigua & Barbuda, Barbados, Grenada, St. Lucia, and Trinidad & Tobago.
35 Such as Jamaica.
36 [1995] WLR 194; (1994) 46 WIR 452.
37 [1987] 39 C.C.C. (3d.) 182.
38 See Professional Codes of Conduct of Antigua & Barbuda, Barbados, Bahamas, Guyana, Grenada, Jamaica, St. Lucia and Trinidad & Tobago. This is also discussed in the Codes of Professional Conduct or Ethics of England and Wales, Australia and Canada. Although not part of the Commonwealth, a similar provision can be found in the Codes of the American Bar Association with regard to the Special Responsibilities of a Prosecutor.
39 (1931-37) LRBG 49.
40 [1976] 62 Crim. AR, 187.
41 (1995) 50 WIR 433 at 436.
42 [1988] 165 CLR, 543, 556.
43 [1992] 1 WLR 446 at 453.
44 [1966] 3 WLR 950, [1966] 3 All ER, 657.
45 The Preamble and Canons 1 through 32 were first adopted August 27, 1908.
46 The Advocates' Society Journal (September 2008).
47 The Advocates' Society Journal, January 2009.
48 [2007] Can L11 31754 (ON S.C.) at para. 24.
49 [1961] 2 QB 366; [1961] 3 All ER 148.
50 [2001] QCA, 58.

PART III

WOMEN AND CHILDREN

CHAPTER 22

THE SYNERGY OF "RIGHTS" CONVENTIONS:

THE CONVENTION ON THE ELIMINATION OF ALL FORMS OF DISCRIMINATION AGAINST WOMEN (CEDAW)

THE CONVENTION ON THE RIGHTS OF THE CHILD (CRC)

THE INTER-AMERICAN CONVENTION ON THE PREVENTION, PUNISHMENT AND ERADICATION OF VIOLENCE AGAINST WOMEN (THE CONVENTION OF BELEM DO PARA)

On 18th December, 1979 the General Assembly of the United Nations adopted the Convention on the Elimination of All Forms of Discrimination Against Women (hereinafter referred to as "CEDAW") which represented the culmination of years of preparatory work and lobbying by members of the Commission on the Status of Women. CEDAW became the vehicle to promote the advancement of women and recognition of their human rights in all fields of development. It urges governments to take appropriate measures to eliminate all forms of discrimination against women. In 1979 ninety-three (93) countries ratified or acceded to CEDAW; today nearly over twenty (20) years later the number has risen to nearly 200.

On 20th November, 1989 ten (10) years later the General Assembly of the United Nations recognising that the Universal Declaration of Human Rights proclaims that childhood is entitled to special care and assistance, adopted the Convention On the Rights of the Child, (hereinafter referred to as "CRC") applicable to all children below the age of eighteen (18) years. CRC seeks to preserve and safeguard the human rights of children, and urges States Parties to take appropriate measures to ensure protection of children against all forms of discrimination or punishment. To date over 186 countries have ratified or acceded to it.

On 9th June, 1994 the Inter-American Convention on the Prevention, Punishment and Eradication of Violence Against Women (hereinafter referred to as "the Belem do Para Convention") was adopted by acclamation at the 24th regular session of the General

Assembly of the Organisation of American States. The adoption of this Convention demonstrated the commitment of the countries mainly from Latin America to revise their laws to ensure specific solutions to the problems of physical and psychological violence encountered by women.

CEDAW and CRC impose on States Parties obligations to undertake all appropriate legislative and other measures to ensure the implementation of the rights recognised in the treaties. Specific issues affecting the well-being and development of women and children are addressed under specific articles of both Conventions, and I shall attempt an examination and comparison of some of these issues. The Belem do Para Convention addresses the problem of violence, and comparisons with the other two conventions will be discussed separately.

CULTURAL PATTERNS AND TRADITIONAL PRACTICES

A major factor hindering women's full enjoyment of their human rights has always been cultural attitudes based on stereotypical beliefs of the role of women in society. These beliefs and attitudes have resulted in women being denied access to education, health care, property, employment or involvement in decision-making. The traditional thinking that informs these attitudes is that women were created for the roles of child-bearing and child-rearing as well as catering to the needs of their male family members.

Traditional practices such as female genital mutilation and payment of dowries have resulted in the deaths of women, and in both instances the victims are invariably young. This necessarily brings both CEDAW and CRC into focus.

One criticism of CEDAW in relation to traditional practices is that it does not specifically urge States Parties to take appropriate measures to eradicate these practices. CRC creditably addresses these practices in unambiguous language. The wording of the relevant articles of the two Conventions is instructive. Articles 2(f) & 5(a) of CEDAW mandates States Parties:

> Article 2(f): to take all appropriate measures, including legislation, to modify or abolish existing laws, regulations, customs and practices which constitute discrimination against women.

> Article 5(a): to take all appropriate measures to modify the social and cultural patterns of conduct of men and women with a view to achieving the elimination of prejudices and customary and all other practices which are based on the idea of the inferiority or the superiority of either of the sexes or on stereotyped roles for men and women.

Article 24(3) of CRC reads as follows:

> Parties shall take all effective and appropriate measures with a view to abolishing traditional practices prejudicial to the health of children.

The differences and emphases in the relevant articles are apparent. Whereas CEDAW in both articles urges States Parties to modify or abolish existing customs and practices and to modify the social and cultural patterns of conduct of men and women, CRC links the effect of traditional practices to the health of children. One such practice of genital mutilation decidedly affects the health of women adversely, but this has not been addressed in the aforementioned articles of CEDAW or under Article 12 where health issues are considered.

A possible explanation for the difference in approaches to these practices in the two Conventions may be that CEDAW was drafted ten (10) years earlier than CRC when presumably the impact and severity of traditional practices on the lives of women were not taken seriously and did not attract world-wide attention. The Committee on the Elimination of Discrimination Against Women at its 9th Session in 1990 adopted General Recommendation No. 14 requesting States Parties to include in their reports measures taken to eradicate female circumcision.

PARENTAL RESPONSIBILITY

Article 5(b) of CEDAW exhorts States Parties to take all appropriate measures to ensure recognition of the common responsibility of men and women in the upbringing and development of their children, it being understood that the interest of the children is the primordial consideration in all cases.

This was again emphasised in Article 16(d) which seeks to eliminate discrimination against women in all matters relating to marriage and family relations by according to all parents irrespective of their marital status the same rights and responsibilities in matters relating to their children, the interest of the children being paramount.

Article 18(1) of CRC mirrors the sentiments expressed in CEDAW by urging States Parties to use their best efforts to ensure recognition of the principle that both parents have common responsibilities for the upbringing and development of the child. It reiterates the primary responsibility of parents or legal guardians for the upbringing and development of the child, the best interest of the child being their main concern.

It is recognised that mainly because of economic constraints on the family income many women are compelled to combine family obligations with working outside of the home. This brings into focus the need for child care facilities, and Article 11(2)(c) of CEDAW seeks to encourage the provision of the necessary supporting social services to enable parents to combine family obligations with work in particular through promoting the establishment and development of a network of child care facilities.

Articles 18(2) & (3) of CRC not only mandate States Parties to render appropriate assistance to parents and guardians in the performance of their child-rearing responsibilities by ensuring the development of child-care institutions and facilities, but also confer on children of working parents the right to benefit from such child-care services for which they are eligible.

SEXUAL EXPLOITATION AND PROSTITUTION

Throughout the years, women have always been victims of sexual exploitation, but in recent times young girls as well as boys are consistently abused. The incidents of sexual exploitation of children are on the rise, and attract world-wide attention. Both CEDAW and CRC exhort States Parties to protect women/children from all forms of sexual exploitation and abuse, and CRC in particular makes reference to the exploitative use of children in pornographic performances and materials.

The relevant provision in CEDAW is Article 6 which requires States Parties to take measures, including legislation, to suppress all forms of traffic in women and exploitation of prostitution of women.

CRC devotes three Articles to this problem, and which due to their importance I shall set out *verbatim:*

Article 34: States Parties undertake to protect the child from all forms of sexual exploitation and sexual abuse. For these purposes, States Parties shall in particular take all appropriate national, bilateral and multi-lateral measures to prevent:

a) The inducement or coercion of a child to engage in any unlawful sexual activity;
b) The exploitative use of children in prostitution or other unlawful sexual practices;
c) The exploitative use of children in pornographic performances and materials.

Article 35: States Parties shall take all appropriate national, bilateral and multilateral measures to prevent the abduction of the sale of or traffic in children for any purpose or in any form.

Article 36: States Parties shall protect the child against all other forms of exploitation prejudicial to any aspects of the child's welfare.

A significant feature of these Articles is that the measures which States Parties are urged to implement are not to be confined to the national level but extends beyond which suggests that States can enter into arrangements with other States in implementing measures to eradicate the sexual exploitation of children. This is commendable, but a sad omission in CEDAW presumably due to the fact that women are regarded as being capable of taking care of themselves. It is hoped that States will avail themselves of these provisions in an effort to remove this scourge from our midst.

NATIONALITY

Article 9 of CEDAW addresses the issue of nationality and accords women the right to acquire, change or retain their nationality on equal footing with men. It also accords women equal rights with men with respect to determining the nationality of their children.

The corresponding article in CRC (Article 7) grants to every child the right to acquire a nationality, and, as far as possible, the right to know and be cared for by his or her parents.

Under the relevant articles of both Conventions States Parties are enjoined to ensure that no change of nationality under any law or otherwise renders the mother or child stateless, and all steps should be taken to preserve an acquired nationality.

Experience has shown that equal treatment is not always accorded to women in the conferring of their nationality on foreigners who they marry. The nationality laws of many countries do not permit the foreign husbands of female nationals to acquire their nationality in the same way as the foreign wives of male nationals. Similarly even though all children born during a marriage automatically acquire the nationality of their fathers, in some countries children born to a foreign mother do not acquire her nationality. The same difference is also evident in the laws governing change of nationality in some states.

One can only hope that in countries where there is this discrimination it will be removed in the foreseeable future.

EDUCATION

Upon an examination of the relevant articles of both Conventions dealing with the right to education (Article 10 of CEDAW and Article 28 of CRC) a common factor is the exhortation to States Parties to ensure access to education at all levels to women and children. In this regard the rights of girl children to education are safeguarded under both Conventions.

There is a significant difference, however, between the provisions of the two Conventions in that whereas CEDAW seeks to eliminate discrimination against women by according them equal access to career and vocational guidance as well as encouraging the elimination of stereotypical roles of men and women at all levels within the education system, CRC seeks to ensure that States Parties make primary education compulsory and secondary and higher education accessible and available to all children; further, it seeks to ensure that States Parties promote and encourage international cooperation in educational matters with a view to contributing to the elimination of ignorance and illiteracy throughout the world, and in this regard particular account ought to be taken of the needs of developing countries.

Article 29 of CRC goes on to amplify the scope of education of children by directing it to the development of their personalities and talents as well as respect for human rights, fundamental freedoms and the natural environment. Education should also be aimed at preparing children for responsible life in a free society in the spirit of understanding peace, tolerance and equality of the sexes.

In the same spirit, Article 17 of CRC addresses the role of the mass media in informing the minds of children, and States Parties undertake to ensure that children have access to information and material from a diversity of national and international sources, especially those aimed at the promotion of his or her social, spiritual and moral well-being and physical and mental health.

Unfortunately, all of this is not reflected in CEDAW which seeks only to eliminate discrimination, but does not direct attention towards the total development of women so that they can function as equal partners with men.

EMPLOYMENT

In order to maintain themselves and their families, women are entering the workforce in ever-increasing numbers. Article II of CEDAW seeks to ensure for them equal opportunities for employment and equal remuneration for work of equal value. It also seeks to ensure safe working conditions and protection of health as well as the right to social security and paid leave. It encourages the provision of necessary supporting social services.

All of these issues are addressed in Articles 3(3) of CRC which ensures that institutions responsible for the care and protection of children conform to established standards in the areas of safety, health, suitability and competence of supervisory staff. Article 26 recognises the right of every child to benefit from social security, and Article 32 recognises the right of the child to be protected from economic exploitation and from performing any work that is likely to be hazardous or to interfere with the child's education or to be harmful to his or her health, or physical, mental, spiritual, moral or social development. It urges States Parties to enact legislation to provide for a minimum age for admission to employment and to regulate the hours and conditions of employment.

HEALTH CARE

In CEDAW health care is addressed under the provisions of Article 12 in a very limited and restricted manner. It seeks to accord to women equal access with men to health care services. However, the general thrust of the Article is directed at women's reproductive function, and refers to the provision of appropriate services in connection with pregnancy, confinement and the post-natal period as well as adequate nutrition during pregnancy and lactation. Other vital areas of women's health are not specifically addressed, and as mentioned earlier unlike CRC it does not link traditional practices such as genital mutilation to women's health.

By comparison Article 24 of CRC which addresses health care is detailed and comprehensive. Apart from recognising the right of every child to the enjoyment of the highest attainable standard of health and to facilities for the treatment of illness and rehabilitation of health, it urges States Parties to strive to ensure that no child is deprived of his or her right of access to health care services. It exhorts full implementation of this right and the taking of particular appropriate measures to diminish infant mortality, provide primary health care, combat disease and malnutrition as well as access to health education, and the development of preventive health care, *inter alia*. Again, as in other articles of CRC States Parties are enjoined to promote and encourage international cooperation with a view to achieving the full realisation of the right to health care, and in this regard particular account shall be taken of the needs of developing countries.

CULTURE AND RECREATION

This aspect of life is considered under Article 13(c) of CEDAW which ensures to women on an equal basis with men the right to participate in recreational activities, sports and all aspects of cultural life in the same way as Article 31 of CRC ensures to children the right to rest and leisure, and to engage in play and recreational activities appropriate to their age; also the right to participate fully in cultural and artistic life.

MOVEMENT OF PERSONS

Article 15(4) of CEDAW accords to women the same rights as men with regard to the law relating to the movement of persons and the freedom to choose their residence and domicile.

This is complementary with Article 10 of CRC which grants to the child and his/her parents the right to leave and enter any country including their own. This right is linked inevitably to that of the parents due regard being paid to the need to maintain family relations and family reunification.

FAMILY RELATIONS

Article 16 of CEDAW ensures to women equal rights in all matters relating to marriage and family relations, and specifically under Articles 16(d)&(f) they are accorded the same rights and responsibilities as parents in matters relating to their children including guardianship and adoption, in all cases the interests of the children being paramount. Article 16(g) grants the same personal rights to women and men to choose a family name, profession and occupation.

These rights are linked in no small measure to the rights of children enshrined in CRC. Under Articles 7, 8 & 9 a child shall have the right from birth to a name, the right to acquire a nationality, and as far as possible the right to know and be cared for by his/her parents as well as the right to preserve family and personal relations as recognised by law without unlawful interference. The issue of adoption and its effects are covered under Article 21.

Article 27 of CRC recognises the right of every child to an adequate standard of living, and places on parents or others responsible for the child, the primary responsibility to secure within their abilities and financial capacities the conditions of living necessary for the child's development.

Another advantage which CRC has over CEDAW is that Article 27(4) enjoins States Parties to take all appropriate measures to secure the recovery of maintenance for the child from the parents or other persons having financial responsibility for the child both within the State Party and abroad, and to assist in this regard States Parties are urged to promote the accession to international agreements. This is most commendable, and if implemented will assist in no small measure the most difficult task women face in seeking to enforce maintenance orders against defaulting fathers.

As far as can be ascertained from an examination of the provisions of CRC the marriage of a child has not been addressed with no stipulations governing the minimum age at which a marriage can be contracted. This omission, however, is compensated for by the provision in Article 16(2) of CEDAW which is to this effect:

> The betrothal and the marriage of a child shall have no legal effect, and all necessary action, including legislation, shall be taken to specify a minimum age for marriage and to make the registration of marriages in an official registry compulsory.

This applies to all children regardless of gender, and is yet another example of the complementary relationship between CEDAW and CRC.

VIOLENCE

Another area which unfortunately is not addressed by CEDAW but which women face every day of their lives in every part of the world is the horrible trauma of violence whether physical, psychological or sexual. The framers of CRC, however, wisely sought to protect children from this scourge under Article 19 which expressly exhorts States Parties:

> to take all appropriate legislative, administrative, social and educational measures to protect the child from all forms of physical or mental violence, injury or abuse, neglect or negligent treatment, maltreatment or exploitation, including sexual abuse, while in the care of parent(s), legal guardian(s) or any other person who has the care of the child.

The Committee on the Elimination of Discrimination Against Women recognising the lacuna in CEDAW, and after examination of reports of States Parties from all geographical regions of the world over a period of ten years, expressed its concern over the ever-increasing incidence of violence by adopting two General Recommendations (No.12 adopted at its eighth session in 1989 and No. 19 adopted at its eleventh session in 1992). In the later Recommendation, the Committee concluded that "not all the reports of States Parties adequately reflected the close connection between discrimination against women, gender-based violence, and violations of human rights and fundamental freedoms". The multi-faceted Recommendation, *inter alia,* urges States Parties in their reports to the Committee to identify the nature and extent of attitudes, customs and practices that perpetuate violence against women, and the measures taken to overcome violence including all available data on the incidence of such violence.

INTER-AMERICAN CONVENTION

At this juncture, I think it apposite to introduce the Inter-American Convention on the Prevention, Punishment and Eradication of Violence (hereinafter referred to as "The Belem do Para Convention") which was adopted by acclamation on 9th June, 1994 by the General Assembly of the

Organisation of American States in Belem do Para, Brazil. The adoption of this Convention demonstrated the commitment of the countries, mainly of Latin America, to revise their laws to ensure specific solutions to the problems of physical and psychological violence encountered by women.

Under Article 2 of the Convention violence against women is understood to include physical, sexual and psychological violence that occurs within the family or domestic unit whether or not the parties share the same residence or that occurs in the community, e.g. rape, torture, forced prostitution, kidnapping and sexual harassment in the workplace, educational and health facilities; it also includes violence perpetrated or condoned by the State or its agents regardless of where it occurs.

States Parties recognise that violence against women prevents and nullifies the free and full exercise of their civil, political, economic, social and cultural rights. They condemn all forms of violence against women and agree to pursue by all appropriate means policies to prevent, punish and eradicate such violence.

An innovative provision for reparation for violence suffered by women is addressed in Article 7(g) under which States Parties undertake to "establish the necessary legal and administrative mechanisms to ensure that women subjected to violence have effective access to restitution, reparation or other just and effective remedies". This is a welcome innovation, and it is hoped that States Parties will give full effect to it by ensuring that procedures are established to which women victims of violence can have ready access.

The synergy of the Belem do Para Convention with CEDAW is exemplified by a comparison of its Article 8(b) with Article 5(a) of CEDAW. Under both Articles States Parties are exhorted to undertake appropriate and specific measures to modify social and cultural patterns of conduct of men and women with a view to eliminating or counteracting prejudices, customs and other practices which are "based on the idea of the inferiority or superiority of either of the sexes or on stereotyped roles for men and women". The only difference in the Articles is that the Belem do Para Convention urges States Parties in modifying social and cultural patterns of conduct of men and women, to include the development of formal and informal educational programmes appropriate to every level of the educational process, and it expresses the view that the idea of inferiority or superiority of either sex and the stereotyped roles for men and women, legitimises or exacerbates violence against women.

A commendable feature of Article 8 of the Belem do Para Convention is the emphasis on education and counselling for victims and perpetrators of violence as well as family members. Programmes are suggested for educating and training all those involved in the administration of justice, police and other law enforcement officers as well as programmes aimed at raising the awareness of the public to the problems of women subjected to violence. Rehabilitation of victims of violence is another commendable feature of the Convention with suggestions for the provision of readjustment and training programmes to enable them to participate fully in the public, private and social life of their countries. Guidelines are also suggested for the media in order to project more positive images of women subjected to violence and to enhance and respect their dignity.

The Belem do Para Convention like CRC urges the fostering of international cooperation for the exchange of ideas and experiences as well as the execution of programmes aimed at protecting women who are victims of violence. In this way, a network of information and programmes can be established as a multi-faceted assault on the scourge of violence with a view to eradicating it. It is a universal problem touching all societies whether developed or developing, and as such needs to be tackled in a concerted manner.

Both CRC and the Belem do Para Convention are of recent vintage when compared with CEDAW, and this may account for the fact that they both make mention of particularly vulnerable groups of women and children, the numbers of which have increased considerably within recent years, and are still on the rise. I refer to migrant, displaced and refugee women and children. Article 9 of the Belem do Para Convention requests States Parties to take special account of the vulnerability of women to violence by reason of, among others, their race or ethnic background or their status as migrants, refugees or displaced persons. Article 22 of CRC mandates States Parties to ensure that a child seeking refugee status or who is considered a refugee receives appropriate protection and humanitarian assistance in the enjoyment of applicable rights set forth in CRC.

The Belem do Para Convention urges consideration of women subjected to violence while pregnant or who are disabled, of minor age, elderly, socio-economically disadvantaged, affected by armed conflict or deprived of their freedom. The rights of the disabled child are given special consideration in Article 23 of CRC with States Parties recognising that a mentally or physically disabled child should enjoy a full and decent life in conditions which ensure dignity and promote self-reliance.

With the meteoric rise in drug use and abuse by the young throughout the world and in an effort to combat drug trafficking, Article 33 of CRC enjoins States Parties to take all appropriate measures to protect children from the illicit use of narcotic drugs and psychotropic substances, and to prevent the use of children in the illicit production and trafficking of such substances.

CONCLUSION

I have attempted to highlight similarities and point out differences particularly between CEDAW and CRC as well as some similarities with the Belem do Para Convention. These three treaties complement each other in no small measure, and together constitute an effective mechanism for enforcing the human rights of women and children as well as being a formidable bulwark against their infringements.

They have their strengths and weaknesses individually and collectively. CEDAW in particular has omitted several areas where women encounter discrimination, and the emphasis on certain aspects of a woman's life has been overplayed while others have been downplayed or omitted. However, in spite of these weaknesses the Conventions are inextricably linked as women and children are biologically. Inevitably discrimination suffered by a woman impacts negatively on the well-being of her children.

It is hoped that States Parties to all of the Conventions will honour their obligations and undertakings thereunder, and that the suggestions of international cooperation on specified issues will be put into effect. This will ensure to women and children throughout the world enjoyment of their rights guaranteed under the Universal Declaration of Human Rights and the Charter of the United Nations.

Belize
October, 1996

CHAPTER 23

BREAKING THE SILENCE

I feel it appropriate to introduce my address to you as we observe International Day Against Violence Against Women with the following poem written by a Bahamian woman named Victoria Coakley, and which was used to introduce the address of the Regional Programme Adviser of UNIFEM, Caribbean Office, Barbados, at the opening of the Regional Tribunal on Violence Against Women held in Barbados recently. It is titled *Break The Silence And Stop Sexual Violence*, and reads as follows:

Night has come and so has my fear,
For a repeat performance I could not bear.
I felt helpless, betrayed and lost
As I turned, twisted and tossed.
Closing my eyes to the horrible sight
Weeping silently as I put up a fight
I was unaware of when he was done
Because when I came to, he was gone.
My memory must be nothing but a bad dream
So I refused to think about what it could mean
I lay awake still locked in my fright
Wishing day would come and gone would be the night
My secret was much too big to keep
I'm a victim of sexual violence
Please help me to break the silence.

"Someone help me" I wanted to scream
I felt so dirty and full of shame
"Don't worry" he had said

As he crept into my bed
"No-one ever need find out
What you and I are all about.
It's our secret don't you forget
For, if you do, you will regret".

How can I break this silence
And the threat of physical violence
There must be someone out there
Who I can talk to about my fear.
I have to do what's right for me
If I ever want to be free.
To continue in this misery and fright
Is to let him believe that he is right.

If this abuse is happening to you
Don't believe there is nothing you can do.
You do not have to bear this alone
Especially in your own home.
Pick up the phone and seek assistance
And ask the counsellor what to do.
Tell them you're a victim of sexual violence
And that you want to break the silence.

For several years now November 25 has been set aside to highlight the ongoing scourge of violence against women. This year is of particular significance in its observance as 1998 marks the 50th anniversary of the signing of the Universal Declaration of Human Rights (10th December to be exact) declaring as it does that all human beings are born free and equal in dignity and rights, and no one shall be subjected to torture or to cruel, inhuman or degrading treatment.

Women have been victims of violence over the years in several situations resulting in assaults (physical and sexual), incest, harassment in the workplace and other forms of abuse. Most of these are unreported and undetected for a variety of reasons – embarrassment, financial and emotional dependency, dishonouring the family name, protection of children, hopelessness, and more frequently fear of retaliation. These are women who are caught in a situation from which they feel they cannot extricate themselves. Some have few options and remain in a hostile environment where they are abused repeatedly because they have no other alternatives.

Hand in hand with physical abuse is psychological and mental torture which includes constant verbal abuse, financial deprivation or excessive possessiveness. All of this may lead to a victim's low self-esteem and feelings of humiliation and guilt.

Most violent acts against women occur in a family situation, and though widespread, it is difficult to assess its extent because of its inherent private nature. For that reason it is very often not reported to law-enforcement authorities, and is seldom the subject of criminal prosecution. It occurs no less frequently in affluent families as in those in the low-income group and also among the aged and the very young.

Abuse of elderly women and children has been on the increase; attention must be focussed on the plight of these vulnerable victims who invariably are incapable of breaking out of the abusive situation and standing on their own.

Violence whether against men, women or children is a breach of one's fundamental human rights for which there ought to be redress. In relation to women and children these rights are protected under two international conventions – the United Nations Convention on the Elimination of All Forms of Discrimination Against Women adopted by the General Assembly in 1979, and the Convention on the Rights of the Child adopted in 1989. States who accede to or ratify these conventions are obligated to enact legislation and take appropriate measures to eradicate violence in all forms. This has led to member states promulgating laws to protect persons caught in the web of violence. There has been much criticism that focus seems to be directed solely on violence against women when in societies men are also victims of violence perpetrated by women. There are, however, legislative provisions which are gender-neutral, and non-governmental organisations which provide counsel and assistance to all victims regardless of gender.

Tribute must be paid to the work of those NGO's which provide assistance by way of counselling and refuge for those afflicted by violence. They provide invaluable service, and must be congratulated for their efforts to relieve the suffering of abused women and men. The newly-formed organisation "Men Against Violence Against Women" must also be congratulated for joining their voices to the appeal for eradication of violence against women. This is indeed commendable as it is crucial that men, particularly young men, be educated that violence is abhorrent and must be eradicated.

Although it is acknowledged that men are victims of violence perpetrated by women particularly within a domestic setting, a disproportionate percentage of violence committed in a family household is inflicted on women whether as wives, lovers or relatives. Available data indicate that between 20% and 60% of women across Latin America and the Caribbean Region have experienced physical or psychological abuse at the hands of their partners in domestic situations. Sexual abuse, particularly rape, seems to be also on the rise with indications that never a day passes without a woman or young girl being sexually violated. Concern has also been expressed about the high incidence of incest in families, the extremely private nature of this crime making it particularly difficult to detect and to prosecute. Sad to say, the majority of victims of this horrible crime are children and young girls who are vulnerable and have few options. They are torn between loyalty to their parents or guardians and fear of reprisals having been threatened with dire consequences if they disclose their violation to anyone. The mothers of these children are also victims torn as they are between loyalty to child and to husband or lover. What a painful dilemma and a nightmare which most parents pray will never afflict their family or anyone for whom they care!

The psychological fall-out of violent behaviour can be far-reaching and long-term. Invariably the child nurtured in a violent environment matures into a violent adult accepting violence as the only means of resolving grievances. The abused child becomes the abusive adult, and the "cycle of violence" continues from one generation to another.

Physical violence has been embedded in the psyche of our society to such an extent that it has become the norm and is regarded as part of our daily lives. Our young people are nurtured in the crucible of violence. They see it in their homes and in our streets. Parents hit out at each other in settling disputes and at their children in disciplining them; small wonder that children and young adults hit each other in anger when differences arise between them.

This horrible trend in our society must be arrested, and arrested now before it consumes us entirely. There are several root causes for violence, and research must be undertaken to ascertain these causes and the depth of the problem. Some reasons may be sociological or economic, some may be due to frustration and a sense of hopelessness with regard to one's station in life resulting in hitting out at those in close proximity.

Apart from research a massive education campaign needs to be embarked upon to educate persons, particularly young persons, that violent behaviour is wrong, unacceptable and a breach of one's fundamental human rights. Young women must also be educated not to accept any form of violent behaviour as being normal. Many feel that an occasional slap by their male friends is acceptable. This if not objected to can lead to more serious assaults. Young men also must be taught that it is unacceptable to inflict any kind of pain or injury on girls with whom they are friendly. Such behaviour is wrong and ought not to be condoned. If a firm stand is taken against it at the outset with perpetrators being reprimanded severely, it will send a clear message that we are breaking the silence.

Religious institutions and organisations must also be enlisted in this campaign against violence. Young persons particularly must be nurtured in and accept the tenets of their religion. Sad to say many of them grow up without any religious belief or training, and this to a large extent is responsible for their callous indifference to the sanctity of human life. Religious leaders need to play a more meaningful role in promoting a campaign of non-violence, and work on bringing the lost sheep back into their fold.

What also needs to be recaptured is the community spirit which pervaded our villages and towns in the not too distant past. We were all our brothers' and sisters' keepers. We looked out for each other. Children were children of the community. They were disciplined by any elder in the village or community without reproach from parents. Discipline was enforced by all regardless of race or social standing. A return to this community spirit is necessary and must be encouraged.

We have to cease regarding violence, particularly domestic violence and abuse of children, as a private matter concerning only the parties involved and to be settled only by them. It is a national issue which concerns everyone; we are all involved, and we can only rid our nation of this scourge if everyone assumes responsibility for the actions of others. We should no longer be spectators to spousal abuse, and we must free ourselves from the cultural mindset that it is the prerogative of a husband or partner to chastise his wife or paramour now and then. If we condone such behaviour we shall be breeding a nation of abusers in the future.

The time to act is now. We are all involved. We shall all be consumed. We may have in place all of the laws to protect women, men and children from violence whether physical or sexual, but unless we are sensitised to the need for action the laws will be meaningless. We can no longer stand silently by and remain uninvolved. We need to break the silence and exhibit zero tolerance for acts of violence committed in our presence. We must aim to promote in our society a culture of non-violence and respect for human rights.

International Day Against Violence Against Women
November, 1998

CHAPTER 24

WOMEN AND VIOLENCE: LEGISLATIVE STRATEGIES

Mankind's predisposition to violent behaviour is legendary, and for as long as men and women have inhabited the universe, anger, frustration and annoyance with each other have had their sequel in assaults, wounds and even death.

Under Article 1 of the Universal Declaration of Human Rights "all human beings are born free and equal in dignity and rights; they are endowed with reason and conscience and should act towards one another in a spirit of brotherhood." This, it is submitted, includes respect for all persons regardless of gender. The all-pervasive problem of violence in all of its hideous forms perpetrated against women in every age group is a flagrant violation of this fundamental human right and has been breached with impunity continuously.

In every corner of the earth, in developed, developing and under-developed countries women are the victims of violence in domestic situations, in places of work or in the streets of cities and villages where they live, work or dwell. In most cases these acts of violence are largely unreported and undetected for a variety of reasons – embarrassment, protection of the family name, financial deprivation, frustration, feelings of resignation, lack of choices, and in some cases the conviction that marital vows or conjugal duties include occasional corporal punishment from their spouses or mates. The violence encompasses not only physical abuse, but also sexual assaults and mental anguish with the resulting psychological scars. Women who are the victims of such abuse are usually maimed for life, and very few ever have the desire or the financial means to seek therapy or sever ties with their abusers; they are trapped with no way out.

INTERNATIONAL STRATEGIES

The highest incidence of violence perpetrated against women occurs in the home and within the bosom of the family. The Convention on the Elimination of All Forms of Discrimination Against Women adopted by the General Assembly in 1979 did not specifically address the problem of violence as it affects women. Over the years this gave rise to grave concern among the members of the Committee on the Elimination of Discrimination Against Women (CEDAW) which is a group of twenty-three (23) experts elected to serve for a period of four years and whose mandate is to monitor compliance with the Articles of the Convention by states who have ratified it. Such states are obligated to submit a report to the Committee every four years indicating measures taken to eliminate discrimination against women.

The concerns of the Committee about the pervasive scourge of violence after an examination of reports of states parties from all geographical regions over a period of ten years was manifested in the adoption of two recommendations, first in General Recommendation No. 12 adopted at its eight session in 1989 and General Recommendation No. 19 adopted at its eleventh session in 1992. The Committee was of the view that "not all the reports of states parties adequately reflected the close connection between discrimination against women, gender-based violence, and violations of human rights and fundamental freedoms", and after a detailed commentary on specific articles a multi-faceted recommendation was adopted in 1992 which, *inter alia*, urges states parties to report on all forms of gender-based violence including in such reports all available data on the incidence of each form of violence and its effects on women who are victims. The Committee also recommended that states parties ensure that laws against family violence and abuse, rape and other sexual assaults give adequate protection to all women, and respect their integrity and dignity. The Recommendation further urges states parties in their reports to identify the nature and extent of attitudes, customs and practices that perpetuate violence against women, and measures taken to overcome these attitudes and practices.

LEGAL APPROACHES

As strange as it may seem, some legal systems did and still do, give husbands the right to chastise their wives; forced and excessive sexual acts were and are still not regarded as rape; in fact, the thinking that informs this right is that upon marriage a wife impliedly gives her consent to any form of deviant sexual behaviour. In many systems, the courts also enforce a husband's right to redress against anyone who commits adultery with or seduces his wife on the ground that he is defending his honour, and if he chastised his wife he was never punished or the sentence meted out to him was invariably light.

The sum total of all of this was the inferior position women held in these societies, and the proprietary rights which men enjoyed over them. Sad to say these attitudes still persist in many societies today. Violence within the confines of the home is generally regarded as a family matter to be settled privately, and not to be aired publicly in courts of law. Law enforcement officials intervene with undisguised reluctance when an abused wife makes a report against her husband at local police stations, and she is very often dissuaded from instituting proceedings. The justification for this reluctance, however, is always reinforced when a frightened and enslaved wife with few options pleads with the court not to imprison her husband or is too terrified to testify against him which results in the charges being dropped.

With this in mind one wonders whether acts of violence against women particularly in the home should be classified as criminal offences in the legal systems of those countries which so classify them. Those who seek to decriminalise such violence suggest mediation and conciliation as a means of dispute resolution with therapeutic treatment and counselling for both abuser and abused. Fostering respect and tolerance of another's point of view, and encouraging self-esteem have also been advanced as alternatives to criminal classification of domestic violence. Very rarely before or after trials are abusers or the abused encouraged by court officials to engage in counselling or mediation sessions. The cases are dealt with in a cold and impersonal manner, and treated as any ordinary criminal matter. The system is regarded as punitive rather than rehabilitative, and the punishment more often than not has a devastating effect on the female victim physically, psychologically and financially if a term of imprisonment or fine is imposed.

On the other side of the coin are those who advocate a retention of criminal justice for abuse against women, and posit that this is the only effective means of combating its escalation. What is defective is the process by which the system is set in motion and its ultimate conclusion. Criminal justice is condemnatory of violence of all forms on all persons regardless of gender, but differences sometimes arise in the punishment meted out to the perpetrator depending on gender. Advocates insist that criminal justice for violence from arrest through prosecution to conviction and severe sentencing is the most effective mechanism for deterring further acts of violence. Of course, in preferring one system over another one ought to have regard to the historical, cultural and economic conditions of the particular society. A system found to be effective in one society may have disastrous consequences if applied in another with different mores and traditions.

LAW ENFORCEMENT

The role of the police in enforcing criminal justice for violence perpetrated against women cannot be ever overstated. In the United Nations report of 1989 on Violence Against Women in the Family, a quote from "Domestic Violence and the Police: Studies in Detroit and Kansas City" by M.Wilt and R.K. Breedlove, indicates one study revealed that police had been called at least once before in 85 percent of spousal abuse and homicide cases and in half of the cases where homicide ultimately occurred, the police had responded previously five times or more.

Though effective, however, in some instances in temporarily halting violent spousal attacks, many women display little confidence in police intervention. They sometimes feel pressured into pursuing cases when all they desire is a stern warning for their abusers, and when such cases do reach the courts they are badgered and humiliated by defending counsel or judicial functionaries which give rise to feelings of guilt and remorse at having initiated the charges, not to mention in some societies ostracism by relatives and friends for having aired "dirty linen" in public.

The humiliation often begins at the investigative stage by insensitive police officers who sometimes hold the view that the abused woman probably provoked the violent reaction of the abuser in some way or that there are insufficient grounds for intervention. The police need to be sensitised to the plight of abused women. They need to be educated to regard any form of violence against women particularly in a domestic situation as a crime like any form of violent assault committed by a man against another man, and not as a purely private and personal matter.

The police in most countries are the only recourse which abused women have when battered and assaulted. They need to understand that the reluctance of abused women to press charges against their male abusers or to testify against them after charges are laid may be inspired by fear of recrimination, family pressure, inability to cope psychologically or financially, low self-esteem or just fear of the criminal justice system with its awe-inspiring court officials. They need to reorient their deep-seated thinking nurtured in traditional male dominance that men are entitled to inflict beatings on their womenfolk now and then to keep them in line and assert their authority.

Young inductees into the police force in most countries do not receive any training whatsoever in handling and investigating reports of violence committed against women whether in the home or as the result of sexual molestation, and so they are ill-equipped to render assistance when confronted with the problem. Consequently, they tend to take the least difficult course by trivialising the reports, by not pursuing investigations or persuading the abused woman to return home and mend fences with her male abuser, or in the case of sexual assaults insinuate that she in some way encouraged the attack.

Against this background one should take a long hard look at legislation pertaining to the investigation, prosecution and sentencing of the perpetrators of violent crimes against women.

This was emphasised at 1985 End of Decade World Conference when paragraph 288 of the Nairobi Forward Looking Strategies for the Advancement of Women urged Governments to "intensify efforts to establish or strengthen forms of assistance to victims of (gender-specific) violence through the provision of shelters, support, legal and other services".

It also urged them to "undertake to increase public awareness of violence against women as a societal problem, establish policies and legislative measures to ascertain its causes and prevent and eliminate such violence, in particular by suppressing degrading images and representations of women in society, and finally encourage the development of "educational and re-educational measures for offenders."

Apart from the provision of forms of assistance for victims of gender specific violence the above stressed the need for raising public consciousness and seeking to ascertain the causes of such violence with a view to preventing it as well as encouraging the rehabilitation of offenders of such violence.

(a) Powers of Arrest

Since the police are the first rung up the ladder of prosecuting offenders in the criminal justice system, one has to ascertain that the legislative powers granted to them in investigating reports of gender-specific violence are adequate.

In most countries, the police have statutory powers of arrest, but may be circumscribed being utilised only if a breach of the peace is threatened or an actual offence has been committed since arrest involves deprivation of the liberty of a person which ought not to be embarked upon lightly. In some jurisdictions, the police tend to proceed against offenders by way of summons rather than arrest. This, however, does not always solve the immediate problems of the abused woman as the male abuser continues to reside in the home with her and may subject her to intimidation before the date required for his attendance in court. In more serious cases of gender-specific violence such as rape no uncertainty with regard to such powers arise, and arrest is usually the norm.

It has been advocated that the police be given wider powers of arrest in cases of domestic conflict based on the fact that arrest is the most effective remedy against a persistent pattern of abuse. It provides the woman with immediate relief from further assaults and brings home forcefully to the abuser the seriousness of his actions and that it will not be treated lightly. Of course, there is always the danger of misuse of this power, and a close watch must be kept to ensure that it is used responsibly.

(b) Powers of Entry

Of course, before an abuser in a domestic situation can be arrested by the police they have to enter the premises where the abuse is taking place, and this raises the issue of police powers of entry. In most countries, these powers are limited based on the conception of a person's home being his castle and private domain to be entered only upon invitation; any unlawful entry is a trespass and a crime not to be lightly encouraged.

In many jurisdictions, the police are given powers of entry on to private property if a breach of the peace is being committed or if they have reasonable grounds to suspect that it is about to occur, but then only with the cooperation of members of the household who alerted them, or if armed with a warrant.

Some countries like Australia, however, have made it easier for the police to enter premises in cases of domestic violence by introducing legislation extending the powers of entry of the police to include situations where an officer has reason to believe that a person on those premises is or may be under threat or attack or has recently been under threat or attack or an attack on such a person is imminent and is not expressly forbidden entry by the occupier. (Crimes Act, 1900 NSW).

TRAINING

There is no doubt that the police in most countries are ill-equipped to handle cases involving violence against women. As stated earlier in this presentation they regard it as a domestic and private matter to be treated lightly. It is therefore imperative that all law-enforcement officials be given special training in investigating gender-specific violence from report to prosecution. There is need for training in relation to attitudes displayed towards victims who invariably are in a state of trauma, shock or hysteria after an attack. Sympathy and understanding should underpin investigations particularly in the initial stages. The surroundings where reports and statements are taken should be relaxing and such as to inspire confidence. Some countries like Brazil have established special police stations staffed by female officers to receive reports from abused women; while this is commendable it is an example of segregation, and can be regarded as an indictment against male police officers who may sometimes be equally if not in some instances more sympathetic to the plight of battered women than female police officers.

It is suggested that training of all police officers in handling reports of gender-specific violence be made mandatory by statute and for all who are recruited into the police organisation regardless of gender. Accurate record keeping and data collection should also form part of the training process as well as satisfactory evidence collection and detailed recording of statements from victims.

COURT SYSTEM

The courts are the next rung up the ladder of the criminal justice system in securing a conviction of a person charged with violence against another, and for female victims can be the most intimidating. They face gruelling and sometimes embarrassing cross-examination by defence attorneys in austere and awe-inspiring surroundings before judges and magistrates dressed in funereal garb and who see themselves dispensing justice in strict accordance with the law.

Most women who are called upon to testify in court about abuses committed against them find this a traumatic experience, and leave with a strong impression that they were on trial instead of the offender, and in some way was responsible for their plight. They also face the humiliation of recounting the sordid details of the attack in cases of rape or the terror experienced at the hands of their abuser in other cases of assault before a courtroom of curious onlookers savouring the unfolding of a salacious soap opera.

Some countries have enacted legislation permitting hearings of rape and other sexual offences *in camera* with only those directly involved being present. This in some measure tends to make the victim feel a bit more relaxed. Much more, however, is required to ensure that court hearings are not intimidatory. It is suggested that as far as possible cases involving violence against women be heard in family courts established to deal with all matters affecting the family, e.g. custody, adoption, maintenance, divorce, etc.

Judicial officials should be sensitised to the predicament in which some women find themselves, trapped with nowhere to go or no one to turn to, and be encouraged to regard gender-specific violence as a serious crime meriting serious penalties for those convicted. In appropriate cases they should encourage both abuser and abused to seek counselling and rehabilitation in order to find other means of resolving conflicts.

In most countries of the world there is some legal remedy available to women who are abused. It could be either civil or criminal or both, and is invariably a creature of statute. So far in this presentation mention has been made mainly of criminal justice, but relief from constant abuse can also be pursued in the civil jurisdiction of the court system. The options include suits for damages for assault and battery, injunctions and protection orders which prohibit the abuser from harassing or molesting the battered woman or even visiting the matrimonial home, separation orders and ultimately divorce for those in marital relationships. In some countries, however, women are prohibited from instituting civil proceedings against their husbands for damages for assault, and until recent times even in highly developed societies under the criminal law a man could not be charged for raping his wife.

Whether the remedies available to women caught in violent relationships are civil or criminal their effectiveness depends on the officials who enforce them, e.g. the police or the Judiciary. Legislative strategies must be developed to ensure that women who are victims of violence can have their causes fully ventilated and their abusers brought to justice by law enforcement and judicial officials who are sensitive to their plight and regard the violence perpetrated against them as being serious and not trivial private matters.

CONCLUSION

All that has been said in this presentation is relevant to women in domestic situations, but is equally relevant to women who are victims of violence wherever committed and of whatever age or station in life. Elderly women are victims of children with whom they reside and on whom they depend for financial and emotional support or from persons in whose care they are placed. There are usually the most vulnerable because of their total dependence on their abusers and their inability to fend for themselves.

The time has arrived for countries of the world to take action to remove the scourge of violence against women in their communities. Although legislation itself will not solve this multi-faceted problem, it will provide a platform from which women can launch a comprehensive attack on this monster in our midst. Countries should be encouraged to enact legislation protecting all categories of women against all forms of violence outside of the regular laws governing assaults. They should also strive to ensure that the laws are enforced and are effective from investigation to sentence, and from initiation of civil suits to compliance with court orders.

Legal remedies alone, however, are insufficient, and must go hand in hand with a change in attitudes to gender-specific violence. In this regard governments as well as non-governmental organisations must undertake training programmes in the formal and non-formal education system as well as with law-enforcement agencies to sensitise the young and the old, particularly males, that regardless of past attitudes and traditions women are not chattels or property capable of ownership, but human beings with needs and emotions who must be respected and treated as equal partners in this complex world of ours.

Magistrates Conference
Georgetown, Guyana
17th May, 2003

CHAPTER 25

JUDICIAL ACTIVISM IN PROMOTING THE HUMAN RIGHTS OF WOMEN

The self-evident fact that women's rights are human rights ought not to be repeated at a forum such as this the theme of which is "Human Rights Today." Over the past quarter century since women's rights have been highlighted, discussed, dissected, analysed and recognised in several international and national instruments, it has now been accepted that any discussion on human rights inevitably will focus on the promotion of the human rights of women.

The main vehicle for promoting these rights is the Convention on the Elimination of All Forms of Discrimination Against Women familiarly known as CEDAW. This multi-faceted international treaty was adopted by the General Assembly of the United Nations on 18th December, 1979, and focussed attention on women's rights in many countries of the world. Within a few years of its adoption several member states of the United Nations had ratified or acceded to it. States parties were obligated to submit initial and periodic reports every four years on progress made in implementing the articles of the Convention. These are considered by a Committee of twenty-three experts elected by States parties and who serve for a period of four years in their individual capacities, and on which I had the honour to serve as member and Chairperson for a number of years.

The reporting obligations of the States parties include providing information on a wide range of issues affecting women – health, employment, education, finance, the family, participation in politics and government, culture, the ever-increasing problems of family violence, female genital mutilation, dowry deaths, women in armed conflict both as victims and participants, trafficking in women, and the problems encountered by rural women. States parties are enjoined to indicate measures taken to improve the status of women and eliminate all forms of discrimination against women in their countries. By ratifying the Convention States parties undertake to embody the principle of equality of men and women in their national constitutions, and to ensure through law and other appropriate means, the practical realisation of this principle. All of this means that the Convention is meaningless unless implemented by the State party.

One has to consider to what extent an international treaty is binding on or enforceable against a State party. Does it form part of the domestic law of the ratifying state, thereby making it enforceable in the national courts? This depends on the relationship of international law to domestic law in a particular state. In some states, domestic law in the national legal system is regarded and treated as being superior to any international treaty which can be enforced only if it is incorporated into the domestic law by the enactment of specific legislation giving effect to it. In other states an international treaty upon ratification is enforceable in domestic courts without specific incorporation, and is said to be "self-executing".

In countries where a treaty or convention is not incorporated into the domestic law its enforceability depends in large measure on the integrity and commitment of the particular state in honouring its international obligations and undertakings by enacting the necessary legislation to ensure enforceability in its domestic courts. This provides a mechanism for a state's nationals to obtain effective redress for violations of their human rights enshrined in those treaties.

As mentioned earlier the adoption of CEDAW by the United Nations General Assembly in 1979 propelled women's rights into the forefront of public scrutiny. In earlier times the rights of women flowed from their status as wives and mothers within a family situation, the main right of a wife being to be maintained by her husband so long as she remained chaste and faithful. The question of according women equal rights with men never came up for discussion, and they were accorded a protective status granted by their husbands. The issue of equal pay for equal work or work of equal value was unheard of. A woman's role was defined as being the child rearer, and so all laws were formulated to accord with this stereotype.

The English common law was imposed on former colonies of the British Empire including all its acts and statutes which perpetuated the stereotypical role of women without exception or necessary adaptation to accord with the peculiar customs and culture of the particular colony.

This sometimes led to absurd results when courts were required to apply the law strictly and follow long-established precedent. A case in point was one decided in 1959 in Trinidad & Tobago when a Muslim marriage was held not to be monogamous in the Christian sense of the term, and a magistrate who had made an order for maintenance against a husband on an application by his wife had no jurisdiction to do so. The reasoning was that the only kind of marriage that entitled the parties thereto to the remedies, adjudication and relief of the matrimonial law of England upon which the Trinidad and Tobago general law relating to marriage was based, was a marriage that was monogamous in the Christian sense of the term.

Being colonies of the then British Empire the influence of the mother country was very strong, and any departure from the settled norms of behaviour was frowned upon as being reactionary. Unrepentant monarchists brooked no interference with long-established precedent which they felt had served us well in the past, and should continue undiminished in form and substance. The conservative view was that the law must be certain and invariable, and any attempt to introduce any liberal interpretation of laws was dismissed summarily even if injustice was the inevitable result.

Although educational facilities and opportunities were available to both boys and girls the latter were not encouraged to pursue higher education which it was felt would inhibit their marital prospects, and the few that were encouraged or persevered to higher educational levels often found themselves pursuing courses in home economics and nutrition, possibly the arts, but very seldom the sciences.

Fortunately, this has changed over the years, and women can now be found in nearly every field of study, and sometimes outnumbering their male counterparts to such an extent that in some countries it has given rise to concern, and discussions centre around finding ways and means of motivating boys and young men.

A widespread and all-pervasive abuse of the human rights of women is violence whether committed in the home, at work or any other place. It may be classified as domestic, sexual harassment or sexual abuse, violence associated with prostitution and dowry deaths, violence against women refugees as well as female genital mutilation arising out of cultural and traditional practices. These issues and others were extensively discussed and deliberated upon at the Fourth World Conference on Women held in Beijing, China, in 1995. Out of these deliberations a Platform for Action was formulated with strategic objectives in identified areas.

One of these was the human rights of women. It was recognised that human rights and fundamental freedoms are the birthright of all human beings, and their protection and promotion is the first responsibility of Governments.

With this in mind the strategic objective was to ensure equality and non-discrimination under the law and in practice, and action identified to be taken by Governments include, *inter alia* –

(a) review of national laws, including customary laws and legal practices in the area of family, civil, penal, labour and commercial law in order to ensure the implementation of the principles and procedures of all relevant international human rights instruments by means of national legislation, and revoking any remaining laws that discriminate on the basis of sex, and removing gender bias in the administration of justice;

(b) review and amendment of criminal laws and procedures, as necessary, to eliminate any discrimination against women in order to ensure that criminal law and procedures guarantee women effective protection against, and prosecution of, crime directed at or disproportionately affecting women, regardless of the relationship between the perpetrator and the victim, and ensuring that women defendants, victims and/or witnesses are not revictimised or discriminated against in the investigation and prosecution of crimes;

(c) strengthening existing or establishing readily available and free or affordable alternative administrative mechanisms and legal aid programmes to assist disadvantaged women seeking redress for violation of their rights.

All of the strategies identified in the Platform for Action are based fundamentally on the articles of CEDAW. Since its adoption by the U.N. General Assembly and its ratification and accession by member states the domestic courts of these states have assumed greater significance and a prominent role in enforcing and giving effect to the rights enshrined in the Convention. The effectiveness of any treaty or constitutional instrument is determined usually by interpretation and pronouncements of the Judiciary of a state. Traditionally the conservatism of the Judiciary was reflected in the reluctance of judges in some jurisdictions to utilise international treaties in their decisions on issues which fell to be determined by them, preferring to tread the safe and well-worn path of precedent. There is always a timidity to launch out into deep international waters in which no one has ventured before, and this was certainly so in relation to giving effect to the rights of women enshrined in international treaties.

Happily, judicial activism is alive and well within recent times. The majority of issues which affect the lives of women on a day to day basis require judicial intervention, and it behoves members of the Judiciary to be familiar with and give effect to the statutes, treaties and legislation pertinent to a resolution of abuses or violation of women's rights. A few examples will illustrate the new trend and the enlightened approach of the Judiciary in the domestic courts of some countries.

There is the well-known *case of Attorney General of Botswana v. Unity Dow* (1992) in which both the High Court and the Court of Appeal upheld a challenge to provisions of the State's nationality law which did not permit a Botswana woman married to a non-Botswana man to pass on her citizenship to the children of the marriage. In the Court of Appeal reference was made to CEDAW which Botswana had ratified, and the status of international treaties and conventions in domestic laws was considered.

In the case of *Dhungana and another v. Government of Nepal* (1999) the Supreme Court of Nepal was called upon to consider a challenge made to Nepali law which provided that while a son was entitled to a partition share of his father's property at birth, a daughter was only entitled to obtain a share when she reached the age of 35 years and was still unmarried. Under Nepali law ratified treaties form part of the domestic law, and the ground of the challenge to the law was that it violated both the guarantee of equality in the Constitution and Article 15 of CEDAW.

In *Aldridge v. Booth* [1988] 80 ALR 1 the Federal Court of Australia dismissed a challenge to the constitutionality of the sexual harassment provisions of the Federal Sex Discrimination Act holding that <u>Article</u>

11 of CEDAW imposed a very clear obligation on Australia to eliminate sex discrimination in employment, and sexual harassment was a form of sex discrimination within the meaning of CEDAW.

The question whether a lower mandatory retirement age for women constitutes sex discrimination in breach of CEDAW was considered in the case of *Nurhatina Hasibuan v. Pty Indonesia Toray Synthetics and others* (1988). The Court expressly adopted the definition of discrimination used in CEDAW which Indonesia had ratified and noted that in the Indonesian community "women are the backbone to support the family economy", and for this reason, an identical retirement age for men and woman was essential thereby recognising the importance of women's labour to society.

The Indian case of *Madhu Kishwar and others v. State of Bihar and others* (1999) is significant because of the dissenting judgment of *Ramaswamy, J.* It involved the succession rights of tribal women. Customary law governing tribal communities provided for succession along the male line to the exclusion of women, and proceedings were launched to determine whether this was contrary to the Constitution and international conventions that protect the rights of women. The majority decision recognised that the customary law of succession discriminated against tribal women, but refused to strike it down. The Court held that it was not desirable to declare customary law to be contrary to the rights of women under the Constitution of India and the rules of succession sometimes provide different treatment that is not necessarily equal. The Court also held that judicial activism in the courts where judges reinterpret provisions beyond the legislative intent should be avoided. It found that it was inappropriate and elitist for judges to enforce on tribal people the principles of equal succession that is enshrined in other personal laws. The role of the courts is merely to advise and point out any legislative gaps to the Executive so that the State, in its legislative role, can attend to any problems.

Ramaswamy, J. disagreed and held that the full rights to the estate of their parent, brother or husband should be granted to women in tribal communities as heirs of intestate succession. He noted that the principles of equality having been ratified by the Government of India in international conventions and declarations should be upheld. He found that the principles of CEDAW had become integral to the Constitution.

This dissenting judgment was an example of judicial activism incorporating international law into both domestic law and the Constitution in enforcing the rights of women.

The cases referred to are just a few examples of a progressive and liberal approach being adopted by courts in many jurisdictions as women's rights assume increasing importance in today's world, and as women participate actively in every aspect of development of their countries.

In concluding this presentation, I adopt an excerpt from a paper delivered by that well-known illustrious jurist, former Chief Justice P.N. Bhagwati of India, at the Asia/South Pacific Regional Judicial Colloquium held in Hong Kong in 1996. The topic was "Creating a Judicial Culture to Promote the Enforcement of Women's Human Rights", and is to this effect:

> Judges have a creative function. They cannot afford to just mechanically follow the rules laid down by the legislature; they must interpret these rules so as to reconcile them with the wider objectives of justice which are encapsulated in the international norms of women's human rights. So long as judges are sensitive to women's human rights and are prepared boldly to advance the law through a process of creative interpretation, women's human rights will be safe.

Gibraltar
2nd – 3rd September, 2004

CHAPTER 26

ACCEPTANCE SPEECH AT CARICOM TRIENNIAL AWARD FOR WOMEN, 2005

Mr. Secretary General, Distinguished Heads and Representatives of Government of CARICOM, Distinguished Opposition Leaders of CARICOM, specially invited guests, ladies and gentlemen.

I wish to express my sincere thanks to Ms. Jacqueline Joseph for that over-comprehensive introduction and detailed citation of my achievements, and I cannot think of a more appropriate person to deliver it, having regard to our long and warm friendship over the years. At one point, I considered seriously just saying "thank you" and taking my seat. It would, however, be extremely remiss of me if I did not place on record my profound gratitude to the Regional Selection Sub-Committee for the Triennial Award for Women and to you, eminent Heads of Government of the Region, for selecting me to be the recipient of this Triennial Award for Women for 2005.

I am honoured to join a most distinguished group of women who preceded me and some with whom I interacted in earlier years in promoting the development of women in the Caribbean. These women worked assiduously and continuously to remove discrimination against women in the Region, and I am proud to have made some contribution with them in this regard.

Over the past twenty-five years much has been undertaken by the governments of the Region to improve the status of the women of the Caribbean. Ministries charged with responsibility for women's affairs have been established in some instance with Cabinet status. One remembers the days when matters pertaining to women were dealt with within an existing ministry with a low profile. Commendably this has changed and women's affairs ministries are properly staffed and operate independently. No doubt more needs to be done in some countries to raise the profile of these ministries.

Governments must be commended for taking issues pertaining to women more seriously than they were in the past, and the fact that the CARICOM Triennial Award for Women has been in existence over the last twenty-one years attests to the serious commitment that the Heads of Government of the Region have towards the women in the Region.

However, several important issues affecting women need to be tackled. There is the ever-present problem of family violence which though, all-pervasive, results in women being the main victims, with the numbers rising in alarming proportions in every state within our Region. Several reasons have been advanced for this astounding increase in violence against women, but it must be viewed against the larger background of violence generally. We have to face the fact that violence has become the main medium for resolving disputes, and strong measures have to be adopted to stem the flood before we are swept away in a tidal wave of death and destruction.

Other problems which affect our female population is the continuing increase of teenage pregnancies attributable in large measure to the absence of parental control. Hand in hand with this is the poor performance of boys in the school system, and who opt for quick dollars engendered by the burgeoning drug trade in the Region. All of this is a spin-off of the fact that most households are headed by single females struggling to maintain a family without financial or parental assistance from recalcitrant fathers.

This is certainly not the occasion to embark on a detailed discussion of these problems which confront women on a daily basis, but it is hoped that they will be noted and action taken to address them in each State within the Region. I am happy to have made some contribution towards improving the status of women in our part of the world, the highlight being my service both as Chairperson and founder member from the Caribbean of the United Nations Committee on the Elimination of Discrimination Against Women which was established in 1984 to monitor implementation by member states of the U.N. Convention of similar name. Over the years we have seen ratification of the Convention steadily increase, and at present nearly all of the Caribbean states have ratified or acceded to it.

Recently I have been given the opportunity to serve the Caribbean in another capacity, that of Judge of the Caribbean Court of Justice. Much has been made of the fact that I am the first woman to serve on this Court, but I am conscious that this carries with it certain responsibilities, chief among them being the ability to administer justice to the people of the Caribbean Region regardless of gender. The gestation period of this Court has been exceptionally long, but its birth is an indication that our independence is complete. It has seen the removal of the last vestige of our colonial past – the abolition of the Privy Council as the final court of appeal of some of the territories of the Caribbean Community. It is hoped that others will follow later.

Over the past few months since the Court's inauguration I have had the opportunity of interacting with my judicial colleagues, and I hasten to assure you that the Court is in the safe hands of a team which is committed to the task, and will work assiduously to justify the confidence which most have demonstrated in the establishment of the Court, and to earn the respect of those who feel the Region has made the biggest mistake. The way will not always be smooth, but determination and dedication will ensure that justice for the peoples of this Region be dispensed fairly without fear or favour, and be based on an understanding of our customs, mores and traditions.

Again, please accept my heartfelt gratitude for honouring me with this distinguished award which I shall always cherish among my most enduring mementoes.

Castries, St. Lucia
July, 2005

CHAPTER 27

THE PROMOTION AND ENFORCEMENT OF WOMEN'S HUMAN RIGHTS WITHIN THE JUDICIAL SYSTEMS OF THE CARIBBEAN

A definition of what constitutes "human rights" may be appropriate before embarking on a discussion of how they can be promoted and enforced in relation to women.

My suggested definition is that they are basic inviolable standards which inhere in every human being and which others are expected to respect and recognise regardless of nationality, race, ethnicity, gender or religion. These rights are closely allied with ethics and morality and reflect the values of a community. They are invariably enshrined within the legal framework of a state and are enforceable if violated.

The Universal Declaration of Human Rights adopted in 1948 by the United Nations was the precursor of several treaties and conventions which have been ratified or acceded to by the member states, e.g. the twin Covenants on Civil and Political Rights and the Economic, Social and Cultural Rights. The Convention on the Elimination of All Forms of Discrimination Against Women is another of them, and will be the focus of this presentation.

Having ratified or acceded to an international treaty or convention implementation can be the most troubling. Questions as to enforceability in the municipal courts of the ratifying state arise. This depends in large measure on the relationship between a state's international obligations and its domestic or municipal laws.

According to the monist theory in international law treaties ratified by a state for the protection of the human person automatically become part of the municipal law of that state. The dualist theory, on the other hand, advocates separation of international law from municipal law, and international obligations of a state are not automatically incorporated into its municipal law which is supreme.

For international treaties to be enforceable in the domestic court system of a state they have to be specifically legislated or adopted into the municipal law.

These theories have been criticised for not reflecting the reality, and are gradually losing ground. Changes in the role and domestic perception and understanding of international law in general and of international human rights law in particular, have led to an increased use of such law in municipal courts.

In countries where a treaty or convention is not incorporated into the domestic law its enforceability depends in large measure on the integrity and commitment of the particular state in honouring its international obligations and undertakings by enacting the necessary legislation to ensure enforceability in its municipal courts. Most of the countries within the English-speaking Caribbean and which inherited the English common law and systems of government adopted the practice of the United Kingdom which followed the dualist theory; hence in our Region international treaties are not automatically incorporated into domestic law upon ratification, and separate legislation and enactment of statutes are required to ensure enforceability in the municipal courts of the state. Of course, the legislation must in spirit accord and not be inconsistent with the State's obligations under the treaty.

Recently, in 2003, Guyana became the exception when its Constitution was amended by the Constitution(Amendment)(No.2) Act with provision for the protection of human rights to the effect that "every person, as contemplated by the respective international treaties to which Guyana has ratified or acceded to, is entitled to the human rights enshrined in those treaties, and such rights shall be respected and upheld by the executive, legislative, judiciary, and all organs and agencies of Government". This is indeed a departure from the traditional process of separate legislative enactments to conform to the provisions of an international treaty. In effect there is automatic incorporation upon ratification whichever approach is adopted to give effect to a state's obligations under a ratified international treaty. There is no doubt that within recent times these treaties are being utilised with increasing regularity in the judicial systems of states with persuasive even though not always legal authority. It is therefore imperative that both the Judiciary and the legal profession as a whole be aware of and become familiar with the well-known international treaties which have been ratified or acceded to by the majority of states within the United Nations family.

THE CONVENTION ON THE ELIMINATION OF ALL FORMS OF DISCRIMINATION AGAINST WOMEN

This Convention familiarly referred to as CEDAW is regarded as the "*fons et origo*" of the promotion of women's rights, and was adopted by the General Assembly of the United Nations on 18th December 1979; it has since been ratified or acceded to by 180 countries or states parties to date. It is often described as an international bill of rights for women, and is multi-faceted in its content covering as far as it could all spheres of women's lives. It defines discrimination against women as:

> any distinction, exclusion or restriction made on the basis of sex which has the effect or purpose of impairing or nullifying the recognition, enjoyment or exercise by women, irrespective of their marital status, on a basis of equality of men and women, of human rights and fundamental freedoms in the political, economic, social, cultural, civil or any other field.

By ratifying states parties commit themselves to undertake measures to end discrimination against women which include incorporating the principle of equality of men and women in their legal systems and national constitutions, abolishing all discriminatory laws and practices, and enacting laws which prohibit any form of discrimination against women. This is reflected in greater detail in Article 2 of CEDAW which can be regarded as its "heart and soul" defining its spirit and intent. Under this Article states parties undertake:

> (a) To embody the principle of the equality of men and women in their national constitutions or other appropriate legislation if not yet incorporated therein and to ensure, through law and other appropriate means, the practical realisation of this principle;
>
> (b) To adopt appropriate legislative and other measures, including sanctions where appropriate, prohibiting all discrimination against women;

(c) To establish legal protection of the rights of women on an equal basis with men and to ensure through competent national tribunals and other public institutions the effective protection of women against any act of discrimination;
(d) To refrain from engaging in any act or practice of discrimination against women and to ensure that public authorities and institutions act in conformity with this obligation;
(e) To take all appropriate measures to eliminate discrimination against women by any person, organization or enterprise;
(f) To take all appropriate measures, including legislation, to modify or abolish existing laws, regulations, customs and practices which constitute discrimination against women;
(g) To repeal all national penal provisions which constitute discrimination against women.

The legal status of women has been addressed in no small measure under articles which guarantee them the right to vote and hold public office, the equal right to acquire, change or retain their nationality and that of their children irrespective of their marital status, and equal rights within a marriage and upon its dissolution, including rights to matrimonial property. The perpetual problem of gender-based violence is not specifically addressed in any article of CEDAW and there is no mandate or obligation on states parties to deal with it. Nevertheless, some articles can be regarded as bearing some relationship to violence even though not specifically making mention of it, e.g. Article 2 and Article 5 which urges states parties to modify the social and cultural patterns and conduct of men and women based on the idea of the inferiority or superiority of either of these sexes or on stereotyped roles for men and women.

As is the norm in relation to most international treaty bodies there is a monitoring mechanism in place to ensure compliance with the treaty by the states parties who have ratified it. For this purpose a Committee on the Elimination of Discrimination Against Women (which is also familiarly referred to as CEDAW, but which to avoid confusion with the Convention, I shall refer to as "the Committee") was established comprising twenty-three experts of high moral standing from the accepted geographical regions of the world, sitting in their individual capacity, and it meets at least twice per year to examine reports submitted by states parties in accordance with their treaty obligations. The Committee also makes recommendations as it thinks appropriate. In keeping with this mandate under CEDAW the Committee at its Eighth Session in 1989 and again at its Eleventh Session in 1992 adopted two General Recommendations (Nos. 12 and 19) on gender-based violence, the latter being more comprehensive and multi-dimensional. Both, however, urge states parties to take appropriate measures to eradicate gender-based violence in all forms.

The interaction in most international treaties is between the monitoring mechanism or committee and the state party. Many of them, however, also provide a complaints mechanism whereby individual citizens of a state party that has ratified a treaty has access to the monitoring body which is empowered to consider complaints and make recommendations for redress of breaches of a person's rights by a state party.

This complaints mechanism is usually given effect to by ratification by a state party of an Optional Protocol to the treaty thereby extending the interaction between the monitoring body and the citizens of the ratifying state party. Prior to 2000 CEDAW had no mechanism for individual women to approach the Committee mentioned earlier for redress of individual violations of their rights. I am pleased to state that there is now in place an Optional Protocol which over time may be ratified by all states parties who have ratified CEDAW. In our Region, only Belize has so far ratified the Optional Protocol, but I hope before long all of the other CARICOM states will do so. Of course, before an individual can utilise the Optional Protocol certain conditions have to be satisfied. Unfortunately, time does not permit me to deal with this in greater detail in this presentation.

Before moving on to enforcement of women's human rights in the judicial system, I think it apposite to mention that within our Caribbean region there is a Charter which has been signed and was adopted in 1997 by the Heads of Government of the Caribbean Community. It is the Charter of Civil Society, which gave effect to a recommendation of the West Indian Commission contained in its report "Time for Action". The Charter lays out in articles recognition of several principles which the Governments commit themselves to respect and strengthen, among which are respect for fundamental human rights and freedoms. Several rights are addressed – political rights, freedom of expression and access to information, equality before the law, women's rights, children's rights, *inter alia*.

Since I am here concerned with women's rights I shall mention those contained in Article XII of the Charter. In summary it states that all women shall have equal rights with men in all spheres, and such rights shall include the right to be afforded equal opportunities for employment and to receive equal remuneration with men for work of equal value, the right not to be discriminated against by reason of marital status, pregnancy or health-related matters which affect older women, and to legal protection including just and effective remedies against domestic violence, sexual abuse and sexual harassment.

Interestingly, the Charter provides for the states to submit periodically to the Secretary General of CARICOM reports on measures adopted and progress achieved in compliance with the provisions of the Charter. One wonders how many citizens of the member states of CARICOM are aware of this Charter, and I suspect the provisions are honoured more in the breach than in the observance. I think Heads of States need to be reminded periodically of their obligations under this Charter. Most of its provisions mirror in large measure the provisions of international treaties which the States of CARICOM have ratified, particularly CEDAW, but is never mentioned or considered maybe because it has no binding sanction.

ENFORCEMENT IN THE JUDICIAL SYSTEM

As mentioned earlier we in the Caribbean as colonies within the former British Empire inherited the English common law and all of its statutes without exception. While some were repealed and amended after the colonies became independent we still maintain to a large extent the practice and procedure of the English court system; in some instances, we still lag behind even though the English system has changed. Many of the old statutes which we inherited as well as the common law perpetuated the stereotypical role of women as being inferior to men and akin to chattels capable of ownership and protection.

Over the years the legal status of women has improved significantly in many areas of their lives although much more needs to be achieved. Archaic laws which perpetuated the inequality of status between men and women have been repealed. However, while the executive and legislative branches of government are obligated to ensure that appropriate measures are taken and laws enacted to enforce the rights of women, it is to the courts and the Judiciary of a state that one looks for protection of these rights and redress for their violation. Laws may be enacted to promote one's rights, but unless they can be enforced legally and violation redressed they will be nothing more than "sounding brass and tinkling cymbal".

There are several legal issues pertaining to women's rights which need to be addressed through judicial interpretation and decisions, e.g. employment laws which discriminate against women in relation to earnings and conditions of work, nationality, inheritance and intestate succession, entitlement to matrimonial property upon dissolution of a marriage, custody of children, the position of women in common law relationships, the ever-increasing problem of HIV/AIDS, termination of pregnancies, the rights of the elderly and of the physically challenged. Most of these issues are addressed directly or indirectly within specific articles of CEDAW, and I shall illustrate from a publication entitled "A Digest of Case Law on the Human Rights of Women" and issued by the Asian Pacific Forum on Women, Law and Development, how the courts in Asia and the Pacific have utilised CEDAW in determining matters concerning the rights of women. The first is the case of *Nushatina Hasibuan v. Pty. Indonesia Toray Synthetics, et al* (1988) in which the Court of Appeal of Indonesia considered whether a lower mandatory retirement age for women constituted sex discrimination, and was in breach of Indonesia's Labour Act which prohibited discrimination on the ground of sex, as well as in breach of CEDAW. The Court upheld a decision of the lower court made in favour of Ms. Hasibuan, expressly adopted the definition of discrimination used in CEDAW, and applied it directly to the circumstances of the case rejecting the argument that it must adapt to local social norms. Reference was made to Articles 1, 4 and 11 of CEDAW.

In the case of *Humaria Mehmood v. The State* (1999) a court in Pakistan was called upon to consider among other issues the meaning and role of consent in a valid marriage under Pakistani law, and held that a marriage without consent is invalid. The Court noted that its findings accorded with a number of international instruments that protect the rights of women, and that Pakistan was a signatory to CEDAW which enjoins member states in Article 16 to take all appropriate measures to ensure equality in matters of marriage and the right to consensual marriage.

Another example of the use of CEDAW is the Indian case of *Mrs. Githa Hariharan and another v Reserve Bank of India and another* (1999) where the issue of sex discrimination under Indian guardianship laws arose. There was a challenge to the Hindu Minority and Guardianship Act 1956, and the Court considered whether it contravened the equality provisions of the Indian Constitution on the basis that they exclude mothers from being the natural guardians of their children during the father's lifetime which was a discrimination against mothers on the basis of their sex. The Supreme Court granted relief by broadening the meaning of the Act rather than striking it down as being unconstitutional, and based its interpretation of the Act on CEDAW. The Court observed that domestic courts in India are under an obligation to construe domestic laws in line with international conventions and norms.

In the area of criminal law particularly in trials for the offence of rape and sexual assault there is a legal requirement that the victim's evidence must be corroborated or in layman's terms must be supported. Judges are mandated to advise juries of the dangers of convicting an accused on the uncorroborated testimony of a victim. Perhaps this came about because it was felt that a woman could easily allege that she was raped, and it is invariably her word against that of the accused. Whatever the reason, it operated against female rape victims to a large extent. Efforts have been and are being made in some jurisdictions around the world to remove the requirement for corroboration in sexual offences, and a case from the Pacific Island of Kiribati illustrates this. *In the Republic of Kiribati v. Tieta Timiti & Rabaere Robuti* the Court was asked to consider whether the rule of corroboration in the law governing rape in Kiribati discriminates against women and was contrary to the provisions of the Constitution and CEDAW. It involved the rape of a woman allegedly by two men whose defence was that intercourse was consensual. The prosecution, even though the victim's evidence was corroborated by three witnesses, argued that the requirement for such corroboration violated the rights of women under the Constitution which guarantees all citizens equal protection under the law without discrimination. The Court was asked to consider the principles formulated in CEDAW and other international instruments that protect the rights of women. Although this case did not result in having the rule of corroboration changed the

Court was presented with the opportunity to consider the claim that the requirement of corroboration is discriminatory against women under CEDAW.

Within the Region in an appeal before the Eastern Caribbean Court of Appeal of *Gladstone Gooderidge v. The Queen* (C.A. No.13/1997) where the Appellant had been convicted for indecent assault of a child aged six years, then Chief Justice Dennis Byron in the course of his judgment made reference to the fact that St Vincent and the Grenadines (where the offence was committed) had ratified CEDAW and hence the international norms that are therefore applicable in the society included the duty of the State to protect the interests of the girl child against domestic violence and sexual abuse.

On the vexed question of spousal abuse where a wife is charged with killing a husband in retaliation for prolonged and continuous physical violence, she is usually prohibited from raising this as a defence to a charge of murder since it is argued that it does not satisfy the requirements of self-defence. This is still so in many jurisdictions, but some have moved towards permitting continuous abuse to be used as a defence. It is familiarly called "battered woman's syndrome". I cannot state with any degree of certainty whether in our Region this is now available as a defence to women charged with killing their abusive husbands or partners. If it is not, one hopes that it will not be long before the criminal laws of our states are amended to permit it.

A feature of life in Caribbean societies is the common law relationship which unfortunately is not always recognised, and until recently very few countries had any laws enacted to protect women in such relationships. Women in these unions were not, and maybe in some jurisdictions are still not entitled to maintenance from their partners nor to any right to property acquired during the relationship except upon strict proof of a specific contribution to its acquisition.

This has changed in some Caribbean jurisdictions, and Barbados must be commended for leading the way since 1981 with the passage of The Family Law Act which makes no distinction between parties in a marital or common law relationship with regard to maintenance; the right to be maintained arises only where the other party in the marriage or union is unable to support herself or himself adequately. The Act applies equally to women and men, and for the first time, I am sure, in the Region there is not an automatic right to be maintained or a corresponding duty to maintain arising solely by virtue of marriage or cohabitation. The Act also imposes an obligation on both parents whether married or in a common law union, to maintain their unmarried children under the age of eighteen (18) years. A similar approach was adopted in relation to rights to property. No distinction is made between matrimonial property and property acquired during cohabitation of persons in a common law union. The Act empowers a Court to make a declaration to title or rights to property in proceedings between parties to a marriage or common law union.

In Guyana, the Married Persons (Property) (Amendment) Act, 1990 empowers a court to make orders concerning property acquired during marriage or a cohabitation, and for this purpose any reference to a "wife" in the relevant section of the Act shall include reference to a single woman living with a single man in a common law union; similarly reference to a "husband" shall include a single man living together with a single woman in a common law union.

The related problem of family inheritance also needs to be addressed. Over the years this has been an area where women have encountered discrimination. Again, women in common law unions as well as children born out of wedlock were not, and in some Caribbean jurisdictions are still not entitled to share in the estate of a deceased cohabitant or father who dies intestate. Their entitlement rests solely on a bequest made in a will by the deceased if he is so minded.

This imposes untold hardship on women in common law unions with men who are married but separated from their wives, and who form lasting relationships with these women sometimes in excess of years spent in a marital union. Upon death of the male cohabitant intestate these women and children of the union could be left penniless, and all of his assets sometimes acquired through the industry and cooperation of the common law wife could be inherited solely by the lawful wife and children of the marriage. In like manner, a lawful wife could be disinherited by a husband who might have harboured undisclosed grudges against her for years by leaving nothing for her in a will. Unlike the common law wife, the lawful wife's position was secure if the husband died intestate.

By passage of the Family and Dependants Provision Act 1990 the position of these women in Guyana has been addressed. The Act empowers the courts to make provision for the spouse, child, child of the family or dependant of a deceased person out of his/her estate. For the purposes of the Act which is gender-neutral any reference to a wife includes a single woman or man living together with a single man or woman in a common law union for seven continuous years immediately preceding the date of death. There is a proviso, however, that only one such union shall be considered for any benefit under the Act. Multiple relationships are not entertained; also, reference to a single woman or single man includes a widow or widower or a woman or man who is divorced.

The Act also provides for a wife, husband, child or dependant who was maintained by the deceased to apply to the Court where a disposition to them made under a will or an entitlement on intestacy is not regarded as reasonable financial provision for the applicant.

I am informed that similar legislation exists in Barbados and hopefully in other Caribbean jurisdictions; if not, I commend this to those states where no such provision is made for the disadvantaged women and children referred to earlier.

At the international level the Committee on CEDAW recognised that there are some countries where the law and practice concerning inheritance and property result in serious discrimination against women who may receive a smaller share of their husband's or father's property upon his death than would their male counterparts. To address this problem the Committee in General Recommendation No. 21 in 1994 urged states parties to include in their reports information on the legal or customary provisions relating to inheritance laws as they affect the status of women in order to ensure that men and women in the same degree of relationship to the deceased rank equally in succession and enjoy equal shares in the estate.

There are a few areas of discrimination which have not been addressed either by legislation or within the judicial systems of our Region to any significant degree as far as I can ascertain. The field of employment springs to mind. Most countries have legislation which protects workers' rights of employment, and provision for payment of wages commensurate with work performance. After years of bargaining, women succeeded in receiving equal remuneration as men for equal work performed. However, this did not always take into account the fact that tasks carried out by women could not always be equated with tasks carried out by men. Article 11 of CEDAW sought to correct this discrimination by introducing the concept of equal pay for work of equal value. It states *inter alia*:

> 1. States Parties shall take all appropriate measures to eliminate discrimination against women in the field of employment in order to ensure, on a basis of equality of men and women, the same rights, in particular:
>
> (d) The right to equal remuneration, including benefits, and to equal treatment in respect of work of equal value, as well as equality of treatment in the evaluation of the quality of work.

At its Eighth Session in 1989, the Committee adopted General Recommendation No. 13 on Article 11 and made reference to the International Labour Organisation Convention No. 100 concerning Equal Remuneration for Men and Women Workers for Work of Equal Value which has been ratified by a large majority of states parties to CEDAW. The Recommendation urges those states parties that have not as yet ratified the ILO Convention No. 100 to do so in order to implement Article 11 of CEDAW fully; further, they should support, as far as practicable, the creation of implementation machinery and encourage the efforts of the parties to collective agreements, where they apply, to ensure the application of the principle of equal remuneration for work of equal value. I remind you here of a similar provision in CARICOM's Charter of Civil Society. In order to implement Article11 states parties should consider the development and adoption of job evaluation systems based on gender-neutral criteria that would facilitate the comparison of the value of those jobs of a different nature in which women presently predominate, with those jobs in which men presently predominate, and include the results in their reports to the Committee.

I have not been able to ascertain whether the labour laws of some or any of the states of our Region have been amended to give effect to Article 11 of CEDAW. If they have not, urgent attention should be given to doing so if women's involvement in the work force is to be meaningful.

Another important area of women's human rights to a large extent has not been given the serious attention it deserves. It is the all-pervasive scourge of HIV/AIDS. One wonders how many states have legislation in place to protect women, and men, from carriers of the virus who intentionally infect others bearing in mind, however, that women are a particularly vulnerable group within marital or other relationships, not very often having the power to insist on safe and responsible sexual practices. The Beijing Declaration which was formulated and adopted at the Fourth World Conference on Women in 1995 addressed the ever-increasing problem of HIV/AIDS, and paragraph 108(b) under Action to be taken by Governments urged them to:

> Review and amend laws and combat practices, as appropriate, that may contribute to women's susceptibility to HIV infection and other sexually transmitted diseases, including enacting legislation against those socio-cultural practices that contribute to it, and implement legislation, policies and practices to protect women, adolescents and young girls from discrimination related to HIV/AIDS.

Action has to be taken by governments in our Region to eliminate socio-cultural practices which contribute to the spread of HIV/AIDS, and if no such action has been taken by some of our Governments I strongly urge them to do so in order to remove this scourge from our midst, and to empower our courts to deal with the consequences which arise from it.

CONCLUSION

In concluding this discourse, I refer again to the Beijing Platform for Action mentioned earlier which can be regarded as a comprehensive blueprint for removing discrimination against women and developing strategies to advance their improvement in all areas of life. One such strategic objective is to ensure equality and non-discrimination under the law and in practice. To achieve this, Governments are required, *inter alia*, to:

> (a) Review and amend criminal laws and procedures, as necessary, to eliminate any discrimination against women in order to ensure that criminal law and procedures guarantee women effective protection against, and prosecution of, crimes directed at or disproportionately affecting women, regardless of the relationship between the perpetrator and the victim, and

ensure that women defendants, victims and/or witnesses are not revictimized or discriminated against in the investigation and prosecution of crimes.

(b) Strengthen existing or establish readily available and free or affordable alternative administrative mechanisms and legal aid programmes to assist disadvantaged women seeking redress for violations of their rights.

The last-mentioned objective is absolutely necessary in the enforcement of women's human rights. Invariably many women are confronted with a dilemma of being unable to afford competent but high-priced lawyers to seek redress for wrongs committed against them because of the need to provide necessities for themselves and their children. This is especially so in the case of female single-headed households. There is a crying need in most of the Caribbean states for state-funded, well-organised legal aid schemes which can provide legal services for the disadvantaged in the society and particularly women who are the victims of recalcitrant husbands and partners who habitually default on payments of maintenance and child support. Promoting women's rights will be meaningless if breaches of these rights cannot be redressed due to women's fragile financial situations. Both Governments and the legal profession in the Region have an unqualified duty to ensure that the disadvantaged can ventilate their rights in the courts of their states.

Ratification of international treaties is commendable, but will avail nothing if the rights which these treaties seek to protect cannot be enforced or protected by those for whose benefit they are ratified. This brings me to the need for education and sensitising judicial personnel and the legal profession as a whole about women's human rights. Over the years this has not been an area with which judges and lawyers are familiar; to be fair women's rights were not regarded as being of any significance, and so were not the focus of special consideration or attention. Happily, we are in a new era, and with women's rights being regarded as any other human right those who administer justice have to focus attention on them, and be sensitive to the need for redress of violations of these rights. In order to do this, there is also a need to be familiar with international treaties generally something which was never before considered relevant in the judicial process. With increasing frequency, international treaties are being utilised to enforce individual rights of the citizens of states which have ratified them. It is therefore imperative for those who administer justice to recognise their significance and give effect to them.

In concluding this presentation, I adopt the following passage from a presentation of that well-known jurist and advocate of women's rights, former Chief Justice P.N. Bhagwati of India at a Judicial Colloquium held in Hong Kong in 1996. The topic was "Creating a Judicial Culture to Promote the Enforcement of Women's Human Rights", a topic somewhat similar to my presentation tonight. He said this, which I humbly adopt:

> Judges have a creative function. They cannot afford to just mechanically follow the rules laid down by the legislature; they must interpret these rules so as to reconcile them with the objectives of justice which are encapsulated in the international norms of women's human rights. So long as judges are sensitive to women's human rights and are prepared boldly to advance the law through a process of creative interpretation, women's human rights will be safe.

Let us ensure that in our Caribbean Region they are and will always be safe.

University of the West Indies
Cave Hill, Barbados
18th November, 2005

CHAPTER 28

CONFRONTING GENDER-BASED VIOLENCE IN THE CARIBBEAN

When one considers the whole issue of gender-based violence one immediately conjures up in one's mind violence against women despite the gender-neutral term used to include the all-pervasive scourge of violence committed against both male and female victims. With increasing frequency, males (boys and adult men) are becoming victims of violence perpetrated against them by females. It is an acknowledged fact, however, that in the overwhelming majority of incidents of violence women are the victims.

The Declaration on the Elimination of Violence Against Women[1], defines violence against women as "any act of gender-based violence that results in, or is likely to result in, physical, sexual, or psychological harm or suffering to women, including threats of such acts, coercion or arbitrary deprivation of liberty, whether occurring in public or private life. It encompasses, but is not limited to, physical, sexual and psychological violence occurring in the family".

This multi-faceted problem which crosses all lines of age, ethnicity and societal positions violates fundamental human rights guaranteed under The Universal Declaration of Human Rights[2], and will be discussed in all of its hideous forms.

VIOLENCE IN DOMESTIC SITUATIONS

The most common and frequently-encountered form of violence occurs in domestic situations; research indicates that women are more likely to be abused, killed or injured within a family setting. It ranges from slaps and kicks to more serious assaults as wounding with knives and other implements sometimes resulting in death. These assaults may be sporadic or consistent on a daily or weekly basis, and invariably are unpredictable with no reference to any act committed by the woman. They may be the result of alcohol or drug consumption by the husband or partner in a family relationship or a personality defect with the abuser seeing the need to inflict pain on the person closest to him.

The rationale for this form of violence is rooted in the historical philosophy of women's subordination and inferiority to men. Women were, and many still are, conditioned to believe in the superiority of their male partners in any relationship; further, they regard everything which occurs within the four walls of a home as being private and not to be disclosed to anyone no matter how devastating. This has resulted in under-reporting of incidents of family violence. A study conducted by Professor Danns and Ms. Shivpersad in 1989[3] revealed that in Guyana only 5.9% of women report incidents of domestic violence to the police. The study also revealed that two out of every three women had been beaten at least once by their conjugal partners.

Women in the main are ambivalent about violence perpetrated by family members. Apart from the private nature of such violence, many women suffer from feelings of guilt believing that they deserve the beatings because of some wrong committed by them. Others refrain from speaking out about the violence because of fear of further abuse or shame and embarrassment, threats of financial deprivation or lack of options. In marital and common law relationships wives convince themselves that their vows or conjugal duties include occasional corporal punishment from their spouses or partners, as frequently glorified in calypsoes and dance hall music.

The impact of psychological and emotional violence is inestimable including repeated verbal abuse, threats, insults, humiliation in the presence of others contributing to low self-esteem and feelings of inferiority which may be in some instances more painful than physical attacks as it is constant and unrelenting. Extra-marital relationships, financial neglect or extravagance, habitual drunkenness, inordinate sexual demands all take their toll on the emotions of partners in a relationship. Unlike physical abuse which is directed invariably at women in the household, all family members may sustain emotional abuse. Children are particularly vulnerable, and even though they may not be victims of the physical abuse, they suffer from lifelong personality defects based on the traumatic experiences of living in embattled domestic situations.

Elderly family members also nurture the additional fear of homelessness or abandonment being frequently dependent on their close relatives for financial and emotional support.

Some theories suggest that low and moderate income families who are housed in cramped and over-crowded conditions are more prone to violent behaviour than families living in spacious and well-appointed accommodation, the reason being that economic hardship and financial strictures impose strains on the conjugal relationship. Relief from these pressures is achieved by hitting out at those closest and acting out all of the frustrations of daily living even in well-heeled families without financial pressures; violence may be a release from emotional or work-related pressures.

In our Caribbean societies drugs and alcohol impact significantly on the incidence of violence in family situations. Invariably women are brutalised by their male partners when in a drunken stupor or under the influence of habit-forming drugs. In some instances, women develop an attitude of resignation to the inevitable beating which will be administered when their partners return home at the end of the day in an intoxicated condition. Again, this resigned attitude is evidence of low self-esteem and psychological manipulation. This goes hand-in-hand in the Caribbean with a myth, which thankfully has to a large extent been exploded that most women enjoy physical violence and regard it as an expression of the male macho image; if not administered periodically it indicates waning affection or the woman's diminished sexual appeal or attraction.

SEXUAL ABUSE

This is the most frequently used weapon in the arsenal of male abusers. Invariably, with some exceptions, the abuse occurs in private. It preys on and affects one's emotions, and leaves behind the deepest psychological scars. It is also ubiquitous in that it can be perpetrated anywhere on any victim regardless of age, gender or social standing. The youngest infant is equally liable to be sexually assaulted as the oldest adult either in the privacy of the home, the workplace or in dark secretive places away from public view. In developing countries, research suggests that rape is an ever-present threat and sometimes daily occurrence for millions of women.

Traditionally rape was perceived as an offence committed by strangers as opposed to relatives. This has changed dramatically with victims being equally liable to be sexually assaulted by family members (parent, sibling or spouse) and by acquaintances or casual friends.

Sexual assaults committed within a domestic situation include incest, which is often not reported due to the fact that it invariably involves a parent or step-parent and child or someone *in loco parentis* to a child. Sexual spousal abuse has in recent times been the subject of open discussion and court intervention. This is a decisive break with tradition and legal theory that a husband cannot be guilty of raping his wife. It was founded on the premise that upon marriage a wife impliedly consents to any form of sexual behaviour by her husband. Modern thinking and judicial pronouncements have reversed this misconception, and husbands can now be found guilty of raping their wives in the absence of consent.

A serious and detrimental spin-off of sexual abuse in today's world is the harmful effect of HIV/AIDS. Research has indicated that many women either as wives, or in common-law relationships contract this potentially fatal disease from their husbands and partners, in some instances transmitting it to their unborn children. Much work needs to be done in this area to sensitise women to the fact that secrecy is not an option where HIV/AIDS is concerned. Shame and embarrassment very often are inhibiting factors in its early detection and treatment particularly when it is contracted from close relatives and within the privacy of the home.

In 2003 in a Framework for Mainstreaming Gender into Key CARICOM Programmes[4] Andaiye identified the fear of violence and economic dependence as barriers to women negotiating safe sex practices, and made reference to the Caribbean Task Force on HIV/AIDS which stated that "Women are at greater risk of contracting HIV in both biological and social terms, as they are both physically more vulnerable and often have little or no power to negotiate safer sex practices with their male partners."

Tina Johnson in a background paper on gender-based violence written for a Human Rights Expert Group Consultation in February 2004[5], expressed these views on the topic:

> Gender-based violence and HIV/AIDS are intersecting epidemics. Women's relative lack of control over their sexual lives and

> methods of preventing HIV and other sexually transmitted infections due to violence or fear of it is one of the main factors behind the spread of AIDS .... This lack of control is experienced not only by women who are sexually assaulted but also by those in relationships where they are unable to negotiate condom use with their partners. Violence both exposes women to HIV infection and limits their ability to participate in and benefit from HIV/AIDS prevention methods and treatment.

Abortions and unwanted pregnancies are the consequential results of rape and sexual assaults on young girls sometimes caught in situations over which they have no control. In many instances, they are scared or hesitant to report acts of sexual molestation committed by siblings or adult male relatives, such as step-fathers or visiting male friends of their mothers. More often than not, mothers are in denial about such abuse preferring not to believe the child rather than face the fact that their male partners are committing such despicable acts on their children.

Outside of the home young girls are equally vulnerable to sexual assaults committed by teachers or fellow students in schools, a trend which is becoming alarmingly prevalent in our Caribbean societies, and the depths of which must be ascertained in order to find solutions. In the case of teachers such acts constitute a betrayal of trust which when discovered should attract the full force of the law.

SEXUAL HARASSMENT

Sexual harassment in the workplace is a not too unfamiliar scenario in our Region. While victims of sexual harassment can be male or female, women suffer disproportionately. Many young women are exploited and forced into sexual liaisons with their male employers to obtain or retain employment. Sexual favours are the *quid pro quo* for permanent job security or advancement. This type of harassment in the workplace frequently destroys a productive working environment and the self-esteem of those who experience it.

Sometimes, however, sexual harassment is difficult to identify particularly in our Region where women regard a touch on the buttocks or risqué jokes as part of our normal social intercourse, and may only treat it as serious when the harassment develops into more aggressive conduct. In less formal employment situations such as domestic service any sexual suggestion or gesture by a male employer will constitute sexual harassment because of the advantageous position and dominance he enjoys in his household.

Overall, the key ingredient in sexual harassment is the authority which the harasser wields over the victim who is usually at a disadvantage owing to her fragile economic position, the current employment being in most cases her only means of livelihood. With this foremost in her mind a victim may be reluctant to confront her harasser or report any unwelcome advances.

The resultant abuse in sexual harassment cases is not only physical, but may have financial implications for the victim's well-being and ability to provide for herself and family.

INTERNATIONAL INITIATIVES

Having identified the incidence of gender-based violence, initiatives and strategies have to be adopted to combat its effect and reduce its prevalence.

The Convention on the Elimination of All Forms of Discrimination Against Women[6] which has been ratified by all member states of the Caribbean Community seeks to remove discrimination against women in all areas where such discrimination is encountered. There was, however, one area which was overlooked and not specifically covered by the Articles of the Convention. This is the area of gender-based violence. The Committee on the Elimination of Discrimination Against Women (CEDAW) which monitors implementation of the Convention by states parties was over the years particularly concerned about this lacuna, and in 1989 at its Eighth Session adopted the first of two general recommendations on violence against women (Recommendation No. 12). The other was adopted in 1992 (Recommendation No. 19) and was more comprehensive than the first. The Committee was of the view that "not all the reports of states parties adequately reflected the close connection between discrimination against women, gender-based violence, and violations of human rights and fundamental freedoms" and after a detailed commentary on specific articles of the Convention, a multi-faceted recommendation was formulated which, *inter alia*, urges states parties to report on all forms of gender-based violence including in such reports, all available data on the incidence of each form of violence and its effects on women who are victims.

The Committee also recommended that states parties ensure that laws against family violence, rape and other sexual assaults give adequate protection to all women, and respect their integrity and dignity.

The Declaration on Violence Against Women (supra) was the result of recognition of the enormity of the problem of violence by governments meeting at the United Nations Conference on Human Rights in Vienna in 1993, and enjoins them to exercise due diligence to prevent, investigate and, in accordance with national legislation, punish acts of violence against women whether those acts are perpetrated by the State or by private persons. The Declaration represents a moral commitment by governments to introduce immediate measures to combat gender-based violence.

In 1994 the United Nations Commission on Human Rights after strongly condemning all acts of violence against women and girls, appointed a Special Rapporteur on Violence Against Women with the mandate to seek and receive information from Governments and other agencies on the causes and consequences of violence against women, and to recommend measures, ways and means at the national, regional and international levels to eliminate violence against women, working closely with other special rapporteurs in this regard. In discharging the mandate the Special Rapporteur was also requested to submit annual reports to the Commission on Human Rights and undertake country visits.

In adopting the Beijing Declaration and the Platform for Action on Women[7] at the Fourth World Conference, governments expressed determination to prevent and eliminate all forms of violence against women and girls which was one of the "critical areas of concern". The Platform for Action recognised that "violence against women is an obstacle to the achievement of the objectives of equality, development and peace and both violates and impairs or nullifies the enjoyment by women of their human rights and fundamental freedoms". One of the strategic objectives was to take integrated measures to prevent and eliminate violence against women, and in so doing Governments were requested, *inter alia*, to "enact and/or reinforce penal, civil, labour and administrative sanctions in domestic legislation to punish and redress the wrongs done to women and girls who are subjected to any form of violence, whether in the home, the workplace, the community or society".

Among the several initiatives which Governments are asked to implement, I regard the following one to be the fortress from which a frontal attack on gender-based violence must be launched. It reads as follows:

> Promote an active and visible policy of mainstreaming a gender perspective in all policies and programmes related to violence against women; actively encourage, support and implement measures and programmes aimed at increasing the knowledge and understanding of the causes, consequences and mechanisms of violence against women among those responsible for implementing those policies, such as law enforcement officers, police personnel and judicial, medical and social workers, as well as those who deal with minority, migration and refugee issues, and develop strategies to ensure that the revictimization of women victims of violence does not occur because of gender-insensitive laws or judicial or enforcement laws or judicial or enforcement practices.

The lead must be taken by Governments in combating and eventually eliminating gender-based violence. A policy which reflects a gender perspective in all governmental programmes aimed at eradicating violence, will result in raising public consciousness and sensitivity to the problem. Similarly, implementing national programmes will encourage and increase knowledge of the causes and effects of gender-based violence. Efforts to eradicate or deal effectively with such violence will be futile if those responsible for implementing policy and executing programmes are themselves not gender-sensitive or committed to the cause. This is particularly so in the case of law enforcement personnel and judicial officers who come into contact with victims of gender-based violence on a daily basis. Concentrated efforts to increase the sensitivity of these persons should be on-going and not sporadic, and must be accompanied by enactment of legislation, which is gender sensitive and provides effective safeguards and remedies.

Recently, The Committee on the Elimination of Discrimination Against Women in examining a report presented by a Caribbean state party, in its concluding comments on the report urged that state to intensify its awareness-raising efforts concerning violence against women, in particular domestic violence, and its unacceptability. It called on the state party "to put in place concrete prevention efforts and sensitization measures, addressed at the public at large", and encouraged the state "to put in place training measures aimed at judicial officers, including judges, lawyers and prosecutors, in order to enhance their capacity to deal with violence against women in a gender-sensitive manner". Other recommendations included ensuring that effective "mechanisms are in place against sexual harassment in the workplace, and that women are informed of their right not to be sexually harassed at work".

In 1995, Commonwealth governments agreed in the Commonwealth Plan of Action on Gender and Development that the elimination of gender-based violence would be one of the priority areas for action. This was followed in 2000 by the adoption of the United Nations Millennium Development Goals by 189 governments worldwide, and the elimination of violence against women was singled out as being integral to the achievement of gender equality.

REGIONAL INITIATIVES

One of the key achievements of the Inter-American Commission of Women was success in having the General Assembly of the Organisation of American States adopt the Inter-American Convention on the Prevention, Punishment and Eradication of Violence Against Women[8], generally referred to as The Convention of Belem Do Para. As far as can be ascertained all of the CARICOM member states have ratified or acceded to this Convention under which states parties condemn all forms of violence against women and agree to pursue, by all appropriate means and without delay, policies to prevent, punish and eradicate such violence.

An oft-forgotten Regional instrument signed and adopted by resolution of all member states of the Caribbean Community is the Charter of Civil Society[9]. This was a result of the recommendation of the West Indian Commission adopted at a meeting of the Heads of Government of the Caribbean Region held in Trinidad and Tobago in October 1992. Under the Charter the Heads of Government declare their resolve "to pay due regard to the principles by which they commit themselves to respect and strengthen the fundamental elements of a civil society". Article XII addresses the rights of women which include the right to legal protection including just and effective remedies against domestic violence, sexual abuse and sexual harassment. Similarly, Article XIII seeks to protect the right of every child against physical or mental violence, injury, neglect or abuse including sexual abuse.

These are laudable principles, and our Heads of Government in the Region must be commended for their wisdom in paying regard to these principles. One gets the impression, however, that they are honoured more in the breach than in their observance. The existence of the Charter is not well known, and has not been disseminated among nationals of the member states. Mention is hardly ever made of it in any forum. Its provisions mirror in large measure those of international and regional treaties such as CEDAW and the Convention of Belem Do Para. The peoples of the Region need to be sensitised and educated about the Charter in order to hold our leaders to strict account in giving effect to the principles which they resolved to follow.

Regional initiatives in the struggle to confront gender-based violence have been taken by the CARICOM Secretariat which has formulated model legislation for adoption by member states with respect to domestic violence, sexual offences and sexual harassment. This leads to discussion of initiatives taken or to be considered at national level.

NATIONAL INITIATIVES

(a) Legislation

Within recent years, several states within the Region have enacted legislation aimed at combating domestic violence – Domestic Violence Acts – based in large measure on the model formulated by the CARICOM Secretariat, e.g. the Domestic Violence Act of Jamaica passed in 1996. These Acts, as does the Jamaica Act, provide for the courts issuing protection or occupation orders aimed at protecting an applicant who is a victim of abuse from further abuse. They also prohibit the perpetrator from entering or remaining in a residence occupied by the victim, or granting the victim the right to occupy the premises forming part of the household. Non-molestation orders may also be made restraining the abuser from waylaying the victim in any public place or being within a specified distance from her or him, and also from making persistent telephone calls to the residence or place of work. The Domestic Violence Act of Trinidad and Tobago (1999) amended the 1991 Act to widen the definition of "domestic abuse" to include psychological, emotional and financial abuse, and recognised visiting and cohabitating relationships.

Countries which hitherto had no separate legislation governing sexual offences have adopted the CARICOM model Sexual Offences Act as well as the Sexual Harassment Act. The latter is comparatively new to our Region, which never regarded sexual harassment as an offence necessitating intervention by the courts. Although the legislation mainly covers situations of sexual harassment by an employer or supervisor in the workplace, it also includes such harassment by a co-worker as well as harassment in education and in relation to persons seeking accommodation from others.

The Organisation of Eastern Caribbean States in 2001 launched a Family Law and Domestic Violence Reform Project Development Agency to reform existing legislation dealing with the family and domestic violence and which formed part of overall Judicial and Legislative Reform initiatives being undertaken in the Eastern Caribbean.

(b) Law Enforcement

Violence within the confines of the home is still generally regarded by law enforcement officers as a family matter to be settled privately, and not to be aired publicly in courts of law. Law enforcement officers intervene with undisguised reluctance when an abused woman makes a report against her husband or partner at local police stations, and is very often discouraged from instituting proceedings being advised instead to go home and patch up matters. Sometimes the justification for such reluctance is reinforced when the frightened abused woman with few options pleads with a court functionary not to imprison the male abuser or is too terrified to testify against him resulting in the charges being dropped.

In such circumstances, courts should be empowered to order mediation with therapeutic treatment and counselling for both abuser and abused, aimed at fostering respect and tolerance of another's point of view. Very rarely, if at all, are abusers or the abused encouraged by court officials to engage in counselling or mediation before or after trials. Cases are dealt with in a cold and impersonal manner, in a system which is punitive rather than rehabilitative. Conviction of the abuser frequently results in financial and psychological loss to the abused woman who is deprived of support for herself and children, if any.

The view has been expressed that criminal justice for violence, from arrest to conviction and severe sentencing, is the most effective mechanism for deterring further acts of violence, and is the only effective means of combating its escalation. This may be so, but rehabilitation must be considered in certain circumstances and situations as a viable alternative.

(c) Training

The role of the police in enforcing criminal justice for violence perpetrated against women cannot be overstated. Though effective in some instances in temporarily averting further violent domestic attacks, many women display little confidence in police intervention. This begins at the investigative stage with insensitive police personnel who sometimes express the view that the abused woman probably provoked the violent reaction of the abuser in some way or is not satisfied that there are sufficient grounds for intervention. Sensitising police personnel to a victim's response to domestic abuse is mandatory in eliminating the scourge of it. They need to be made aware that violence committed on persons in domestic situations is a crime like any form of violent assault committed by one person against another and is not a purely private and personal matter. In relation to women victims in most countries the police are the only recourse which they have when battered or assaulted.

Police personnel need to reorient their thinking and attitudes nurtured in traditional male dominance that men are entitled to inflict beatings on their women folk now and then to keep them in line and assert their authority. Young inductees into the police service in most countries do not receive any training in handling and investigating reports of violence committed in the home or as the result of sexual molestation, and so are ill-equipped to render assistance when confronted with the problem. Consequently, they tend to take the least difficult course of trivialising the report and not pursuing the investigation rigorously. Sympathy and understanding should underpin investigations, and the surroundings where reports are made and statements taken should be relaxed to inspire confidence.

Recognising the need for training and improving the response of the police to gender-based violence, the Guyana Police Force earlier this year in collaboration with the Ottawa Police Service of Canada embarked on a project aimed at sensitising participants to the whole problem of domestic violence. The respective officers exchanged experiences, and the members of the Guyana Police Force received training in interviewing victims and managing a report from the time it is made. Such training should be mandatory for all recruits into police organisations, and accurate record-keeping as well as data collection should also form part of the training process.

In 2003 an Ad Hoc Committee on Domestic Violence was appointed by the Attorney General of Trinidad and Tobago to prepare an investigative and procedural manual specifically tailored for the use of police investigators responding to reports of domestic violence. A wide range of resources, both human and physical were identified as well as strategies including the establishment of a domestic violence unit in each division of the police service. It was recommended that on-going training on domestic violence be provided for every officer throughout his/her career.

(d) Court Systems

The courts are the final rung up the ladder of the criminal justice system in securing a conviction of a person charged with violence against another and found guilty of doing so; for female victims, this can be the most intimidating. They face gruelling and sometimes embarrassing cross-examination by defence attorneys in austere and awe-inspiring surroundings before judges and magistrates dressed in black garb and dispensing justice in strict accordance with the law.

Most women who are called upon to testify in court about abuses committed against them find this a traumatic experience, and leave with a strong impression that they were on trial instead of the offender and being in some way responsible for their plight. They also face the humiliation of recounting the sordid details of the attack in cases of rape or the terror experienced at the hands of their abuser in other cases of assault before a courtroom of curious onlookers savouring the unfolding of a salacious soap opera.

I have not been able to ascertain whether all countries of the Region have legislation in place permitting hearings of rape and other sexual offences to be heard in camera in the presence of only those directly involved. The CARICOM model Sexual Offences Act certainly provides for it, and so does the Domestic Violence Act of Jamaica which is commendable having regard to the personal nature of such proceedings.

Consideration should be given to the establishment of user-friendly family courts well-equipped to handle sensitive domestic matters. Such a court has been established in Trinidad and Tobago as a pilot project, and has met with great approval and deep appreciation from both visitors and those who have to use the facilities. Hopefully, such courts will become the norm in the rest of the Caribbean.

An issue which requires urgent attention is the adequacy of staffing of courts which deal with gender-sensitive matters particularly in the criminal jurisdiction. Victims of rape and other sexual assaults usually encounter court staff who are cold, impersonal and sometimes intimidating. The time has come for the testimony of rape victims, particularly the very young, to be given by video or behind screens to avoid the trauma of face-to-face contact with the abuser. Admittedly providing user-friendly facilities in courts comes with a large price tag, but adequate financial resources must be made available by governments in their budgetary allocations to the administration of justice. The same must be considered in providing training both for staff and judicial officers as is proposed for law enforcement officers.

The remedies available in the courts for gender-based violence fall mainly within the criminal jurisdiction, e.g. the offences of rape and sexual assault as well as ordinary assault and battery. Legislation pertaining to domestic violence in some instances provides for courts to exercise a quasi-criminal jurisdiction. Apart from this, civil suits can be brought against perpetrators seeking damages for assault or injunctive relief or eventually matrimonial proceedings.

Whether the remedies and relief sought by victims of gender-based violence are criminal or civil, their effectiveness depends in large measure on the officials who enforce them. Initiatives must be developed to ensure that victims of violence have their cases ventilated fully and heard expeditiously. Delay in hearings is not a luxury which victims of violence can afford both from a physical as well as a psychological perspective. The wounds inflicted may heal within a short span of time, but the scars remain until the end of time. The trauma of an assault is not easily forgotten, and the speedier the trial the quicker the recovery can begin. Judicial officers must bear this in mind when fixing hearings, and police officers must be prepared to complete their investigations of the case at the earliest opportunity.

(e) Research and Data Collection

Recommendation 19 formulated by the United Nations Committee on the Elimination of Discrimination Against Women indicated data collection as one of the factors which states parties should include in their reports on the subject of violence against women.

No one can reasonably doubt that the Caribbean as a whole is plagued by the multi-faceted problem of gender-based violence. If efforts to eradicate it are to be effective, the dimension and extent of such violence must be ascertained. This cannot be undertaken by individual states acting in isolation, having regard to their limited financial and human resources. Research and data collection although the responsibility of each state, must be undertaken at a Regional level, perhaps by the CARICOM Secretariat if not already so undertaken. Data collection should include, for example, police and court statistics on reports made and penalties imposed on perpetrators. These statistics should be updated periodically, and form the basis for collective action after being reviewed by a designated entity within the Region.

The time has come for a Regional summit to consider the problem and devise solutions for excising this canker which is persistently eroding the fabric of our individual communities.

(f) Education

An important tool in the ongoing struggle to eradicate violence is inculcating in both victim and offender mutual respect, gender sensitivity, tolerance and the acquired skills of peaceful conflict resolution. These values should be incorporated into the educational curricula at all levels in the formal school system as well as in informal educational programmes. Much work also needs to be undertaken in sensitising the media to the whole issue of gender-based violence as being acts of criminality with long-term effects on the victims rather than opportunities for sensationalism and titillating journalistic commentary.

Above all, women and young girls in particular have to be taught that they are victims of, rather than participants in, violence, and need to report such incidents. In this regard, Governments and other agencies should undertake legal literacy campaigns to inform women of their rights, and educate them specifically about domestic violence.

NON-GOVERNMENTAL INITIATIVES

Most of the initiatives discussed earlier relate to Governments with whom the main responsibility lies to confront gender-based violence and eradicate it. Non-governmental organisations, however, have played and need to continue to play a positive role in combating such violence. These organisations' involvement is multi-dimensional, ranging from the provision of shelters, refuges and hot-lines to conscious-raising programmes and support groups.

These initiatives were undertaken mainly by women NGO's, but in recent times male

NGO's have joined the battle against gender-based violence, and have been organising groups such as Men Against Violence Against Women. One such organisation has been formed in Guyana with the objective of educating men and boys to respect the rights of women and develop anger management and dispute resolution skills. There also exists in Jamaica an organisation, Fathers Inc., no doubt with similar objectives.

This type of organisation must be encouraged throughout our Region to remove the perception that the battle against gender-based violence is to be fought only by women; all are involved, and all are consumed.

A very significant contribution to the struggle against violence comes from the Church, specifically from the World Council of Churches which in 1998 decided upon a Decade to Overcome Violence, and identified the most vulnerable groups as being women, youth and children. Margot Kässman[10] in a book entitled *Overcoming Violence: The Challenge to the Churches in All Places* indicated that few church leaders see domestic violence against women as a major question to theology, yet more and more Christians are coming to see that the churches are called to be at the forefront of the movement against violence affecting women and children. The influence of the Church (and I include here all other religions) should not be underestimated.

Its teachings and tenets abhor violence, and its followers regard religion as a panacea for the ills that affect society. Church groups with wide-ranging membership across gender, race and age are fertile soil for the growth of the core values of respect, compassion and concern for the welfare of others. The Church must harness its large reservoir of influence and channel it towards combating the evils of gender-based violence.

CHILDREN

No discussion on violence particularly in family situations will be complete without consideration of its effect on the most vulnerable group of persons – the children. The effect of violence on them whether direct or indirect, is incalculable. The child nurtured in a violent environment becomes an abusive or mal-adjusted adult who regards violence as the norm. As mentioned earlier, where the child is the subject of physical abuse, the emotional and psychological scars remain long after the wounds are healed.

The Convention on the Rights of the Child[11] which has been ratified by all countries within the Caribbean Region, under Article 19 requires states "to take all appropriate legislative, administrative, social and educational measures to protect the child from all forms of physical or mental violence, injury or abuse, neglect or negligent treatment, maltreatment or exploitation, including sexual abuse, while in the care of parent(s), legal guardian(s) or any other person who has the care of the child." All that has been discussed in relation to adults in violent situations applies in equal measure to children. The same initiatives should be taken to protect children from violence particularly in family situations and from sexual abuse, which though intolerable when adults are victims, is reprehensible and unforgivable when committed on children, particularly those of tender years which seems to be occurring with increasing regularity.

Although not the focus of this paper, it is opportune to mention one area of physical violence against children which is condemned by the Committee established to monitor compliance with the Convention on the Rights of the Child. It is corporal punishment inflicted on children whether in the home or in schools. After general discussions, begun since 2000, the Committee at its 42nd Session held in June 2006, issued a General Comment which focuses on corporal punishment and other cruel or degrading forms of punishment, and which urges states parties to prohibit and eliminate this practice as early as possible, by legislative, awareness-raising and educational measures.

CONCLUSION

The multi-dimensional problem of gender-based violence has been discussed as far as it is possible to do so within the confines of a few pages. There is so much more to this problem which needs to be addressed, and solutions identified. Nevertheless, whatever these are at the end of the day, it requires determination, dedication and commitment of the leaders of society and the political will of Governments to eradicate this problem. Further, women's fragile economic positions provide few options when seeking to extricate themselves from violent situations. Women's poverty needs to be addressed as a matter of urgency.

Roberta Clarke in a publication in 1998,[12] from which I derived much assistance, expressed these views in the section on Conclusions and Recommendations:

> Any attempt at solving violence against women must also take notice of the section of the female population whose efforts to leave situations of violence are severely impaired by economic poverty. While violence against women occurs in all classes, in all regions, there is no disputing that the economic crisis reduces a woman's power to resist. Women with few resources have less options.

There are also the ever-present issues of deep-rooted and stereotypical attitudes towards gender-based violence. Unless these are changed and more progressive thinking adopted, the battle to eradicate such violence will be lost. This attitudinal change has to begin in the homes and communities of our respective countries by inculcating in the young the values of self-worth and human dignity.

Lucille Mathurin Mair Public Lecture Series
Jamaica, 2006

Endnotes

1 Adopted by the United Nations General Assembly on 20 December, 1993, G.A. Res. 48/104.
2 Adopted by the United Nations General Assembly on 10 December, 1948.
3 Domestic Violence and Marital Relationships in the Caribbean: Guyana based study, Women's Studies Unit, University of Guyana, 1989.
4 Plan of Action to 2005 prepared for the CARICOM Secretariat.
5 Sponsored by the Commonwealth Secretariat, London.
6 Adopted by the General Assembly of the United Nations on 18 December, 1979.
7 United Nations Fourth World Conference on Women, Beijing, China, September 1995.
8 Adopted by the General Assembly of the Organisation of American States on 9th June 1994.
9 Adopted by Heads of Government of the Caribbean Region on 19 February, 1997 in Antigua.
10 A Bishop of the Evangelical Lutheran Church, Hanover, Germany.
11 Adopted by the United Nations General Assembly on 20 November, 1989.
12 Violence Against Women in the Caribbean: State and Non-State Responses.

CHAPTER 29

PROGRESS IN THE CARIBBEAN REGION ON COMMITMENTS TO CHILDREN'S RIGHTS

Before launching into a discussion on the topic of this address I wish to thank the CARICOM Secretariat for inviting me to be one of the keynote speakers at this Special Meeting of the Council of Human and Social Development on the subject of children, our most important assets into whose hands the future of our world will be entrusted. This is a fact which very often we tend to forget in our interactions with and treatment of children. We disregard totally the impact our actions and patterns of behaviour have on the psyche and character of those entrusted to our care.

The vehicle which has driven the world's attention towards solving the problems faced by children internationally and which has come to be regarded as a Bill of Rights for children, is the United Nations Convention on the Rights of the Child[1] (later to be referred to as "the Convention") and which entered into force on 2nd September, 1990 after the requisite ratifications. Though not automatically enforceable under the domestic law of states embracing the dualist system which requires international treaties ratified by the Executive to be enacted into the domestic law by legislation, (Suriname being the exception) the Convention was ratified by all CARICOM states by 1995.

The years since entry into force of the Convention saw the adoption of two other important United Nations instruments impacting on the well-being of children – the Millennium Declaration[2] and A World Fit for Children.[3]

Here in our Caribbean Region over the past ten (10) to twelve (12) years initiatives have been ongoing giving rise to commitments by governments and other agencies to protect and safeguard the rights of our children, beginning in 1996 with the Belize Commitment to Action for the Rights of the Child, the Regional Symposium on Juvenile Justice in 2000 in Trinidad and Tobago, and a Special Meeting of the Council of Human and Social Development held in 2002 which recommended a Regional Framework for Action for Children's Rights and Development with specific targets to be achieved within the period 2003-2006. The time frame for attainment of the goals of this Framework is 2015.

A Regional Task Force on Child Rights and Child Protection was established comprising representatives from member states and civil society as well as development partners with a mandate to, *inter alia*, ensure a coordinated regional approach to effective child protection mechanisms and juvenile justice systems, and provide a forum for interchange of experiences and ideas.

As far as can be ascertained the issues of disciplinary practice, juvenile justice, violence in schools and institutions as well as children affected by migration have been addressed by the Task Force, but there are still several areas of concern still outstanding.

With this background of conferences and symposia several questions arise such as where do the children fit into all this and what are their needs in an adult world? At the Children's Forum of the Belize Conference in 1996 fifty-two (52) children speaking on behalf of the children of the Region formulated several recommendations (a "wish list") pertaining to the following:

- education
- health
- employment
- crime
- rehabilitative punishment
- social issues
- protection from abuse
- breaking communication barriers
- public awareness about the Convention
- after-school training programmes for teenaged parents
- 24-hour "hot lines"
- motivation and building of self-esteem
- participation in recreational events

That list reflected the children's views and opinions on every issue after full discussion, with areas of concern being directed to the relevant authorities, governments and those administering the judicial systems, the security forces, their parents, and even themselves. Governments were urged to improve education systems and allocate adequate funds to health care while providing opportunities for employment.

Those children expressed the view that those who administered the criminal justice systems needed to display greater sensitivity to their situations and focus on rehabilitation in imposing punishment. The same applied to the security forces who needed to perfect their public relations skills. The message to parents was to break the communication barriers and start to listen to their children. This is intimately connected with the other message to parents to be more responsible and less neglectful of their parental duties. What those children considered of great importance was general awareness of the Convention which in their opinion may avoid violation of their rights by parents, other children or society at large. It is not without significance that governments' action plan in fulfilling the commitments made at that meeting in Belize in 1996 was to "establish or intensify programmes that effectively implement the commitments countries assumed in signing and ratifying the Convention on the Rights of the Child, particularly compliance with Article 4.

Having perused the relevant documentation on goals to be achieved and strategies to be adopted I wish to focus on a few issues which in my view are increasingly of concern in our Region, and which should be addressed consistently and not sporadically. This is not meant to detract attention from other pressing issues such as health care, education and employment of children which are equally important, but just to highlight the following:

- Child abuse including sexual abuse
- Violence in all of its forms
- Child prostitution and pornography
- Teenage pregnancies
- Use of children for drug trafficking and soliciting financial donations
- Absentee fathers and their failure to maintain their children.

In the twin instrument to the Convention born unusually nearly thirteen (13) years later and entitled "A World Fit for Children", governments at a special session of the General Assembly of the United Nations on Children reaffirmed their commitment to protect the rights of children by upholding certain principles and objectives, such as putting children first by ensuring that their best interest be of primary consideration, leaving no child behind by removing all forms of discrimination affecting them, and protecting children from harm and exploitation. This latter objective leads me to make mention of the Optional Protocol to the Convention on the Rights of the Child, on the sale of children, child prostitution and pornography [4] which unfortunately to date has been ratified by only two Caribbean states with three others being signatories. Over the years prior to its adoption states parties having become gravely concerned at the increase in international traffic in children and the widespread practice of sex tourism in relation to girl children in particular, agreed to incorporate all such practices as offences in their criminal justice system, and also to adopt appropriate measures to protect the interests of children who are victims of sexual exploitation.

These commitments were reiterated in A World Fit for Children with additional affirmations, such as, identifying and addressing the underlying causes giving rise to trafficking and sexual exploitation of children, and raising awareness of the illegality and harmful consequences of such practices.

Recognising that commitments made by governments at summits and conferences invariably are relegated to the dump heap soon after they are made, follow-up actions and assessment were provided for in that document with specific provisions for developing as a matter of urgency (if possible by the end of 2003) national and, where appropriate, regional action plans with specific time-bound goals and targets in the Plan of Action formulated in the document to create a world fit for children.

ABUSE AND VIOLENCE

Within recent years individually and collectively our states of the Region have been beset with an alarming rise of violent incidents with children being increasingly the victims. The innocence of childhood where their only concerns should be keeping healthy, learning and interacting with their peers in playful encounters, has been replaced by the trauma of dodging bullets (if fortunate enough) and experiencing the constant verbal and physical assaults of adults in hostile environments. Others face the all-too-familiar scourge of deviant sexual abuse in dysfunctional households – fathers and step-fathers committing acts of incest on trusting and unsuspecting girls and boys of tender years who have been prematurely catapulted into the adult world of sexual activity or are witnesses to daily violent and physical encounters between parents or those *in loco parentis*. These incidents lead inevitably to children committing acts of physical violence on and sexual experimentation with each other. Lack of parental control or misguided perceptions of the role of a parent leads to children developing character traits which encourage the use of violence as means of settling disputes or survival and coping skills in a world which they perceive to be hostile. As they advance into adolescence they live by the mantra – "get you before you get me". It is survival of the fittest, and anger always close to the surface erupts on commission of simple acts which are misconceived as provocation or disrespect.

Inevitably this has given rise to a large increase in the number of children and young adults running foul of the law, and being prosecuted for such serious crimes as rape, wounding, manslaughter and murder. As a result, the juvenile justice system in some states of our Region become overburdened and understaffed. For the more serious crimes such as rape and murder these young offenders sometimes face trial as adults in adult courts. Most of the legislation pertaining to juveniles in some states is archaic and in need of drastic reform. So too, the support services within the system which need to be staffed with suitably qualified personnel; also, where appropriate, the utilisation of procedures other than deprivation of liberty should be employed.

As will be mentioned later in the paper, in October 1996 in Belize states in the Region committed themselves to reviewing and revising relevant laws to comply with the Convention, more specifically Article 3, which provides for treatment of children when detained and their rights in the court system.

In September 2000 at the Regional Symposium on Juvenile Justice key recommendations for reform were suggested, *inter alia*, utilisation of measures to divert juveniles from the criminal justice system, and establishment of juvenile family courts or strengthening of existing juvenile courts.

To date, I am informed only three states have embarked on harmonisation of their laws concerning juveniles or undertaking some degree of legal reform. The speed of reform of the juvenile justice system must be accelerated in the best interests of the children of the Region.

DRUG USE AND TRAFFICKING

There is another scourge stalking our communities – the pervasive use of habit-forming drugs and its by-product of trafficking which spawns mules and "swallowers" attracted by lucrative payments for transhipment out of the Region mainly to the metropoles of the developed world. Poverty in the main is the incentive for young men and women taking the risks inherent in embarking on these potentially dangerous enterprises. Rising costs of living and inadequate job opportunities coupled with a misplaced sense of priorities in regulating one's finances all contribute to the ever-increasing drug trade. In all of this, children are caught in the middle, and are sometimes also utilised as couriers and foot soldiers for drug dealers.

The tentacles of the drug trade have reached into the fabric of every state in the Region spawning the formation of gangs in our communities with rivalry among them resulting in early death of young male adolescents. The proliferation of guns and ammunition which is the Siamese twin of the drug trade is another cause of the early demise of our youths when they fail to conform with the rigid codes within the gangs. In most instances young boys find within a gang the discipline, comfort and understanding which may be absent in their own families. These gangs become their families sometimes with disastrous consequences. Day by day we witness the wanton destruction of young lives cut down in their prime. Urgent concerted action is required at the Regional level to arrest and eradicate this canker from our midst.

I was particularly moved by a news report which I read in a recent edition of a newspaper in Trinidad and Tobago, and which I extracted for its vivid portrayal of what I have just mentioned. It was one woman's plea to save our youths by a graphic display of red paint stained on her clothing and representing the blood of her nation's children being spilt daily. She called on those in authority to pass the necessary legislation to protect the rights of the child. I regard this as serendipitous coming as it did just when I was preparing this paper.

The entire problem of violence in all its forms needs to be addressed collectively by the Heads of Government of the Region maybe through their respective representatives and civil society at a meeting called for that purpose, and solutions found to save the lives of our male adolescents. To do so will be fulfilling the mandate imposed on states parties by Article 19 of the Convention to take all steps to protect children from all forms of physical or mental violence, injury or abuse. I have learnt that the issue of crime in the Region was discussed at the recent Inter-Sessional Heads of Government Meeting in The Bahamas, and a summit is to be held. It is hoped that the whole problem of violence at all levels will be discussed, and I am of the view that participants should include civil society and NGO's as well.

PROSTITUTION AND PORNOGRAPHY

Equally abhorrent is the growing practice of luring young children mainly girls into prostitution and pornography. The advent of this despicable plague which stalks the world no doubt prompted the adoption of one of the Optional Protocols to the Convention mentioned earlier which entered into force on 18 January, 2002. This canker has found a place in our communities, and our children have fallen prey to the baser instincts of predators and their insatiable desire for filthy lucre. With frequent regularity, our girl children are being lured into prostitution even across our borders. Sad to say, parents are sometimes complicit in deals selling their children for financial gain or more despicable, living off the earnings made from prostituting them. Commendably some of the states within our Region have enacted legislation against trafficking in persons, and those which have not are urged to do so with despatch consistent with Article 3 of the Optional Protocol and Articles 34 & 35 of the Convention.

The other hideous aspect of sexual abuse of children which has invaded our communities is pornography and titillating sexual practices. I have learnt with horror that this has crept into our school systems where teen-aged school girls and boys indulge in these practices captured on mobile phones which proliferate in classrooms, and are now the medium for spreading pornography. Both parents and teachers (particularly the former) seem to have lost control and authority over children under their care. This too has to be arrested before it becomes the norm in our schools and societies. Ratification and implementation of the Optional Protocol on this issue is not an option; it is obligatory and an imperative.

TEEN-AGED PREGNANCIES

The continuous decay of the moral fibre of our societies is also evident in the increasing number of teen-aged pregnancies – children giving birth to children. Every state of our Region has seen the rise of this phenomenon. What do these children who themselves are in need of care and protection have to pass on to their offspring? What values can they inculcate in them? Very often these teen-age girls drop out of school, and enter adult life without completing formal education. They have no skills, and find it difficult to subsist economically being invariably dependent on one or other parent; if not, they find themselves involved in other relationships which lead to the birth of other children, completing a vicious circle out of which they cannot extricate themselves. Help is needed if they are to re-integrate into society, and in keeping with Article 24 of the Convention states are obligated to develop preventive health care and guidance through family planning services. If possible, such children should be given the opportunity to resume their education and secure coping skills to enable them to provide financially for themselves (Article 39). The next issue follows logically from this one.

ABDICATION OF PARENTAL RESPONSIBILITIES

The large number of female single-headed households in our Region is adequate testimony of the neglect and failure of men in our society to undertake their responsibilities as fathers particularly in visiting relationships. Some women find themselves in the unfortunate position of dependence on more than one putative father for financial support which invariably is never forthcoming. Children particularly boys enter adolescence and adulthood without the guidance, love and care of a father which sometimes forces them into the arms of gang leaders who they regard as father figures. This was an area of concern of the Committee on the Rights of The Child which monitors compliance with the Convention in one report from the Region. The Committee in examining periodic reports of states parties identifies areas of concern and makes recommendations. Mothers throw up their arms in despair when they can no longer cope with the twin burdens of nurture and discipline thereby leaving adolescents to fend for themselves. The result – a generation of angry young men, teen-aged female prostitutes, and street children soliciting alms. What a dire prediction of the future of our Region!

One wonders whether the absence of religion in the lives of our children is conditioning their interaction with persons who cross their paths. The tenets of all religions as practised in our part of the world are in large measure based on respect for human life and forgiveness for perceived wrongs. Most young adults live in environments devoid of any religious instructions whatever, and regard life as cheap and disposable. The leaders of all religious institutions need to re-assess their influence on the lives of young adults. A pro-active approach is essential to save our children and appeal to their innate humanity.

In like vein, we all look back with nostalgia to the era when children in a village or community were nurtured and reared by all members of that village or community who exercised discipline regardless of the familial relationship to a child. It took that village to raise a child. Such community spirit has disappeared and has been replaced with an attitude of selfishness and individuality, the approach being - mind your own business. Again, a recent newspaper report exemplifies graphically the present attitude of parents to community discipline. A man lost his life after scolding two four-year olds (not his children) for breaking two eggs belonging to someone else. A parent of one of the children became so incensed that a quarrel ensued which later resulted in the man being killed by unidentified gunmen who entered his home that night, all over a reprimand given to two small children. What a senseless loss of life! A re-assessment of this approach is required, and a return to communal responsibility.

The Convention recognises the right of every child to a standard of living adequate for the child's physical, mental, spiritual, moral and social development (Article 27) and the primary responsibility rests on the parents (both of them) to guarantee that right within their capacities and financial capabilities. Fathers have to step up to the plate and face up to their financial responsibilities. Recovering payment of court-ordered child support is a frustrating exercise in every state of the Region. Procedures to facilitate recovery of thousands of dollars owed by defaulting fathers must be a priority of state personnel. This was another area of concern of the Committee in reports from a few states in the Region, and recommendations were made to improve the situation.

INCREASING AWARENESS AND IMPLEMENTATION OF THE CONVENTION

Among the wishes of the children at the Forum in Belize in 1996 was the promotion of awareness of the Convention among their siblings, parents and teachers in order, as they claim, to make the school and home environment more "child friendly". This is also one of the goals of the Regional Framework for Action, and in all of the reports submitted to the Committee on the Rights of the Child dissemination and public awareness of the Convention was an area of concern and a recommendation to have this corrected in keeping with Article 42 of the Convention.

Implementation of the Convention seems to present some difficulties for the states of the Region. I have ascertained that to date only Belize and Jamaica have incorporated the Convention into their domestic law. Guyana by an amendment to its constitution has mandated the executive, legislative, judiciary and all organs of Government to respect and uphold the rights enshrined in international treaties which Guyana has ratified and which includes the Convention under discussion.

In the reports examined by the Committee one recurring concern was the slow pace of reform of existing legislation as well as the enactment of new legislation to conform with the Convention; invariably recommendations of the Committee included a comprehensive review of laws pertaining to children particularly with regard to abuse, violence and neglect.

It is a matter of personal concern that states of the Region are not honouring their reporting obligations upon ratification of the Convention. Only a few have submitted initial reports, and those who have, did so sometimes a decade after ratification; also second and other periodic reports remain outstanding. It does not seem as if the full import of ratification of treaties is appreciated. It carries with it the responsibility to comply with the obligations undertaken under the treaty. Dialogue with states parties who ratify is essential in monitoring compliance with the provisions of a treaty, and this is carried out with the monitoring mechanism established under the treaty, usually a Committee of independent experts elected by the states parties. Submission of initial and periodic reports by states parties to the Committee is the only means whereby it can be ascertained whether a ratifying state is complying with its obligations and implementing the provisions of the treaty. Without examination of these reports the true position of progress being made in implementation cannot be assessed. Ratification therefore becomes meaningless.

If we are serious about improving the status of children in our Region and ensuring that they are raised in a safe and healthy environment free from violence, drugs, abuse and fear we have to hold ourselves accountable by taking seriously our obligations under treaties we ratify, and complying faithfully with their provisions. States should also heed the recommendations made by the Committee in its comments on their reports, and seek to give effect to them by positive implementation.

In the Belize Commitment to Action for the Rights of the Child a few of those commitments made by states are paramount:

- generate and sustain the necessary political will to protect child rights;
- set up or strengthen national mechanisms;
- review and revise relevant laws to fully comply with the letter and spirit of the Convention;
- establish mechanisms to enforce laws;
- establish or intensify programmes to effectively implement the commitments assumed when signing and ratifying the Convention.

These reside mainly within the remit of governments, and the first will inform the success of the others. Without the political will nothing can be achieved. Budgetary allocations for implementation of programmes aimed at alleviating poverty, establishing national machinery, revising laws and improving health care, to name a few, have to be consistent and foremost in the hierarchy of priorities.

To date, can all of the states of the Region seriously acknowledge that these commitments have been honoured? Only a few of the states seem to have taken steps to review, revise or enact laws to comply with the Convention although some attempt has been made or is being made in a few others.

The Convention may have been the vehicle which attracted world-wide attention to children's rights, but it is the political will of nations which is the fuel that will propel it to its destinations in the long journey towards ensuring effective social development of our children and their maturity into responsible adults. We must find that political will or all will be lost. We must act now. Time is not on our side. Our children are suffering. Let us heal the wounds and set them on a journey of progress in this twenty-first century thereby creating a Region fit for our children.

CARICOM Secretariat
Special Meeting on Children of the Council of
Human and Social Development (COHSOD)
Guyana
March 17th – 19th, 2008

Endnotes

1 Adopted by the U.N. General Assembly on 20 November, 1989.
2 Adopted by the General Assembly in September, 2000.
3 Adopted by the General Assembly under Resolution S-27/2 on 10 May, 2002.
4 Adopted by the U.N. General Assembly on 25 May, 2000.

CHAPTER 30

FOREVER INDEBTED TO WOMEN: THE POWER BEHIND THE THRONE

.... and the rib which the Lord God
had taken from man, made he
woman, and brought her unto the man.

This quotation is taken from Cap. 2 Verse 22 of the book of Genesis, in the Bible, the holy book of the Christian religion. It explains the creation of mankind and the evolution of woman from the body of man. It has also been postulated by men of olden times and even some in modern society that this justifies the secondary role women must play to men.

From time immemorial women have been regarded by some as being inferior to men.

In earlier times, they were looked upon as chattels and items of property to be bartered or exchanged. This is still the norm today in some societies where they have no rights, only duties - duties to their husbands, fathers, brothers and male superiors, duties to be obedient, disciplined, respectful and compliant. They are expected to cater without question to all of the whims and needs of their menfolk, reasonable or unreasonable, and in some societies, they are still the "hewers of wood and drawers of water", performing all menial and arduous tasks in addition to household chores, e.g. working in the fields tilling the soil in the heat of the day with their babies often strapped to their backs.

The irony of this situation is that several women accept their positions as being inevitable and pre-ordained. They dedicate their lives to making the lives of men comfortable, never regarding their work as chores or unpleasant or degrading tasks. They are content to care for their children and cater to the needs of their families despite long hours of work under primitive conditions.

In some societies of the world women are subjected not only to the dominance of their husbands, but also of the entire family. A wife married into the household of her husband falls under the discipline and control of the matriarch of the family, and is expected to obey every order and perform every task without question. Invariably these wives are child brides whose future is decided and husband chosen while they were still of tender years. If the "bride price" or dowry does not live up to expectations the hapless "bride" very often is chastised or sacrificed, the explanation frequently being that she committed suicide.

Of course, one has to view the position of women in the context of the times and the societies in which they live. In biblical times and in centuries thereafter women needed the protection of their menfolk. They were not educated and trained to cope in a world which was male-dominated. Men went to war, men hunted, men provided the food for their families and made all decisions concerning the welfare of the family and the community. Women were not required to make any important decisions or even to think independently or differ from rules laid down by the head of the household who was always male; to even think of defying him was tantamount to sacrilege. In spite of what to us today would seem to be a situation of tyranny and which in large measure still exists in some societies, women were content and relatively happy; many even today will tell you that they would not change this for anything. They have been conditioned to think in this way; their mothers and grandmothers before them accepted this way of life and were contented. They regard the new generation of so- called "liberated" women as upstarts and rebels who wish to usurp the role of men. The important question to be decided is – should we try to change these women and redirect their thinking and way of life? Should we try to import new values into their lives or impose on them what we think they ought to have? Who are we to judge?

It is axiomatic that in the world in which we live nothing stands still. Change is inevitable and very often enures to our advantage if we are to progress and develop. The role of the majority of women worldwide has certainly changed dramatically over the years invariably for the better due in large measure to an increased awareness of and sensitivity to the rights of women. During the last century in some developed societies women were given the right to vote and to participate in choosing those who governed the affairs of state. They were accorded the right to own property, and in some instances jointly with their husbands, in other cases, in their own right. They were given the opportunity to hold positions and offices previously held exclusively by men. This has increased exponentially over the years, and has seen the percentage of women as heads of state and government becoming the norm rather than the exception.

As the societies of the world developed women's roles changed dramatically. The standard of living of families improved as technology which increases at a frenetic pace has made life easier making it possible to own and enjoy amenities which hitherto were beyond the reach of most. This necessitated larger financial output and increased incomes which resulted in more women joining the work force. As a result, they have had to balance employment with caring for their families, a feat which sometimes requires superhuman effort. Some critics of women who work outside of the home have advanced the view that the children suffer morally and psychologically when the mother's steadying influence is absent for the greater part of the day. Delinquency is sometimes a result of both parents being away from home and children being left to fend for themselves for several hours. However, in some communities such as ours in the Caribbean, fortunate to enjoy the benefits of the extended family, the care of children of employed parents is entrusted to aunts, uncles, grandparents, and even helpful neighbours. This has alleviated in large measure the burden cast on working women, and has helped them to contribute substantially to the financial stability of their families.

Another problem that has reared its head within recent times and which has compelled women to enter the work force is the steady increase in the number of single-parent households with women being the sole bread-winners. This is sometimes a result of men's abdication of their financial and other parental obligations as fathers, and a misguided perception that they ought not to be solely responsible for the upbringing of any children they may have sired. Some may argue that this attitude is attributable to the fact that women have become less dependent on men for financial and even emotional support choosing to care solely for their children. The women's answer to this is that they have been forced to seek employment to maintain themselves and their children because of the irresponsibility of errant fathers. Whatever the reason and wherever the blame falls the irrefutable fact is that the number of female-headed households has increased significantly particularly in the Caribbean Region. Invariably these women lack marketable skills and are not equipped to secure highly remunerative employment; consequently, they are forced to seek jobs which push them into the low-income brackets with long working hours under poor conditions, not to mention being subjected to exploitation and sexual harassment by unscrupulous employers.

This dual role of breadwinner and caregiver exemplifies women's superhuman capacity, and justifies the adage that "*the hand that rocks the cradle rules the world*". These women somehow over the years have oft-times produced leaders in our societies who, in some instances, belatedly become acquainted with a father who was never part of their lives, but who exhibits great pride in the achievements of sons or daughters to whose development and education he never contributed. These women truly and in a very real sense are the powers behind the thrones on which their children sit. Of course, the reverse invariably occurs.

Some of these children reared by a single mother fall between the cracks and run foul of the law into a life of criminal activity. In these instances, the unfortunate mother is the only one who stands by her child in a court of law, sometimes seeking leniency and rising to his/her defence in spite of clear evidence of guilt. This exemplifies a mother's unwavering loyalty to her offspring even though facing shame and embarrassment.

Over the past three or four decades women have moved into nearly every sphere of activity. They can be found in the traditional professions as well as in non-traditional fields of employment which had been the sole preserve of men in earlier times – engineers, mechanics, astronauts, boxers in the field of sport, heads of government in the political arena, and leaders in the religious sphere.

In this regard the meteoric rise of women in some of the established churches has been most significant. Traditionally women comprise the large proportion of the membership of churches, and here I am referring to the Christian churches. All of the religious organisations within a church are maintained by women. They work assiduously with male pastors and priests being called upon at any time to serve and preserve the whole fabric of a church including organising Sunday school classes for children. The success of these religious bodies depends on women's continuous support. Women have been the fund-raisers for church organisations – cake sales, tea-parties, fairs, working with dedication and commitment to augment the funds of the church in order to assist the poor and needy in the congregations. Truly, powers behind the throne. Yet despite their vital role in the congregations only within recent years have we seen the advent of women into the hierarchy of some of the established churches, and this has been received sometimes with undisguised hostility and antagonism. Some progress has been made, for instance, about two or three years ago a woman was promoted head of the Episcopalian Church in the United States of America. Within our Caribbean Region in the Anglican dioceses women priests have gained acceptance and are now the norm. It is also the same in other Christian denominations with the exception of the Roman Catholic Church.

The greatest contribution made by women apart from giving birth was molding young minds in the field of education. Many leaders and academics in our societies owe their success to and reminisce about their kindergarten and primary school teachers who were invariably women, and who exerted unwittingly tremendous influence on impressionable minds. The values which are so much a part of their adult lives were nurtured and inculcated by those dedicated teachers of years gone by. Sad to say this seems to be a dying breed in today's money-grabbing world. Their selflessness and devotion to duty were their only reward, and certainly not equal to the paltry salaries they received in those days. Their students are forever indebted to them for molding their characters and influencing their choices in later life.

Women's influence is also exerted in the workplace. An efficient secretary (nearly always a woman) is priceless and worth her weight in gold. Successful male managers and executives are lost without the services of their secretaries. They are the life blood of the office, and organise their boss in every sphere of his working life which sometimes results in clashes with that other woman in his life whose role and influence I shall now consider.

An oft-repeated adage and truism is that behind every successful man there is a woman, reference here being to his loyal and faithful spouse. Many women sacrifice their own careers in order to advance the careers of their husbands, offering support and encouragement when the going gets rough and failure seems imminent. They sometimes carry without complaint the burden of caregiver for the entire family sacrificing their own needs in order to ensure that their mates fulfil their ambitions and continue upward mobility in their chosen fields of endeavour - the power behind the throne. We have also seen instances of women standing by their men at all costs, being at their side in moments of crisis sometimes involving infidelity, with a brave face while perhaps seething with anger inwardly, and portraying an appearance of unity in adversity. These men should forever be indebted to these faithful, selfless women.

In relation to positions of leadership in the field of politics women's contribution is immeasurable. In countries with thriving democracies women work tirelessly to have men elected to parliament and as heads of government. During election campaigns who comprise the largest proportion of attendees at rallies and political meetings? Who trudge daily house to house to persuade potential voters to vote for their parties' candidates who to a large extent are usually men? Commendably within recent decades women's participation as candidates at elections has increased substantially, particularly within our Region; in fact in some states legislation has been enacted to provide for a certain percentage of candidates fielded by a party to be women. This period in world history will be recorded as the most eventful with at least seven women serving simultaneously on the world stage as heads of government and a few as leaders of opposition parties in parliament.

A few months ago, the world watched with interest the struggle by Hillary Clinton to become the first female President of the United States of America. A large majority of women were rooting for her although an equally large number were not so enthusiastic. Personally, I felt proud that a woman was striving to be head of the most powerful nation in the free world, but alas, it was not to be, at least not just yet; maybe some day in the not too distant future. After all, women hold up half of the sky. However, we can be content that the glass ceiling has been shattered, and in some places broken by other female heads of government. Someone remarked, possibly quoting Hillary herself that "eventually it will be unremarkable for a woman to become President of the United States; when you stumble, get right back up and proceed; someday a woman will be launched into the White House; right now there are about 18 million cracks in that glass ceiling representing the persons who voted for [Hillary]". Right now, also there are thousands of women working to have the two male candidates elected – the power behind those thrones.

Apart from a woman's role as wife, mother and caregiver, she carries the portfolio of economist and financier within the home ministry. Women are magicians, adept at stretching one dollar and converting it into several sufficient to satisfy the needs of their families. Who searches the newspapers for bargains and sales spending hours walking from store to store to discover the one with the lowest price on items? I am convinced that the economies of the countries of the world would be much healthier if all finance ministers were women. They sacrifice their own needs in order that a child or other family member may have food or clothing which they sorely need but never seemed possible to acquire.

I had a classic example of a woman's propensity for financial management when delivering a lecture sponsored by the Barbados Public Workers' Cooperative Credit Union on the celebration of its 36th anniversary, and as part of its Memorial Lecture Series honouring Olive Trotman. This remarkable woman's dedication and commitment to the Credit Union transformed it from a small savings society in 1970 with a capital of only $1732 and operating out of a suitcase which has been preserved as a momento, to a highly successful bank with assets with over $400M today. My tribute to her was summed up in one phrase – never underestimate the power of a woman, and which epitomises the strength of women in any undertaking in which they are involved.

It would be remiss of me not to make mention of the part played by women in the trade union movement especially since this lecture is one in the series organised by the Hugh Lawson Shearer Trade Union Education Institute to honour Caribbean Union women in particular. Whenever the words "trade union" are mentioned one immediately thinks of a group of men in the work place taking on management, demanding increased wages, and better working conditions. A woman never enters one's mind except as part of the membership, never as the leaders, very rarely sitting around the bargaining table. However, whenever industrial action is undertaken, for example, when a strike is called or rallies or marches are staged, women are always in the forefront, supporting the leaders, bearing the brunt of the action, making the sacrifice of foregoing wages or distributing strike relief. In their unswerving support for their leaders, they spare no quarter in carrying out decisions without thought of the effects on themselves or their families. There are, however, a few women within the Region who have served successfully as leaders of trade unions, and have held positions of influence particularly in the public and teaching service organisations. We salute and pay tribute to these women at this time.

As a related issue mention must be made of the large number of women who are still not unionised, these being domestic workers, performing duties of a personal nature in the privacy of homes, and apart from earning low incomes are sometimes subjected to indignities of a sexual nature from male employers. This category of workers is difficult to unionise with possibility of dismissal being the main disincentive. Although they may not be powers behind any thrones we are forever indebted to them for the invaluable service they provide.

Any discussion concerning women's role in families must inevitably revolve around the whole issue of poverty which is usually defined as not having enough income to provide basic needs such as food, clothing and shelter. Data and statistics have shown that when one considers poverty the vast majority of those who live below the poverty line are women; in fact, the majority of the 1.5 billion people living on US$1.00 per day or less are women. The gap between men and women caught in poverty has given rise to the term "the feminisation of poverty". Many women, very often those of single-headed households, barely eke out an existence, surviving in appalling living conditions with their children and oft-times on one meal per day if they are fortunate to have it.

Feminine poverty derives from a variety of circumstances - as inheritance from parents who themselves faced life-long poverty, abandonment by male partners either through divorce or refusal to honour financial commitments to their children for maintenance, no coping skills or inability to pull oneself out of the quagmire of poverty, lack of formal education or just surrender to the forces operating against them whenever they attempt to rise above their existing situations resulting in low self-esteem and resignation to the inevitable.

The poverty of women must be addressed as a matter of urgency. Governments of the Region must put in place measures to address the problem. The Beijing Platform for Action adopted at the Fourth World Conference on Women held in China in 1995, identified the eradication of the persistent and increasing burden of poverty on women as one of the critical areas of concern requiring special attention and action by governments; in fact according to the Platform for Action "more than one billion people in the world today, the great majority of whom are women, live in unacceptable conditions of poverty, mostly in the developing countries". Among the United Nations Millennium Development Goals is the eradication of poverty the aim being to reduce by half the proportion of people living on less than US$1.00 a day, and to achieve full and productive employment and decent work for all including women and young people.

Returning to the Beijing Platform for Action, in the discussion on women and poverty it was recognised that "women contribute to the economy and to combating poverty through both remunerated and unremunerated work at home, in the community and in the workplace". It noted that "the empowerment of women is a critical factor in the eradication of poverty". Governments were urged to take action to "develop and implement anti-poverty programmes, including employment schemes, that improve access to food for women living in poverty and introduce measures to integrate or reintegrate such women into productive employment".

It is incumbent on governments to implement the action suggested in the Platform for Action in order to ensure that women have adequate economic and social benefits arising from unemployment. Women's empowerment being crucial in minimising, if not eradicating, their poverty provision of access to economic and educational opportunities is essential and critical in encouraging them to take advantage of these opportunities.

The debt of gratitude owed to women throughout the world can never be repaid even at low interest rates – the debt owed as nurturer, care-giver, housekeeper, counsellor, adviser, financier, peace-maker and other roles too numerous to mention. These roles are gifts for which no repayment is required except loyalty, appreciation, love and affection. What women certainly do not deserve is abuse, mental and physical, and other dastardly acts of violence. The ever-present, all-pervasive scourge of gender-based violence has become commonplace in all spheres of life affecting women and girl children of all ages. It is part of the whole regime of violent behaviour stalking all our communities and which must be arrested before we are all consumed by it. The most common and frequently encountered acts of violence occur in domestic situations mainly in the home, and range from slaps and kicks to more serious assaults such as wounding.

The problem is widespread and varied being not readily susceptible to precise evaluation because of its inherent private nature. It is very often not reported to law-enforcement authorities, victims being invariably deterred by the consequential embarrassment of prosecutions in severe court proceedings, and preferring to suffer in silence rather than reveal the sordid details of violent abuse to total strangers.

Sexual abuse is the most frequently used weapon in the arsenal of male abusers, and it preys on and affects one's emotions leaving behind deep psychological scars. A serious and detrimental effect of this form of abuse is the pervasive and potentially life-threatening scourge of HIV/AIDS. Research has indicated that many women either as wives or in common-law relationships contract this deadly disease from their husbands and partners, in some instances transmitting it to their unborn children. Shame and embarrassment are very often inhibiting factors in early detection and treatment particularly when it is contracted from close relatives within the privacy of the home.

One cannot readily ascertain all of the reasons for violence directed at women, but several factors may contribute to it. In our Caribbean societies, as in others there is a close link between domestic violence and alcoholism with both women and children being victims of all forms of abuse committed while the offender is heavily intoxicated; the use of habit-forming drugs has similar effects. In some instances,-women develop an attitude of resignation to the inevitable beating which will be administered when their partners return home at the end of the day in an intoxicated condition. This resigned attitude is oft-times evidence of low self-esteem and psychological manipulation, and goes hand-in-hand in our Region with a myth that most women enjoy physical violence as an expression of the male macho image. What a fallacy, propounded no doubt, by arrogant and self-opinionated men!

It is time women call in the debts and promissory notes owed to them by men, and demand a halt to the escalating rise in violent behaviour. It is time women, particularly young teenaged women, take a stand and wake up to the realisation that they have options in a world which is on the fast track of change. In addition to being the powers behind the thrones on which men sit, the awareness must be conveyed to women that they can sit on the thrones themselves. They can be whatever they want to be. This must be driven home forcefully to young women who need to acquire greater self-esteem and self-worth. Invariably through naiveté or a flawed value system dependence on men is perceived as the gateway to personal financial gain mainly through alliances with gang and drug leaders. For many the road to progress and self-development through independent effort is too long and arduous when compared with the easy road to financial aggrandisement through largesse from male benefactors even if one loses one's self-esteem and integrity in the process. They must be encouraged to grasp the numerous opportunities offered and available for personal advancement in whatever field of endeavour they may choose. Low self-esteem and self-worth must be replaced and bolstered by confidence in one's ability to grow and develop.

When according to the Christian scriptures God made woman from the rib of man, I am sure He intended that they should complement each other. Although I chose the theme of this lecture to reflect the indebtedness to women who are powers behind the throne, and believe me, many, many of us are, I advocate a repositioning from being behind the throne to being alongside it. Women's roles over the decades have changed in large measure from being solely bearers of children and household helpers to being equal partners in all aspects of relationships, blazing trails for themselves and sitting on thrones of their own.

Whatever course the economic and social trends of the world and of our communities may take in the future, one thing is certain, and that is, that the position of women will evolve exponentially, and will never stand still. There will be improvements in some areas and setbacks in others, but whatever happens we have to be prepared to meet the challenges of a frenetically-changing and technologically-driven world in this twenty-first century.

The University of the West Indies
The Hugh Lawson Shearer Trade Union Education Institute
Mona, Jamaica
Speech delivered in Antigua
10th September, 2008

PART IV

WOMEN AND CHILDREN

CHAPTER 31

THE ROLE OF JUSTICE IN THE SEARCH FOR GLOBAL PROSPERITY

At first blush one may wonder at or be dubious about the connection between justice and prosperity, and I must confess that when I was asked to speak on this topic I suffered momentary apprehension, and doubted my ability to speak sensibly on so abstract a subject. I still feel some degree of apprehension as I stand here, but I hope that at the end of my presentation the relevance of justice to global prosperity will be much clearer. Of necessity, I shall draw on my experience of the operation of justice in our society, but justice is a universal concept applicable to all mankind regardless of nationality or geographical location. Justice, of course, means different things to different people, and it may take different forms. There is justice according to law, and there is justice according to the norms of society or social justice.

In a publication given to me and entitled "The Prosperity of Humankind", Baha'u'llah avers that "justice is the best beloved of all things", and it calls for fair-mindedness in one's judgments, for equity in one's treatment of others, and is thus a constant if demanding companion in the daily occasions of life.

This brings me to the question – what is justice? There could be many definitions depending on the perspective of each individual. If a resolution of a problem leans in favour of one person that individual will consider justice to have been done; if it does not an injustice was committed. However, in its ordinary meaning it connotes fairness or equitable treatment whether administered in a court of law or by the State or even in our everyday dealings one with the other.

In every civilised society laws are enacted to regulate human behaviour either between individual and individual or between individual and the State. If there were no laws our societies would descend into anarchy and chaos with the strong and powerful terrorising the weak and helpless. These laws confer rights and impose obligations in relation to the person, property or liberty of the citizens of a state, and regulate human conduct with regard to the enjoyment of familial, social, political, religious, economic, cultural and other human rights.

In western-styled democracies such as ours there are three branches of the State – legislative, executive and judicial. The legislative branch enacts laws, the executive branch executes them, and the judicial branch interprets and administers them. The judicial branch is separate and distinct from the others, and enjoys independence from political pressure or interference. A strong and independent Judiciary is a bulwark against repression in any well-ordered society, and offers protection to the individual citizens against infringements of their human rights whether by another individual or by the State.

Confidence in our judicial system can never be over-emphasised, and every citizen is entitled to expect that justice will be done when he or she approaches our courts for redress of wrongs committed against them or for offences for which charges are instituted against them. However, it must be admitted that within recent times public confidence in our judicial system seems to have been eroded, and many doubt the ability of the system to vindicate their rights or redress their wrongs. One hears all too frequently the comment that it is futile and useless to approach the courts as nothing will be done and the only winners are the lawyers who extract small fortunes from persons who can ill-afford the cost of litigation. The pessimism giving rise to these comments is born of frustration at the length of time taken to achieve results, misunderstanding of how the system works, and a new phenomenon of lost and misplaced court documents and the consequential effects on the outcome of litigation, not to mention the dishonesty of some of those employed within the system.

Conceding that there may be some justification for the erosion of confidence in our judicial system, much of it can be attributed to a lack of appreciation of how the system works. There is still the popular conception particularly of litigants that justice must be swift, sharp, speedy and easily dispensed. One files a complaint today whether civil or criminal and one expects that it will be resolved within a matter of days. Many assume that the assembly line system operates where the matter is fed in at one end and the perfect result comes out at the other end. Alas, nothing is further from the truth. In order to regulate effectively the administration of justice there are rules of procedure which must be followed. Time limits are imposed for the filing of claims, counterclaims and defences. In the criminal jurisdiction, the maxim "everyone is presumed innocent until proven guilty" is the foundation of our criminal justice system. Therefore the fact that someone has been charged by the police with the commission of a criminal offence does not mean that he is guilty. The police or prosecutor has to prove beyond reasonable doubt that he or she is guilty, and certain rules of procedure have to be followed. There is no short cut to justice.

It is often difficult for the layman to understand the intricacies of the judicial system, and this leads to suspicion that justice is not being done. This is particularly so in the civil jurisdiction of our courts where the rules of practice and procedure as well as the rules of evidence may seem complex. A person who has suffered loss of his land by unauthorised trespassers or someone who sustains injuries in a traffic accident may be dismayed that it could take years for them to obtain redress by way of damages for the loss suffered or an order for the eviction of the trespassers.

After the pleadings have been filed and an action becomes ripe for hearing due to the large number of actions being filed daily delay is encountered in having the case heard. Judges of the High Court carry a heavy case load of both civil and criminal matters apart from matters heard in Chambers and a summary court called "Bail Court" in Guyana where on any one day the total number of matters listed can reach 200 or more. It is necessary to read and examine in detail all of the documents filed in connection with each claim and hand down a well-reasoned judgment or make an order which affects a person's liberty or property worth millions of dollars. A judge's decision does not always have to be right, but it must reflect deep thought and consideration of the issues with which he or she has to grapple.

It is not an easy task; it calls for constant dedication, reflection, serious reading and contemplation, detailed consideration of the law applicable to the facts, and above all an abiding sense of justice. A judge is expected to do all of this in relation to every matter that comes before him or her, and when one considers the heavy workload one can appreciate the resultant delays. I am by no means attempting to excuse the law's delays which is exemplified in the maxim "justice delayed is justice denied". I am merely trying to give you a picture of the task facing a judge whenever he or she is called upon to adjudicate.

Apart from the ever-increasing workload there is the shortage of efficient support staff. Gone are the days when a judge could rely implicitly on the competence of his/her clerk to draft an order of court accurately and have it entered within a matter of days or be able to advise a judge, particularly a new one, on the rules and procedures in conducting a trial. Because of the low level of salaries in the Public Service there is a rapid turnover of staff with persons leaving for more lucrative jobs; also applicants with high level qualifications are not attracted to positions in the judicial system for the same reason. It is hoped that in the near future this will change and standards will be improved.

In administering justice in some instances judges have not only to balance the competing claims of the litigants before them, but also must have regard to the interests of society as a whole. How will the decision given in a particular dispute affect other members of a community or residents of a particular neighbourhood or the morals of society? Justice therefore does not only proceed from the individual, but arises within society. All judges are products of the society in which they live, and consciously or unconsciously their decisions are influenced in varying degrees by the environment around them as well as the mores and traditional value systems under which they were reared. Public opinion also may exert some influence on judicial decisions. If the public conscience is outraged at the commission of an unlawful act or the terror created by the criminal activity of an individual or group of individuals, a judge may after ensuring that all legal requirements are satisfied feel the need to reflect this public outrage in the severity of the sentence or quantum of damages in the hope that it will act as a deterrent or smooth the ruffled feathers of a disturbed and concerned community. This is not, of course, to advocate that the feelings of society must always influence the decisions of the courts; this is exclusively the province of the judge who determines a matter as he or she sees fit according to law. However, the eminent jurist Jhering expressed the view that "law is an instrument for serving the needs of human society, and the success of the legal process is to be measured by the degree to which it achieves a proper balance between competing social and individual interests." This view is worthy of consideration, and a simple example will suffice.

The government intends to sink a well on a particular portion of land legally owned by an individual, and which will enure to the benefit of the community as a whole. This, however, collides directly with the landowner's right of enjoyment of his property, and is also an infringement of his right to own property. There are laws laid down by statute which confer on the State the right to compulsorily acquire property for public works which will benefit a community and to pay compensation to the landowner for the loss of his property. The landowner may be dissatisfied and approaches the court for redress. A judge hearing his case has to balance the rights of the landowner to enjoy all of his property unhindered against the rights of the community to safe and potable drinking water. The learned judge is required to achieve a proper balance between the competing claims of the individual landowner and the societal interests of the community as a whole. It is not always easy to hold the scales of justice evenly, and sometimes it may weigh more heavily in favour of doing what is necessary for the overall good.

For the law to be effective it must be certain. An individual is entitled to know what the outcome of his case is likely to be, the vagaries of witnesses and human error excepted. He is entitled to know how the law will be applied in a given set of circumstances. In order to achieve certainty in the law there has been built up over the years a considerable body of precedent, i.e. cases where the legal principles applicable to the facts of those cases were enunciated and laid down by judges and which guide future judges in deciding cases the facts of which give rise to the same legal principles. If a litigant can refer to an earlier case in which the same principles of law were applicable even though the facts are not identical he/she will have a reasonable expectation that the case will be decided in like manner. These precedents bring certainty to the law when the rights of parties or the guilt or innocence of an accused person falls to be determined.

There is also in law the concept of what jurists call "natural justice", and a body of precedent has been built up around this concept. You may ask quite rightly what is natural justice? Isn't all justice natural? Isn't it natural to be just? In law, however, this concept has a special meaning. That great and eminent judge Lord Denning discussed it in the case of *Kanda v. Government of Malaya* (1962) A.C. 322, and explained that the rule against bias and the right to be heard are the essential characteristics of what is often called natural justice. He said that they are the twin pillars supporting it, and the Romans put them in the two maxims – "*nemo judex in causa sua*" and "*audi alteram partem*" (translation – no one must be a judge in his own cause, and the other party must be heard). Lord Denning summed them up in two words – impartiality and fairness.

The effect of this is that a person or tribunal called upon to pass judgment on anyone must be unbiased and impartial, and have no personal interest in the outcome of the proceedings; in other words, he must not be a judge in his own cause. The other limb of natural justice means that everyone is entitled to be heard before being condemned, i.e. he must be given a fair hearing. Although there are no written rules governing these twin pillars of natural justice a body of precedent over the years has ensured that they are applied whenever the circumstances dictate, e.g. if an employee is dismissed without being told the reason for his dismissal or without a charge being laid against him, or if the person laying the charge is himself the person hearing the charge.

I venture the opinion that these two concepts are the pillars of natural justice because they arise from what is naturally fair and just. It is natural for both sides in a dispute to be heard before it is determined, and it is also natural that no one should be a judge in his own cause.

So far I have concentrated on justice according to law and how it operates in our judicial system. Justice, however, is a concept which affects all aspects of our daily lives, and is demonstrated in our day to day dealings with each other. There are areas in our daily activities which are not controlled or governed by laws, but by unwritten conventions or rules of conduct and by the expectation that we shall be accorded just treatment when transacting business or dealing with fellow citizens. This expectation also extends to our dealings with functionaries of the State. One expects that the time-honoured virtues of honesty, integrity, reliability and trust will be observed and respected. One expects that one's word once given will be adhered to and that persons will act in good faith. One expects that equal treatment will be meted out to all citizens alike regardless of race, colour, creed, gender or political affiliation. Very often we hear the comment "that is not fair" when someone scores an unwarranted advantage over another. This is another way of saying that justice was not done.

Having listened and I hope absorbed all that I have said about justice you must be asking yourselves how does all of this help in the search for global prosperity? Prosperity in the normal, accepted sense connotes success, and of course, global means universal or world-wide, so the question to be answered is "can justice play a role in the search for world-wide success?" My answer is in the affirmative since fairness and equity can only lead to universal success. This may sound utopian and a pipe-dream; maybe it is, but if everyone in his/her family, neighbourhood, community and country strives to act fairly and observe the biblical exhortation to "do unto others as you would that they should do unto you" which means being fair and treating everyone as you would like to be treated, the results may be startling. From these small beginnings, the spiral effect will be felt world-wide in an ever-widening circle. Just and fair-minded treatment affects one's mental well-being positively which in turn has a direct effect on one's outlook and approach to life. This will lead inevitably to prosperity and success in one's undertakings, and hence to a prosperous world.

In the materialistic world in which we live we tend to measure prosperity or success in terms of personal wealth and the amenities which this wealth can provide us. Prosperity, however, embraces health, contentment, personal satisfaction and peace of mind which are all by-products of a just and well-ordered society. Let us all resolve henceforth to be fair and impartial in our treatment of others, and so ensure prosperity not only in our small communities but in the larger world beyond our shores.

Bahai Seminar
July, 1995

CHAPTER 32

THE ANGLICAN DIOCESE

Thank you for inviting me to address you as you celebrate your Diocesan Festival on matters pertaining to the Diocese.

What is the Diocese of Guyana? The diocese comprises the Bishop, Clergy and the Laity. The clergy are the priests and deacons, and the laity are the people, vestries and wardens. The Bishop is the spiritual head of the Church and of the clergy, and the Chancellor apart from being legal adviser to the Bishop is the highest representative of the laity in the hierarchy of the Church.

There is also the Registrar of the Diocese who is responsible for preparing the licences and other legal documents of the Diocese. Both the Chancellor and the Registrar are appointed by the Bishop, and must be communicants of good standing in the Church. It is a requirement that the Chancellor must be a lawyer, and although the Regulations of the Diocese do not require the Registrar to be a lawyer traditionally he has been.

The business of the Diocese is entrusted to a Diocesan Council which comprises the Bishop, the Chancellor, the Registrar, the Archdeacon, the Trustees, the Dean, representatives of the clergy and laity elected at Synod and three representatives of the rural deaneries of Demerara, Essequibo and Berbice.

The Council meets once per month and among its duties are:

(1) advising the Bishop on all matters connected with the administration of the Diocese;
(2) receiving reports of all committees and preparing the agenda for Synod;
(3) fixing the amount of Synod assessment;
(4) appointing members to the Committees of Council, e.g.

Buildings Committee, Finance Committee, Synod Committee; Communications Committee, Stewardship Committee and Lands Committee, etc.;

(5) receiving financial accounts of the Diocese.

Apart from the Diocesan Council there are the Trustees of the Diocese -four in number in whom all of the property of the Diocese, movable and immovable, is vested. This includes all lands owned by the Churches within the Diocese. They can sue and be sued on behalf of the Diocese. They too are elected at Synod. No land can be sold or divested without the permission of the Council and the Trustees.

Now about Synod. Synod is the annual meeting of the three orders of the Diocese, i.e. the Bishop, the Clergy and the Laity as well as the Chancellor, Registrar, Trustees, the Diocesan Secretary and Treasurer. Each parish is required to send to Synod between one to four representatives depending on the number of electors in the parish. These persons are normally elected at the annual meeting of the parish as you may know.

Synod is held normally in the month of May over a period of three days and commences with a roll call and mass at the Cathedral on the afternoon of the first day at which the Bishop gives his charge to the Synod representatives. Matters pertaining to the Diocese are discussed, working groups debate a chosen topic and make recommendations. The annual budget of the Diocese is laid before Synod and discussed, and elections to the Diocesan Council are held.

It is an opportunity for members of the Anglican Communion to meet and become acquainted with both clergy and laity from the interior locations and parishes as far distant as Rupununi. These priests and representatives sometimes spend days travelling to attend Synod, and it is the major event in the Diocese which all clergy and lay representatives are expected to attend.

Apart from the Diocesan Council there is a Diocesan or Administrative Secretary who is responsible for the day-to-day running of the business of the Diocese and for arranging meetings of the Council and Synod. He operates out of the Diocesan Office which is located in Georgetown and with a small staff. He is an important person in the Diocese as he deals with every aspect of the business of the Diocese and the parishes within the Diocese. It is a full-time occupation, and very demanding.

There is also the Diocesan Treasurer whose responsibility is to regulate the finances of the Diocese. This is not a full-time employment, but requires commitment and dedication to duty.

One must not forget, of course, the Diocesan Magazine which keeps us informed about happenings in the parishes of the Diocese. This is published by an Editorial Board with a hard-working editor. It is hoped that parishes will continue to submit information about their Churches so that we can keep the magazine going.

Now, last of all I must tell you about the office of Chancellor, a post which I hold, and maybe the reason why I was asked to speak to you this morning.

As I stated earlier, the Chancellor is the highest office of the laity in the Diocese, and is appointed by the Bishop. Among other duties the Chancellor issues faculties for the erection of new churches, substantial extensions or alteration of existing churches, the demolition or removal of churches, and all alterations or removal of any part of a church, e.g. the altar, pulpit, lecterns, organ or even pews; also, the erection or removal of permanent memorials in churches and the removal of corpses or tombs from churches or churchyards.

Now you may ask quite rightly what is a faculty. It is in simple terms a permit or licence to alter any part of a church or church property. In effect, no part of the church should be removed or altered without obtaining a faculty from the Chancellor. This is provided for in the Regulations of the Diocese and a procedure is laid down for the grant of a faculty. I recall granting a faculty for extensions to this Church, and the procedure was followed. An application was made to me, and a notice exhibited in the Church. If there are no objections the faculty is granted. Any alterations to the fabric of the church without the grant of a faculty is unlawful and against the Regulations. In fact, for the construction or substantial alteration of a church building a plan or sketch must be submitted with each application.

In addition to issuing faculties the Chancellor administers oaths to newly ordained priests and deacons, and as stated earlier advises the Bishop on all matters concerning the interpretation of the Rules and Regulations of the Diocese.

I hope I have been able to give you some idea of how the Diocese of Guyana operates. There is also the Provincial Synod of the Dioceses in the Province of the West Indies which meets every three years, and is attended by all of the Bishops, representatives of the Clergy and the Laity from all of the Dioceses of the West Indies. The Diocese of Guyana elects its representatives to the Provincial Synod at the local Synod immediately preceding the date of the Provincial Synod which is held in one of the provinces of the West Indies.

The Diocese in any country is as strong as its members, these being the Bishop, the Clergy and the Laity each playing an important role in ministering to the spiritual needs of its followers. We are all involved. It is not the exclusive responsibility of the Bishop or the Clergy. The laity or members of the church are equally responsible for the success or failure of your parish. We all need to ensure that our parishes serve the needs (spiritual and otherwise) of the community in which we live. Let us rise to the challenge and make the Anglican Community stronger and more effective.

Diocesan Festival
25th August, 1997

CHAPTER 33

GRADUATION ADDRESS UNIVERSITY OF GUYANA

About six weeks ago with a degree of recklessness which I regretted the next moment, I accepted an invitation from the University to deliver an address to the graduating class of 2002. It was reckless since I had indicated that I had absolutely no idea what one could say to graduands who had spent between one to four years within the cloistered walls of an institution of learning amidst lecturers who they were tired of listening to and examinations which they hoped they will never have to write again. Instead of giving me some way out of the dilemma in which I found myself, upon inquiring about what should be the subject of the address I was told quite blithely that I could speak on whatever subject I chose providing it did not exceed 15 minutes. I gave the assurance that I had every intention of being as brief as possible and not run the risk of everyone shaking their watches every minute to ensure that they were still working and had not stopped.

Upon sober reflection, however, I concluded that I had an obligation, nay, a duty to impart some advice to persons who were embarking on a new phase of their lives, in some instances, entering the uncharted waters of the world of work for the first time. It is a duty which I humbly undertake with the fond hope that what I have to say will in some way guide you as you embark on your chosen fields of endeavour.

I commence by posing a question to you, graduands. What induced you to embark on a course of study at the university? I am sure that the answers will be as varied as they are students. Some of you may say that you enrolled at the university because you felt that a degree or diploma would guarantee better employment or a secure future. Others may say that they needed to pursue a course of study which was their life's ambition; yet others may have been propelled in that direction by ambitious parents or guardians who themselves never attended university, but feel strongly that their offspring should take advantage of the opportunity to further their education.

Whatever your reasons for enrolling, from the moment you attended your first lecture you made a commitment not only to yourself but to this institution of higher learning. You were committed to attend classes regularly, you were committed to turning in your assignments on time, you were committed to relentless study and steadfast dedication to duty. The fact that you are graduating today is eloquent testimony that you honoured those commitments, and realised your dream. This, I am sure, was not achieved without setbacks and obstacles. There must have been times when you thought seriously of quitting or dropping out when the going was rough, when fees were difficult to meet, when domestic demands impinged heavily on study-time and delivery of assignments, when transportation (financial and actual) was a nightmare. In spite of these setbacks, however, you persevered and overcame the difficulties. You drew on your inner strength no doubt with the support and encouragement of your family and friends. You survived, you scaled the mountain and now you are at the summit. You are basking in the afterglow of success and achievement. You have been awarded a certificate or diploma which testifies that you have satisfied the examiners in your chosen field of endeavour, and can now be regarded as being knowledgeable in the subject.

I now pose another question – what next? What lies ahead after today's celebrations are over, when the euphoria has subsided, when stark reality sets in? What do you plan to do with the paper which attests to your qualification? Have you made any plans or thought at all about the future? Most of you will answer in the affirmative; you have made plans maybe to enter the world of work by finding employment commensurate with your newly-acquired qualifications; others who are already employed maybe hope to be promoted in the hierarchy of the institution where you work doubtless with increased remuneration; yet others intend to pursue further studies if not at their alma mater, at institutions of higher learning overseas.

This can be a crucial stage in your life particularly for those of you entering the world of work for the first time. It demands serious attitudinal adjustments. You are no longer a student; you are now an adult with a responsibility to perform creditably in keeping with your newly-acquired expertise; much is expected of you; you have much to offer. You have to put into practice the knowledge acquired over the years within the hallowed walls of this institution and imparted to you by long-suffering lecturers. You will find that contrary to what you thought, the assignments and examinations were the easy part; the hard part now begins. You will encounter in the work place persons who think they are or actually are more experienced than you even though not as qualified. You have to make the mental adjustment to cope with situations where experience supersedes qualifications. Do not make the cardinal mistake of assuming that because of the certificate or diploma on which the ink has barely dried, you are now the fount of all knowledge and have the answers and solutions to all problems. If you do, you may have a rude awakening. You will come face to face with the realities of a rough world out there.

Avoid the arrogance which invariably is the hallmark of those who have earned the right to place certain letters after their names, and which look good on your curriculum vitae. Admittedly, a certain amount of intellectual arrogance is good and tolerable; avoid, however, lording it over others who have not had the opportunity or good fortune to pursue higher learning, but spent years acquiring practical skills and developing expertise in their chosen fields.

Wherever you may find yourselves, it will be a learning experience. It will require a large degree of practical common sense as opposed to academic knowledge. It has been said that common sense is the knack of seeing things as they are, and doing things as they ought to be done; also it is a thousand times better to have common sense without an education than to have an education without common sense. You will find that you will need to draw on your reservoir of common sense more than your academic ability in interacting with colleagues or solving day-to-day problems which may arise in the workplace. These are the realities of life.

One has to develop and work on inter-personal relationships when interacting with those around you. These are not skills which are taught as part of the school curriculum unless you major in psychology or some related subject. Even so, the practical and the theoretical do not always synchronise. What one learns from a textbook or lecturer oft-times does not always work in the practical world. There are some things in life which can only be learned by experience. This applies in every sphere of activity – in the workplace, in the home, among friends and relatives. I am sure that you encountered situations while at university where common sense and a practical approach to solving everyday problems worked wonders.

All that I have mentioned earlier applies equally to those who are already gainfully employed and even to those of you who intend to pursue higher academic qualifications. This brings me to an important goal which all of you should strive to attain – the goal of excellence. Too often mediocrity is the acceptable norm with the perennial cliché "This is Guyana", as if this is meant to be the ultimate goal to which all Guyanese should aspire, and represents our own brand of doing things in half measures. The world is now a global village of which we are a part; as such we must be prepared to compete on equal footing with persons of excellence in our chosen disciplines in other parts of the world. We therefore have to equip ourselves with the requisite skills to take our places in a rapidly developing world where the knowledge one acquires today may be irrelevant tomorrow. Excellence has to be the goal to which we all aspire. We have to drag ourselves out of complacency and cease being satisfied with second-best. There is no place for mediocrity in today's world; only the best survive.

The achievement of your life's ambition from this campus where acquaintances were made and friendships forged may evoke in some of you feelings of nostalgia as you leave. Others may experience feelings of relief and yet others total indifference. Whatever you may feel on this day you are now indebted to this institution of higher learning. Some of you may dispute this as you paid financially at great personal sacrifice. University education is no longer free, and therefore there are no obligations.

This is an erroneous and misguided conclusion when one considers the economic costs of keeping an institution such as this on an even keel and up to acceptable academic standards. One tends to take every day things around us for granted. Have you ever thought of the costs of maintenance, provision of office supplies, preservation of the campus environment and its surroundings, not to mention seemingly ordinary tasks as cleaning classrooms and lecture halls? I mention this to alert your attention to the fact that much has been invested in your education, and much is expected of you. You are obligated to give back to this institution and your country some of what you have acquired. Do not turn your back on this fine place of learning and all that it stands for. You are an investment, and your country expects returns from its investment. Sadly, in today's world such qualities as loyalty and gratitude are in short supply, and one tends to forget good deeds all too quickly. We live in a self-centred world where no one feels obligated to anybody. The attitude is that I succeeded because of my own efforts, and not from what others did for me.

This university needs its graduates both as lecturers and supporters. By being loyal to this institution you are being loyal to your country.

As you leave at the end of this memorable day in your lives, do not let this occasion be one which you remember only for the certificate you received or the pictures you took in flowing academic gowns. Resolve within yourselves to make a commitment to assist this institution in every way you can. Be loyal to your *alma mater*; contribute in whatever way you can to build on the foundations laid by those who preceded you. In the history of academic institutions this university is still in its infancy. It therefore needs to be nurtured and cherished. It needs its graduates. Never forget it, and never forget that whatever you achieve in the future had its genesis on this fine campus. Keep its memory alive as you ascend the ladder of success. Again, I exhort you - do not feel that you have arrived at the pinnacle and know everything there is to know because of your newly-acquired skills. Much, much more knowledge awaits you out there; do not rest on your laurels. Go on to greater heights. You can and will succeed.

Heartiest congratulations to all of you, and best wishes for the future!

University of Guyana
9th November, 2002

CHAPTER 34

HISTORY OF THE LAW COURTS OF GUYANA

As one travels north or south along the Avenue of the Republic, in the capital city of Georgetown, Guyana, one cannot but be struck by an imposing building east of the eastern carriageway of the Avenue, which houses the several courts of law where justice is dispensed daily and within which two centuries of records of historical legal importance are kept.

This impressive edifice is known officially today as "The Law Courts", but in earlier times was known as "The Victoria Law Courts" having been opened on May 24, 1887, the birthday of Her Majesty, Queen Victoria of England. The Queen also celebrated her Jubilee Year in 1887. Consequently, a statue of the Queen standing erect in front of her throne in full regalia, with orb, sceptre and crown, was placed on a plinth on the western lawn of the Courts east of the eastern carriageway of the Avenue of the Republic.

Historical records reveal that it was designed by Baron Harco Hora Siccama and drawn by C. Castellani although the accuracy of this has been challenged. It is L-shaped in design with covered verandahs, and occupies two floors – a ground floor which houses the Supreme Court Registry and the upper floor which houses the courts and judges' chambers. There was also a tower on the southern end of the building. Over time additions have been made, but the original character of the building has remained the same.

In a publication entitled *"Caribbean Heritage: Architecture of the Islands"* (Darkstream Publications, 1996) at page 108, the Victoria Law Courts is described thus:

> Ground floor masonry walls and tall cast-iron columns support the upper level, timber-framed superstructure. The low horizontal

> roofs are given dramatic emphasis, at key points, by large boldly designed elements. An eclectic building whose spirit is Gothic. The tall building, with its strong exposed timber framing and steep helm roof is rather German in character.

A publication entitled *"Historical Georgetown"* by Sheik M. Hassan and Universal Bookstore, 1997, describes the style of the upper floor as being reminiscent of the timber-framed buildings popular in England during the 16th century with its exposed studs and X-bracing, and though designed along the earlier classical style of the Roman and Greek eras, it reflects Victorian architecture in its cast-iron columns, steep roofs and dormers.

Within recent memory and shortly after attainment of Republican status, the majestic statue of Queen Victoria was removed from its plinth and taken to the back of the Botanical Gardens where she rested for a period of time. However, a few years ago she was resurrected, and after some rehabilitation resumed her place on the plinth in front of the Law Courts (minus her left hand and orb) even though the name "Victoria" no longer forms part of the nomenclature of the Courts.

Although a building to house the Courts of Justice of Guyana was opened in May 1887, a court system was in place much earlier administered by the Dutch and later by the British separately in the counties of Demerara, Essequebo and Berbice. The following excerpt from "The Legal System of Guyana" by Dr. M. Shahabuddeen, S.C., at page 35 provides an insight into the historical development of the court system in the early 19th century:

> The court system which emerged in Demerara and Essequebo was as follows: There were three courts in existence, namely, the Supreme Court for the trial of criminal and civil cases, a Commissary Court for the trial of petty debt causes, and a Roll Court to deal with interlocutory matters relating to actions pending in the full Supreme Court.

Dr. Shahabuddeen states further that later by Royal Order-in-Council made on June 20, 1831 it was directed that "the Court of Criminal and Civil Justice of Demerara and Essequebo, and the Court of Civil Justice and the Court of Criminal Justice of Berbice, shall henceforth be holden by and before three judges and no more." These were to be the Chief Justice and second and third puisne judges.

These two Courts of Civil Justice, i.e. Demerara and Essequibo, and Berbice were given exclusive jurisdiction in any civil case in which the sum or matter in dispute exceeded the value of £20. However, by Ordinance No. 21 of October 12, 1844 the Supreme Court of Civil Justice of Demerara and Essequebo was united with the Supreme Court of Civil Justice of Berbice under the style of the Supreme Court of Civil Justice of British Guiana. Similarly, by Ordinance No. 11 of 1870 the Supreme Court of Criminal Justice of Demerara and Essequibo and the Supreme Court of Criminal Justice of Berbice were united and called by the title of the Supreme Court of Criminal Justice of British Guiana. Finally, by Ordinance No. 8 of 1893 the Supreme Court of Civil Justice of British Guiana and the Supreme Court of Criminal Justice of British Guiana were united under the style of the Supreme Court of British Guiana. This in fact was the precursor of the present High Court of Guyana.

Both the magnificent edifice and the court system where and under which justice has been dispensed have endured throughout the years. Hand in hand both the structure and the system will endure for many centuries and succeeding generations.

Chancellor of the Judiciary
July, 2004

CHAPTER 35

SOCIAL JUSTICE AND HUMAN RIGHTS

The two concepts of Social Justice and Human Rights have been used complementarily, and social justice has sometimes been regarded as being based on human rights and equality. Social justice is not always easy to define, and may mean different things to different people. Several writers and theorists have defined it in a variety of ways, for example, as a concept of a society in which justice is achieved in every aspect rather than merely in the administration of law; as the way in which human rights are manifested in the everyday lives of people at every level of society, and also as a concept used to describe the movement towards a socially just world.

Doing what is just means treating everyone equally and fairly without distinction based on race, gender, religion or social standing. This indeed conforms with the inalienable rights of every human being guaranteed by the Universal Declaration of Human Rights adopted by the United Nations, and accepted by all member states. In our Caribbean Region all of the constitutions have provisions for the protection of the fundamental human rights and freedoms.

Social justice imposes on states and their various entities and institutions an obligation to act fairly in their interactions with citizens in all spheres of activity. Although this obligation falls mainly on a state other sections of society are also under a similar obligation, e.g. the private sector, trade unions, religious bodies and any entity which operates within society. Social justice imports the principle that man is basically good, that a person of good intent should not be harmed, and one should treat others as one would like to be treated.

Returning to the concept of human rights, one can define a right as an entitlement, a privilege or an immunity, and for every such right enjoyed by an individual there is imposed on another a corresponding duty not to interfere with or disturb that individual in the enjoyment of that right. Some of these rights are inherent and cannot be withdrawn or removed by anyone, e.g. the right to life, work, personal liberty, protection and certain freedoms such as those of expression, religion or conscience, association and movement, to name a few.

Of necessity, social justice has to be viewed in the context of social issues which arise in any society, and which confront individuals on a daily basis. Inevitably these issues will be intertwined with people's human rights. In our Caribbean societies, the most current social issue in my considered opinion, is the ever-present scourge of violence in all of its forms which seems to be rising exponentially with the wanton destruction of human life. I note that this was one of the issues discussed extensively by this Commission and by the dioceses, and I endorse the recommendations listed in the report of the Commission at its meeting in June 2006.

There is, however, another important aspect of violence which has become a social issue to be taken very seriously, and which is a violation of one's inherent human rights – the right to personal liberty which is increasingly under threat by acts of terrorism exemplified in some of our Caribbean communities as kidnappings and abductions for ransom even of children. I view any threat to the liberty of any person as an act of terrorism once it puts that person in fear for his life. The right to personal liberty is one of the fundamental rights guaranteed under all of the Commonwealth Caribbean constitutions, and one's liberty can only be taken away by operation of law, for example, by commission of a criminal offence. The recent trend of depriving individuals of their liberty by force must be condemned unequivocally and urgent steps taken to eradicate this canker from our midst. Hand in hand with this is the equally abhorrent phenomenon of abducting young girls and adolescents and luring them into prostitution with offers of lucrative employment. This is a breach of a basic human right of freedom from slavery and forced labour which is protected under most of the constitutions of the Region. The problem is exacerbated when these young victims are taken out of a state's jurisdiction to other countries and their passports retained by their abductors.

These acts have implications for our Caribbean community and the movement of persons within the Region for illegal purposes. The laws of sovereign states must be respected, and even though the member states of CARICOM commit themselves to the goal of free movement of their nationals within the Community, this has to be within the laws of each state. The abduction of nationals of one state for the purpose of trafficking or other illegal activity in another has serious implications for the security of our Region, and requires urgent attention. This is an issue which the Church, using this term collectively, needs to address.

When the World Council of Churches held its 9th Assembly in Brazil in February 2006 at which I had the honour to represent our Province, terrorism was one of the issues which the Public Issues Committee discussed. In the context of overall violence of which terrorism was one example one recommendation was:

> to encourage interfaith initiatives to mobilise alternate responses to terrorism that do not rely on violence; reject all attempts to justify acts of error as a response to political and social problems and play an active role in the prevention of conflicts by serving as an early warning system and by building a culture of peace for life.

Eradicating breaches of human rights in whatever form is the responsibility of all sections of a society. Safeguarding and protecting young adults from sexual predators, traffickers and potential kidnappers who spread terror among unsuspecting victims requires a concerted effort.

Alternative dispute resolution without court intervention and in a non-legal context needs to be adopted in the urban and rural communities of our Region to sensitise our people both young and old that there are other methods of settling disputes without resort to violence in any of its hideous forms. This was discussed in the Commission's report referred to earlier. Where are the elders in rural communities whose roles in bygone days were that of mediators in family and other disputes or disciplinarians of errant youths who committed minor infractions when compared with serious crimes of today? The children and young persons of a village belonged to everyone and could be reprimanded and punished irrespective of family connections. Indeed, it took a village to raise a child. Those of us who grew up in that era reflect with nostalgia on the pride of place which such virtues as respect, honesty and integrity were accorded in our upbringing. Guns were weapons reserved for the military and utilised only in times of war between nations far removed from the peace and tranquillity of our small, safe communities where we found comfort and solace. How times have changed! These communities are now war zones with guns being the weapons of choice in resolving simple disputes or differences of opinion in harmless arguments.

Something is terribly wrong in the states of our Region. Physical attacks and violence against each other is the norm and accepted method of venting our anger which is always just below the surface. Literally stepping accidentally on someone's toes can incur wrath which results in death. Human life is expendable and worthless. We have inevitably to ask certain questions – how and at what point in time did we arrive at this stage? When did the Church lose its influence, when did we lose our humanity? Of more importance is the question – what can we as individuals and collectively as members of the Anglican Communion do to restore the old order and value system and excise the cancer of hatred, malice and wanton destruction of human life from our midst?

These are questions which must be answered and solutions found over the days of this Synod. It is only by frank discussions we can ascertain the depth of the problem in our several dioceses, and make decisions on the ways and means to reverse the downward slide to obliteration of our young people by gun warfare and other forms of violence.

All that I have mentioned earlier applies in equal measure to another scourge stalking our lands – the ever-present scourge of domestic violence with women being the main victims. Churches and particularly priests, in the past played a significant role in resolving domestic disputes, but, alas, in resolving marital problems the courts have become the first option rather than the last resort. Tolerance and respect for the points of view of others need to be emphasised along with parental responsibility including honouring financial obligations within a family relationship.

I endorse and wish to reiterate consideration of the recommendation of the Commission that a study on violence within the Province be initiated in order to ascertain its depth and extent with a view to developing appropriate strategies to eradicate it.

It is hoped that at the end of this Synod we will devise coping mechanisms for the myriad problems and issues which confront our societies and which will ensure that social justice is not only a catch phrase, but will guarantee equality of treatment to all and respect for the human rights of every person within our Region and Province.

Provincial Synod of the Church of the West Indies
Antigua
24th – 30th November, 2007

CHAPTER 36

TOWARDS UNIVERSAL ACCESS: STRENGTHENING THE MULTI-SECTORAL COALITION ACTING RESPONSIBLY IN THE PREVENTION OF HIV/AIDS

Before commencing this address, I wish to extend my heartfelt gratitude to the Pan Caribbean Partnership Against HIV/AIDS (PANCAP) for inviting me to address its Ninth Annual General Meeting in these very exotic surroundings, on a subject of which, I confess, my knowledge had hitherto been quite limited. I pondered after recklessly accepting the invitation about what I should say, and it occurred to me that in dealing with a scourge which has caught and embraced the whole world in its tentacles, prevention should be foremost in the minds of all involved. This is certainly within the theme of your meeting: "Towards Universal Access: Strengthening the Multi-Sectoral Coalition." I have added a sub-theme "Acting Responsibly in the Prevention of HIV/AIDS."

Four decades ago this topic would have had no relevance to our Caribbean society, and would not have been considered appropriate for discussion having regard to the taboos concerning topics of such a personal nature. Fast forward to the present, and observe the changes that our societies have undergone. One cannot now have too much information on this scourge of HIV/AIDS which is plaguing our people, particularly young men and women, and to a large extent children who contract the disease while still in their mother's womb.

I note that the Caribbean Regional Strategic Framework (CRSF) 2008 – 2012 is a call to the nations of the Caribbean "to accelerate their individual efforts against HIV," and "take a more country-centred approach recognising that success in individual country programmes is essential for overall regional success in achieving universal access to HIV prevention, treatment, care and support." Six priority areas have been identified, and my attention was drawn to the first which I regard as being the top priority of the priorities. It involves creating "an enabling environment that fosters universal access to HIV prevention, treatment, care and support services." This enabling environment embraces reducing the stigma and discrimination associated with HIV/AIDS, and encountered by victims on a regular basis from close relatives, friends and the public at large. The one single attitudinal problem which inhibits victims from seeking medical attention in the early onset of HIV is prejudice, and fear of ostracism. This is intimately connected with our culture and traditional socialisation. Before amplifying on this aspect of the prioritised areas of concern reflection on international efforts directed at prevention and combating this deadly disease is appropriate.

In 2001, Caribbean states were among those at the General Assembly of the United Nations which adopted the Declaration of Commitment on HIV/AIDS. Having noted, *inter alia*, their deep concern that the global emergency and one of the most formidable challenges to human life and dignity as well as to the effective enjoyment of human rights, and that by the end of 2000, 36.1 million people worldwide were living with HIV/AIDS, 90 percent in developing countries, declared their commitment to action to address the HIV/AIDS crisis having regard to the diverse situations in different regions of the world. I note with particular interest that recommended action included strong leadership at all levels of society, specifically by governments.

Earlier that same year the Regional Heads of Government adopted their own Regional Declaration of Commitment and issued "a solemn call to bring together the resources of all partner governments, regional institutions, civil society including those living with HIV/AIDS, the private sector and international partners to create supportive environments for the prevention of HIV infection and for mitigating the impact of the disease." I am informed that this led to the launching of PANCAP. It mirrored directly the U.N. Declaration which had urged universal regional support for initiatives on HIV/AIDS and specifically made reference to PANCAP in our Region. At the national level, a time line of 2003 mandated ensuring, *inter alia*, "the development and implementation of multi-sectoral national strategies and financing plans" which address the epidemic in forthright terms, confronting stigma, addressing gender and age-based dimensions, and eliminating discrimination and marginalisation, goals which I consider of immense importance in creating an enabling environment.

The Declaration of Commitment of 2001 was reaffirmed in 2006 at the United Nations General Assembly Special Session on AIDS, (UNGASS) the main focus being to review progress achieved in realising the targets set out in the Declaration of 2001. The result of this Meeting was another multi-faceted Political Declaration which acknowledged that many of the targets had not yet been met, and what I find to be of particular interest, that they remained deeply concerned by the overall expansion and feminisation of the pandemic, that women represented half of all people living with HIV, and recognised that gender irregularities and all forms of violence against women and girls increase their vulnerability to HIV/AIDS. Further, grave concern was expressed that "half of all new HIV infections are among children and young people under the age of 25, and that there is a lack of information, skills and knowledge regarding HIV/AIDS among young people." Hand in hand with this was a further grave concern that 2.3 million children are living with the dreaded disease and the lack of paediatric drugs in many countries was hindering efforts to protect the health of children. I have learnt that at that Special Session the Caribbean delegation led by Prime Minister Denzil Douglas of St. Kitts and Nevis committed the Region to the achievement of universal access to HIV and AIDS-related prevention, treatment and support services by 2010.

In further reference to international conventions and declarations pertaining to the HIV/AIDS pandemic it is apposite at this juncture to consider two United Nations Conventions pertaining to women and children and their relevance to the AIDS pandemic. Although these groups of persons are by no means singularly affected, together they form a significant group of victims who are continually at risk. Article 12 of the United Nations Convention on the Elimination of All Forms of Discrimination Against Women mandates states parties to take all appropriate measures to eliminate discrimination against women in the field of health care, and in this regard at the 20th Session in 1999, the Committee on the Elimination of Discrimination Against Women (CEDAW) established to monitor compliance with the Convention, formulated and accepted a comprehensive General Recommendation No. 24 which recognised that the issues of HIV/AIDS and other sexually transmitted diseases are central to the rights of women and adolescent girls to sexual health, and as a consequence of unequal power they are often unable to refuse sex or insist on safe and responsible sex practices. Women in prostitution are also particularly vulnerable to the risk of contracting HIV/AIDS and other sexually transmitted diseases. States parties were urged to ensure the right to sexual health information, education and services for all women and girls and particularly the rights of both female and male adolescents to sexual reproductive health education by properly trained personnel in specially designed programmes that respect rights to privacy and confidentiality.

This General Recommendation was the latest and most comprehensive of earlier Recommendations on HIV/AIDS emanating from CEDAW, and complemented, and was no doubt motivated, by the Strategic Objectives and Actions adopted as part of the Platform for Action accepted at the United Nations Fourth World Conference on Women held in Beijing, China, in 1995. One of these objectives in relation to women's health was "to undertake gender-sensitive initiatives that address HIV/AIDS and other sexually transmitted diseases." Several issues were identified as action to be undertaken by Governments among them being ensuring the involvement of women, especially those infected with HIV/AIDS in all decision-making relating to the pandemic, and reviewing and amending laws and practices that may contribute to women's susceptibility to HIV infection; also, encouraging all sectors of society as well as international organisations to develop non-discriminatory HIV/AIDS-related policies and practices.

Children are victims of HIV/AIDS for several reasons – contracting it from birth and from sexual interaction with carriers as well as those growing up as orphans having been deprived of both parents. The United Nations Convention on the Rights of the Child (Article 24) recognises the right of children to "the enjoyment of the highest attainable standard of health," and urges states parties to ensure the provision of necessary medical assistance and health care. There is no specific reference in the relevant Article to HIV/AIDS, but in 2003 the Committee on the Rights of the Child issued a multi-faceted and wide ranging General Comment on HIV/AIDS and the rights of the child. The objectives sought to promote and strengthen the human rights of children in the context of HIV/AIDS which impacts heavily on their lives affecting as it does all of their human rights, for example, the right to non-discrimination, and the right to life, survival and development.

The Comment discussed the most frequent cause of HIV/AIDS among infants and young children – mother to child transmission occurring during pregnancy, delivery or through breast-feeding.

It recommended as preventive measures the provision by states parties of anti-retroviral drugs, appropriate antenatal, delivery and post-partum care, as well as voluntary counselling and testing services. Children as victims of sexual and economic exploitation attracted comment with emphasis on girls and boys who are deprived of the means of survival and development through being orphaned by AIDS. In the quest for survival they encounter sexual exploitation through prostitution and trafficking with girls being the primary victims. This state of affairs applies not only to those who are orphaned, but also to those caught in violent and abusive situations which increases the risk of their infection of HIV/AIDS through rape or sexual molestation. All of this emphasises the dire and immediate need for universal access to HIV prevention.

In tracking progress made in achieving the Millennium Development Goals the current position of Caribbean states based on the national Government reports of a few in relation to combating HIV/AIDS indicates that it is possible for the goals to be achieved if some changes are made. This has to be considered when viewed along with the Underlying Principles of the Regional Strategic Framework (2008-2012) that there can be no overall regional success without successful national programmes; a more country-centred approach must be adopted in measuring regional success.

Returning to creating an environment conducive to prevention and awareness of the pandemic in our Caribbean region, one has to consider our customs, traditions and lifestyles. In the main we have historically inherited through colonisation conservative values with regard to sexual conduct and relations between men and women. As mentioned at the commencement of this address any discussion on an issue pertaining to sexual behaviour would have been taboo and off limits years ago. This to a large extent informed our negative reaction to any HIV positive person. Our instinctive reaction was one of scorn and shame; in fact this attitude was not confined to our society, but was a universal one. However, whereas the developed world adapted much more quickly with tolerance for HIV/AIDS victims, progress in this direction took much more time in our part of the world. We were and maybe still are not as tolerant in our approach nor forgiving in our reactions to what we consider inappropriate sexual behaviour and immorality which invariably may be one of the causes of contraction of the disease. We regard victims of HIV/AIDS as being sexually deviant preferring an unacceptable lifestyle. This is intimately intertwined with strong religious convictions which are not easily shaken. The result of these strong views and opinions has been ostracism and stigmatisation of HIV/AIDS victims with close relatives denying them care and comfort; in fact, in some instances denying any familial relationship.

Much work needs to be undertaken to effect attitudinal change to victims, particularly young victims, and thereby removing prohibitions against them seeking medical treatment. I was alarmed to learn from perusing PANCAP's Caribbean Regional Strategic Framework 2008-2012 issued in September 2008 that the Caribbean has the second highest HIV prevalence rate in the world after sub-Saharan Africa. Statistics indicate that there is a higher rate of infection among men, but the proportion of women infected is increasing, and the incidence of HIV infection among women aged 15-24 years is 3 to 6 times that of men.

This sends a stark message to all of us in the Region that we are losing our future adults to indiscriminate sexual activity and this downward slide has to be arrested. The CRSF made the point with which I am in whole-hearted agreement that "risky sexual behaviour such as transactional sex, commercial sex, multiple and concurrent sexual partnering, casual sex, cross-generational relationships, and inconsistent condom use all contribute to the HIV epidemic." Sexual experimentation is the norm among our teenagers today adopting the lifestyles of those in the developed world via the media through songs, music, shows and television programmes. Impressionable minds yield to the temptation to experiment totally oblivious or ignorant of the consequences. The world has shrunk becoming one large village through advanced technology moving at a frenetic pace; what occurs in distant geographical regions is transmitted instantaneously to another region. It is in this environment that our children are being nurtured mainly in positive ways, but also with negative consequences.

As mentioned earlier in 2006 the leaders of the Region at UNGASS made certain commitments to be achieved by 2010, among these being increased knowledge of HIV transmission between youths as the most "at risk" population, and reducing the age of sexual initiation among pre-teenagers by increasing the use of condoms among adolescents and young adults. If this can be achieved by 2010 we will have crossed a significant barrier in creating an enabling environment towards universal access to HIV prevention. This remains one of the most challenging of the priority areas identified by CRSF – challenging because it involves re-educating a whole generation to act responsibly having regard to their natural physical and emotional impulses. Unpalatable as it may be to conservative and religious members of our Caribbean societies condom use should be encouraged among young adults as a safeguard against contracting HIV. This is not to denigrate the traditional teachings of responsible sexual behaviour and abstinence which should continue to be the first option, but in the realities of life there are always those who fall prey to the temptations of others; they have to be protected from their weaknesses and be encouraged to act responsibly.

This leads to consideration of another factor influencing the spread of HIV/AIDS. In our societies peer pressure and some societal norms expect young boys to display their sexual prowess and prove their manliness at an early age which results in their exerting pressure on their young female counterparts to indulge in sexual activity sometimes utilising force to prove their sexual competence. There is also the wanton use of habit-forming drugs and alcohol consumption at an early age with no regard to the deleterious effect such substances may have on their mental capacity to act responsibly.

In the midst of all the social issues contributing to teenage infection is the plight of women in our Region caught in the HIV net by forced sexual intercourse (rape) or unwitting consensual liaisons with male carriers. Add to the mix the ever-increasing horror of violence which many women face on a daily basis, sometimes inflicted for denial of sexual favours. Poverty is also a major contributing factor in the contraction of HIV infection by young and adult women in dire economic circumstances who resort to prostitution or form alliances with seemingly prosperous men in their communities. In most of our Caribbean countries high unemployment and the low purchasing power of wages, if any, force a significant number of women with children to seek financial assistance from multiple male partners sometimes resulting in HIV/AIDS being transmitted to offspring, and exemplifying increased feminisation of the epidemic.

The economies of the Caribbean being in very large measure dependent on the tourist industry the transmission of the virus may also be attributable to carriers from overseas enjoying our sand and sea with wanton abandon. In all of this one must not forget that young boys are also at grave risk from homosexual activity encouraged not only by tourists but also from within their own communities. These are the realities with which we have to grapple in creating an enabling environment.

Other express commitments by leaders of the Region in 2006 to be achieved by 2010 related to the increase in the number of women receiving a full course of antiretroviral therapy in an effort to reduce mother-to-child transmission as well as the increase in persons with advanced HIV infection also receiving antiretroviral therapy. Fulfilling all of these commitments may seem unattainable. There may be success in some areas and failure in others. Some countries may report overall progress while others may report only moderate success. It must be remembered that "the core premise of the new CRSF is that an effective response to the HIV epidemic primarily depends on the commitments, capacity and leadership of the Region's national authorities." A more country-centred approach is the objective of the CRSF for 2008-2012 since overall success in achieving universal access to HIV prevention rests in the hands of every nation of the Caribbean.

In tackling this monumental task the burden does not lie, or cannot lie solely on the shoulders of governments. Civil society and non-governmental organisations are obligated and owe a responsibility to the respective nations to prevent continuing spread of the epidemic. All sectors of society must be involved; all will be consumed if no action is taken. This was recognised in CRSF of 2002-2006 when listed among the lessons learned was that the commitment of political and civic leaders at regional and national levels is necessary for the successful implementation of programmes in order to achieve universal access to HIV prevention. In fact, the need to mainstream all sectors including civil society was recognised by Dr. Denzil Douglas, Prime Minister of St. Kitts and Nevis in the foreword to the 2008-2012 Framework.

At the UNGASS Against AIDS in 2006 one of the major objectives outlined in the General Assembly's resolution was the maximum active participation of civil society, the business community and the private sector, and in fact an unprecedented number of civil society organisations was granted special accreditation to the Special Session. Civil society's partnership at national and regional levels is a *sine qua non* to the success of HIV prevention, and is an imperative which no one can ignore. The burning issues of early teenage sexual activity and abuse, gender-based violence, stigmatisation, elimination of discrimination and marginalisation, to name a few, are areas specifically within the remit of non-governmental organisations, civic and religious groups.

Further note is taken of another lesson learned from the implementation of the 2002-2006 CRSF, that is, that legislation in many countries which criminalises homosexuality and sexual acts committed on girls and boys below the legal age of consent tend to constrain HIV programmes resulting in an environment which inhibits disclosure of HIV status. Indeed, in most Caribbean states legislation is enacted to protect under-age girls and boys from sexual predators, and any form of sexual activity between persons of the same sex is regarded as a criminal offence. Laws are in place for the protection of the citizenry of a country, and one recognises that the stigma attached to these vulnerable and "at risk" groups may inhibit either reporting of the offence or if reported and action taken, reluctance to seek help if infection follows. There is no easy way to solve this dilemma. The laws have to be upheld and enforced, but strategies have to be found to encourage those who are victims of these traumatic sexual experiences to seek help. An environment which inspires confidence has to be created. In this regard support from social workers at the national level must be encouraged.

Now about PANCAP specifically. The whole reason for PANCAP's existence is partnership. It was created "to provide a unified vision and direction among all partners in reducing the spread and mitigating the impact of HIV in the Caribbean, and to coordinate the programmes and activities of partners at the regional level." I am informed that a record number of partner agencies and observer organisations will be attending this Ninth Annual General Meeting. This continuing upward spiral in participation in your annual meetings is a clear manifestation of the increasing confidence in PANCAP as an organisation, and recognition quoting from a World Bank Report published in 2005 that "PANCAP is the single most important entity in the fight against

HIV/AIDS in the Caribbean." Similar sentiments were expressed on the critical positioning of PANCAP in 2006 Report of the Caribbean Commission on Health and Development.

I take this opportunity to applaud the architects of this unique Pan Caribbean movement for the vision which inspired its formation, and which seeks to embrace the English, French, Dutch and Spanish-speaking countries of the Caribbean. I extend heartiest congratulations on the achievement of your ninth year of existence. The fact that PANCAP was specifically referred to in the United Nations Declaration of 2001 attests to its importance and impact.

Encomiums must be showered on PANCAP for the progress made in significant areas since its establishment. These include:

- Stabilisation of the presence of HIV infection across the Region, particularly early signs of a decline in at least three countries;
- Significant decline in mother-to-child transmission of the infection;
- Moderate progress in treatment, care and support;
- Rise in the level of knowledge of the cause of HIV infection.

This suggests that PANCAP and its partners are on the way to achieving by 2012 their stated goals of reducing by 25% the estimated number of new HIV infections as well as mortality due to HIV, and the social and economic impact of HIV/AIDS on households. We cannot, however, be oblivious to the fact that the HIV prevalence rate in the Region is still one and one-half times that of the global average, twice that of North America and Eastern Europe, and more than five times that of Western and Central Europe.

The 2001 United Nations Declaration identified strong leadership at all levels of society as being essential for an effective response to the epidemic. One of the Guiding Principles which Caribbean countries are expected to endorse and apply is political commitment to achieve a sustained and effective regional response to HIV. Unless there is the political will regional success in achieving universal access to HIV prevention, treatment and care will remain a distant dream. Success demands an effective regional political response to mobilisation and management of resources whether human or financial.

At this juncture, I wish to emphasise the absolute importance of continued financial investment in PANCAP. I have been made aware of the extraordinary financial support given to PANCAP by the international development partners from its inception, and that much of its successes have been through the generosity of these development partners. Meaningful and lasting partnerships are the foundations on which progress is built, and this applies in no small measure to PANCAP achieving its objective of providing a unified vision in reducing the spread and mitigating the impact of HIV in the Caribbean, particularly in the face of the social and economic challenges facing developing countries such as ours. It is hoped that the financial support to PANCAP will continue despite the growing inclination of partners to shift their development priorities away from HIV/AIDS, and thus either reduce or discontinue funding to PANCAP. The result would be a catastrophe for the achievement of the indicators for universal access, the reality being that the Caribbean will never be in a position to achieve them relying on its fragile individual economies. Strengthening the multi-sectoral coalition in the Caribbean is an imperative which cannot be ignored or brushed aside.

This is an impassioned plea to all financial partners for your continued support to PANCAP as it strives to make the theme of this meeting a reality – Strengthening the Multi-Sectoral Coalition in its quest for universal access to HIV prevention, treatment, care and support. You can do it. We all can do it. Yes, we can.

Best wishes for a successful meeting, and continued progress in the future.

Pan Caribbean Partnership Against HIV and AIDS
PANCAP Coordinating Unit
CARICOM Secretariat
Ninth Annual General Meeting Grenada
28th- 30th October, 2009

CHAPTER 37

THE CHRISTIAN PRIEST TODAY A LAYPERSON'S PERSPECTIVE

In order to analyse a layman's expectations of a priest one must begin by assuming that those expectations are based on one's belief in the Christian religion and its tenets. So I shall begin by asking the question – why are we Christians?

The answer may vary from person to person – some may say that the question is wholly unnecessary and self-evident. We are Christians because we have been inducted into the Christian faith as followers of Christ who died to save our sins. We are Christians because our parents before us were Christians, and we were brought to the church to be baptised, following in our parents' footsteps although we had no say in that decision. We may be Christians because on assuming adulthood we made the conscious decision to embrace the Christian religion.

Other reasons may vary depending on the individual; we may have been attracted to the particular church at which our friends worshipped or after hearing an impressive sermon delivered by a charismatic priest. Whatever the reason, there must have been something and some inner satisfaction that made us continue to be Christians. This in large measure may relate to our spiritual adviser from whom we garner much comfort and solace when facing enormous challenges in our lives.

This brings me to the subject on which I am expected to speak – "*What does a layperson expect from a Christian priest in today's world*?" The emphasis should be on the last words. It is beyond dispute that we live at present in a world that is moving at a frenetic pace. Days seem to be shorter with less time to accomplish all the tasks we impose on ourselves. Caught up in this frantic rush is the ever-changing value system, and an insatiable need to acquire worldly possessions at the expense of traditional Christian values. Many Christians who regard themselves as being faithful to the tenets of their religion sometimes fall victim to temptations which are ever present.

What role must a priest play in all this turmoil swirling around us today? The traditional role of a parish priest has not changed basically. These include ministering to the spiritual needs of the members of the parish, being present at mass, performing traditional rites of baptism, burials and preparing younger members for confirmation as well as uniting couples in marital bliss. Communities were smaller, and everybody knew and was familiar with each other in a village or town. Children belonged to communities, and the main virtue was respect for elders, particularly the priest within a parish. He was called upon to serve as mediator in disputes either between families or with neighbours. His word carried weight. He was expected to preserve and protect traditional values.

Sad to say this has changed over the years. People's reverence and respect for the Church and its tenets are no longer as sacred as they used to be. The world has become more practical than idealistic, more tolerant of views and opinions which in the past were frowned upon. Because of this, our young people in particular need to be reminded that certain core Christian values never change. In this regard the role of a priest today assumes even greater importance than that of one in the past. The lines between right and wrong have become blurred. Every wrong seems to find justification in the minds of some today. The traditional value system has become skewed, and needs to be pulled back on track. The Church has a major role to play in pulling this runaway train back on the Christian line.

I posit the view that from a layman's point of view the role of a priest is much more difficult in that no help seems to be coming from the homes where many of our youths are nurtured and where values are formed. There is no guidance or direction; hence the Church in many instances has to provide that guidance and point them in the right direction. This process requires patience, understanding, empathy and fortitude. It requires time and effort, not to mention sacrifice, and the ability to be a substitute parent in situations where no parental influence is being exerted.

In my view the pastoral role of a priest in today's world needs to be more all–embracing and far-reaching than it was in the past when life was more placid and we operated under a universally accepted code of behaviour; when there was adherence to law and order, and elders were accorded respect which they had earned and deserved.

The priesthood requires commitment and dedication to a vocation as well as unstinting service to parishioners whose expectations sometimes exceed the limits which are achievable. Priests have to be able to supply solutions to problems which beset not only their parishioners, but the society in which they reside. This could sometimes be overwhelming having regard to the number of churches one priest may be required to serve. The battle for reform and inculcating Christian values will only be won by reaching out to those who need to be brought back into the fold or be persuaded that change will enure to their benefit. Outreach programmes may be the answer and the road our Church needs to take if it is to succeed in its primary objective to win hearts and souls for Christ, and to create a better life for its followers.

We cannot wait to be visited; we have to make the visits and seek out those who have fallen through the cracks. In this regard we are losing the battle to other less formal denominations that have perfected the art of winning over persons, particularly, the youth to their way of preaching and making a joyful noise to the Lord. We do not necessarily have to adopt their strategy completely, but our outreach to members of our communities has to be dynamic, persuasive and convincing. The days of sitting back and expecting persons to join our churches are over. Two or three decades ago those who professed the Christian faith were members of the established churches – Roman Catholics, Anglicans, Methodists, Congregationalists, Seventh Day Adventists, to name a few. Now there are numerous choices. A new church springs up every few months, and amazingly they attract many to their cause.

We need to ask ourselves the key question – why? We are too self-righteous and maybe a bit arrogant in assuming that being an established church everyone will flock to us. We have to realise that we are operating in a completely new environment. Of course, this goes hand in hand with the approach and attitude of our priests. I regard the priesthood as a vocation rather than a job. It requires full-time commitment even under the most trying conditions. I echo Archdeacon Spencer's words yesterday, that you go where you are needed, and not where you want to go. You have to bow in submission to God's will. It is a life of service to God without boundaries, without time limits, sometimes without appreciation or gratitude. In spite of the trials and tribulations I am sure that there is the self-satisfaction in some instances of having improved the lives of others when one sees undisguised gratitude and happiness reflected in the faces of contented parishioners and a child or young person who you have succeeded in rescuing from a life headed for disaster.

Yesterday some time was spent discussing a Code of Conduct for our clergy. I cannot anticipate what the reports from the groups will reveal, but from a personal standpoint I think it is a step in the right direction. Every discipline today sees wisdom in providing guidance to those involved in interactions with the public. In my own sphere of activity and as head of the Judiciary a Code of Conduct was formulated for our judges and magistrates way back in 2002, and at present, I am involved in doing the same for our Caribbean Court. Even at that level it is necessary. This has nothing to do with lack of trust or assumptions that one cannot conduct oneself properly. It is intended as a guide on how to deal with problems when confronted with certain situations which may arise in our vocations.

The proliferation of social networking in recent times inspired the need for codes of conduct. Facebook and other social networking sites are fertile ground for a range of negative activity and gossip. Marriages have been wrecked by exposing salacious details of intimate, personal incidents either to create embarrassment or seek revenge. In any vocation or profession one is constantly under a public microscope which attracts a wide range of comment or discussion ranging from admiration to condemnation. Whatever office of trust one holds, upholding one's personal ethical code cannot be overstated. Responsibility for upholding that code rests at all times with the individual. We ought not at any time have to teach anyone about what constitutes good behaviour, but sad to say, in today's world this has become necessary.

The lay persons of our Church expect our priests to be exemplars of good behaviour, and role models to everyone in a community. It may seem a heavy responsibility having regard to the frailties of human nature, but it is a burden which the vocation demands and which must be borne courageously and with implicit faith in God to be your guide.

In closing, I adopt the scriptural quotation appearing at the beginning of the document circulated for discussion on the code of conduct:

> *... as He who called you is holy, be holy yourselves in all your conduct. (1 Peter 1:15)*

May God continue to richly bless each and every one of us in our respective vocations.

Annual Synod of the Anglican Diocese of Guyana
27th -29th May, 2012

CHAPTER 38

ALTERNATIVE DISPUTE RESOLUTION AT THE INTERNATIONAL LEVEL

From time immemorial disputes and disagreements have arisen between individuals as strangers, within families, as neighbours, at places of work, and between nations. Over time methods have been found to resolve these conflicts peacefully, but sometimes with disastrous results. Reliance has often been placed on the wisdom of elders in a community to offer advice and steer warring factions in the right direction for a peaceful resolution of disagreements. In countries such as India and those in the African continent, where there were no structured judicial systems communities formulated their own methods of settling disputes, and which proved very effective over the years. This form of dispute resolution still exists at present with members of some communities preferring their disputes to be settled privately rather than in the public arena of civil courts.

Over the years, however, formal judicial institutions were established with the responsibility for administering justice between disputing parties in order to resolve conflicts. As expected the volume of matters requiring judicial intervention and consideration increased exponentially as populations grew and became more diverse racially and culturally; differences in religious beliefs have also given rise to conflicts oft times with fatal repercussions.

Dissatisfaction with the judicial systems in developed metropolitan countries, but even more so in developing countries with large, unmanageable judicial dockets due to limited numbers of judicial officers and the need to balance national priorities in the distribution of scarce financial resources, led to the fashioning of systems for resolving disputes as alternatives to established and formal judicial processes. These include but are not limited to arbitration and mediation also known as conciliation with procedures which were much more informal and relaxed with less cumbersome and rigid rules of admissibility of evidence and recording of testimony. One key element of the alternative forms of dispute settlement is that they are consensual and not confrontational. They require the agreement of the parties to be operational; if there is no agreement there can be no settlement or resolution of a dispute. Mediation requires the agreement of the parties on selection of a person to hear the respective contentions of both parties and offer guidance in resolving difficult issues. The mediator is as the term suggests the person in the middle guiding both parties to an amicable settlement of disputes. There ought never to be contention, only agreeable resolution.

Arbitration, however, is more closely related to traditional litigation in that an arbitrator is expected to resolve the dispute after hearing both parties and making a finding which may be enforceable in the courts. Whatever mode of dispute resolution one selects the objective must always be the speedy termination of disagreements which may have remained unresolved over a considerable period of time.

This paper will address examples of institutions which have adopted alternative forms of dispute resolution and which sometimes operate in conjunction with established adjudicative court systems and tribunals.

THE UNITED NATIONS COMMISSION ON INTERNATIONAL TRADE LAW

This Commission (UNCITRAL) was established in 1966 as a subsidiary organization of the United Nations to hear and determine arbitrations in relation to international trade disputes, but now also hears and determines arbitrations between private individuals and sovereign states. The General Assembly's mandate was to further the progressive harmonization and unification of international trade law having considered it "desirable that the process of harmonization and unification of the law of international trade should be substantially coordinated, systematized and accelerated". In pursuance of this objective preparing and promoting the use and adoption of both legislative and non-legislative instruments in key areas of commercial law is vital and important, one of these areas being dispute resolution. To this end UNCITRAL model laws on international commercial arbitration were formulated and adopted with amendments over the years since 1985. Non-legislative texts include rules for conduct of arbitration and conciliation proceedings.

Members of UNCITRAL are selected from Member States of the United Nations, and represent different legal traditions and levels of economic development. Structure of the Commission ensures that the various geographic regions and principal global economic and legal systems are represented, this being in compliance with United Nations traditions.

THE EUROPEAN CONVENTION FOR THE PEACEFUL SETTLEMENT OF DISPUTES

In 1957 the Council of Europe having considered that the aim of the Council was to achieve greater unity between its members resolved to settle by peaceful means any disputes which may arise between them, and agreed to submit to the judgment of the International Court of Justice all international legal disputes concerning, *inter alia,* the interpretation of a treaty and any question of international law. This, however, in no way affects the parties to disputes concerning other issues agreeing to resort to conciliation before that of judicial settlement. Article 4 of the Convention provides for conciliation in certain circumstances, and when a dispute arises which falls within the scope of Article 4, it shall be referred to a Permanent Conciliation Commission previously set up by the parties concerned. If the parties agree not to have recourse to that Commission, the dispute shall be referred to a special Conciliation Commission agreed upon by the parties. The task of the Commission is to elucidate the questions in dispute and to endeavor to bring the parties to an agreement.

Apart from conciliation parties to a dispute may also have recourse to arbitration if the parties agree to this or if attempts at conciliation fail. An Arbitral Tribunal may by agreement or otherwise be constituted.

THE ADMINISTRATIVE TRIBUNAL OF THE COUNCIL OF EUROPE (ATCE)

This Tribunal formerly the Council of Europe Appeals Board, is an international administrative court competent to hear complaints of the serving and former staff members of the Council of Europe, and was established in 1965. Under Article 59 of the Staff Regulations complaints concerning administrative acts may be submitted to the Secretary General, and if not satisfactorily resolved Article 60 provides for an appeal to be lodged in writing with the Tribunal.

Either on the initiative of the Secretary General or at the request of the staff member complaints can be referred to an Advisory Committee on Disputes which can formulate its opinion for the consideration of the Secretary General no doubt before a decision is made and before an appeal is lodged with the Tribunal. This Committee which comprises four members, two appointed by the Secretary General and two elected by the Staff Committee is completely independent in discharging its duties, and formulates its opinion based on legal considerations and any other relevant matters after consultation with the persons concerned.

THE WORLD TRADE ORGANISATION (WTO)

It is generally accepted that dispute settlement is the central pillar of the WTO, and its unique contribution to the stability of the global economy. Disputes between member states over breaches of WTO agreements or failure to honour obligations may be resolved by utilization of the multilateral system of settling disputes which involves abiding by the procedures under the Dispute Settlement Understanding (DSU) and the judgments of the Dispute Settlement Body (DSB).

In 1994 WTO members agreed on an Understanding on Rules and Procedures Governing the Settlement of Disputes (DSU). The first step in the process involves consultation between the parties to disputes which may in a majority of cases result in acceptable resolution of contentious issues. Statistics indicate that consultations are effective in resolving a significant number of disputes. Failure, however, to resolve the issues may result in recourse to the DSB panels and ultimately to the Appellate Body of the WTO. The DSB comprises representatives of all WTO members, and is responsible for administering the DSU by overseeing the entire dispute settlement process.

An appeal can be filed against the report of a panel to the Appellate Body only on issues of law and legal interpretations, and is heard by three members of the permanent seven-member Body who may uphold, modify or reverse the findings and conclusions of a panel. Marion Panizzon, in her book, "Good Faith in the Jurisprudence of the WTO", concluded that the possibility for an appeal makes the WTO dispute resolution system unique among the judicial processes of dispute settlement in general international law.

Significantly, WTO in the DSU pays special attention to the problems and interests of developing countries particularly with regard to safeguarding their concerns at hearings by panels. Provision is made in the DSU for a panel to comprise at least one panelist from a developing state when a dispute involving a developing state is being heard. Similarly, the stipulated time for consultations before a panel is convened may be extended, and the time for a developing state in a dispute to make submissions before a panel may be relaxed. One can surmise that the rationale for leniency is acknowledgement of the fact that developing states may face serious difficulties in preparation of their cases and lack of competent personnel which developed states do not normally encounter.

THE UNITED NATIONS CONVENTION ON THE LAW OF THE SEA (UNCLOS)

This Convention came into effect in 1994 in a spirit of mutual understanding and co-operation by States Parties to settle all issues relating to the law of the sea. Article 279 of the Treaty imposed an obligation on States Parties to settle any dispute between them concerning its interpretation or application by peaceful means in accordance with Article 2.3 of the Charter of the United Nations which enjoins member states to "settle their international disputes by peaceful means in such a manner that international peace and security, and justice, are not endangered." Article 280 of UNCLOS further provides for settlement of disputes by any peaceful means chosen by the parties outside of Articles of the Convention.

Where under certain obligations in general, regional or bilateral agreements between parties to a dispute which may involve the interpretation or application of the Convention, Article 282 at the request of the parties permits acceptance of an agreed procedure in lieu of the established procedure providing that the result will be a binding decision.

In the spirit of encouraging peaceful resolution of disputes between states Article 284 of the Convention provides that a State Party in a dispute may invite the other party or parties to submit the dispute to conciliation in accordance with provided procedures or other conciliation procedures. Annex V is dedicated to the conciliation procedure which includes the constitution of a conciliation commission.

The International Tribunal for the Law of the Sea (ITLOS) was established to adjudicate on disputes concerning the application and interpretation of the Convention and to render advisory opinions.

Article 288 refers to the jurisdiction of all of the possible compulsory dispute resolution bodies, and provides that each shall "have jurisdiction over any dispute concerning the application or interpretation of the Convention which is submitted to it in accordance with this Part" and that each "shall also have jurisdiction over any dispute concerning the interpretation and application of an international agreement related to the purposes of the Convention which is submitted to it in accordance with the agreement". In addition Annex VI, Article 21 provides a wider jurisdiction for the Tribunal, and provides that "the jurisdiction of the Tribunal comprises all disputes and all applications submitted in accordance with the Convention and all matters specifically provided for in any other agreement which confers jurisdiction on the Tribunal".

THE INTERNATIONAL CENTRE FOR THE SETTLEMENT OF INVESTMENT DISPUTES

This Centre (ICSID) is one of the five organisations which comprise the World Bank Group, and is regarded as one of the leading institutions for the resolution of international investment disputes. Research reveals that it was established under the Convention on the Settlement of Investment Disputes between States and Nationals of other States (the ICSID Convention), a multilateral international treaty which entered into force on October 14, 1966. As of January 20, 2013, 158 States had signed, and 147 Contracting States had ratified the Convention.

The primary purpose of ICSID, whose governing body is the ICSID Administrative Council, is to provide facilities for the conciliation and arbitration of international investment disputes, both of these forms of dispute settlement being entirely voluntary and requiring the consent of both the investor and the State concerned. The jurisdiction of the Centre under the Convention is defined as extending to any legal dispute arising directly out of an investment between a Contracting State and a national of another Contracting State which the parties to the dispute consent in writing to submit to the Centre. Significantly, such consent having been given it cannot be withdrawn unilaterally, and becomes a binding undertaking; in fact, the Rules provide that consent of the parties to arbitration under the Convention is deemed to be consent to arbitration to the exclusion of any other remedy.

ICSID is an impartial facilitator of dispute resolution with no power to decide cases. This is exclusively the role of independent and impartial tribunals comprising expert arbitrators and conciliators appointed to hear evidence and determine the outcome of a dispute on the basis of the facts and the law presented by parties to the dispute. It must be noted that the arbitral proceedings are separate and independent from the work of the World Bank Group. In most instances, the tribunals consist of three arbitrators, one appointed by the investor, one by the State, and the third (the presiding arbitrator) appointed with the agreement of both parties. Statistics indicate that approximately 40% of ICSID cases are settled or discontinued before a final ruling is made.

THE ADMINISTRATIVE TRIBUNAL OF THE INTERNATIONAL LABOUR ORGANISATION

This Tribunal came into existence at the time of the League of Nations, and also served the International Labour Organisation whose mandate was to provide guarantees that the officials employed by the institutions over which it had jurisdiction at that time would enjoy protection against arbitrary acts committed against them by their employer. The Statute of the Tribunal provided for the hearing of disputes of any other international organization meeting the standards set out in the Annex of the Statute one of them being that it must be intergovernmental in character. A complaint is receivable by the Tribunal if it is a final decision and all internal appeal procedures have been exhausted. This rule has always been strictly applied according to the relevant case law. Exhausting all internal procedures means utilizing all of the legal channels that are available to an official within the rules of the organization before a final decision is taken. Apart from the Staff Regulations providing for compulsory appeals procedures, there may be less formal procedures available, e.g. conciliation, mediation or an ombudsperson, to enable an amicable settlement of the dispute to be reached.

THE ADMINISTRATIVE TRIBUNAL OF THE ORGANISATION OF AMERICAN STATES

The Statute of the OAS Administrative Tribunal provides for recognition by the Tribunal of the finality of all settlement agreements, releases, agreements to arbitrate, and agreements to seek conciliation or mediation, and it may not reopen, review or adjudicate the issues finally resolved by those agreements or procedures, absent the express consent of all parties thereto (Article VII). Notwithstanding this, however, the Tribunal reserves the right to vacate a decision or award in whole or in part where an award exceeds the maximum indemnities that may be imposed by the Tribunal or the award was procured by corruption or misconduct of the arbitrators or failed to follow the material provisions of the Rules of Procedure.

The Rules provide that before submitting a case to the Tribunal, the parties may seek to settle their disputes by means of any form of arrangement or voluntary agreement, including arbitration, conciliation, mediation, and settlement (Article 16: General Principle). They also provide that the result of any of the aforementioned agreements shall be accepted by the Tribunal as binding upon the parties, and shall not be reviewed or reopened unless such is requested in writing by all the parties or unless any of the conditions in Article VII of the Statute apply (Article 17).

THE ADMINISTRATIVE TRIBUNAL OF THE INTERNATIONAL MONETARY FUND

The Statute of this Tribunal provides for the hearing of applications by members of staff challenging the legality of administrative acts of the Fund adversely affecting them, and Article V stipulates that such an application may be filed only after the applicant has exhausted all available channels of administrative review. The exhaustion of such channels is deemed to have taken place when certain stipulated conditions have been satisfied; such channels shall also be deemed to have been exhausted when both the Managing Director and the applicant agree to submit the dispute to the Tribunal. Article VI provides that an application challenging the legality of a decision shall not be admissible if filed with the Tribunal more than three months after all available channels have been exhausted, or in the absence of such channels, after the notification of the decision.

THE INTERAMERICAN DEVELOPMENT BANK ADMINISTRATIVE TRIBUNAL (IDBAT)

With the recent amendments to the IADB Statute and Rules of Procedure, the former Conciliation Committee was abolished and mediation made compulsory before embarking on a hearing before the Tribunal. In this regard the Staff Rules have been revised with the aim of resolving conflicts by open dialogue. The purpose of the new conflict resolution mechanisms being part of the Bank's policy is intended to take into account the interests of the parties in a conflict, and to achieve better collaboration between the staff and the Bank.

In this regard both the revised Statute and Rules of Procedure of the Tribunal provide that complaints are only admissible for hearing within 120 calendar days of the exhaustion of all other remedies required within the formal system for the resolution of employee grievances as conditions for access to the Tribunal.

Staff Rule PE-323 which addresses Labor Relations and Conflict Resolution Mechanisms provides for the appointment of an impartial, independent and qualified Mediator to assist parties in conflict in reaching informed and voluntary agreements, and an impartial and independent Ombudsperson who will act as a confidential source of assistance in the resolution of work-related issues and/or grievances. The Ombudsperson is part of the informal conflict resolution mechanisms of the Bank. The Staff Rules also provide for informal mediation which is a voluntary, confidential and non-adversarial mechanism aimed at promoting communication between employees and management. To achieve this a Mediation Secretary will be appointed by the Bank, and shall be an independent and impartial official with no decision-making powers, and only an advisory role in making suggestions and recommendations to the parties.

THE UNITED NATIONS DISPUTE TRIBUNAL (UNDT)

The former United Nations Administrative Tribunal was replaced by the United Nations Dispute Tribunal, and on 16 December, 2009 the U.N. General Assembly by resolution approved new rules of procedure which provide under Article 15 that at any time during any proceedings brought by a party including at the hearing, the Tribunal may propose to the parties that the case be referred for mediation, and may suspend the proceedings. Where a presiding judge proposes and the parties consent to mediation, the Tribunal shall send the case to the Mediation Division in the Office of the Ombudsman for consideration. The parties on their own initiative can also decide to seek mediation, and so inform the Registry in writing. During mediation further hearings are suspended. The new Dispute Tribunal is the first tier in a two-tiered system of dispute resolution, and appeals can be brought from decisions of the Tribunal to an Appeals Tribunal. This new procedure was the result of the General Assembly in 2007 deciding to introduce a new system for handling internal disputes within the United Nations, and after extensive discussions on the issue of the administration of justice, and recognition that the existing system no longer met the needs of the Organisation, the General Assembly acted on the report of the Secretary General. The goal of the revised system, *inter alia,* was to place stronger emphasis on resolving disputes through informal means before resorting to formal litigation.

THE COMMONWEALTH SECRETARIAT ARBITRAL TRIBUNAL

The Statute of this Tribunal was originally adopted by Commonwealth Governments on 1st July, 1995 and later amended with the latest amendment being on 16th May, 2007. The jurisdiction of the Tribunal extends to hearing and determining applications brought by members of the staff of the Commonwealth Secretariat, the Secretariat itself, and other persons who enter into contracts with the Secretariat, and allege the non-observance of the terms of a contract. The Tribunal is also competent to hear and determine an application involving an international or intergovernmental Commonwealth body or organization which meets the criteria set out in Annex A to the Statute.

The Tribunal shall only consider an application if in relation to a contract of service, the applicant has exhausted all other remedies available within the Secretariat or other body or organization including the redress of grievance procedures specified in the contract or in relevant Staff Rules, and the application is filed within a period of ninety (90) days after the occurrence of the event giving rise to the application, receipt of notice that the relief asked for or recommended will not be granted or receipt of notice that the relief will be granted if such relief shall not have been granted within one month after receipt of such notice. Notwithstanding the aforementioned the Tribunal may consider an application where all other remedies have not been exhausted where the Tribunal determines that the remedies available cannot adequately address the issues raised in the application.

THE INTERNATIONAL CHAMBER OF COMMERCE DISPUTE RESOLUTION SERVICES

The ICC is another leading provider of dispute resolution services for individuals, businesses, states and international organisations seeking alternatives to court litigation. The range of these services includes arbitration administered by the ICC International Court of Arbitration. The Court although not a judicial one, comprises 100 members from about 90 countries, carries out functions assigned to it under the ICC Rules of Arbitration which include assessing whether there is a prima facie ICC Arbitration agreement and monitoring the arbitral process from filing of a request to the notification of the final award. In addition there is the ICC International Centre for ADR which is the administrative body that oversees the ICC ADR. The Centre works with parties to establish dispute resolutions that satisfy their specific interests.

THE ADMINISTRATIVE TRIBUNAL OF THE ASIAN DEVELOPMENT BANK

The Statute of this Tribunal similar to the IADB Tribunal provides in Article II that no application by a staff member of the Bank shall be admissible unless the applicant has exhausted all other remedies available within the Bank except in exceptional circumstances if the applicant and the President of the Bank have agreed to submit the application directly to the Tribunal.

THE ADMINISTRATIVE TRIBUNAL OF THE AFRICAN DEVELOPMENT BANK

The Statute of this Tribunal, like the other Tribunals mentioned earlier provides that no application by a staff member will be admissible unless all other available remedies are exhausted, and in similar vein like the Asian Development Bank Tribunal, unless the applicant and the Bank agree to submit the application directly to the Tribunal.

Apart from those already referred to there are other established alternative dispute organisations and arbitration facilities worldwide, such as the London Court of International Arbitration headquartered in London, but which may sit anywhere if so requested. Its services also include mediation which is regarded as a negotiated settlement usually conducted and concluded with the assistance of a neutral third party, the process being voluntary without any binding decision or enforceability. Similarly, the International Centre for Dispute Resolution offers all forms of dispute resolution with a wide range of services.

The New York Arbitration Convention embraces two functions, the recognition and enforcement of foreign arbitral awards and the referral by a court to arbitration. It applies to awards not considered as domestic awards and not only awards made by arbitrators appointed for each case but also those made by permanent arbitral bodies to which the parties have submitted. In relation to its second function under the Convention a court of a Contracting State, when seised of a matter in respect of which the parties have made an arbitration agreement, must, at the request of one of the parties, refer it to arbitration unless the arbitration agreement is invalid.

A review of the aforementioned Tribunals and other dispute resolution mechanisms indicates that amicable resolution of disputes arising between institutions and their employees has become the overarching objective in trade and other disputes. Litigation seems to be the very last resort after everything else has failed. The pursuit of settlement by agreement can enure only to the benefit of all involved, and lead to a more harmonious environment whether at the international or domestic level of commercial activity, or within interpersonal relationships in every sphere of life.

Although the resolution of disputes of any nature may embrace several alternatives, conciliation and mediation remain the least expensive and facilitates dialogue at the initial stages. The parties at the minimum no doubt will agree to talk and consider the possibility of a resolution of their disputes. Nothing is lost, and if the talks fail there are other alternatives. Courts throughout the world, particularly in developing countries have resorted to or are encouraging their courts to have recourse to dialogue before finally going to trial or to arbitration. It is hoped that the benefits will have the effect of increasing the understanding of parties that no problem is ever irreconcilable if the parties have the commitment to resolve their differences peaceably.

IADB 30th Anniversary Observance
December, 2013